Blessed Assurance

A Postmodern Midwestern Life

Marcelline Hutton

Zea Books
Lincoln, Nebraska
2019

Copyright © 2019 Marcelline Hutton
All rights reserved

ISBN 978-1-60962-155-1

doi 10.32873/unl.dc.zea.10903

Set in Callisto, Myriad, Vladimir Script, and Castellar initials.

Zea Books are published by the University of Nebraska–Lincoln Libraries

Electronic (pdf) ebook edition available online at
https://digitalcommons.unl.edu/zeabook/

Print edition available from
http://www.lulu.com/spotlight/unllib

UNL does not discriminate based upon any protected status.
Please go to http://www.unl.edu/equity/notice-nondiscrimination

> *When I am writing,*
> *then I am being most of all.*
>
> Fyodor Dostoevsky

> *The past is never dead. It's not even past.*
>
> William Faulkner

> *The past is beautiful because one never realises*
> *an emotion at the time. It expands later, and*
> *thus we don't have complete emotions about*
> *the present, only about the past.*
>
> Virginia Woolf

> *Man is born broken.*
> *He lives by mending.*
>
> Eugene O'Neill

Marcelline Hutton (left), with mother Madeline and sister Kathryn, c. 1960.

Contents

	Acknowledgments	6
	Introduction	7
I.	Childhood	12
II.	Youth: Joy and Alienation, 1950s	51
III.	College, 1958–1962	65
IV.	Graduate School at Iowa, 1962–1975	82
V.	Married Life in Kansas City, 1976–1979	146
VI.	Divorce: Finding My Own Voice in Graduate School	162
VII.	Teaching: 1980s and 1990s	187
VIII.	Life in Lithuania	214
IX.	Blessed Assurance: Retirement and Old Age	275
X.	Mother's Cooking Legacy	318
XI.	Conclusion	328

Acknowledgments

I am grateful to the following people for their friendship, support, love, prayers, and encouragement as I wrote this autobiography: Mary Roseberry Brown, Gwen Colgrove, Madhumita Gupta, Marg and Chuck Felling, Linnea Fredrickson, Miriam Gelfand, Elly Hart, Beth Hemmer, Kathryn Hutton, Walter Hutton, Birgitta Ingemanson, Michael Johnson, Faye Kartrude, Elaine Kruse, Robbin Lowe, Alexa Maples, Kent Nelson, Paul Royster, Larry Ross, Donna Swischer, Tom Tiegs, Jerry Thompson, and my son, Martin.

Introduction

In writing my autobiography, I have come to realize that while the crises in my life were personal, they were also part of a larger cultural shift in America from traditional to postmodern, with its lack of authorities. I was born into a simple but democratic working-class environment in La Porte, Indiana, in November 1939. I went to college from 1958 to 1962, when history was still taught from the viewpoint of male political elites. I lived through several cultural revolutions: an academic revolution when women's history, working-class history, and black history became new forms of study and research; a feminist theological revolution; and the sexual revolution of the 1960s and '70s.

Taking account of postmodernism makes my personal struggles more understandable. Initially, I thought a simple chronological explanation of my life as a woman moving from working class to middle class academe would suffice as a document for future historians. As I began with this approach in mind, I soon found that life was more dynamic and writing, life, and love messier than I expected. None of these are neatly experienced or expressed. So when my friend Elly Hart observed that my life is an improvisation, I was surprised. Then I thought that improvisation is a bit like Hegel's dialectic: thesis, antithesis, synthesis. However, instead of seeds of destruction initiating this process, I think it was seeds of dissatisfaction that led to change in my life. While Hegel posited the Zeitgeist moving the historical process along, I think it's been the Holy Spirit nudging me. We become conscious of something and then begin to change our minds and actions. Since I am a historian, I organized my memoirs as chronologically as possible. However, sometimes a theme wanders into later decades. I hope the terms *improvisation* and *dialectic* allow for and facilitate these diversions and digressions. Or perhaps it's as Virginia Woolf suggests: we realize the importance of an emotion or event only much later.

Memories for this autobiography have come in a variety of ways, some unsolicited. For years I have been awakened by Clio, the muse of history, in the middle of the night with an idea for a paper or book. I have learned to keep a pad of paper and pen next to my bed so that when I am "kissed by Clio," a phrase coined by Goethe, I don't have to get out of bed but can just reach up, turn on my light, and write down the insight that has come to me. If I don't do this, I often can't retrieve it in the morning. Of course, I prefer having these ideas in the daytime when I am writing at my table, but writing, like life, is unpredictable. Intuitions and interpretations don't always come on command. Yet the computer makes writing additions and subtractions easier. Life and writing can be mysterious and messy.

I usually write the outline of a book on a yellow legal pad and develop it in detail. I work this way as long as I can. Then, all of a sudden I find myself inserting new material into the text that I have already typed into the computer. For example, at a concert one evening, I found myself musing about the nurturing role of trees. So, I turned to the section about growing up in La Porte and added material about the trees sheltering our home. This idea was not on my mind when I initially wrote about my childhood. It came later. As Faulkner said, the past really isn't even past. It sneaks into the present. With the aid of my computer, I can make these changes.

As a historian, I was trained to write impartially in the third-person singular: it, he, or one, and it has been a considerable shift writing "I," first-person singular, in this memoir. I found it almost impossible to do this when an editor suggested I do it for my book *Falling in Love with the Baltics: A Travel Memoir* a decade ago. Today it is easier but still a stretch. Some years ago when I told a friend about my dilemma of using "I" instead of "she," my friend gently reminded me that I could do this because I do it every day in my journal. This was true, but my journal was for private consumption, not public, as memoirs are.

I may have felt emboldened to write up my story because I had assembled the accounts of many Russian women in my last two books *Remarkable Russian Women in Pictures, Prose and Poetry* (2013) and *Resilient Russian Women in the 1920s and 1930s* (2015). In these works I used the memoirs, diaries, and reminiscences of many Russian women to show what their lives were like. At some point, I realized that future historians won't know how women lived in twentieth-century America unless women write down our stories as evidence.

Looking back over my spiritual life, I can see that it too has been influential and dynamic. In the Episcopal *Book of Common Prayer*, there's a phrase in the communion service of God's offering us "new and unending life," and today I am grateful for this. However, this was not always the case. Looking back on my life, I can see that while God was continually offering me new life in terms of personal growth, study, relationships, jobs, adventure, and travel, I didn't always accept it or appreciate it. I was sometimes frightened of the new and clung to the old familiar ways. Reared during the 1940s and '50s in a working-class household, I imbibed traditional culture and remained a traditional person in many ways. When I was growing up, my culture told me it was acceptable for a man to be ambitious and achieving but not for a woman. Society viewed such women as uppity, stepping outside their "place." Indeed, it wasn't always clear what my "place" was. This book is an effort to locate my "place" in my society, family, and religion. Sometimes it's an upsetting and unsettling journey. Sometimes the blessings are unexpected and inspiring.

Changing my traditional core values to postmodern ones has not been easy, whether studying in graduate school, experiencing divorce, adopting feminist theology, or taking a new teaching position. Each situation could be awkward. When I was young, I was naive and unaware of the unwritten social contracts involved in negotiating life. I sometimes felt bewildered by my husband's middle-class friends and family or in academe because I wasn't familiar with that culture. My own willfulness and unwillingness to change often got in the way of being transformed and accepting new life. Sometimes giving up a dream—like being a missionary to Africa, staying married to my husband, or getting tenure at the University of Texas at El Paso—was painful and took a long time to process. I often just didn't want "new life." Yet, the Spirit seemed to nudge, restore, refresh, and revive me. Often I didn't comprehend the new life Providence was offering, but today I am a little more mindful of it. Upon reflection, I can now see that getting divorced led me to become my own person, learning to think for myself instead of relying upon my husband's ideas and opinions. Likewise, not getting tenure did not ruin my life but only thwarted my career in Russian history. Still, not getting tenure allowed me to travel extensively in Eastern Europe and to visit St. Petersburg several times when I was teaching in Lithuania. I wouldn't have had those adventures if I had stayed in El Paso. So, today I can be grateful for the "hard" experiences, although I wasn't at the time. These reminiscences, then, are an account of my life—growing up, adventures, challenges, connections, transitions, and transformations—that I fondly and not so fondly recall. They also show how class and gender played out in my life in the mid and late twentieth century.

Growing up, I experienced stability in my extended family, neighborhood, school, and church. This center held together until I went to graduate school in 1962. Such stability was helpful because while my father's alcoholism, anger, and financial irresponsibility were demoralizing factors in my early life, my mother and siblings as well as my extended family and the wider society of La Porte, Indiana, provided cohesiveness. Certainly, my mother's self-sacrifice, altruism, and hard work, as well as the reassuring presence of my older brother and sister supplied an environment of caring, belonging, and safety in the midst of our slightly crazy, repressed family life. My mother stressed the importance of eating three good meals a day, which she diligently prepared for us. She also instilled in us cleanliness, order, discipline, deferred gratification, frugality, and work—all virtues that have undergirded the rest of my life. She also inspired a lifelong love of walking, which has kept me mentally and physically healthy. While my father's alcoholism, ranting, raving, and threatening behavior were frightening, his presence also provided protection and safety. We were not homeless, and he was better than no father at all.

One of my most painful childhood experiences was being silenced. My mother's family all believed in children being seen but not heard, at least not in adult company. My sister also "shushed" me at times. Today I can understand her wanting to socialize me by teaching me not to talk too loudly, but as a child I felt put down and conflicted about expressing myself. Certainly the alcoholic family notions of "don't talk, don't feel" also muted me. As a woman, I often felt stifled by patriarchal figures in my family, my marriage, and the male-dominated history profession. Still, there were times and places for self-expression: singing at school and church, playing games in our neighborhood and at school, frolicking in the snow in winter, and enjoying the lake in summer. Later, there were opportunities to express my ideas in papers in college and graduate school and now in books in retirement.

These reminiscences also came about because a friend pestered me about writing my autobiography. At first, this seemed an egotistical thing to do. However, as I had just finished two long books about Russian women, I didn't quite feel like beginning another extensive historical work that I had been brooding about, so it seemed like a good time to undertake what I thought would be a short project. I really didn't think it would take very long to write up my story. I knew I'd encounter some difficult passages about the crises in my life—the end of youthful idealism, the disintegration of my marriage, and the end of my teaching career, but I thought I could handle those topics and move on fairly quickly. Of course, everything is more complicated and takes longer than expected. So has writing these memoirs—it's been almost three years. But there have been unexpected psychological, social, and spiritual insights, which I have appreciated.

I've discovered that traveling, listening to music, and cooking and baking have been consolations in my life, and that's been surprising. Writing these memoirs has also given me a greater appreciation for my mother and son and more compassion for my father, former husband, and myself. It's been fascinating to see that while I adopted modern intellectual ideas, I retained some of my mother's traditional values, such as the dignity of work, frugality, cooking, and entertaining. I've been amused to observe that I adopted my father's love of the grandiose. While he liked to treat his friends to drinks in the bar instead of bringing his money home to his family, I discovered that I too have been attracted to the grand gesture. In retrospect, my desire to be a missionary in Africa may have stemmed from grandiosity as well as self-sacrifice. My attraction to the grand and glorious in Russian history may have originated from my father's and my love of the grandiose. For decades I loved dressing with dramatic flair, and this too may be related to the desire for the grand gesture.

A religious retreat a few years ago also motivated me to write these recollections. During the retreat, we drew pictures of our religious journey, breaking it up into ten-year intervals. Reviewing my life in these decades, I noticed surprising blessings in each period of my life—many of which I had been unaware. This autobiography encompasses more than my religious life, of course, and I have to admit that each period has had a mixture of banes as well as blessings. As a youth, I wasn't familiar with Jeremiah's scripture about God's plans to prosper me and give me hope. Yet, somehow I intuited this. I have certainly believed in the beneficence of God, even when I have felt uncertain, mystified, and bewildered. So on with the story. I hope it interests you.

CHAPTER I

Childhood

"Be it ever so humble, there's no place like home."

I was born in La Porte, Indiana, sixty miles east of Chicago, November 19, 1939, the third child to my parents Madeline and Lee Hutton. Below is an early photo of my parents, taken before any of us children were born. Sad to say, I never saw them look so carefree. Economic recovery from the Depression in the United States had not yet begun in the late 1930s, and it was a hard time to raise a family. Only now do I appreciate the difficulties my parents experienced during World War II and the following decades.

My parents' first child was a son, Walter Lee, named for my Swedish grandfather, Walter Johnson, and for my father, Lee James Hutton. My brother was born April 29, 1937. He was a great and good influence on me, very protective—the best kind of older brother. A year after his birth, my sister, Kathryn Patricia, was born. She was named after our Swiss/German grandmother, Catherine Iselman Johnson. My sister's birthday is May 7, 1938, so she's a year and a half older than I. Since my sister and I were so close in age, more sibling rivalry existed between us than between my brother and me, yet we've also been emotionally supportive of each other. I was named Marcelline Judith, after my aunt Marcelline Johnson, later Breese, who was living with my parents when I was born. I don't know where the name Judith came from—perhaps from Judy Garland in *The Wizard of Oz*, which was popular in 1939. When I was a child my mother called me Judy since she thought

Lee and Madeline Hutton,
La Porte, Indiana, 1936

it would be simpler for school. She was correct because teachers and principals always mispronounced Marcelline when making formal announcements.

To the right is an early photo of the three of us: my brother in the middle, my sister on the left, and me on the right. This picture was taken at my grandparents' farm near Kingsbury, Indiana, when we were little. I assume I was three or four, since I was about as tall as my sister at the time of this picture.

As a child, I remember looking at the pictures of my brother and sister that were taken at a photography studio and thinking, "Why isn't there one of me like that?" Since I was the youngest child, I wondered if I was unwanted, and that's why there were no photos of me. Only in middle age did I realize that such pictures were expensive, and my parents had little extra money by the time I came along. A cousin recently gave me a baby picture of my sister that I used to admire.

The other thing that bewildered me as a child was why my birthday was in bleak, barren November. I couldn't understand this since my mother and brother had birthdays in beautiful, sunny April, and my sister and father in May when the trees and flowers were blooming. As a child, I didn't know who to fault for this arrangement. I never spoke to my mother about it because she was always busy working, cooking, or cleaning, and I sensed she wouldn't like my interrupting to ask this question. It may have been this mystery that made me a little lonely and wistful as a child. It certainly didn't help me understand my place in the universe very well.

Kathryn, Walter, and Marcelline, Johnson farm, 1940s

Kathryn as a baby, La Porte, 1938

Early Childhood Memories, 1940s

I recall my father once complaining that during the Depression he worked for twenty-five cents an hour cleaning wallpaper for a wealthy family on "the Avenue." When I was growing up, many of the wealthiest people in La Porte lived in large brick mansions on Michigan or Indiana Avenue. My parents envied and resented them. I didn't completely understand this class antagonism until later. I knew we were poor, but it took me a long time to realize that I'd grown up working class. It was a source of shame for many years because most Americans deny class structure and insist we are all middle class. Once I became a well-educated professor and by definition middle class, I realized that I really needn't have been so ashamed of my working-class background or tried so hard to disguise it. But I was fifty before I no longer felt this way. By then I appreciated the generosity of the working class, had a position as history professor, and had adjusted to being middle class.

One of my first memories is going to view the body of my great-grandfather, John Iselman, when I was three years old. I remember seeing him in his coffin, but I didn't understand what death meant. This great-grandfather died at the age of eighty-five. I remembered hearing stories of my great-great-grandfather, Frank Letcher, who lived to be 101. So, as a child, death was fairly meaningless to me since no one close to me had died and people in our family lived a long time! My experience was different from that of my son, who lost both grandfathers before he was three years old.

The other early memory I have is of lying ill on the living room couch in our house. The doctor came to see me, and I remember lying there on the sofa thinking this strange man was a doctor but not knowing quite what that meant. In that image I can also see the Franklin stove in the living room which kept us warm and cozy. It stood on the wall opposite the davenport. Later my father, who was a furnace man, installed radiators in each room and a boiler in the basement to heat the water for the radiators. We moved to this house during World War II, when I was three years old. My mother lived there from 1943 until 1995, and this house provided stability for us. To the right is the earliest picture of me, at age three, before moving to Norton Street.

Marcelline, house on Woodward Street, about 1943

Until reading J. D. Vance's memoir *Hillbilly Elegy*, I hadn't appreciated the stability that living in the same house for decades provided.[1] I discounted how hard my mother worked to keep our family together. I remember her saying that she "wore her fingers to the bone" providing for us, but I didn't really understand what sacrifices that entailed for her. I didn't recognize the relentless work that providing us with food meant for her. While my father's alcoholism and ranting and raving were adverse childhood experiences, my mother's stoicism kept us anchored and helped mitigate the chaos and shame my father created in the household.

My mother was complex. She worked hard and was never paid if she was ill, so she went to work no matter how bad she felt. Her jobs were physically demanding, and she sometimes denigrated the soft lives of intellectuals, whom she thought lived in the ivory towers of academe. She sometimes said things like "the longer you go to school, the less common sense you have." While she wanted us all to do well in life, that meant going to college and getting a good job, not necessarily becoming intellectuals. So while I clung to some of Mother's traditional values, I slowly slipped into an admiration of the intellectual life and away from some of her views. As a youth, I vowed to be different from her. I didn't want to be the meek martyr/victim she was. I wanted to be strong and not let others trample on my feelings. Yet, Mother was supportive, and despite her anti-intellectual views, she came to my college and university graduations. She never told me she was pleased with my accomplishments, but one of her friends confided in me when I was in my fifties that my mother had been proud that I had gotten a PhD in history. So, I was glad to eventually learn this.

An endearing incident involving my mother happened when I was closing up her house to move her to El Paso in the mid-1990s. I was sorting out her papers when I found the first postcard each of us children had sent to her when we first went to college. I had no idea that she had saved them all those years. That was a sweet surprise.

As a child, I remember our little house snuggled among huge trees, which provided a sense of protection. I wasn't conscious of this, but I somehow felt the trees sheltering us as I was growing up. We had maple trees lining the sidewalk on the periphery of our property, a tall tulip tree, a fir tree, and an enormous elm tree near my parents' bedroom. On the alley, we had a cherry tree that I could climb, so I liked it and was disappointed when my mother had it cut down because the cherries were wormy. We also had a medium-sized apple tree between the house

---

1. See J. D. Vance, *Hillbilly Elegy: A Memoir of a Family and Culture in Crisis* (New York: HarperCollins, 2016).

and the garage, and its branches were low enough for me to climb. We also had lilac trees outside the kitchen and bathroom windows, and two enormous pear trees dividing our property from that of our neighbors. I used to try to sell pear blossom corsages on our street corner for twenty-five cents when I was small, but no one ever bought them. All these trees provided shade in the summer and beauty in the spring and fall. I was always sorry when a tree had to be cut down. It felt like losing a companion. I didn't verbalize these thoughts to anyone, not even myself, but somehow I experienced their presence and then their absence.

The streets around our house and in nearby neighborhoods were lined with maple trees that kept us cool on hot summer days as we walked uptown and partially shielded us from the wind and rain on the cool days. They also beautified our hikes with their bright orange, gold, and red leaves in the fall, making a canopy of color as we walked to elementary and high school up Niles Street. I felt protected by them as a youth. While I strode quickly to school so as not to be late, I often strolled slowly home in the afternoon savoring the experience of being sheltered by their branches and colorful leaves. Perhaps on a subliminal level I was aware of their energy flowing over and nourishing me. The trees were a benign force guarding the whole town. Upon reflection, I realize that the trees were akin to angels watching over us, as in the Negro spiritual "Angels Watching Over Me."

In the fall, my father and brother raked leaves into huge piles, and sometimes we were allowed to make a fire to roast marshmallows. Our house was situated on the corner of Norton and Niles Streets. While Niles was a well-paved main street, Norton was poorly paved and lacked curbs, so I guess my father thought it was a safe place to burn the leaves. Despite my pleas, we roasted only marshmallows, not hotdogs, in the leaf fires. My dad always considered burning the leaves a potential fire hazard, and we didn't linger too long in this activity. Still, it was the only form of cookout that we ever had, and it was a cozy and close time since we did it as a family.

On Niles Street, we used to roller-skate, and we sometimes jumped into the huge piles of leaves that people had raked in front of their homes. In retrospect, I am surprised they never shouted at us for doing that. We lived in a pleasant, lower-middle-class neighborhood. Many of the neighbors, like us, were buying their homes, but some rented. It was a good, safe place to grow up.

Looking back, it's fascinating to remember the Boy Scouts tapping the sap of the maple trees in the town. They turned the sap into maple syrup, which they sold. In many ways, trees in La Porte signified abundance, beauty, and protection. Our city, called the Maple City, was a wonderful place to live. The following picture below the remaining maple trees near the living room in our house decades later. Thinking about these trees has made me remember a line from John Milton: "They also serve who only stand and wait." It seems that the trees were literally and figuratively standing, waiting, and guarding us.

Our Niles Street house, without many of the trees of my childhood

Today, I have slightly different views of trees. I still see them protecting me, but I value their physical beauty more. In the spring I love their pale green leaves as they bud open and the beautiful blossoms of fruit trees more than I did as a child. In the fall I appreciate the sun shining through the leaves in the late afternoon, heightening the colors. Indeed, I enjoy looking at the trees and their changing colors more now than previously. Presently, I live on a street lined with huge oaks in Lincoln, Nebraska. I enjoy gazing at them through my living room and kitchen windows or from our terrace when I eat supper outside. I especially like seeing the squirrels scamper around them as they play in the yard.

Another childhood memory was my parents' struggle to buy a ton of coal each fall. In those days, a coal man drove a truck to the side of the house and used a slide to push the coal through a basement window. I had no idea how much the coal cost, but it seemed to be a lot since my parents argued over getting the money for it. I think they ordered two tons to begin the winter.

Years later, in 1968, when my husband, son, and I were living in Southampton, England, we had a similar financial struggle with having enough money to buy a hundredweight of coal. To my surprise, the English coal man carried the coal in a huge gunnysack on his shoulders to put in our shed. We used the coal to make fires in the evening because there was no central heating in the large old Victorian house we rented. It turned out that coal made much warmer fires than wood, but it also cost more, and we had only fifty dollars a month to live on at that time. I also remember the coal man asking me for a few pounds plus a "tanner." I had no idea what a "tanner" was. When I held out my hand with some coins, one turned out to be a sixpence. I had never heard that term before. It's like the archaic American expression "two bits" for a quarter.

Christmas could also be an occasion for parental disagreements. My father always liked to buy an extravagant Christmas tree. It usually cost about $2.50, which my mother probably needed for food, clothing, and shoes for three growing children. The tree my dad bought was often too tall, and he had to cut a foot off the top of it. All of this arguing upset me.

Another time, I heard my parents carrying on about dolls my dad had bought for my sister and me. He had stashed them behind the enormous cookstove in our kitchen. We seldom used this stove because we had a modern gas stove at which my mother did her daily cooking and baking. We used the cookstove only to burn paper on fall mornings when it was cool but not cold enough to start the boiler. For us children, the cookstove was a sort of giant toy where we could play with fire. This particular Christmas, I heard my mother complaining to my dad about spending money on dolls when she needed it for food. Then I saw the boxes behind the stove, and I got the feeling that I didn't deserve presents.

Since then, I have always had a hard time telling anyone what I wanted for Christmas or my birthday. I internalized the notion that I wasn't worthy of gifts. This experience along with many others led to feelings of low self-esteem, which I struggled with the remainder of my life.

On a more positive note, I remember my father always decorating the tree with a Santa Claus I had made in first grade. It was a simple figure that I had colored red and attached to a Santa face the teacher had given us. As I got older, I couldn't understand why my dad always insisted on having this ornament on the tree. I became ashamed of it as I grew up, thinking it rather primitive, not as elegant as the store-bought ornaments. Only in writing my personal history have I come to realize that my dad wanted to include the Santa Claus figure because I had made it, and it was precious to him. Sadly, I didn't understand that I was precious to him too. He never told me.

While my family always had plenty to eat and warm, clean clothes to wear, thanks to my mother's hard work, my parents' arguments about money eventually made me realize that we were poor, and that didn't feel good. We weren't poverty stricken like some classmates at school, but while we didn't look any different from children on "the Avenue," since we had good food and clothing, eventually I realized that our social and economic lives differed considerably. In our culture, poverty was considered a stigma. I learned that even if we were poor, we mustn't appear poor. We should always dress nicely, and I did this all my life, even though as an adult dressing nicely meant frequenting thrift shops instead of department stores. Eventually, it became a burden trying to appear middle class when I wasn't, but I was so used to "trying to pass as middle class" I hardly noticed when I had succeeded. I can remember decades later when I first heard of a Russian play titled *Poverty Is No Crime* by the nineteenth-century writer Alexander Ostrovsky. I found it hard to believe that anyone would think poverty wasn't a crime or a stigma. So many Americans still think it is.

As a child, I didn't feel poor all the time, just when I couldn't pay the $2.50 book rental fee when a new school year began. My mother didn't always have the money for them. She earned only one dollar per hour and could barely pay the grocery bill and the utilities on her meager wages. Since my dad spent the money he earned treating people in the taverns, we soon learned that only our mom could help us pay the book charges. In Indiana, students had to rent their textbooks, and we never took our books home from school.

As an adult, I was astonished to hear friends talking about having homework in elementary school. We didn't have homework. Maybe the principals didn't believe in it in those days, or maybe the authorities feared we might not return the books if we took them home. Who knows? In retrospect, I think it was enough for us to study at school and then learn informally at home. I learned to add, subtract, and multiply while playing cards with my brother and sister on winter evenings. Perhaps it was this informal education playing with my sister and brother that made elementary school so easy for me.

Years later I read Dutch historian Johan Huizinga's book *Homo Ludens* (Man playing, 1938).[2] In it, he endorsed play, explaining how ubiquitous the word is—that is, we play games with rules like chess, cards, dice, or football, and we play the piano or other instruments. Children play hooky; adults play it safe, play at life, play roles, play by the rules, play the stock market, engage in foreplay, and so forth. We also engage in word play, puns, jokes, and so forth. Huizinga thought play provided meaning, risk, experience, and fun. Certainly, playing was important in my early life.

Winter: Playing in the Snow

One of my happiest childhood memories is playing in the snow. At home, I'd don my wool ski pants, coat, headscarf, mittens, and boots to go outside to

---

2. Johan Huizinga, *Homo Ludens* (New York: Harper Edition, 1970).

make snow angels in our backyard. We lived on a corner, so we had a big yard but also lots of snow for my dad and brother to shovel. La Porte was often the snow capital of Indiana, since we received lots of lake-effect snow from Lake Michigan, which was only fifteen miles away. Sometimes I played in the snow by myself, other times with my sister or brother. With them, I enjoyed making snowmen. Some of my brother's friends, the Dadlow boys, who lived at the other end of our block, built snow forts or igloos, and they invited my brother and me to play with them. I adored playing in these snow structures. On the way to school, I also found it exhilarating to skip and slide in my warm snow pants and wool coat. Moreover, if I fell down, this padding prevented me from hurting myself or getting wet.

At school, we sometimes played fox and geese in the snow. Someone made a circle with spokes in it, and we took turns being the fox and geese. It was fun running and chasing each other. It was exciting trying to escape the fox, or capturing the geese if I was the fox. Snow made life magical. It transformed whatever it touched—the playground, our yard, the street. Sometimes it formed a cocoon over the entire town. It made life cozy. I loved playing in the snow. I recently cleaned some rugs by sweeping them with snow. I thoroughly enjoyed this activity and later realized it was a way of playing in the snow.

The most fun I have had in the snow as an older adult was learning to walk in snowshoes. I did this at Hamilton College in Clinton, New York, where I taught Russian history and Western civilization during the academic year 1987–88. Clinton is near the Great Lakes, so we had lots of snow there too. The college provided free skis and snowshoes to students and faculty, and I learned how to snowshoe on the golf course opposite my apartment. I fondly remembered one of my favorite childhood radio shows *Challenge of the Yukon* (later *Sergeant Preston of the Yukon*) and the sergeant's dog, Yukon King, as I trudged around the golf course. I felt like a heroine strutting around, imitating my hero Sergeant Preston, who had worn snowshoes in his work as a Canadian Mountie. Early in the morning before teaching, I enjoyed the vista of the golf course, the whiteness and cleanliness of the snow covering everything in sight. I suppose it was an Emersonian Transcendental experience. Growing up attached to trees, lakes, and snow, I fell for the Transcendental ideas of Emerson and Thoreau that I read about in high school.

In elementary school, we played a variety of games at morning and afternoon recess. Girls occupied one half of the playground and boys the other half. In groups of two or three, girls drew hopscotch squares on the pavement and hopped in the boxes. We also played jacks in small groups. One of my favorite games was skipping rope, especially Double Dutch, which involved two heavy ropes that two girls twirled while the rest of us jumped in and out, reciting various rhymes. None of these games were taught in class. We learned them on the playground and made up rhymes ourselves. I can't say that I made up any of the rhymes, but some of my classmates did. It still fascinates me that this informal education coexisted with our formal instruction. One of my favorite playground games was dodgeball. The entire class participated, usually with a teacher present. We played it a bit like baseball, throwing a ball to a kicker at home plate. That person kicked the ball as far as he or she could, then ran the bases to score a run.

Looking back, I can see that my parents had very different play styles. My father enjoyed going to the zoo in nearby Michigan City to watch the monkeys. My mother didn't enjoy this activity, so she never went. I only marginally liked the zoo but enjoyed participating in an "outing." I remember sitting in Dad's work truck eating chips while he was inside the bar having a drink. This seemed to be his way of celebrating a holiday. Maybe drinking culture represented my dad's form of play. I don't know.

My mother was more serious. She worked very hard and never drank liquor, which if she had might have made her more playful. She had lived during Prohibition, and many churches prior to World War II frowned upon drinking, so she grew up in a teetotal culture. None of my relatives drank in my presence, and we never had alcohol at our joint family holiday dinners. Indeed, alcoholism carried a terrible stigma in my childhood culture. Mother's entertainment was making a special dessert and serving cake and coffee to friends and relations who dropped by to visit. I think her Nordic heritage also constrained her playfulness. What has surprised me, despite my resolve to live differently from my mother, is that like her I have baked cakes and served tea to my friends as my form of entertaining wherever I have lived: in Iowa City, Kansas City, El Paso, Klaipėda (Lithuania), and Lincoln.

Summertime

Summer play could also be magical. Pastimes my sister, playmates, and I enjoyed included picking rhubarb stalks with their enormous leaves, strolling around with them, pretending they were umbrellas. We also made dolls out of the colorful hollyhocks growing in the alley next to our yard. We used toothpicks to fasten the buds as heads to the bodies of the hollyhock flowers, which if held upside down resembled long gowns. We also chased and captured butterflies. The son of one of our neighbors collected butterflies, so we used to capture them and put them in jars to give to him. At night, we played games like kick the can with older neighborhood kids, and we caught fireflies. One night I was very naughty and put a jar of fireflies with the lid off in my dad's bedroom where he was sleeping and then shut the door. I don't remember being punished for this deed, but I must have been. I can't remember if I bragged to my sister about this incident or not.

My mother's usual punishment for me was banishment. I don't remember her ever spanking us. We normally congregated around the kitchen table, but when I talked back to her or was the least bit "lippy," my mother would send me to my bedroom. I hated this. I always wanted to be part of the family or neighborly circle. This was an awful punishment for me. Often the adults would sit at the table, talk, drink coffee, and eat cake or cookies, and we children would have milk and cookies. I liked having the snack, but I also loved hearing the adults gossip, and I wanted to hear what they were saying. I must have had a bit of impishness in my personality because I can remember being banished from the kitchen periodically even though I can't remember what I did wrong. I didn't rebel very often or openly because I spent most of my time trying to be "Miss Goody Two-Shoes." Still, occasionally, this playful part of me surfaced, and it still does.

Another childhood experience I remember is Mother telling me "Run outside and play." If my brother or sister were not outside too, I didn't know quite what to do. I felt lost but didn't know how to tell my mother. She was always busy working and didn't like being challenged. When I got older, I knew to go to Aunt Marcelline's to play with my cousins Jean and Jane, but when I was very little they didn't live close by.

At the Lake

In the summer when my mother was working at Coddington Garment Factory, Aunt Marcelline used to take her two daughters and my sister and me to the beach at Stone Lake. Occasionally, we took the bus, which cost only a dime, but we usually marched the entire two miles to the lake with my aunt carrying a suitcase containing an army blanket and towels. We swam and played in the water. We always went to Stone Lake because Clear Lake was designated for fishing and Pine Lake for sailing. There was a yacht club at Pine Lake, but that was for people with money, and I never knew anyone who went there to drink, dine, or sail. Perhaps it was for the people who lived on "the Avenue." The social demarcations in our town were pretty clear-cut, but it was only as a teenager that I realized only the well-to-do went to the yacht and golf clubs. None of our neighbors or relatives went to these places, so I didn't feel left out.

Had I lived in my hometown as an adult, I'm sure I would have chafed at all the social restrictions. However, once I went to college, I never returned to live year-round in La Porte. So, in my mind's eye, it was a happy place to grow up.

Other summer fun included the Johnson family reunions held at Fox Park across the street from Clear Lake. Being part of my mother's extended family provided stability in my life, and the family reunions were times we all got together. Many of my aunts, uncles, and cousins lived on farms, so I didn't often see them since we lived in town. Only about five of my cousins lived in La Porte. It was always fun to have the great feasts at the reunions and to play together on the park swings and merry-go-rounds. I think the older boys and men played baseball while the women set out the food. Below is a picture of me and my cousins at a Johnson family reunion when we were young.

Johnson family cousins, Fox Park, 1940s

The above photo shows my brother on the top row right, and our cousin Sonny next to him. I am in front of my brother, in the second to the top row on the right. My friend Connie is to the left, and my sister Kathryn next to her. My sister and I wore matching sunsuits that our mother had made for us, but I was already taller than she. My cousin Jean Breese is next to me holding up another cousin. This picture was probably taken in the mid to late 1940s when I was about seven or eight years old. Later, even more cousins appeared.

At the Movies

Another great influence in my life was the movies. The first movie I ever saw was *Gone with the Wind*. I saw it with my mother and sister when I was a preschooler. It had a tremendous impact—the drama of Scarlet and Rhett, the pain of the wounded Confederate soldiers and their operations without anesthetic, the music—all pretty graphic for a child. Growing up before TV, I spent a lot of summer afternoons at the La Porte, Fox, or Roxy movie theaters. In retrospect, I can see that the movies were a cheap way to entertain children. I loved the westerns, which were popular in the 1940s. My favorite cowboy was Hopalong Cassidy, second favorite Gene Autry. I didn't much like Roy Rogers. I remember Hopalong Cassidy wearing black shirts and pants but riding a white horse. He epitomized the hero. In those days, the movies were in black and white, and the heroes always beat the outlaws. I suppose they symbolized the knights of old, only in western garb. This reinforced simplistic either/or thinking, common in children.

I never developed enough psychological distance in viewing movies, and I was and still am terribly upset by violence or torture. I failed to ever develop an ability for critical analysis of films. From adolescence I was a sucker for romantic novels and movies. Unfortunately, I internalized the romance I saw in them and yearned for it, even though I saw precious little of it in the marriages in my family or community. The idealization of romance influenced me more than the reality I lived in. Still, movies helped me process my feelings, and I easily cried while watching them. Today one of my favorite TV channels is Turner Classic Movies, especially the black and white films from the 1930s, and I still cry when watching the sad ones.

The movies in my hometown cost twelve cents for children, ten cents plus two cents tax. On Saturdays at the Fox Theater, there were always double features and programs for the kids between the two shows. The manager tossed candy bars into the audience during the intermission, and of course I secretly hoped to catch one of them but never did. There were also pie-eating contests held on stage. I always wanted to participate in these, but only boys did that. There was no announcement saying "Only boys can do this," but it was understood that it was their preserve. It was a bit like my brother taking the train to Chicago when he was a teenager. He could do that because he was a boy. As a girl, I knew I couldn't do that. I learned early and often that men and boys ruled the wider public world. Of course this set up some dissonance within me since children were treated pretty fairly at home, school, and church. I knew my brother was the apple of my mother's eye, but I also knew that I was my father's favorite. However, being the favorite of an alcoholic did not have too many advantages. My dad never gave us money, and if we wanted to go to the movies, we asked our mother. I remember her sighing and saying: "I'm down to my last red cent, but you can have it." I never knew what "red cent" meant. I did know it meant we were poor. I think now it meant a token from wartime rationing.

I also remember losing my birth certificate at the movies. I was tall for my age, and the managers often asked me if I was under twelve. When I said "Yes," they didn't always believe me. This was embarrassing, and I hated not being believed. So I started taking my birth certificate to the movies as proof of my age. Of course I lost it because children didn't carry backpacks or purses in those days. We only took enough money for the movie and maybe a treat. I always bought Milk Duds because the chocolate-covered caramels lasted a long time. I don't remember ever buying popcorn because we had plenty of that free at home.

I also recall the Roxy Theater having an enormous crack in its ceiling. It seemed awfully close to the huge chandelier which hung from the ceiling. It gave the feeling that the chandelier might fall on us. Since it was in the middle of the ceiling, it was hard to avoid sitting under it. Going to the movie there, I often wondered if I was safe. Watching the old version of *Phantom of the Opera* (not the musical) made me feel eerie, and the crack in the ceiling intensified the terror. Now I wonder if maybe we liked being frightened.

The most embarrassing moment I had at the Roxy was when my mother once had me paged. I had to go to the telephone to speak with her. She was angry at me and made me come home from the movie. I didn't think I had left without her permission, but I must have. Anyway, I felt disgraced being summoned away from the theater and my name announced for everyone to hear.

Before TV, my sister, brother, and I sometimes went to see free movies at the downtown YMCA on Saturday mornings. They were usually old comedies from the 1930s, like those by Laurel and Hardy or Our Gang (later the Little Rascals). The rascals were a group of ragtag kids with a wagon and a dog that had a black ring around his eye. Their adventures usually got them into trouble. Still, they were humorous. At the time, I didn't realize how predictable the plots were. We all just sat on the floor and enjoyed ourselves at the Y.

The greatest mistake I made in going to the movies was confusing the movies' actions with reality. I was pretty gullible and thought people really behaved as they did in the films. I thought men—the subjects—only fell in love with beautiful, sexy women—the objects of their affections. Had I looked around me, I would have seen this wasn't so, but as a teenager I feared no one was going to fall in love with me since I had blemishes and was tall and gangly, not cute and curvy like the actresses. I also thought men showed their love in rough, predatory, demanding, patriarchal ways, like the character Lewt in the film *Duel in the Sun*, which I saw when I was young and impressionable. When I saw this film again on TV recently, I was surprised to notice that Lewt's brother was gentle and quiet, like Ashley Wilkes in *Gone with the Wind*. Of course these men were not the only heroes in the films I saw. I did observe gentle and romantic men like Pierre and Prince Andrei in *War and Peace*. Still, I came away from the movies with pretty confused, sexist ideas about the roles of men and women. While rewatching *Duel in the Sun*, I was glad to observe that in my deteriorating marriage my husband and I did not literally kill each other, as a couple did in the film, but rather dueled with hurtful words and passive-aggressive behavior.

Elementary School

School was one of my favorite places. I felt safe there. No alcoholics like my father or the man next door acting crazy. No shouting. I remember everyone at Lincoln Elementary School being well behaved, and I felt at ease in that environment. My elementary school friend Peter Cumerford recently reminded me that some students misbehaved by spending their money on candy instead of paying for the milk we drank each morning. He even remembered one girl in our class being spanked by the teacher for this misdemeanor. I didn't recall this incident at all, so it's good that I sometimes check with friends and relations as I write these memoirs. Yet, my brother recently confirmed my remembrance that most of the pupils at Lincoln School were well behaved. We were all a little afraid of the principal, Mr. Crum. I think the episode Peter recollected was the exception, not the rule, at our school.

My brother and sister paved the way for me at school. Playing cards with them probably taught me numbers before I went to kindergarten. Filling in coloring books with my sister also taught me colors. Learning the ABCs in kindergarten was easy. Much of what we were taught in kindergarten I already knew, but I wasn't bored. I loved painting at an easel with a brush and a bottle of paint. This was a new and exciting experience for me. Even if I felt bored, family life had taught me to behave and be quiet around authority figures like teachers and my elders.

Looking back, I don't remember if I already knew how to read before I entered Mrs. Bell's first-grade class, but I recall practicing words like "cat" and "dog" on plain three-by-five-inch cards. We began with simple readers—the Dick and Jane series with phrases like "See Spot run." Soon, we advanced to larger books with more words and paragraphs per page. This is when I almost got into trouble. I loved to read ahead and hated waiting while other students took turns reading aloud. We were supposed to keep a paper bookmark under each line as it was being read. Even today I can picture my classmate Tom Jacobs standing and reading out loud to the class. We seldom stood to recite, but reading out loud was the one time we did. We were not supposed to skip ahead in our book, but I couldn't resist reading quickly to see how the story was developing. I would usually read several pages ahead. The trick was to turn back quickly to find the place my classmate was reading from before the teacher called on me. I remember not getting caught many times. Perhaps it was only this once, when Tom was reading. It was pretty embarrassing that I couldn't pick up where he had left off. Basically, I was rule oriented and usually behaved in school. I remember how proud I was to become a monitor when I was in one of the higher grades. I also remember how intimidated we all were of Mr. Crum, our principal.

First grade class, Lincoln Elementary School, 1940s: Marcelline (back row, middle), Pete Cumerford (back row, second from right), and Tom Jacobs (first row, second from left).

Recently, I have become aware of how my teachers represented stability in my life. Unlike today when students frequently have substitute teachers, this almost never happened in our elementary school. Our teachers were disciplined, showed up, and expected us to do the same, so we did.

I loved learning to read. It was a lot more fun than practicing writing in cursive or spelling. I didn't mind those other subjects, but I adored reading or being read to. Still do. I remember in fifth grade one of our teacher helpers, Mrs. Fey, would sometimes read to us. It was enthralling. I discovered I could get lost in a book and enter another reality. While I loved playing outside and was well coordinated, what I loved doing most was reading. One of the happiest times in my childhood was getting my public library card—my passport to other worlds. I soon learned I could go anywhere in the world in a book. I read the usual children's books like the Swedish *Flicka, Ricka, and Dicka* and the American stories of *My Friend Flicka* and *The Box Car Twins*. Later, I graduated to books like *The Brooklyn Kid*, a baseball story. At about twelve, I realized that the books about male heroes didn't quite fit me and was delighted when a neighbor gave me several books in the Nancy Drew series. Soon I turned to historical romances. Little did I realize as an adolescent that these novels would influence me to study history and to pursue romance my entire life. Indeed, I didn't perceive how enticing history would prove to be and how it would later lead me to be "kissed by Clio," the muse of history.

Twice I remember writing stories when I was in elementary school and junior high, but they were not well received. In the third grade I wrote a short story, but I don't remember much about it. I showed it to our teacher helper, Mrs. Fey, and she rebuked me for writing it. For some reason, she didn't like it, and I felt so ashamed that I never wrote anything for a long time. I felt so put down that I never showed anyone my work for many years. Indeed, in college it was painful to turn in papers, never knowing if they were good enough. Even when I received an A on a paper, I tormented myself that I surely didn't deserve it. I certainly didn't major in English with a desire to write. Yet, despite all my inner doubts, I was somehow drawn to writing. It turns out that I mentioned wanting to be a writer in my high school yearbook. Decades later, I was shocked to see these words when some friends showed me the comments.

When I reminisce, I remember loving to learn and being good at it. I can't say I loved learning to write in cursive with a scratchy pen and black ink, but I did it along with my classmates. I especially loved learning something new—like long division, or adding long columns of figures in my head without paper or pencil. Our fifth-grade teacher helper, Mrs. Fey, encouraged this. She would shout out a string of numbers and then ask us to raise our hand when we had calculated the answer in our minds. Everyone wanted to be first with the answer, and often I was. Having reread an analysis of Huizinga's work, I realize that this signified a form of playful learning for me. When I got the answer first, I felt proud. I really enjoyed being the teacher's pet. This sometimes meant I helped with the bulletin board or erased the blackboard. I liked being the teacher's helper. Maybe my teachers let me help them because they realized my family life was difficult. Who knows? School was also nice for me because I never heard any arguments.

At home, my father's drinking and alcoholism often made mealtime unpleasant since he repeatedly provoked arguments with my brother. I suppose my father may have resented my brother because he was my mother's favorite. Maybe my father wanted to be her favorite. Who knows? I know I longed to be her favorite, but I never felt I was. For whatever reason, Dad seemed to pick a verbal fight with my brother at suppertime. At our round oak table, my brother sat at the 12:00 position near the stove, my sister at the 3:00 near a cupboard, father across from Walt at the 6:00 position near the sink, and mother at 9:00 near the cookstove. I was sandwiched between Mom and Dad at the 7:30 position nearest the door. No doubt sitting so close to my father made me aware of his anger. I was frightened when he shouted. I remember once my mother telling me to always put ice in my dad's water glass and to put bread on the table. Otherwise, he wouldn't sit down to eat. I resented these directives, and as a result I never had ice in my water nor bread on the table for supper when I became an adult. While my dad seldom picked on me at dinnertime, I didn't like it when he blustered at my brother. It wasn't very calm when Dad was home, unless he was eating breakfast in the morning by himself, reading the paper in his armchair in the living room in the evening, or "sleeping it off" in bed or on the living room floor.

To be fair to my father, I must include two good experiences I had with him when I was in junior high school. I don't remember if this was before or after I attended the CFO Camp at which my Sunday school teachers and I prayed for him. Anyway, my sister and brother had saved money to buy a hot water heater and a shower, and we all wanted to be able to bathe in the bathroom instead of the tin washtub in the kitchen. Being younger, I didn't earn as much as my siblings, so I don't remember giving money to the project. But because I could "get along" with our father, my contribution was to work with him on the plumbing project. My dad was very skillful at any sort of furnace or plumbing installation, just not good at providing for us and modernizing our house. I remember it was summertime when we did this work, and I helped him saw some thick sewer pipe. I didn't mind being the "gopher" because I liked going down into the cellar for Dad's tools. I liked the musty smell there and some of the implements he had. He mended his own shoes and had metal shoe forms and equipment set up for doing that. I liked to poke around in his stuff and especially to play with the grinding stone used to sharpen knives and tools. It was a different world from upstairs in the kitchen, which was my mother's domain. In retrospect, I'm not so sure I did much work. Maybe my assignment was to encourage our father and keep him on task until the project was completed.

Sometime after our work together on the plumbing project, our father bought or rented a secondhand shop a few blocks away from home on Scott Street. He asked me to help him sell the goods, like watches, in the shop, and I loved doing that. At the same time, I felt a bit conflicted about working there because such shops were not common, and there was a stigma associated with them. I actually felt a bit ashamed to work in such a place. So part of me felt proud to work there and help the customers and another part felt uneasy about it. I don't think I was ever concerned about being robbed. In those days, La Porte was a pretty safe place, and I felt physically safe in the store, even when I was alone. Obviously, not a lot of money was to be made in this enterprise, and I think I worked there only a few months before the shop closed.

Because I had never talked to anyone about these events, I decided to check with my brother to make sure I was recalling them accurately. He assured me I was, and I asked him a bit about our father. He worked with our dad and our uncle Lloyd on various projects and had a different relationship with them. I was shocked when he described Dad as a "soft" drunk. Not the adjective I would have chosen, but it shows how we can live in the same household yet have very different experiences and interpretations of life there. While I loved our father, I was also frightened of him and resented our poverty and the stigma of his alcoholism. After the age of twelve, I felt terribly shamed by him and his behavior. I certainly didn't see him as a "soft" drunk because I remember him ranting, raving, and intimidating us. Moreover, Dad had a swearing litany that used to embarrass me. If he was upset, he would swear "Those goddamned Dagos" or "Polacks" or "kikes," and so forth. I knew this was not nice, but only much later did I realize this was his litany, and he didn't necessarily believe it. It was the braggadocio of men like him. In contrast, I never heard my mother swear or express any prejudice.

Since our mother came to sleep with me some nights, I assumed Dad was menacing to her, and this heightened my fear of him. Only recently, while sitting in a plane waiting for it to be repaired and dying for a drink to help me relax, did it occur to me that perhaps my father needed alcohol to get through life. I had never reflected on that before and felt more compassionate about him. So writing these memoirs has become a healing experience in many ways.

Likewise, I only discovered after my mother came to live with me in El Paso, and we talked, that she had almost died when I was born. She had nearly bled to death at my birth. So I now think she may have been sex avoidant to save her life. I hadn't known any of this when I was young because in our family no one ever talked about sex. Now I wonder if mother may have come to sleep with me because she was trying to avoid intercourse and maybe not because my father was physically abusing her. Of course, I'll never know for sure.

Ballet Lessons

My mother provided good activities for my sister and me. I participated in Girl Scouts and loved selling Girl Scout cookies. I liked going house to house and asking people to buy the cookies. Great-aunt Lizzie lived just a few blocks away, and I always stopped at her place. I suppose she bought a box from me every year, since I always went there. My mother also bought me a membership at the YMCA, where I learned to swim and play on the trampoline. Today, I still use a small trampoline during my morning exercises because it's fun and good for the body. Our mother also paid for my sister and me to have ballet lessons. My sister was diligent and soon learned to dance on her toes. She had beautiful pink toe shoes, and I envied her. However, I was a little lazy and didn't practice as she did. I somehow thought I could practice my tap dancing routines in my head, and I did sometimes, but it wasn't the same as practicing with my feet. I was always tall for my age, and my mother said she hoped that the ballet lessons would help my posture. She didn't want me to stoop, and I never did until decades later. There are pictures of me in one of my tap dance outfits and my sister in her toe shoes. I was about eleven or twelve in the early 1950s.

Marcelline in tap shoes and costume, La Porte, 1950s

Kathryn in ballet toe shoes and costume, La Porte, 1950s

When we were growing up, my brother was tall too: 6 feet 5 inches while in high school. While it was considered a good thing for a boy to be tall, it wasn't so good for a girl in my generation. In those days, the social norm was for men to be taller than women. Since I was tall, I was a threat. I didn't mean to be, but at 5 feet 8 inches in junior high and 5 feet 9½ in high school, I was. I had a complex about being tall, but it wasn't something my family discussed openly. My mother may have discussed it with her family and friends, and that may be why she provided me with ballet lessons, even though she had so little disposable money.

In retrospect, I realize that I hated being tall most of my adult life. I was as tall as my sister from the age of four. Socially, I wanted to fit in, but I didn't. By adolescence, my loathing of my body supplanted my feelings of being poor. By that time, I had jobs, earned money, and didn't feel so poor—just felt like an outsider because I was so tall and skinny instead of curvaceous and cute, or normal and medium-sized. Even though I had a healthy body, I managed to hate it because it wasn't the one I thought was popular. In 2014 I read Cyndi Dale's book *Attracting Your Perfect Body through the Chakras*, and it helped me accept my tall body as the perfect one for me. What a relief to finally be grateful for the tall, healthy body that I had lived in for so many decades. It's strange how we torture ourselves!

Halloween

We were always glad when Halloween came. We liked going trick-or-treating around the neighborhood. It was usually pretty cold at the end of October, so we always had to wear our coats over our costumes. I don't recollect our buying outfits to be a princess or a pirate. We didn't wear our ballet outfits because it was too cold. My sister and I seldom disguised ourselves or engaged in any tricks. We did our trick-or-treating when we were in the upper elementary grades and possibly junior high. By high school, we had jobs at night, so we quit then.

I remember one of the Dadlow boys once dressing up as Aunt Jemima. He blackened his face and wore a turban and several layers of clothes to look fatter. We didn't recognize him when he came to our front door. He was the exception, however. I don't recall my brother ever dressing up as a special character.

Our favorite treats were candy bars, and we liked getting a lot of them. My sister and I usually took a medium-sized brown paper bag for collecting and quit when the sack was half full. Our least favorite treats were apples or cookies, and we got our fair share of them. Our very least favorite was having a bowl of peaches at a neighbor's dining room table. That was not our idea of a treat!

My brother and his friends often took a pillowcase and filled it with candy. They were not limited to our neighborhood as my sister and I were, but they roamed the avenues and affluent areas in search of great treats. They did well but sometimes played pranks too—soaping the windows of stingy people—but nothing too nasty that I ever heard of. Years later in El Paso, my neighbor told me that growing up in rural Iowa, she and her friends had sometimes done mean things on Halloween. They tipped over a fellow farmer's outhouse. That stunned me. No one I knew did such mean things, but we didn't live in the roughest part of town, so I don't know what happened there.

Shadows on My Sunshine

When I look back on my early childhood, I tend to see the happy events and activities. My mother sheltered us from our poverty as well as she could, but there were reminders that my father's alcoholism adversely affected our family. Unlike really poor families, we always had very good, freshly cooked food and well-balanced dinners. In those days, most food was organic, locally grown, and wasn't so contaminated with additives and antibiotics as it often is today. Although my mother probably hadn't heard the Latin phrase for "healthy minds in healthy bodies," she did believe in eating nourishing food and exercising. Mother's proverb was "if you're going to work, you have to eat." Perhaps that came from her farm background. Work was certainly extolled in our family. Mom worked from seven or eight in the morning to five o'clock. She then returned home to her unpaid work of cooking and cleaning for our family each evening. In the morning, she usually left cooked oatmeal for our breakfast if we wanted it. Also, we could have dry cereal and milk if we wanted. When I was in high school I remember frying three pieces of bacon to eat with toast for my breakfast. I couldn't digest eggs very well, so I never made those at breakfast. Sometimes I took a fried egg sandwich for my lunch if I was eating at school in the winter. Mother also left supplies for us to make lunch. We could heat up canned soup, cook Mrs. Grass noodle soup, or make sandwiches from lunch meat, peanut butter and jelly, or whatever we wanted to create. There were always abundant food supplies, including fruit and cookies or cake for dessert.

We also dressed well and never had shabby clothes or shoes. Mom sewed us dresses when we were little and employed a dressmaker when we were in elementary school to make matching outfits for my sister and me: skirts and weskits or vests, and sundresses for the summer. She always bought us new spring and winter coats because there weren't thrift shops then. Nor were there neighborhood rummage sales in those days. Those emerged decades later in the 1960s.

The chief reminder of our poverty, as previously mentioned, was when school began. Being unable to pay the $2.50 rental fee for my schoolbooks in elementary school made me so ashamed. My mother charged our groceries but paid for them at the end of every week. That was OK. No shame there. I felt ashamed when I couldn't take the money for my books to school—not the first week and often not the second or third week either. I felt so bad when the teacher repeatedly asked me for the money, and I couldn't give it to her because my mother didn't have it to give.

Most of her life my mom worked really hard but only earned one dollar per hour, without any paid holidays. No wonder I became intellectually attracted to trade unionism and socialism when I read about them in college. From her meager wages, she bought the groceries and paid the utilities and mortgage payment on our house. Sometimes she got behind on the utilities, and the gas and electric company turned off the electricity. This was another source of shame. Not only was it inconvenient not having electricity but shameful as well. Like many others, I internalized a sense of shame at my father's alcoholism and our poverty. But eventually I learned to shame myself. However, this was something I observed long after childhood. Since Mother worked fulltime, I don't remember her reading to us or cuddling us, so I didn't miss it as a child. But I did do those activities with my son when he was little. By then, I realized how important hugs were and wanted to raise him differently. As a child, I didn't understand that my mother's way of showing love and affection was in cooking us good meals and baking delicious desserts.

Family Holidays

When I look back, I wonder how my mother was able to manage as well as she did. I remember her telling me that her mother had always taken all her wages when she was a young woman, and the implication was that she hadn't liked it. She certainly didn't take any of our money. Indeed, she never even suggested that we contribute to the family income, even though we could have. As I look back I think she should have asked us each for five dollars per week toward the grocery bill. That would have given her a bit more to pay the utilities and other bills.

Indeed, I never knew how she scrimped and saved to buy us Christmas presents. I noticed when I was older that she usually had a Christmas Club Plan, a special account at the bank that she used for saving each week for the forthcoming holiday. I don't know when she began that habit. Once she bought us a child-sized blackboard set on an easel. Ordinarily we had lots of fun playing with it. Unfortunately, I once caught my finger on it, lost a nail, and had to wear a piece of bacon around my finger until the nail grew back. Another time she bought us a plaster of paris set to make small figurines of Mickey Mouse and the seven dwarfs from *Snow White*. We had to mix the plaster with water and then put the wet mixture into rubber containers to let the plaster harden. When it did, we could empty the contents by inverting the rubber holders and pulling the figurines out. We then painted the white plaster figures. I think this entertained us on winter holidays. We also played cards, Monopoly, and store. Playing store meant dragging all my mother's cooking supplies out of the cupboards and placing them on our small wooden table. Then we took turns selling and buying the salt, sugar, and other items.

On winter evenings, since we didn't have homework, my sister and I colored in our ballet coloring books or played card games like rummy. We made fudge or popcorn to eat as we entertained ourselves while mother cleaned up the kitchen. In retrospect, I can see that playing cards was not only entertaining but good for our minds since we added, subtracted, and multiplied various number combinations in our brains. Even as an adult, I played rummy with my mother and son when we visited her in the summer or at Christmas. Some summers, my nephew Eric came from New York City, and then the four of us enjoyed playing cards together.

In junior high, canasta was the rage. I would sometimes go to my friend Jane Davis's house, and we played all day, often till nine or ten at night. My mother would get a bit irritated at having to walk to the neighbors to get me at night. She was probably tired from working all day, cooking dinner, tidying up the house, and then having to go to Jane's house to collect me. We didn't have a telephone

Marcelline (back row, right) at cousin's home in the country, 1950s

or car most of my young life. So, we literally walked to our friends, neighbors, or relatives to see them or gather up one another. Some of our neighbors didn't have a car or phone either, so that wasn't a cause of shame. The picture shows me when I'm in junior high school. The cousin on the left is only about a year younger, but it shows how tall I was for my age, especially compared to her.

Housework and Chores

I can't honestly remember how old I was when my mother required my sister and me to help with the housework and laundry on Saturdays. I didn't mind hanging up the clothes, especially when it was warm outside. Hanging them upstairs in the winter wasn't as much fun. There wasn't much heat in our attic, and it was pretty close quarters working under the low down-sloping ceiling. What I hated was cleaning our bedroom and the living room each week. We had to dust and polish all the furniture. I didn't like dusting or polishing. They were boring. Moreover, we had a lot of furniture in our bedroom: two twin beds with headboards, a vanity, a chest of drawers, a desk, and pictures on the wall. In the living room, we had to dust and polish the wooden feet of the overstuffed chairs and couch, our mother's desk, a large floor-model radio, a case for some encyclopedias, and our father's smoking stand, which stood next to his armchair. The smoking stand had several parts, and each section had to be taken apart and cleaned. One section was for cigars, which our dad didn't smoke, and two small round sections were for cigarettes. Our father smoked but not in the house. I do recall his smoking in the basement though. It's ironic that I now have this small piece of furniture in my living room, as a memento of my childhood. I asked my mother about the stand when she moved to El Paso, and she told me that Dad had received it from a customer when he did some furnace work for him. I never realized such barter took place then.

Our vacuum was never the best, even though my mother bought it new from a door-to-door salesman. She was a sucker for these salesmen who came each week to collect a small amount until the item was paid. She also bought us World Book encyclopedias, which we never used. I'm not sure why I didn't use the encyclopedias—perhaps it was because I preferred reading fiction. Later, I used the reference books at the library, which had the Encyclopedia Britannica that was a cut above ours. I'm sure mother thought she was doing us a favor by providing them, but the sleazy book salesman somehow made using them unattractive. My brother remembers our father chasing the salesman down the street one time because he hadn't fulfilled his bargain regarding the yearbooks we were supposed to receive as part of the deal. I didn't recollect this incident, but I can imagine that it happened.

My mother washed clothes every week, and this meant changing our bedding each week too. That wasn't much of a chore, but moving all the furniture around so we could change the room design was a real bother. It was usually my sister who wanted to change the furniture in our bedroom. This meant moving the dresser and vanity out of our bedroom into the living room. Then we had space to slide the twin beds and desk around. Finally, we could move it all back in. I don't know why my sister liked doing this; I guess because she liked cleaning house, and I didn't. I think we equally despised washing the windows, which we had to do all too frequently. Mother was a stickler for cleanliness and tidiness.

Now, I appreciate those qualities, but as a child I didn't. Our house was more than a hundred years old, and each window had many panes of glass—two rows in the top half of the window with three panes each, and two rows in the bottom with three panes. We smeared some sort of pink liquid onto each small pane of glass, let it dry, and then wiped it off. If I was on the outside, I never got all the streaks wiped off, and if I was inside, I seemed to miss some spots too. I wasn't very good at washing windows. Moreover, there were lots of windows—three in our bedroom, three or four in the living room, two in the kitchen, and one each in the bathroom, my parent's bedroom, and my brother's bedroom. I don't think we ever had to clean the windows or furniture in our parents' room. Mother did that. However, we did have to clean our brother's small room because he worked on Saturdays and wasn't home to participate in the cleaning chores. Needless to say, I resented having to change my brother's bedding. It didn't seem fair.

Later, in Kansas City, I was astonished when my twelve-year-old son volunteered to wash the windows. There too we had some windows with very small panes of glass, and he didn't seem to mind washing them. He also cleaned the bathroom, another chore I detested. Odd, how we are constructed and respond differently to housework.

Our mother did certain tasks like washing and stretching the lace curtains that hung at our bedroom and living room windows. She had to dye them an ecru color and then put them on special stretchers set up in the backyard. She did special tasks like this in the spring and fall general cleanings. I was my mother's helper and was usually sent to the store to buy the ecru dye for the curtains. The advantage of being her errand girl was that I got to choose which cookies to get at the store. Until we had a vacuum, she also hung the large living room rug outside on the clothesline to beat. I had almost forgotten about this until I lived in Lithuania and saw women beating their rugs outside to clean them. They didn't have vacuums either. (A couple from Lithuania Christian College and I bought a vacuum cleaner together and shared it. I was fortunate to have it.)

I didn't mind helping my mother with the ironing. I was good at that, and she sometimes asked me to do the "press work," clothes that required pressing but didn't need to be dampened first. This usually included my dad's work clothes. Since he was such a big guy—6 feet 3 inches tall and huge around the waist from cirrhosis—his clothes took quite a while to press. So, I usually preferred ironing my smaller blouses and skirts. They were often starched and dampened, so when I ironed them they looked really nice. Strange to say, I still love ironing. I find it soothing. I can see what I've done, and that's refreshing because intellectual work is so invisible.

I remember once in Kansas City my son asking me to show him how to iron. He was a teenager, and I was shocked. I had never seen a man iron and didn't know what to do. I remember not showing him, and then feeling bad afterward, especially after his father and I had divorced. I had rigid stereotypes regarding men's and women's work. Only later did I relax these ideas. I thought it was OK for men and women to cook, but I believed washing dishes and ironing was women's work, just as cutting the grass and shoveling the snow was men's. No doubt these were the functions I saw my mother and father perform at home, and I thought this was a universal rule. While my father cooked his own breakfast since he often rose at four or five to leave to do furnace work, he didn't cook for our family. My mother did that. Moreover, my aunts and uncles behaved in similar ways. I never saw an uncle cook or iron nor an aunt shovel snow.

I was surprised when talking to some friends lately when they said they were taught to iron beginning with small items such as handkerchiefs. I had never heard of that. I guess I just learned to iron by watching my mother do it and then imitating her. It wasn't hard. I suppose the same was true for cooking. My mother didn't teach me to cook, but I saw her do it for years, and it didn't seem hard when I married. I checked out a recipe book from the public library and tried various dishes to see what my husband liked best. It proved to be Balkan cooking—that is, dishes like rice pilaf and moussaka. So that's what I prepared whenever I cooked something special.

When my sister and I were growing up, our mother worked at Coddington's, a textile shop that made women's apparel. She pressed open the seams on skirts, vests, and jackets. Some garments had a minor flaw, and they were called seconds. Mother often bought some of these skirts for us for one dollar each, so we had lots of well-made, fashionable skirts. We used our babysitting money to buy blouses and sweaters to go with the skirts. In junior high school, our home economics teacher taught us how to make gathered skirts with a zipper, so we had plenty of summer clothes too. In those days, material or yard goods were fairly cheap, and I enjoyed making myself lots of pretty summer gathered skirts. I had learned how to hem a skirt for one of my Girl Scout badges, one of the more useful skills I learned in Girl Scouts.

Mother, our yard, 1950s

During my childhood, there was not much compassion for alcoholics like my father. Indeed, most of my relatives considered alcoholism a moral failure, and they shunned my father. Some of my relations were pretty self-righteous: people like my dad were the sinners but not them. He was never included in any of my mother's family gatherings. Initially, I didn't notice that my dad was not attending these family affairs—not the summer family reunions, Thanksgiving, Christmas, or Easter gatherings. Only later did I realize that my dad always stayed home in bed and slept. My mother always brought him food from the feast, but it wasn't the same as having him with us.

During the years when I was twelve to fourteen years old, I cleaned house for my great-aunt Mary on Saturday mornings. She often told me tales of how awful my father was because he drank and supposedly went to prostitutes. As a result of our poverty and my relatives' condemnation, I felt very wounded and conflicted about my dad. Part of me loved my father because he was my dad, and certainly the Ten Commandments encouraged me to honor him. All these conflicting attitudes made me feel confused. So I was very relieved one summer when my Sunday school teachers Edith McClellan and Flossie Coddington invited me to attend a CFO church camp (Camp Furthest Out) with them. There, I asked if it was all right to pray for my father, and they said "yes." What a relief. In our family, the children went to Sunday school, and my mother went to church, but we didn't say grace at meals or pray at bedtime. Yet I knew that prayer was powerful and wanted to find a way to express my love for my father. So this camp was extremely helpful in resolving my inner conflicts about Dad. Like many families, ours never talked about prayer, so I was surprised years later when I brought my mother to live with me to discover that she prayed when she cooked and baked. I had never known that before and was quite touched when she told me how she always prayed before putting her cakes and cookies into the oven. Now I too ask God's blessing on my activity, whatever that is: baking, writing, even walking these days.

It was thirty years after praying at the CFO meeting that I heard of the program Adult Children of Alcoholics (ACOA) and found solace for my injured inner child. By that time my father was dead and could never shame me again. Long after my father's death, I realized that I could shame myself and make myself miserable. It was sixty years later that I heard of CFO again and attended it in Nebraska. Again, it was a very prayerful, healing experience.

Somehow I had internalized my second-class status as the child of an alcoholic, and it made me horribly shy in new social situations. My mother also suffered from low self-esteem, so I internalized some of her social behavior as well. As the third child in an alcoholic family, I am termed the "lost" child in ACOA language. I certainly felt lost in social situations. It was incredibly painful for me to ask for a job. Often, my sister or brother would get me a job at the place where they worked. When they found an opening for me, I always took it, but I could barely utter the necessary words to apply for it. I was similarly stymied in making new friends and often "inherited" my sister's old friends. She was the rebel in the family and good at making friends outside the family circle, while I was not.

My brother was the fair-haired achiever in the family, in both academics and sports—on the football field and basketball court. He took the hardest courses in math, physics, chemistry, history, English, and always earned the highest grades. He was also a good basketball player and received a college basketball scholarship. He had to work from the age of ten to earn money for his clothes, shoes, and spending money, so he didn't have as much time as some of his friends to hone his sports skills. Yet, he must have been a natural to do as well as he did. I think his coaches were also great role models for him. Recently, he told me that his high school basketball coach gave him some suits when he was a senior because he needed a suit to attend the senior banquets that were always held in honor of each graduating class. Until writing these memoirs, I never asked him if he suffered from being the adult child of an alcoholic. We learned the lessons "don't ask," "don't talk," and "don't feel" early on. So, we never spoke about those issues growing up.

Talking to my brother about life recently, I have begun to see that he had quite a fine, analytical mind even when he was in high school. When he told me how he evaluated other high schools that he visited when playing basketball around the state, I realized that he was much more observant than I was at that age. I was also surprised to hear him say that because he was a midyear student, he profited from that. He entered high school in January and enrolled in small classes for algebra and other subjects. He also indicated that he got to play sports a semester longer than most others because he didn't graduate until 1956. He said he always studied during his study halls and that he often had two periods for study hall because of the way his midyear schedule worked out. I had never been aware of any of this when we were growing up. Now, however, I can see why he didn't need to study at home because he had two hours to do so at school. Of course, many students simply squandered their study hall time in pranks, but my brother didn't. He worked after school and played sports, so he did his studying at school.

My sister was as smart as my brother and me, but she never seemed to care enough about school to excel. In college and later, I found that my sister possessed a more philosophical mind than I, and as an art therapist she is very perceptive. She just didn't care that much about school. As a result, our nuclear and extended families did not praise her for getting good grades as they did my brother and me. Still, she was more socially integrated than Walt and I. She tried out to be a cheerleader, attended the school dances, and went to the prom, which my brother and I never did. In high school, I belonged to the "Club of the Unkissed" and shied away from school dances because I felt like a broomstick on the dance floor.

Reading Jane Mayer's book *Dark Money* for the Lutheran Women's Book Club the other night, I noticed that Charles Koch was sent to Culver Military Academy, which is in Indiana. This triggered a memory of attending a high school dance after a Culver–La Porte football game. I was standing around feeling like a wallflower when a really handsome, tall cadet from Culver approached and asked me to dance. I was dumbfounded yet pleased. When we started dancing, I felt rigid and ungainly. Taking tap lessons had not prepared me for social dancing, and no one else asked me to dance that night. Needless to say, I felt so ashamed that I never attended another high school or college dance. In old age I vowed I would marry the man who could teach me to dance. I didn't after all because it turned out that although a fellow taught me to

Kathryn in prom dress, 1950s

foxtrot and I loved doing it, we had nothing in common to talk about. That was disappointing!

While my sister made lots of friends in junior and senior high school, I stuck to my cousins or inherited her cast-off friends. My sister was often invited to slumber parties, and once in a while I was too. However, we couldn't invite friends to our house because we never knew how our father would behave. Dad sometimes had shouting tantrums, and we never knew when these would occur or what would trigger one. Once he got mad when Kathryn and I were doing the dishes, and he shouted "Stop arguing. Just throw the damn dishes outside." Then he threw some plates out the back door. We were frightened. Obviously we knew enough not to invite anyone home to a slumber party. Our father was too unpredictable. While my sister entered into the larger world of high school, friends, and dances, I retreated into books. I felt safer reading.

My sister and I also differed in other ways. I was more rule oriented and she more rebellious. When our mother came to live with me in El Paso in the 1990s, she told me that when my sister was seven years old she had asked our mother to divorce our father. That astounded me. I would never have thought of such a thing, and if it had entered my mind, I never would have said it. I also remember my sister asking our mother to cook more captivating food. I loved most of the meals mother cooked—typically Midwestern meals of roast beef or chicken, potatoes, vegetables, salad, homemade noodles, rolls, and dessert. My sister wanted more unusual food, like spaghetti, pizza, and chop suey. I remember our father telling us not to make him any pizza. He wasn't eating "that." My sister also rebelled in other ways. In the house, she would put on her headscarf and boots to wear to school, but then she slipped outside to the garage and left them there. She didn't want to wear them because headscarves and boots were not popular in her circle of friends. I found this weird and wore my winter clothes because they kept me warm, and I was younger and shielded from such attitudes. In junior high school, I thought my sister sometimes ditched her home economics and physical education classes because she didn't like them. She'd write a note excusing herself from school and forge our mother's signature. I don't know if our mother ever found out. I was pretty surprised but didn't tell on her. Recently, I discovered that aspects of these classes made my sister physically ill, and that's why she refused to go to them. I hadn't known that and had misjudged her behavior. In old age, I am discovering that I have sometimes made mistaken judgments of people because I thought I knew why they were doing X or Y, but I really didn't. It's fascinating how we come to self-knowledge!

Unlike my sister who rebelled directly at times, I usually obeyed all the rules, even if I resented them. I was passive-aggressive and later rebelled vicariously through others—my friends, my husband—and even through ideologies, such as socialism and feminism.

Church as a Child

One of my favorite childhood memories is going to the Methodist Sunday school. I can't remember exactly how old I was, but I remember the beauty, acceptance, and safety I felt there. On the way to my Sunday school class, I always passed an enormous, breathtakingly beautiful stained glass window of Jesus with children gathered around his knees. Standing in front of it, I could imagine him blessing me too. It was all so enchanting. Indeed, it was the only stained glass I had ever seen, and its warm message impressed me. The light and colors enthrall me, as did the seated Jesus stretching out his arms to the children.

In Sunday school our teachers often told Bible stories using felt figures on a small easel. The figures captivated me because they stuck to the board and didn't fall off. The stories and figures were almost magical. In class, we also memorized psalms. When we had memorized Psalms 23 and 100, we received a King James version of the Bible with our name inscribed in it. It was special having my own Bible because the flyleaf was black paper, and my name was written in white ink. Wow! I had never seen that before or since. Mine said: "To Judy Hutton from the Methodist Church, 1949."

A third memorable thing about Sunday school was the fun we had on the way home. In good weather, my brother, sister, and I stopped at the Civic Auditorium playground, swung in the swings, and hung from the trapeze and monkey bars. I remember this so fondly because my brother and sister were with me, and I felt very safe and happy playing with them. We had fun playing outside together when the weather was warm. Looking back, I don't suppose our mother would have been happy having us play in our "good" clothes, but she didn't know since she was home working.

Sunday Dinner

When we arrived home from Sunday school, our mother was busy preparing our big Sunday dinner. We usually had chicken, roast beef, or "city chicken," which was a combination of beef, pork, and veal cooked on a skewer. When we had roast beef, mom usually cooked potatoes, onions, carrots, turnips, and homemade noodles with the beef. When she made noodles, she hung the dough to dry from one of the straight-backed oak kitchen chairs. Sometimes I'd sneak a bite of the noodle dough, and it tasted so good. With dinner, she usually served bread-and-butter pickles that she had made during the summer. She also prepared homemade cloverleaf dinner rolls and some sort of scrumptious dessert. The dessert could be burnt sugar cake, peach pie, or butterscotch or lemon meringue pie. The burnt sugar cake was unique. She caramelized white sugar in a cast iron skillet to give it an unusual flavor. All my family and relatives loved this particular cake, and I did too. Looking back, I can see that we were blessed to eat organic food. No one called it that, but the milk and meat were not adulterated with antibiotics as they are today. Moreover, fruits and vegetables were often locally grown. Living near Lake Michigan meant that orchards were protected, and there were lots of apple and peach orchards nearby. In the summer, strawberries, blueberries, and melons were also plentiful. Moreover, since they were grown locally, they were all tree and vine ripened and tasty to eat. Sweet corn, green beans, tomatoes, and squash were also local crops. Our relatives who lived on farms often provided us with these nutritious vegetables. In those days, we had such healthy fruit and vegetables only when they were in season. In the winter, mother often made potato or split pea soup from scratch. Nothing came out of a box. Only in the winter did we have canned vegetables, and often they were mother's own green beans and tomatoes that she had preserved during hot summer evenings after working eight hours at Coddington's and after preparing the evening meal for five people.

Mom even made sweet rolls on Sundays. These were made from the same dough as the cloverleaf dinner rolls, but they were baked in round cake pans, not individual muffin tins, and they were frosted with caramel icing and pecans. She prepared the bread dough by setting it to rise on the kitchen radiators. When I was older, she let me help make the caramel rolls. She even let me experiment a bit by adding jam instead of cinnamon and sugar to some of the rolls to see how they would turn out. I loved doing this, but often she was in a hurry to make the dinner and dessert, and she didn't want me interfering and slowing her down. Moreover, she often made the pies early in the morning when I was asleep or in Sunday school, so I never learned how to make piecrust with lard, as she did. The result is that I seldom make pies because my crust is not as tender and flaky as hers was. I usually make pie using only a graham cracker crust, such as for cheesecake. That I can make. It's easy and pleasant for summer.

Visits from Grandpa Johnson

Other good memories I have from early childhood are the visits of my Swedish grandfather Walter Gustavus Johnson. He often came to town on Saturday to do the family shopping—buying the groceries, shopping for clothes at Low's Department Store, and so forth. Apparently my grandmother did not like shopping or was too busy for it. Grandpa Johnson stopped to see his various children and grandchildren, and he always had spellbinding stories to tell. I loved his tall tales. My favorite was about how his boat laden with gold was coming to the United States from Sweden, and we were all going to be rich. This seemed true to us, because he always gave us twenty-five or fifty cents, and that was a lot of money in those days. He always enjoyed a piece of cake or pie and some coffee that my mother served him, and his visit was a special event. Needless to say, I had very fond memories of my grandfather, and he lived to be eighty-five—outliving my own father, who died at sixty-seven, and my father-in-law, who died at sixty-two. So it was a little odd that my son had a great-grandfather but no grandfathers when he was young.

Earning Money

Because my mom worked so hard and earned so little money, it was important that we earn money ourselves. I suppose my idyllic childhood came to an end when I first started earning money by babysitting. Initially I babysat for the two children across the street. I was ten years old and they were younger, three and five or perhaps five and seven years old. I was surprised to discover how differently the Teeter family functioned from ours. They had a lot more money than our family did. They had a car and a telephone that we occasionally used. Yet they were frugal in odd ways. While they had a huge Buick, since the father was an insurance agent, the children did not have beds or a bedroom. In contrast, my sister and I each had our own bed and matching maple furniture. The children, Terry and Thyra, slept on benches in their father's office. So, I got out their blankets for them in the evening, and Mrs. Teeter put away the bed clothes in the morning. Also, the children had to eat everything on their plate. If they didn't, it was put in the fridge until the next meal. We never did that. If we didn't like what my mother prepared, she told us to make ourselves a peanut butter sandwich but not to complain. We never had to try vegetables and food we didn't like. Any food left over from dinner was given to our dog, Lady. So, we never had leftovers. My mother always cooked a fresh meal each night.

We could always have as much as we wanted—an extra hamburger, piece of minute steak, or pork chop—but we weren't supposed to waste food. Since we had a dog, extra mashed potatoes and gravy went to her. I was surprised years later to discover that people bought special dog and cat food. We never did.

Despite their unusual childrearing practices, Mrs. Teeter did some things I admired. She sewed her own clothes with an electric sewing machine, and she let me use it too. What I recollect as most unusual were the Christmas cookies she made. She made sugar cookies shaped like Santa Claus, but she decorated hers with colored frostings. She used a paintbrush to apply red frosting for Santa's coat, cap, and pants; white frosting for his beard; and black frosting for his belt. I thought this was so neat. I vowed to myself that I would do that when I grew up, but I never did. My mother made tasty oatmeal, peanut butter, and chocolate chip cookies and about ten other kinds for the holidays, but she didn't decorate them like Mrs. Teeter did. Mom only scattered colored sprinkles on our Christmas cookies.

One other amusing recollection I have of babysitting with the Teeter children was reading them the *Uncle Remus* Br'er Rabbit stories and correcting the dialect in the text. When I came to double negatives and other incorrect grammar, I automatically changed it because I knew it was wrong. I thought children should not hear such English. Maybe this was the teacher in me emerging at the tender age of ten. Looking back, it seems strange that when I listened to the stories of Br'er Rabbit and the tar baby on the *Uncle Remus* records that my cousins Jean and Jane had, I didn't feel the need to correct the language. Somehow I distinguished between spoken English and the written word.

I realize now that babysitting and earning money changed my life. It meant I was more grown up and didn't have to ask my mom for money to go to nearby Scholl's dairy with my friends and sister to buy an ice cream cone. Also, I sometimes saved my money for something special. In the sixth grade, I remember buying some pretty green pumps with a very low heel that I wore to school. I thought them so chic, although I didn't know

Marcelline in saddle shoes, outside our house on Niles Street, 1940s

the word then. I guess I loved them because my mom always bought serviceable saddle shoes for me, as the picture shows.

While I tried to be a model child, I wasn't. My mother was terribly self-sacrificing and hardworking for her children, but sometimes she could be a bit wintry. I remember once when I was in the sixth grade, my mother sat me at the kitchen sink to wash me—this was before we had hot water and a shower—and she scolded me. I don't recall what I had done to offend my mother, but it must have been awful since she rarely criticized us and never hit us. I suppose I must have lied about something serious. She told me to shape up and threatened to send me to the girls' reformatory in Indianapolis if I didn't. That frightened me. The result was that I silenced and repressed myself still more. I was already pretty shy in social situations, and this verbal attack from my mother scared me. I decided I had better withdraw more and just read. That seemed better. Years later when I had brought my mother to live with me in El Paso, I asked her about this incident. I still wanted to understand why she had threatened me, but she said she didn't remember anything about it. I knew I hadn't made it up, but I still don't understand it and had repressed it until recently. Three explanations come to mind: first, I may have been acting out, as my dad sometimes did, only he could get away with it and I couldn't. Second, my mother may have been going through menopause and wasn't in a good mood. Third, more likely, I may have done something really bad and just repressed it. I recollect my sister once telling me I had slapped a classmate in the face on the playground, but I didn't recall ever having done that. I do remember later becoming friends with both of those sisters because we attended the same school and church.

Since my brother and sister were older, they got paying jobs before I did. They often accused me of being lazy and spoiled, and that made me feel bad. In our family, working and earning money were virtues. The more you worked and the more money you earned, the more virtuous you were. The exception was my dad. As a furnace man, he worked hard and of course earned good money, more than any of us; but he spent it all at the bars buying drinks for other guys, and he didn't contribute much to our family economy. He usually rose early around four or five and made himself steak and potatoes because he worked long days taking out a furnace and putting in a new one. He was considerate of others, not wanting to leave a family without heat for more than a day if he could help it. However, he wasn't so kind to his own family. We never prospered from his work and high wages. Years later, I married a man who didn't drink, and who worked long hours, but he resembled my father in being stingy to his family.

By the time I was twelve, I was able to follow in my sister's footsteps and work for a babysitting agency. We earned twenty-five to fifty cents per hour. Working and earning money probably made us all more independent. It certainly signaled the end of childhood. Thinking about this recently, I realized that my brother's going to work, and then my sister's too, undermined the coziness of our family life. No more time together playing cards and eating popcorn and fudge in the evenings. I felt family closeness again only at Christmas when we sat in a semicircle around the tree exchanging gifts. Then I felt that coziness. What I didn't know then and learned later when I entered the ACOA program was that children in alcoholic families often don't have much childhood. They have to behave responsibly because the alcoholic parent doesn't.

In retrospect, it seems that I had a rather carefree childhood until I was ten or twelve. Then I became more aware of the implications of my father's drinking and arguing. Still, compared to homeless children today, who don't even have beds, I can see that I had stability in having a home. None of us discussed our father's drinking. Relatives might comment, but we never talked about it. I never talked to my mom or my sister about our father's drinking and the devastation it caused. "Don't feel" and "Don't tell" were the unwritten bywords. I grew up pretending everything was OK. I never learned to tell my father how much his drinking and our poverty hurt me. Decades later, I failed to tell my husband when he hurt my feelings or shamed me. As a child, I had internalized male abusive language, and it took years for me to learn to accept my feelings, articulate them, and defend myself.

As a child, I discovered I could have and express feelings safely at church but not at home. I loved the exhilaration of singing beautiful hymns and anthems at church, but I didn't sing around the house very much. My mother sang softly when she ironed in her bedroom, and I remember lying on my parent's big bed, watching her iron and listening to her sing. Like most children, I heard the words "'Round yon Virgin" in the carol "Silent Night" as one word. Even today, I choke up when I hear a group singing this carol. I think of my mother who sang this song so sweetly. She died in 1997.

While mother didn't pray out loud at home, she inculcated good values in me by her generous and gentle treatment of others. She also told me some of her adages. I remember her saying once, after my dad had brought home some disreputable fellow for a drink, "I like everybody, but I may not like their ways." I thought the stranger looked pretty disgusting, even a little scary, and was surprised at my mother's broadmindedness. Today, I try to be as kind as my mother was, but I usually think to myself when dealing with someone offensive, "This person is also a child of God. God loves them more than I ever can." This means that even if I can't really love the offender right now, I know God does. My acceptance is often more grudging than my mother's. But she was an amazing, long-suffering person, able to separate the sin from the sinner. Sometimes I'm more like my father—angry, rejecting, and resentful. Another time I recall mother making me share my Popsicle with a friend on the back porch. I didn't really want to do it because we didn't get treats like this from the store very often, but she insisted that we always share our food with those around us, and we always did. One of my cousins recently remarked that he never came to our house without mother offering him something to eat. I try to emulate this behavior too, and I know that my son is also very generous sharing food and drink with others.

When I was young, I also remember loving to sing in school. It was easy for me to learn the melodies and memorize the lyrics, and I adored belting out the old favorites. In retrospect, I don't suppose my classmates enjoyed my singing so loudly. Yet it was a safe release for me and a chance to use my voice. I didn't feel silenced then, as I did so much of the time.

I suppose the alcoholic family's "don't feel" rule was another reason I enjoyed losing myself in a book—living in another more expressive emotional reality. It was a safe way to experience feelings vicariously. Today I enjoy reading novels by Rhys Bowen, Elena Ferrante, Gail Godwin, Jan Karon, Amy Tan, and Jennifer Winspear; historical novels by Hillary Mantel, Ken Follett, and Amor Towles; and mysteries by P. D. James, Donna Leon, Henning Mankell, and Louise Penny. Like a drug, they temporarily transform ordinary life into a more romantic, tantalizing, or mysterious place. I often read two or three such books a week.

Films and TV have a similar effect, but they are not as portable and satisfying as a book. Of course smartphones and Nooks are portable and do provide entertainment, but I still prefer holding a book in my hands. My family bought a TV set when I was in junior high, but I had enjoyed listening to radio programs like *Our Gal Sunday* during lunch in the summertime, *Sergeant Preston of the Yukon* after school, and *The Lone Ranger* in the evening during the winter. On Sunday afternoons I often listened to scary mysteries like *The Green Hornet* and *The Fat Man* in my brother's bedroom, since he had a radio.

TV shows like *Howdy Doody* did not satisfy my imagination as radio programs did. They were boring. I didn't care for TV comedians like Jack Benny or Sid Caesar. The only TV programs I liked were the sentimental *I Remember Mama*, which I watched with mother on Saturday nights, and the films featuring the clever detective Charlie Chan, which I had watched with Dad on Sunday mornings after Sunday school when I was in elementary school. In high school on Friday nights I enjoyed watching romantic movies with one of our neighbors. My sister liked popular music shows like *The Dick Clark Show* and its "American Bandstand Top Ten," but this didn't attract me since I didn't go to dances.

My two favorite radio shows were *The Lone Ranger* and *Our Gal Sunday*. I admired the Lone Ranger as a hero and loved his loyal sidekick, Tonto. I was surprised years later to see a short story by the Native American writer Sherman Alexie titled "The Lone Ranger and Tonto Fistfight in Heaven." That was an unexpected perspective on their relationship. His novel *The Absolutely True Diary of a Part-Time Indian* was also surprising and bittersweet. The 1950s radio serial *Our Gal Sunday* presented a woman in love with an English lord and the uneven course of their relationship because of their class differences. I believed this soap opera a little too much and later thought that my husband with his English mother and relatives would transform my working-class life into something much better. How wrong I was. I thought him debonair, like the gentlemanly Ashley Wilkes in *Gone with the Wind*, but he turned out to be tougher, more like the character Rhett Butler.

CHAPTER II

Youth: Joy and Alienation, 1950s

Church as an Adolescent

One event that signaled the end of my childhood was my decision to be baptized and confirmed as a member of the La Porte Presbyterian Church when I was twelve years old. I can't remember when my mother switched from the Methodist to the Presbyterian church, but it was sometime while I was in elementary school. According to my brother, our mother's departure was part of a general exodus from the Methodist church caused by some problem with a minister there. The fact that I myself decided to be baptized and confirmed indicates my serious nature when I was young. About the time I became a member of the church, I also joined the choir at the Presbyterian church. We met for practice on Wednesday nights and sang on Sundays. I could sing on key and sang alto but could only sing this part if I sat next to a strong alto who could read music. I always heard the melody of the sopranos in my mind, and it was hard for me to harmonize. I could see the notes for the altos but didn't know how to produce them. I felt awkward about this but never thought of taking singing lessons so I could read music and the alto part. This problem plagued me even when I went to college and sang in the college choir. After a semester of feeling insecure about my singing, I quit and never sang in a choir again until I lived in Kansas City, two decades later.

Despite my uneasiness about singing alto properly, I kept singing in the choir in junior and senior high school because I loved doing it and the wonderful way it expressed my joy at Christmas and Easter time. I especially resonated with hymns and anthems in minor keys, which we often sang during Lent. I loved singing the hymns because we sang them in unison. I could easily hear and sing the melody. It was glorious and majestic. Years later, I was surprised to find that my Mennonite friends, with whom I taught at Lithuania Christian College in Klaipėda, Lithuania, during the years 2000–10, harmonized when they sang hymns. They grew up in churches without organs and learned to harmonize as youngsters. Occasionally some of the Mennonite men would perform in a barbershop quartet style for our offertory, and that astounded me. Prior to their performance, I had heard such groups sing only secular music.

One of my fondest memories is our youth choir having a recital and then going on a tour under the direction of Mrs. Marion Williams, our director. We sang Haydn's "The Creation," and the alto part was not so hard to follow, so I felt confident during the performances. I'll never forget the opening bars:

> The heavens are telling the glory of God,
> the wonder of His work displays the firmament.

The music was glorious and grand. I knew my part reasonably well, and it was the first time I ever wore a long formal. I think we bought them from neighborhood girls who were Catholic and had participated in some big weddings. The long gowns also signified being grown up, and that was exciting for a thirteen-year-old.

Mrs. Williams arranged for our youth choir to go on a tour to Dearborn and Detroit, Michigan, to perform at Presbyterian churches there. We even crossed into Windsor, Canada, from Detroit, and I was impressed to be visiting a foreign country. It was an awesome experience for a naïve girl from La Porte, Indiana. In 1952 Windsor looked pretty poor compared to the United States, but when I revisited it in 2013, it was lively and flourishing. My sister also sang in the choir and went on the trip, but I never asked her if it had the same impact on her. I guess this was the alcoholic family rule of "don't talk." I'm not sure.

Our choir director was an amazing person. Although she was married with children, she taught music in junior high school and also directed the youth and senior choirs at the Presbyterian church. She was a creative and open person. She encouraged a young fellow who played the cello to accompany our choirs in their anthems and to play duets with the organ for the offertory. The cello plus the organ really made our performances powerful. She was the sort of teacher we had in our school system: thoughtful, kind, talented, professional, and caring. I was surprised once when my brother commented on how professional our French teacher, Miss Dick, was. I had assumed all teachers were like her—professional and proficient yet fun and caring. She had studied in France and continued to take trips there to polish her spoken French. The motto in her classroom was "On parle français ici"—One speaks French here—and she taught us to read, write, and speak French. We also had a French name we used in class. Mine was Roxanne. My brother's was Yves. I thought our names made us intriguing. We could also sign up for a French pen pal and write our letters in French. This was fantastic, especially when I discovered that my pen pal made mistakes in grammar. "Wow!" I thought, "even the French make mistakes."

The result was that my two years of high school French made second-year college French a breeze. A consummate teacher, she taught us French numerals by having us play bingo in French. Learning how to quickly say numbers like sixty-seven, seventy-eight, or ninety in French helped us learn to think in French. It was excellent practice and sharpened our minds. Our French and Latin teachers also taught us Christmas carols in those languages, and my hunch is that learning to sing in a foreign language helps one speak it. We learned "Jingle Bells" and "Adeste Fideles" in Latin class. We learned "Minuit Chrétien" and "Il Est Né Le Divin Enfant" in French class. We also learned other songs and hymns in those languages, which made learning those languages playful. Miss Dick, like many of our teachers, gave "good" students extra work. She suggested my brother read Victor Hugo's *Les Miserables*, which he did during his study halls, and assigned me some novels by Jules Verne, which I read. Here is my brother's graduation picture from La Porte High School (LPHS).

Years later when interviewing Aunt Marcelline for a family history project, I learned about some of my high school teachers because my aunt had studied with them twenty years earlier. I found the pictures of my Latin teacher, Mrs. Russell, and my French teacher, Mlle. Dick, as young women endearing. I only knew them as seasoned, middle-aged women. My aunt, much to my surprise, had belonged to the high school travel club, and there she discovered that her European history teacher, Miss Davis, had made many trips to Europe to study European culture. I was flabbergasted she

Walt Hutton, LPHS, 1956

had been so adventurous because I had thought of her as an old fuddy-duddy since she made us take verbatim notes of her lectures. It was also strange to see my tough, white-haired American history teacher, Frankie Jones, as a young woman with bobbed hair in the 1930s. By the time I went to high school, she was a veteran teacher, ruled the class with iron discipline, and made us not only memorize the preamble to the Constitution but also analyze films about the TVA dam project. She was demanding but fair, a good combination.

Adolescent Discoveries

In junior and senior high, I realized that I could not associate with certain girls without getting into trouble. I became aware that if I remained friends with those headed toward drinking and wild parties that they might lead me onto dangerous paths. I felt as if I had to be very careful and decided I'd better try to remain "Miss Goody Two-Shoes." It was also when I was about twelve that I recognized I could no longer play with my brother's friends. In earlier times we all played happily. But when I was about twelve and they were fourteen or so, something happened. They became too rough for me. Boys that I had earlier enjoyed building snow forts with had changed. One of my brother's friends began throwing snowballs with ice and stones in them. This was not fun. He also threw them too hard. At the beach in the summer, the neighborhood boys started dunking me and holding me under the water too long. This scared me. The message I got was "Boys are dangerous. Avoid them." Little did I know then that a girl withdrawing from dominant male culture was normal at that age.

There were two boys in my elementary school class who were gentle and who might have become my boyfriends had they stayed in La Porte, but they moved away before junior high began. One of the boys, Norman Trost, often gave me a ride home from school on his bike. This was so sweet. But I was too innocent to see this as a possible budding romance. He lived a block away, and I just thought he was being neighborly, and maybe he was. I now wonder what my life would have been like if I had had a boyfriend like Norman Trost or Jimmy Terhune in high school. What if I had had a normal adolescence instead of the repressed life I led in high school and college? What would my life have been like if I had not gone to college but had stayed in my hometown and married a local boy? Who knows? In retrospect, I can see I was blessed to love reading and studying and that this led me to go to college and graduate school, which expanded my horizons.

Odd Forms of Adolescent Romance

As a teenager, I didn't fall in love with a boy but with books and ideas. Reading remained my favorite hobby. I especially enjoyed historical romances. They were a two-for-one experience—the vicarious romance between a man and a woman, and an exotic setting in a foreign locale. The ideas I was attracted to were Transcendentalism and being a teacher missionary to Africa. The latter seemed romantic because it involved some self-sacrifice. Upon reflection, I can see that this desire also possessed some of the grand gesture that my dad liked making. I wasn't conscious of that part of my personality then. In writing these memoirs I have noticed this about myself. My most mundane romance was with my bike. I loved the freedom it gave me.

Romance of the Road: My New Bike

I remember being in the sixth grade when I received a bike for Christmas. It was the best present I had ever gotten. Until then, I had ridden my brother's. He was generous in letting me use his. I loved riding into the countryside as far as I could go. I never thought of danger. There wasn't as much traffic on the roads then as there is now. My bike represented freedom, and I could ride to the beach by myself and stop at the Dairy Queen to buy a five-cent ice cream cone on the way home. This small purchase represented luxury to me. I don't remember riding my bike to school very often. I don't know why. I guess we preferred walking. I can remember strolling home from school, reading a book as I ambled along because I knew the way and there weren't many objects to stumble over. In those days, people maintained their sidewalks because we used them to walk to work as well as to school. Only a few people in our neighborhood had cars. In 2008 I retraced my old route from the library to our house and was shocked to see the sidewalks on Niles Street cracked, broken, and dirty. Today everyone drives. In 2008 when I stayed at my aunt's, I was often the sole pedestrian as I walked uptown to the public library.

Romance of Youthful Idealism

At some point in high school, perhaps in my junior year, I decided that I wanted to become a teaching missionary to Africa—no special country, just Africa. I was ignorant that Africa consisted of more than fifty countries. I think I wanted to sacrifice myself as a missionary instead of just teaching in an ordinary American school. Teaching there seemed romantic, altruistic, and exceptional. Perhaps I was influenced by the model of Albert Schweitzer, the famous organist and theologian who earned a degree in medicine to become a doctor and missionary in Africa. All this occurred in the mid-twentieth century, before the time of President Kennedy and the idea of the Peace Corps, but perhaps the idealism was similar. Perhaps I saw the movie about Schweitzer in the early 1950s and was influenced by it. I do remember talking to my minister about my "calling to be a missionary" and coming under care of presbytery as a future church worker as well as praying with him about this decision.

CHAPTER II

Romance of Transcendentalism

I still remember my English teachers, who assigned us excerpts from American writers like Ralph Waldo Emerson and Henry David Thoreau. I fell in love with their Transcendentalist ideas. What is there not to love in Nature with a capital N? Living in a town like La Porte with its magnificent maple trees, lakes, and bountiful snow, it was easy to love Nature. I often wonder today how young people are driven to experiment with drugs and alcohol when Nature is so dazzling in much of the United States. A sunrise, a sunset, a beautiful moon still stir my soul, and I can't quite figure out why Nature doesn't speak to young people today. Maybe it does, just not to everyone, or not so deeply. Many youth seem to have a more fragile psychic state today, as the higher rates of drug overdose and suicide suggest. Of course, many youth are ardent environmentalists, so Nature does speak to them.

Reading Jill Ker Conway's autobiography *The Road from Coorain* helped me realize how environment can shape our outlook. She grew up in the harsh outback of Australia, where she was haunted by images of terribly destructive drought, marginal farms, and even outlaws. She realized this landscape shaped the inner landscape of her mind. Her emotional life was dominated by images of great drought.[3] In contrast, I grew up in a rather lush physical environment in northern Indiana with luxuriant trees; attractive lakes for fishing, swimming, and sailing; and a healthy climate with sufficient rain that produced bountiful fruits and vegetables. My environment provided simple abundance, making it easy for me to believe in a providential God. Indeed, there was even an abundance of game, and I remember my brother hunting ducks and rabbits, which we then ate for supper. Rabbit tasted like chicken to me, and I wasn't squeamish about eating it. No one minded his killing the wild rabbits because it seemed part of the natural order of things. Much later I wondered who cleaned those rabbits. I don't know if it was my dad or my mom. I was sure glad I didn't have to.

Historical Romances

In junior high school I felt socially left out. What I really liked reading were historical romances, which provided an alternative reality. My aunt Marcelline Breese, who was sort of my second mother and lived just two blocks away, subscribed to the Book of the Month Club, and I avidly read all her Frank Yerby

---

3. See Jill Ker Conway, *The Road from Coorain* (New York: Vintage: 1989), 218–19.

novels. His books were set in the antebellum South, often in New Orleans. I also liked secretly reading romance magazines like *True Story*, which I bought with my babysitting money and hid from my mother. I read them surreptitiously when I was a teenager. By twelve, I was able to check out books from the adult section of the library. When I heard about a racy movie based on the book *Forever Amber*, I decided to check out that novel and read it. I hid it in my desk at school when I was in junior high, and I read it on the sly during class when my teacher wasn't looking. I'm sorry to say I probably wasn't paying much attention to my lessons during the week I read that book. I remember rushing through my assignments to read it. Later in high school, I found European history engrossing because I had read so many historical novels. History helped me put all the information from the novels together in a meaningful way. Then I began to understand not only where France, England, and Scotland were but something of the genealogy of the kings and queens, and how a particular novel fit into a broader historical picture. In high school, I saw the movie *War and Peace* with Audrey Hepburn, Mel Ferrer, and Henry Fonda and fell in love with Russian culture. I read Tolstoy's novel, and although it's a cut above most historical romances, it clearly was historical and a romance. It also made me appreciate Russian history. Although many other amusements and activities, such as knitting, embroidering, bicycling, and swimming came into my life, reading remained my favorite pastime. Indeed, reading still acts like a drug for me, and I jokingly say that I read my way to a PhD in history.

Confidence from Jobs and Sports

In adolescence, my life was outwardly circumscribed by going to school during the day and to work in the afternoons or evenings. The summer I was fourteen, I was able to take a better-paying job than babysitting. My brother helped me get a job working at Bernachi's Produce Company, putting vegetables in bags. It was assembly line work, and we mainly put green onions into plastic bags. To make it challenging, I used to race some of the other girls to see who could bag the most in the shortest time. Silly me. I didn't realize I was increasing the work tempo, and not everyone wanted to do that. The next year, my brother helped me get a place at Carringer's Dairy where he worked. I remember both jobs paying seventy-five cents per hour, a marvelous wage. At the dairy I worked some evenings, some Saturdays and Sundays. However, the dairy was thirty-seven blocks from our house, and it was a long, cold walk in the snow at night in the winter. If I rode my bike, I could get home faster, but

I got colder than walking. I remember coming home in the dark but not being scared, since that is what we did. Not having a car, we always walked to and from work. Neighbors did too.

After working at the dairy for a year or two, my sister helped me get a position as a cashier at Leroy's grocery store, which was downtown and much closer to our house—only about ten blocks away. Moreover, sometimes Mr. Leroy gave us a ride home when we closed at ten at night. I appreciated this during the winter. I remember this job paid one dollar per hour, and I was very proud to earn this amount. I earned about twenty dollars per week and tithed two dollars a week to the church. This made me feel very grown up. My self-image benefited from having a job at the grocery store since the owner and other workers liked me well enough. They didn't look down their noses at me because I came from the working class part of town and lacked social graces. As long as I did my job well that was all that mattered. This experience probably helped salvage some of my battered self-esteem. The affirmation of my teachers and fellow workers kept me anchored and functional. My outer mask showed me smiling and happy on the outside, as the following high school picture indicates, while inside I felt insecure.

Marcelline, LPHS, 1956

With the onset of adolescence my spirit of play disappeared. I felt inferior, like an ugly duckling. I suffered from the low self-esteem of an alcoholic's daughter. So, work gave me some independence and self-definition. Even if I felt in low spirits while walking to the grocery in the evening, by the time I arrived there I felt better. At that time, I didn't know that exercise was good for my mind and spirit as well as my body. I walked because that was how we got around, and I didn't discover the many benefits of walking until much later. Moreover, when I worked from six to ten at night at the grocery store, I made my own supper, often a pork chop sandwich, and this freed me from conflict around the supper table, where my dad often provoked arguments. Freed from that family chaos was a benefit of working that I recognized while reading Vance's book *Hillbilly Elegy*.

It also helped that I excelled at school. This gave me a sense of well-being too. Joy in life consisted of reading bewitching novels, learning fascinating material at school, and participating in church activities. I wasn't miserable since I lived vicariously in the historical romances I read. Indeed, I loved my course in European history that I took when I was a sophomore because it helped me understand the worlds of the novels I read.

In retrospect, I can see that being good at sports also provided some self-confidence. We didn't play organized girls' basketball or volleyball in La Porte in those days, but we did have pick-up baseball games, gymnastics some evenings at the high school, and archery as a competitive sport for girls. I was good at archery and once went to a state archery contest at Purdue University. That was because our women's physical education teacher, Miss Cosand, who sponsored our archery group, drove us there. I grew up in the days before Title IX and the regulations that make sports available to girls as well as boys. While my brother went all over Indiana playing basketball, sometimes staying overnight if the school was far away, girls didn't do that. Years later, I was surprised to find that the state of Iowa sponsored girls basketball, and Nebraska allowed girls volleyball as a competitive sport. This was so different from the Indiana where I grew up.

Social Attitudes

At one point, several of my sister's friends wanted to be airline stewardesses. I sure wanted to do this too, but I was too tall to fit the stewardess guidelines. By eighth grade, I was already five feet eight inches tall—too tall for the airlines' regulations. Perhaps it was about this time that I began to internalize my self-loathing for being too tall. I had heard that the actor Alan Ladd was short and had to stand on a box when he played opposite actresses who were taller than he. That showed how our culture valued men being taller than women.

I thought myself too tall and too skinny—not at all like the Hollywood starlets or school cheerleaders who were curvaceous, cute, and short. I remember feeling so physically inadequate. Nor did I feel better when people made remarks like "Oh, you should be a model. You're so nice and tall." I was rather photogenic, but I didn't know that term. I just knew that my pictures didn't really reveal my flaws. Indeed, I was dumbfounded recently when a friend told me that my high school graduation picture was "glamorous." I certainly never felt glamorous. Little did others know that I felt too unattractive to be a model. My sister and I never talked about these feelings, nor did my cousins and I.

Once, I remember my cousin Sonny Keller telling me that his friends thought I was eighteen years old when they saw me walking down the street, and I was only twelve! So, once more, I didn't feel as if I had a normal adolescence. Now that I'm older, I realize that most kids struggled in adolescence. Not everyone felt "normal." At the time, I thought I was the only one with these problems because I never talked to anyone about my feelings.

As a teenager, I discounted myself. My pretty blonde hair of childhood had darkened to a mousy light brown. Sometimes I had pimples, and I felt like a tall, skinny freak. I certainly didn't know that most teens worried about their physical appearance. Sixty years later, reading Sherman Alexie's *The Absolutely True Diary of a Part-Time Indian* was a revelation. He too had suffered from low self-esteem and worried about his physical appearance. No doubt obsessing about one's appearance is normal for teenagers; I just didn't know that since I never talked about my personal problems with anyone. By adolescence, I no longer needed my family to silence me; I had learned to do that to myself. However, I learned to wear a smiley face in public, as my graduation picture shows.

Marcelline, graduation picture, LPHS, 1958

Doing Well in High School

High school was pretty easy for me. Although I had a good mind, I wasn't conscious of it and didn't value it. I quickly memorized Latin vocabulary, the conjugations of French verbs, and the bones in the body for biology tests. Yet, I would have given a lot to be pretty and popular instead of tall and brainy. While Latin, French, history, and biology came naturally, math didn't. Algebra entailed struggle, even though I got A's in it. Geometry was harder. I had internalized the notion that just as women were not supposed to sweat, girls were not supposed to struggle intellectually. So I avoided calculus and trigonometry, physics, and chemistry. I don't know where I picked up those ideas, but I remember in college avoiding philosophy until my senior year. Again, I thought philosophy was "hard," and I shouldn't have to struggle with it. Somehow, languages and the social sciences were easy subjects for me in high school and college, but science and math were harder—to be avoided. Later, when studying Soviet history, I noticed that girls and women there studied math and science. Many became doctors and engineers before and after the 1917 revolution. Decades later in Lithuania, I discovered that one of my best Russian friends had trained as an engineer as a young woman during the 1970s.

Today, I've read enough psychology, especially books by Carol Gilligan, including *In a Different Voice: Psychological Theory and Women's Development*, to know that my experience was not unique. Many girls withdraw from the wider culture around the age of twelve. Many internalize the idea that the active life is the boy's sphere and avoid following the male path.

Fortunately, several of my high school teachers took an interest in me. Their encouragement meant a lot. My French teacher, Mlle. Dick, gave me extra French books to read. I was quick at memorizing verb endings, and reading in French was easy. However, I wasn't as good at listening and catching the meaning of words orally. The down side of my teachers' validation was that I didn't realize others did not necessarily share this view. One of my more painful high school experiences was applying to study abroad in France. This was a chance to live with a French family for the summer and improve my conversational French. Over the years, several La Porte High School students had participated in this program and had profited from it. However, they were middle class. I hadn't imagined doing this myself, but my Latin and French teachers encouraged me to apply for this award. They suggested I ask my minister for financial support from the church, which I did after much soul searching. However, when I was interviewed by a local pastor, I could tell I wasn't passing his scrutiny. I recall his asking me if my family subscribed to magazines, and I had to say "No." My dad read the *La Porte Herald-Argus* newspaper every evening, but I didn't. My brother bought the *Chicago Sun-Times* on Saturday to follow the sports, but I only read the comics on Sunday in the South Bend paper and Aunt Marce's *Ladies' Home Journal*. I don't recall the other questions in the interview, but I knew I hadn't passed muster despite my teachers' glowing recommendations. This was my first school-related failure and minor identity crisis. In retrospect, it showed me the disconnect between my teachers' approval and the lack of social acceptance by others.

Until this experience, I had understood class differences but not class prejudice. This was an awakening. I hadn't realized that some middle-class people did not want lower-class people moving up. I knew that my parents resented "people on the Avenue," but I hadn't realized that this attitude could work both ways. My teachers were all middle class, and many were liberal-minded. They encouraged bright students regardless of class to go to college. They were not prejudiced and expected us to move up in the class system, although no one used that term.

At the time, it was painful to realize I wasn't good enough to get the award, and that didn't feel good. While my teachers didn't discriminate against me for being working class, I realized that some townspeople did. I was hurt by this event. When the girl selected to go to France fell and broke her leg, the committee still did not appoint me to take her place. The injustice rankled a long time. I suppose this is why I included it in these reminiscences.

The failure to get the study abroad award deepened my sense of shame and self-loathing. I wasn't clinically depressed, just deeply hurt. At the time I thought I would have improved my conversational French if I had been immersed in French culture. I hadn't realized I possessed such a thin veneer of social and cultural capital. I certainly didn't know those terms then or understand much about class relations. I probably wasn't prepared to represent my hometown and live with a French family. Maybe my manners were not fine enough. Who knows? I just couldn't face having been judged and found lacking. It was not a nice experience. Perhaps if I had spoken to one of my teachers or my minister about this rejection, I might have been able to understand and accept it. But I didn't do that. I had been brought up with "don't talk" and "don't feel." My lower-class origins made me continue to fear rejection, and I didn't know how to express my feelings to others, even those who loved me. I didn't change this behavior until late in life with the help of a counselor in Lincoln, Nebraska.

Indeed, I'm still learning to share my feelings with appropriate friends instead of pretending that everything is fine. The other day a friend asked me if I hadn't valued being smart in high school, and I said "No, I didn't." Perhaps it was because of this experience that being smart wasn't enough to get the award that I wanted. Also, I probably never thought of myself as "smart enough" since I suffered from low self-esteem. Writing about this experience has shown me that while my teachers judged me one of the bright ones, I didn't do that myself.

Growing up, no one supervised my reading, so I didn't read classics by Jane Austen or modern books by J. D. Salinger. Had I done so, I might have realized teenage angst and alienation were common. However, reading Tolstoy's *War and Peace* did influence my future study of Russian history in college and graduate school.

Personal Struggles

It's strange how fear of Dad's unpredictable alcoholic behavior hampered my life. Part of me wanted to be a normal teenager and ask a boy to the girls' formal dances. But I was too shy and frightened of rejection. Moreover, working at night prevented me from attending Latin or French clubs that met in the evenings and where I might have made like-minded friends. Part of me yearned to participate in those activities, but another part of me silenced that voice. Fear of new social situations constricted my behavior. I had no one to talk to about these feelings. I didn't know I could have gone to a guidance counselor or to my minister. No one I knew did that in the 1950s. Everyone in my family kept their thoughts and feelings secret and pretended life was OK. Such pretense came at a high cost, however. While I repressed my feelings, my dad "acted out" his anger at the world on his family. He swore, ranted, raved, and scared us all, so I never challenged him. My mother also did not invite confiding. She was very busy: working full-time since I had been about six years old, managing the house, washing the clothes, cooking every night for a family of five. She was also pretty straightlaced and moralistic. I didn't know how she would have responded to my sharing feelings with her, so I kept them to myself. She wanted us to "be good," but the message I internalized was "be perfect." Trying to be perfect proved another way to beat myself up and repress dark feelings.

At the end of my senior year, I dated a young minister who had been teaching a course in Christianity through a released-time program I took at the high school. When the class ended, I was surprised that he asked me out. We dated all summer before I went to college. He liked kissing me and holding me, but my affectionate and sexual feelings were pretty repressed. I was proud to finally have a boyfriend, but I wasn't "in love" with him. He was kind and nice, but I didn't feel romantic about him. Having seen too many romantic movies and read too many romance novels, he didn't fit my swashbuckling image of a romantic hero. So he didn't release my tightly held emotions. I was disappointed when I returned from college at Christmas and found he had another girlfriend. I sure didn't like being rejected and cast aside, even if I wasn't "in love" with him. Feelings are so complicated.

Graduation

Aunt Marcelline graciously allowed me to have my high school graduation party at her house. I can't recall now whether my brother and sister had done this too. The incentive was having a pleasant place to celebrate my graduation without having my dad around drunk. My aunt had a better furnished living room and dining room, and we served cake and a punch made from sherbet, Hawaiian Punch, and ginger ale. We thought the punch quite lovely, although adults probably found it commonplace. In those days, even wedding receptions featured only cake, coffee, and nonalcoholic punch. Most Protestant gatherings at that time did not include alcohol. Certainly no one served alcohol to minors. Later, at Park College in Missouri, our banquets and parties also included punch. Only when I was a senior in college did I discover that some of the "wildest" boys drove to Kansas to drink in private clubs. Very few of the girls had cars or went along to drink.

At my high school graduation party, I remember receiving some very nice presents—a pretty blue and white duster from my Sunday school teachers, Dwight and Sue Handley, and a delightful clock radio from my parents. I treasured both items, and they lasted several decades. Of course, some friends and relations gave me money, which I saved for college. My aunt Iva and uncle Kenny Johnson drove my sister and me to Parkville before college started, and that was a tremendous present.

CHAPTER III

College, 1958–1962

Getting Ready for College

In the late 1950s we could still send a trunk on the train from La Porte, Indiana, to Parkville, Missouri. My Sunday school teacher, Edith McClelland, who lived in retirement at the Ruth Sabin Home, suggested my sister and I each take a sturdy nineteenth-century wooden trunk from her basement. We painted the trunks grey, printed our names and address on the top in heavy black paint, and wallpapered the insides. I recall one of us finding a half dime dating from the 1850s, but it had a hole in the middle of it, so it wasn't valuable. I kept my trunk for decades and used it whenever I moved. I retained it until I divorced in 1979 and then left it in Kansas City with my former husband. Somehow, my sister's trunk came to me in El Paso in the late 1990s, when I moved it and some of my mother's furniture there. I kept it until I sold my house and moved to Lithuania in 2000.

Park College: A New Persona

Going to college was a liberating experience because I felt I belonged. I met more people like myself: not tall skinny girls but ones who liked learning and playing sports. Park College was a small, liberal arts, Presbyterian-related school located near Kansas City, and it featured girls' sports teams as well as boys'. We didn't have fraternities or sororities but boy-girl clubs, which everyone could join. It was through these clubs that sports, dances, and dramatics took place. Some members of the Parchevard Calliopean Club (PCC) wooed me when I first arrived. I was flattered that they wanted me in their club. At the time, I didn't realize that they wanted me for my athletic skills, for which I had received a Girls' Athletic Association award in high school. I proved an eager beaver when it came to sports participation. I had never played field hockey or girls basketball, or bowled, but I enjoyed learning and playing these team sports. I had swum before but not in competitive races as we did at Park. That was a new experience. Girls' basketball was a challenge because it was played on only half of the court. I had never heard of it or played it since we didn't have it in Indiana. But I learned to do it and played it well enough. I felt accepted and appreciated for participating. Eventually, I realized that I didn't need to be an outstanding sportswoman, just part of a team to compete against the other clubs.

Classes

My first few years at Park did not undermine my traditional working-class attitudes and approach to life. I felt as if I fit in, and my courses were not overly demanding. My freshman courses included Western civilization, French, the history of education, art and music appreciation, freshman composition, world literature, physical education, and choir. I had studied European history in high school, and my history of education and art appreciation classes covered the same time periods, so I found my Western civilization course enthralling and easy. Professor Ellery Hulbert seemed incredibly suave. He came from the East Coast, which made him almost foreign to me. He smoked a pipe and had a wry sense of humor. How could I not be impressed by this sophisticated man? Intellectually, Dr. Hulbert and I were on the same wavelength, and I found his essay tests fascinating, fun, and challenging. Unfortunately, not all the students in this required class felt the same way. Some fell asleep in class, and many did not do well on his tests. So, he wasn't the most popular professor on campus, except to me. It was thirty-five years later when I realized I'd probably had a crush on him—when a friend told me how common this was.

It turned out that I also impressed Professor Hulbert, and he assigned me an independent study for the second semester of Western civilization. All I had to do was quickly read the text, take an exam over it, choose a paper topic, and consult with him once a month about it. Another bright student also did this, and I felt honored to study so closely with him and Professor Hulbert. I chose to write about the development of trade unions and socialism in England, France, and Germany during the late nineteenth century. I was drawn to this broad comparative topic and ended up writing a 100-page paper. In retrospect, I suppose I was attracted to the plight of workers because I saw my mother work so hard for so little money. As I have mentioned, she earned only low wages and never had a paid holiday. I was not attracted so much to Marxism as an intellectual system because I was impressed by the struggle of workers to find social and economic justice. German Lassallean Socialism and French Utopian Socialism promised greater social justice and gender equality, and it was these forms of socialism that enticed me.

Two decades later I wrote my dissertation on the broad topic of Russian women's lives titled "Russian and Soviet Women, 1897–1939: Dreams, Struggles, and Nightmares." My first book, *Russian and West European Women, 1860–1939*, was also a comparative history of English, French, German, and Russian women, based on census data from the 1890s, 1920s, and 1930s. It included their labor force participation, education, and marital status. It covered literary works of those eras and analyzed their social, educational, economic, and political struggles, dreams, and nightmares. So, I continued to resonate with broad, comparative, historical topics.

During my junior year at Park, I took Professor Hulbert's Russian and Soviet history classes. While I had initially fallen in love with Russian history after seeing the movie *War and Peace* as a teenager in 1957, my fascination deepened as I studied it. Part of its attraction was its sense of "otherness." It was grander than anything in the Midwest. Moscow and St. Petersburg, as described by Tolstoy and Dostoevsky, were more exotic than any places I had known in my limited Midwestern life. Russian culture beguiled me because it was more expressive than the subdued Nordic culture I grew up in. Only years later did I realize that Russian history embodied not only great mercy, largesse, and self-sacrifice but also terrible sadness, suffering, and cruelty.

College Regimen

In college, I lived a rather Spartan, methodical life. I usually went to bed at ten and got up around seven. It never occurred to me to skip breakfast or any other meal. The food seemed satisfactory to me, and I was amazed to hear students complain about the "mystery meat" of the day. It seemed ordinary to me. The only real change was that I learned to drink coffee and soon drank it at each meal. Wednesday breakfast was my favorite because we had Danish sweet rolls. Usually we had an assortment of cereal or eggs and fried potatoes. But I loved the Danish. I vowed to myself that when I graduated, I would have sweet rolls every morning for breakfast, but I never did. Today I still eat oatmeal with fruit and nuts. It's tasty and nutritious. Presently in Lincoln, Nebraska, I live only a block from a Hispanic bakery, but I seldom go there to buy the inexpensive breakfast pastry. Sweet rolls are no longer my choice for breakfast as I imagined they would be when I was in college. How our tastes change!

I had grown up eating three meals a day and did so at college and the rest of my life. At Park, food was plentiful and part of our room and board that we paid for by working fifteen hours per week for the college. Park was fairly unique in the late 1950s and '60s because it retained its original purpose of being a work college and required all students to work for a $250 reduction in their yearly $500 room and board charge. Since I had received a $500 tuition scholarship, this meant that I needed to earn only $250 each summer to pay for my schooling, which totaled $1,000 per annum. This was a blessing because it was before the days of student loans. Moreover, girls made only that much during the summer. Boys often earned more and still do. The work requirement at Park produced considerable gender and class equality, and I appreciated that. Some students came from well-to-do middle-class families that could afford to pay the $500 tuition and $500 for room and board, but my parents were too poor. Having worked from the age of ten, I was surprised when one of my middle-class roommates told me that although she had never had a job, she found working at Park gratifying. Since I had saved only a few hundred dollars during high school, I was fortunate to receive tuition scholarships and not end up in debt, as so many students do today.

At Park, I usually had three classes on Monday, Wednesday, and Friday from nine till noon. Then we had lunch. There were fewer afternoon classes—labs for biology, physics, or chemistry; choir; art and music appreciation. In the late afternoons, we played field hockey in the fall and basketball, bowling, or swimming in the winter. After our sports activity, I often took a nap and then took a shower and went to supper. As a freshman, I waitressed from five till seven each weekday. We served seated suppers, and we set the tables and served the food family style in bowls. This was how I fulfilled ten of my fifteen hours of work program commitment. The other five hours I worked as a janitor cleaning the lounge in one of the men's dorms, one hour an afternoon Monday through Friday. This work consisted mainly of dusting the furniture—nothing hard or heavy. I got to know the housemother there, and she invited me to go with her to a photography studio to have my picture taken when she had her sons' done. It's one of the few pictures I have of me at Park College, so I include it here. I'm a little more somber and not so smiley but still reasonably photogenic in this photo.

During the fall and spring, I enjoyed seeing the sunset after supper while on my way to the library to study. In winter the sun set at about five o'clock as I was walking over to the dining room to work, so I was blessed to see the sunset then. We had magnificent sunsets because we were situated on a hill and could see the sun set over the Missouri River below the college and the town of Parkville. The campus consisted of several hundred acres at that time, and most of us enjoyed walking the trails, especially those that led to a bluff where we could see the river from above. It was also refreshing to amble along the riverbank, find a huge boulder, sit down on it, and then watch an enormous tree trunk float by in the water. Coming from a town of three lakes, I was glad to find water so near. Most of us at Park had been nurtured by the Transcendentalist writers in our American literature classes in high school.

I'm sure I wasn't the only student there enjoying Nature with a capital N on walks around the campus. Indeed, this was a free activity that many participated in. It's still part of me, and I feel blessed to have written the beginning of my reminiscences in Fort Lauderdale, Florida, where I rented a room in a house on one of the canals on the Intracoastal Waterway near the Atlantic Ocean. It was so lovely writing on the enormous patio surrounded by palm trees and tropical foliage—like being in Paradise. It was a bit rainy and overcast in February 2015, but March turned out to be warm, sunny, and breezy—just right.

Marcelline, freshman year at Park College, 1958–59

My sister transferred to Park for her sophomore year—the year I was a freshman—and she was able to earn enough to pay her way too. Our brother had gotten a basketball scholarship to the University of Colorado at Boulder, so he was the first to earn his way through college. After two years, he decided college basketball was too intense, and he earned a tuition scholarship because of his good grades. He also worked while finishing his education. I didn't think much about it at the time, but in retrospect I realize it was quite a feat that our poor family had three college graduates, since my parents could not help us financially. Perhaps it shows how anxious we were to escape our hometown and family life there? It may have been a combination of many factors: ambition, encouragement from teachers and family, and an open society and culture. Of course my mother provided moral support by writing to us each week and by sending us chocolate chip cookies to cheer us up. Moreover, our mother didn't ask us to stay home, get a job, and help her with the mortgage and other household expenses. She encouraged us to develop ourselves and lives. Not all my relatives did so. Some of my aunts kept their children tied to their apron strings, encouraging them to live close by even though they could have afforded higher education for them. Some of my cousins also went to college when I did and obtained degrees. Fortunately for my sister and me, our uncle Kenny Johnson used to send us twenty dollars at Christmas so we could take the train home for vacation. Our mother just didn't have the money to spare, nor did we. In those days, twenty dollars was a lot of money. That's hard to believe sixty years later.

Vacations

When I was in college, my mother worked in a bakery, and her boss often hired me to help as a cashier during the Christmas season. I loved doing this because I had enjoyed working as a grocery clerk, and this was similar. While I was socially shy, I wasn't reticent when I had a clearly defined role. I didn't have to go to work as early as my mother, and I got to eat as many of the donuts, apple slices, and other desserts as I wanted. This was pretty sweet in the literal and figurative sense of the word. After the store closed on Christmas Eve, the owner always gave my mom several cream pies and dinner rolls, which we took to the Johnson family Christmas dinner.

My mother had seven siblings, and all but one married and had children. So I had many cousins, and there were lots of adults and children at the family dinners. There were so many of us that we didn't fit into anyone's home, so we rented a hall in the country owned by the Grange for our potluck Thanksgiving, Christmas, and Easter dinners. My aunts took turns preparing the turkeys, potatoes, vegetables, pies, and cakes. It was always a feast but a bittersweet time for me. I felt honored that they asked me to say grace before the meal. I could pray extemporaneously but always felt a little odd that my father was not included in these festivities. He was persona non grata, so we always took him a plate of food for supper at home. My grandmother did not approve of drinking, so he was never invited to her home or these family gatherings. As a child I wasn't aware of this arrangement, but by the time I was in college, I understood my dad's exclusion, and it dimmed the festive joy for me.

College Life, 1958-1962

Initially, my college classes—especially European history, French, and English—were as easy as my high school courses. I had more papers to write for them, but I usually liked doing this, despite the angst about whether my interpretation was "OK." A few courses were a bit of a struggle. I remember art appreciation being a challenge. We read some art critics and then criticized a painting ourselves. I thought I understood art historian Bernard Berenson's book and ideas, but they weren't absolutely clear when I tried to apply them to a painting in my paper. While I earned A's in my history and language classes, I may have received an A– in art history.

I also recall my history of education professor accusing me of using material from a blurb in one of my papers. I was insulted because it wasn't true. But the experience saddened me and fed into my low self-esteem. I didn't have a confidante to share this event with and felt miserable for a while. I had never cheated in my schoolwork or papers and felt so bad to be accused of doing something like that. No wonder I was later attracted to Dostoevsky's novella *The Insulted and the Injured*.

Another disappointment was getting a B in choir. It's what I deserved, of course. While I could follow the melody of the music and could sing on key, I was an alto and was supposed to harmonize. I found this difficult to do unless I stood next to a strong voice and could follow her lead. I was ignorant of the mechanics of singing, and I didn't know that I could have taken singing lessons and learned how to read music and harmonize. I didn't know how to give myself permission to improve my situation and learn new ways of solving my problems. It was as though I had an inner censor that prevented me from remedying my situation.

This happened in other areas of my life too. I often didn't know how to ask for help when I needed it. Some of the assumptions I grew up with were "suffer in silence," "don't let on about problems and weaknesses," "pretend everything is OK," and "don't ask questions about how to change things." The strong role of denial in my alcoholic family meant I disowned what was inconvenient or hard to understand. I ignored my shyness with new people and situations as well as my inadequacy as an alto. It was decades later that I heard someone say that we should listen to the other parts when singing. Wow. That was a discovery. So, while I always loved singing and still do, I'm more aware of how complex harmonizing is. I also know that training as well as talent are involved. When I was young, I thought it was only talent, and that certain people just naturally knew how to harmonize. I spent decades denying my ignorance of certain things, did the best I could, and avoided the rest. I guess part of growing up means recognizing how complex life is, not keeping everything bottled up inside, talking about it with others, and seeking solutions to my problems, not just letting them fester.

While I came face to face with my limitations as an alto singing in the choir, I also learned a lot about music at Park. Our choir director was an exquisite organist, playing prodigious pieces by Bach, Buxtehude, and Mozart as preludes and postludes at Sunday church. He also taught the music appreciation course that later enhanced my life so much. In addition to magnificent organ solos on Sundays, there were chamber music concerts at the college, and Park students could usher for the Kansas City Symphony and enjoy its concert for free. I had not known much about symphonic music before taking the music appreciation course and before coming to college, because La Porte was too small to have a symphony orchestra. I really enjoyed learning about classical and modern music. I especially remember falling in love with Bach's "Passacaglia and Fugue in C Minor" when I first heard it in our class. It was powerful and hypnotic. My kind of music! Years later, I got a tape of it and listened to it every night for months. In that class and in choir, I also came to appreciate classical composers like Haydn, Handel, and Mozart. Twentieth-century modernists like Stravinsky and Schoenberg didn't enthrall me as much. They turned out to be an acquired taste but are enjoyable today.

Little did I realize in 1959 how much the music appreciation course would enhance my life. It became one of the greatest influences on my life after graduation. At the time I understood the aesthetic appeal of music, but I didn't know of its therapeutic aspect. It was years later that I heard of music therapy and realized that I had been treating my misery with classical music for years. Somehow I subliminally understood the healing aspect of music. My fascination with Russian history later opened the door to the music of Tchaikovsky, Rimsky-Korsakov, Glinka, Mussorgsky, and Borodin as well as Soviet composers Rachmaninoff, Stravinsky, Shostakovich, and Prokofiev.

My freshman roommate also contributed to my music education. She had a small record player, and every night she'd play Gershwin's "Rhapsody in Blue" for me. She liked to stay up late to study, and I liked to study at the library and go to bed early. Listening to "Rhapsody in Blue" every night enabled me to go to sleep while she did her homework. I found Gershwin's music powerful and seductive. Listening to a live performance recently recalled this incident to me. It reminded me how masterful and enchanting the piece is.

In college, I was also a product of my generation of women who are sometimes called drifters. Decades later I read a book by Collette Dowling called *The*

Cinderella Complex in which she argues that in the 1950s women were taught to wait for Prince Charming to come along and rescue them instead of being agents of change themselves. I certainly drifted along in classes that were effortless for me—the social sciences and languages. I breezed through French, history, economics, and political science. I enjoyed psychology but avoided studying it in depth, lest anyone think I had psychological problems and was studying it for that reason. We used to joke that only disturbed students majored in psychology. In denial, I couldn't admit that I was wounded and needed therapy. It wasn't a popular thing to do. Who wanted to appear weak and wounded? Eventually, I ended up majoring in the social sciences with a history concentration. I think it was then that I was "kissed by Clio," the muse of history.

I thoroughly enjoyed my first course in Russian history with Professor Hulbert and especially writing a long paper about the liberal Russian gentry-class reformers. I admired them and fell even more in love with Russian history. I found it grand and glorious. It was harder to appreciate the Bolsheviks since I had given my heart to the nineteenth-century social revolutionaries who worked to improve the lives of the peasants. It took a long time for me to make peace with the Bolshevik victory of November 1917. Only later did I do that.

I also loved my economics classes. I remember writing one very good paper titled "The History of Business Cycles." It fit in with my freshman paper on workers and trade unions in the nineteenth century, although the subject was economic systems, not workers. I enjoyed the research tremendously, and my paper was so good my economics professor asked to keep my copy of it. This was before the days of photocopying, so I never reread the paper to see why it was so good. I just recall being honored that my professor wanted it. Feeling low in self-esteem, I couldn't believe my paper was so brilliant, just that it was good.

Needless to say, it's taken decades for me to honor my intellectual talent and insights. I always wanted to do well and shine, but I didn't really think my ideas, interpretations, or writing were ever top notch. I guess I was always looking for outside validation instead of esteeming my own thoughts and ideas. But, this is probably an existential situation dealt with by many students. I just didn't know this when I was young.

I knew from my performance on standardized SAT tests that I was not brilliant. I often scored 88 to 93% on these, not 99%, and this knowledge kept me humble in college despite my good GPA. Of course I did well in ordinary courses and often scored 100 on tests in my classes, but I interpreted this to mean that when I did well the subject was really easy, that I had done the homework on time, and studied enough for my exams. I never gave myself credit for doing well. I just assumed it was easy for everyone, but some students didn't apply themselves. I didn't know then that we have different aptitudes for learning subjects. I didn't understand that not doing well on my physics exams meant that I lacked an aptitude for and a familiarity with math and science, not that I lacked intelligence generally. Instead, I felt that there was something wrong with me that I could get A's on our lab experiments but not on the exams.

Inner Struggles

At college, I sometimes felt inferior around smart boys and middle-class students. I discovered that I didn't do well in these situations. At the time, I didn't realize that my feelings sometimes got in the way of doing well in a class. I realize this only in retrospect. I remember feeling uncomfortable in a Victorian English class I took at Park. It was a small class—about eight or ten students—but filled with smart upper-class fellows and English majors like my sister. My sister and I took this class together and shared the books. It didn't work out very well because we both wanted to read the assigned text at the last moment. Moreover, feeling inferior to the brilliant boys contributed to my doing only average in the course.

Another problem with the class, or my attitude toward it, was that I didn't really respect the professor, Eleanor Douglass. She wasn't very dynamic, and I found the subject matter boring. We didn't read any of the great novels by Jane Austen, Charles Dickens, William Thackeray, Anthony Trollope, or George Eliot. Instead, we studied literary critics like Matthew Arnold, Thomas Macaulay, Thomas Carlyle, Arthur Clough, and John Ruskin. I was probably not sophisticated enough to appreciate the material that we covered. Reading about bourgeois philistines seemed dull and unimportant. It still does. I thought there was something wrong with me, not the course, because I seldom found a course boring. The older guys in the class were history honor students, and I was probably intimidated by them. I certainly didn't shine in that class.

Little did I know then that in graduate school I would be surrounded by confident, competent, challenging, middle-class men, just like them. Today it is hard to know whether it was their gender, class, or competitive manner that undid my fragile self-confidence. I hadn't been used to competition in high school nor in the first two years of college. I really wasn't prepared for this aspect of male behavior in academe, so when it emerged, I shrank away from class participation and didn't apply myself very well. I didn't study as diligently for this course as I did others. Later, in graduate school, I was also turned off by male competition. I somehow felt defeated before I began.

During high school and college, I often identified myself as a student, a sort of neuter gender. But sometimes and in some places, I couldn't ignore gender differences. I guess some men just oozed masculinity, or some male students were more aggressive and competitive than I was used to. In most of my college classes, I wasn't terribly aware of the gender factor, but in graduate school I could not ignore it. In my graduate history classes, I was often the only woman, so it was harder to overlook this issue. Also, in graduate school, some of the men were older and married, quite unlike in undergraduate school.

Social Life

At Park the prevailing notion was that we were a community of scholars, which implied some equality in our search for truth. We felt this in the classroom and on other occasions. At public lectures and other venues, people did not always agree. Professors as well as students discussed international affairs in the International Relations Club. Our physics professor was a pacifist, and he often disagreed with our political science professor who believed in "Realpolitik." Park had only 350 students, and many departments had only one professor. This was the case in biology, chemistry, physics, political science, philosophy, German, art, and music. In history we had two historians, one American specialist, Stanley Urban, and one Europeanist, Ellery Hulbert. The English department had about three professors because they had many majors. Generally, we learned it was OK to differ in our opinions, to defend our views, and to respect those who differed from us. It seemed to me that our common search for truth was the significant thing, and that competition for grades was not so important since almost everyone who studied did well.

In college my social skills were rudimentary, but none of my friends minded. I had one friend, Marsia Alexander, who was an art major. She was an enchanting person, having grown up as the child of Presbyterian missionaries in Chile. She spoke Spanish as well as English. Only years later did she mention to me that she read English very slowly, and the novel by Tolstoy that I lent her took her ages to read. This shocked me because I had no idea she read slowly when she was a student. Some of my friends, like Alice Coates, were much more sophisticated than I. Alice had read the poetry of Lawrence Ferlinghetti, so when he came to speak in our dorm lounge, she knew all about him and his work. Needless to say, I had never heard of him, never having read American writers after World War I since that was as far as my high school literature class went. We read poetry by Edna St. Vincent Millay and Edwin Markham in the 1920s but not modern writers or the beat poets like Allen Ginsberg, Jack Kerouac, or Norman Mailer. Indeed, I was surprised years later in graduate school to realize all the men in my husband's circle were devotees of these men. When I read some of Norman Mailer's writings in the 1960s, his dominating male–female relationships repulsed me.

Park had a variety of clubs that we could participate in, and I attended International Relations Club, French Club, and History Club. While the French and History Clubs were rather sedate affairs and met monthly, the International Relations group met weekly and could become controversial and contentious, touching on contemporary political issues. History Club met at our professors' homes, and we had tea and cookies as we calmly discussed various historical topics. French Club could be fun with singing and the opportunity to speak French with each other. Our International Relations advisor, Professor Hauptman, was a Polish émigré and very dynamic. He spoke with a heavy accent, which attracted me. Indeed, we had several émigré professors: one was Dr. Manuil, our dean of Academic Affairs who was from Romania; another was the economics professor who hailed from Jamaica. In retrospect, I think I found them all intriguing. I adored Dr. Hauptman, and I appreciated his classes. He was one of the most energetic and fascinating professors I ever knew, but his views were too conservative for me. I respected Hauptman but never became a political science major. However, he had a coterie of devotees who swarmed around him, almost worshipping him.

Studying

After supper, I usually went to the library to study for a couple of hours. Sometimes I needed to learn French verbs or read a chapter in my history text, listen to a record for music appreciation class, or research a paper for a political science class. We usually had ten short papers in our political science courses but fifteen- to twenty-page page papers in other classes. If I had a long paper to write, I often checked out the relevant books and took them to the dorm to read and mark with a pencil so I could erase the marks later. I never used the three-by-five cards for my research that professors later advised in graduate school. Then and now I like having a nest of books or papers around me when writing.

I lived at the girls' dorm called Herr House my sophomore, junior, and senior years. On the top floor of the dorm was a large study hall with an enormous wooden table. I usually left all my books there and worked sporadically on my papers in silence because very few people used the room. When it came time to write a paper, I sometimes skipped all my classes for a day or two to concentrate on it. I didn't skip many classes so wasn't penalized. I loved the simple yet cozy atmosphere of this upstairs lounge. While anyone could use it, it soon became "my study." There were a few wooden chairs at the long desk and perhaps a few soft, stuffed chairs at either end of the room. Someone donated a toaster, and a few of us took a break at nine in the evening to make toast and jelly. We obtained the bread, butter, and jelly from the cafeteria and made our own snacks. However, we never had coffee at this hour because we usually went to bed at ten or so. These were the days before microwave ovens and popcorn. From what I hear, dorm life is quite different today. Many students have their own refrigerators, microwaves, and TVs. We had one TV in the downstairs lounge and one at the Student Union, but students seldom watched it. Few students had record players or records. Our lives were Spartan and simple but full and good.

Special Friends

As a freshman, I had two Japanese friends: Michiko Taniguchi, a psychology major from Kobe, Japan, and Irene Osuga, a Nisei Japanese student from Denver, Colorado. It was fun cooking seaweed and rice in the dorm kitchen when we were freshmen, and I loved hearing their absorbing stories. I was stunned when Michiko told me that she could never marry when she returned to Japan after college because her culture considered her polluted for having come to the United States to study. That shocked me. Likewise, I was disheartened to hear Irene's story about her family's internment during World War II by the American government. I had never heard of this growing up in the Midwest. We didn't have many Asians in our population, and our history books certainly did not mention any dishonorable actions of our government. Our texts never mentioned the horrors of slavery and racism, our broken treaties with Indians, or the imprisonment of Japanese citizens during World War II. I grew up saying the Pledge of Allegiance to the flag and feeling proud of being an American. It took several decades for me to realize the social, economic, political, and educational atrocities committed in the name of the American government against our society. Even today it's not easy coming to grips with "the long, dark shadow" of racism in American history and society or with the white privilege I was born into.

During my time at Park, I helped correct the grammar in Michiko's papers. Most students at Park helped each other when they could. It was a very cooperative environment. Michiko and I were also partners in our physics lab work, and we did our experiments together. I corrected the writing in her lab reports. I suppose this was part of my desire to be a teacher. Certainly these experiences kindled my life-long love of international students and professors.

At Park, I found the foreign faculty and students captivating. As I've mentioned, Dean Manuil was from Romania and spoke with a fascinating accent. Our political science professor, Dr. Hauptman, was from Poland, and he too spoke in an intriguing way. One of my economics professors was a black man from Jamaica, and his British accent and manner beguiled me. He seemed English, not American. He didn't stay at Park very long, perhaps because Parkville was a racist community and maybe it wasn't comfortable for him. While the college staff and students were tolerant, Missouri was a pretty prejudiced place in the 1950s. It was difficult for black men to get their hair cut in Parkville. They had to go to a segregated area in Kansas City to do this.

Still, it's good to see that society has changed in the sixty years since I left Parkville and Kansas City. Presently, Park has many black students who commute from Kansas City, and it has several black American professors. However, Kansas City remains a very segregated place in terms of its black and white populations. Troost Avenue remains the dividing line between the two groups, and the public school system remains highly segregated. In the 1970s, when I returned to live in Kansas City, most black and Latino students attended the community college, while whites attend the University of Missouri–Kansas City and private schools like Rockhurst University. However, the city has elected a black mayor and more black politicians in recent times. So, change happened, but not completely since neighborhoods and schools remain segregated.

At Park, there were also a few students from Iran, Turkey, Japan, and even Korea. Those from Iran always referred to themselves and their language as Persian. I found them exotic. The foreign fellows were good at soccer and helped the Park team, which played other nearby small liberal arts schools like William Jewel College. I was friendly with a Turkish woman named Seven. She was a junior or senior when I was a freshman and a philosophy major—very smart. I loved walking in comfortable silence with her along the railroad tracks which skirted the Missouri River or talking with her. It was only decades later that I realized that I suffered from what Edward Said dubbed "Orientalism," viewing the other as exotic. I clearly did that.

One of the nicest parts of college life were the friendships that developed and the education that took place outside the classroom. While some students dated, not everyone did. Some, like me, belonged to the "club of the unkissed." Many students were serious and went on to graduate school. They didn't come to college just to have a good time and snag a husband but to study and develop themselves and their talents. Indeed, none of my friends sat around talking about a date or lack thereof. We may have felt a bit left out of the dating scene, but it didn't seem to matter as much as it had in high school.

I had very few dates, and would have liked more, but I think I was too naïve. While I sparkled in the classroom, I was a dud as a date. As a freshman, I remember a fellow in my Western civilization class asking me to go walking on the trails on the outskirts of the college. We did a few times, and then he told me he was engaged to someone back home. I felt awkward about this and didn't go walking with him anymore. I didn't know then that men and women could be friends, and they didn't have to be romantically interested in each other. It would have been helpful to have had a male friend to talk to sometimes, but I didn't have one.

I remember as a sophomore a student whom I admired asking me to go to our art professor's house in Kansas City for an evening of conversation and fun. I was romantically attracted to this student, and I was scared and uneasy once we arrived. I don't remember saying anything clever or impressive. I recall feeling dumbstruck and embarrassed on the ride back to Park College. As a result, no more dates with this guy followed. Eventually, he found someone a little more sparkly and savvy than I was. Only in graduate school did I encounter someone who attracted me as much romantically and intellectually.

When I was a junior, I recollect having a date with a fellow history major. He took me out and asked if he could kiss me goodnight at the end of the evening. Feeling a little cocky, I said, "No," and he never asked me out again. I certainly lacked finesse. Now I realize that I could have said, "I would be interested in kissing you, but not on the first date." I didn't know much about kissing, flirting, or any of the rules of the dating game.

Looking back, I can see that I was frightened of my own sexuality, as well as his. It was uncharted territory for me. Having repressed this aspect of my life, I didn't really know how to deal with it. Only in graduate school did I unleash this part of me, with serious consequences. Indeed, it's only in old age that I am beginning to make friends with this aspect of myself. I do remember being very disappointed during my junior year when a woman from the Presbyterian Board of Missions came to Park to interview me about being a missionary. She told me bluntly that I could never marry if I went to Africa to serve as a teacher. I was stupefied at this news. I knew I wasn't a Hollywood beauty, but I also knew that deep down I wanted to marry and have a family. While part of me doubted I was pretty enough to marry, another part of my traditional self longed for the fulfillment of that dream. So, after her visit I knew I could kiss the dream of being a missionary goodbye. Then I pondered what I was going to do if I didn't go to Africa.

I remember my sister being not as repressed as me. She had a crush on a fellow at Park, and they dated a bit. As in high school, she attended the college dances while I didn't. But she never confided in me about her dating experiences. I guess it was part of the alcoholic family rule of "don't talk, don't feel." Most of my friends—Marsia, Alice, Irene, and Michiko—also didn't date, and it seemed OK. Since we all belonged to the "club of the unkissed," we didn't feel left out as we had in high school.

Religious Life in College

During my years at Park, I didn't experience many challenges to my traditional religious views. The spirituality of the place helped me. Going to church on Sundays and Wednesdays strengthened me. Being at a church-related college like Park, I never felt alienated or my faith threatened, as I did later in graduate school at a secular university. Not many students were majoring in religion, but students were required to take one class in the Old Testament and one in the New. I read Søren Kierkegaard's book *Fear and Trembling* and wrote my semester paper on it when studying the Old Testament. The book and the professor for the class were challenging but didn't undermine my beliefs. Indeed, the professor was pretty gentle when he questioned some traditional beliefs.

One year the Religion in Life Program sponsored a psychologist. After listening to some of his talks, I decided to go see him and ask about my father. I told him about my mom and dad, and he helped me see my father in a more compassionate way. I had hoped that he could help me understand my family life, and he did. In those days we didn't have the language of "dysfunctional family," even though I knew from experience what it was. I remember going home that Christmas and kissing my father hello. I had never done that before, and it was a liberating action. I had never understood my mother as the martyr/victim in their relationship, and that was hard to accept, but I could see some truth in that analysis.

Little did I know that I would later imitate my parents' marriage in some ways: idolizing my husband and allowing him to bully me while following in my mother's footsteps to become the martyr/victim. Although a therapist in Iowa

City in 1979 suggested to me that I and my spouse might share some of the traits of our parents, I didn't believe it. It took many years for me to digest this truth. Only long after my divorce could I see some of the similarities between my parent's marital behavior and my own—that is, men under-functioning and women over-functioning. After fifteen years of marriage, when I felt pushed to the edge, I found I could give way to rage just as my father had done, but I could do this completely sober. I didn't have the excuse of being drunk to shout and scream at my husband as my father had done at his family. As a young woman I had promised myself a very different life from my parents, but I only partially succeeded.

CHAPTER IV

Graduate School at Iowa, 1962–1975

"Bewitched, Bothered, and Bewildered"

A rriving in Iowa City in the fall of 1962, I initially felt bewitched not only by the study of Russian history but also by a young graduate student named John with whom I fell hopelessly in love. I also felt bothered and bewildered by my study of Russian history. I was bothered by the male graduate students who seemed so much more accomplished than I and who excelled in repartee and one-upmanship. Yet I remained beguiled by Russian history and culture.

After the disastrous visit from the Board of Missions official at Park College in 1961, I had rethought my future. Now I no longer planned to be a missionary, and I was disappointed in myself. What was I to do? Did I still have a calling? My history professors at Park suggested I go to graduate school. That didn't seem quite as grand as being a missionary, but it did seem to be the best choice. My favorite professor, Ellery Hulbert, who taught Russian history, suggested I study this subject. I was amenable since I had been enthralled by Russian history since high school. Brought up in a repressed Nordic Midwestern environment, I loved Russia's grandiose history and culture.[4] My readings had introduced me to remarkable nineteenth-century Russian reformers, radicals, and revolutionaries. Likewise, Dostoevsky's novels and Tchaikovsky's music had also worked their magic on me. Reading Russian literature and taking two courses in Russian history at Park had piqued and deepened my interest

---

4. Amor Towles in *A Gentleman in Moscow* also noted the Russian love of the grandiose. In one segment he says: "In Russia, whatever the endeavor, if the setting is glorious and the tenor grandiose, it will have its adherents." Towles, *A Gentleman in Moscow* (New York: Viking, 2016), 46. It's interesting that a writer noticed the same quality in Russian culture that I identified as a historian.

in the culture. I was impressed by the gentry-class reformers and found them to be honorable, attractive figures. The self-sacrifice of the Russian intelligentsia serving the peasants as teachers and doctors was also commendable. They seemed bold and beautiful. Moreover, while some Russian writers depicted weak, superfluous men, they also portrayed strong, attractive female characters who captivated me.

Finally, the United States government in 1962 was building up Slavic departments in Midwestern universities to counter Sputnik, which the Soviets had launched in 1957. Since the government was offering fellowships to study Russian history, I applied to the University of Iowa and was awarded a National Defense Educational Act (NDEA) Fellowship to study Russian history. I was proud yet bewildered to receive a tuition scholarship plus a $2,000 grant for living expenses. I was overwhelmed at the prospect of being paid to study. I couldn't believe I deserved the money. My low self-esteem created a lot of mental static about getting this fellowship. Perhaps it was my working-class background or my gender, but I didn't know that women won honors like this.

Self-doubt reared its ugly head, telling me I wasn't worthy of it. So when I arrived in Iowa City, I was struggling with various old "ghosts." While part of me was yearning to respond to new beginnings, another part was fearful and hesitant. Improvisation was stymied. I was unaware of the unwritten social contracts that grad school involved. While I hadn't committed too many faux pas in college that I knew of, I was still socially shy and inept at small talk. In undergraduate school, it had been enough to be a good student, but at faculty parties at the University of Iowa, a student needed to shine, and I didn't. I was like a mouse, whereas my friend and future husband John dazzled others with his witty New York banter.[5] Until that party, I hadn't realized that to make it in academe, it helped to be male and middle class. I had been unaware of these prerequisites. Indeed, it was only many decades later that I heard the term "social capital" and understood more about the differences between working-class and middle-class behavior. Only later did I read that men possessed more social capital than women. So it was a gender as well as a class issue. I felt a vague uneasiness about these issues on some subliminal level, but I was a pretty unconscious person. Of course, none of these gender or class issues were overtly discussed. This was the time before social history and feminism.

---

5. In the interest of family harmony, I decided to omit John's last name. One of his relatives was irate about this chapter, so I thought it best to omit the family name.

Chapter IV

Initial Unhappiness at Iowa

Looking back, I can see that in 1962 I felt double-minded and disillusioned about higher education because of a "run-in" I had experienced with the president of Park College during my junior year. My situation resembled that of the fellow in the film *Indignation* when the character was roundly put down by a dean for thinking for himself. As a junior I'd had a demoralizing experience with the president about attending our midweek secular chapels, and I lost that battle. I had argued that some of the speakers were lackluster, poorly informed, and not worth our attention. He argued the opposite. Since I had stopped attending these required events, I was put on probation and called before the deans of the college. I was punished for standing up for my analysis of the speakers which had been sharpened by three years in college. I became disenchanted when I was rebuked and disciplined for expressing my views. I felt silenced once again. The deans omitted my name from *Who's Who Among Students* and blackballed me from the women's Honor Dorm.

As a result, I felt dispirited during my senior year in college and had a hard time finishing one of my papers. I was disappointed in myself for breaking my vow to go teach in Africa as a missionary. I felt uneasy and guilty about this. By my last year in college, I had written so many papers I was "burned out," although I didn't know this term. My mind and body rebelled against writing more long papers. Having the president come to my oral exams at graduation was the final straw. What an insult to have him checking up on me and making me nervous by suddenly appearing at my orals. I had never heard of this before. Even though I graduated cum laude from college, I wasn't very happy about it. I did not want to shake the president's hand when I received my diploma, but I forced myself to do so as I walked across the stage. For all these reasons, I didn't feel psychologically free to enjoy the new life graduate school offered.

I wasn't in a very good frame of mind or spirit to begin a new life in graduate school. I felt so overwhelmed and undeserving to be awarded an impressive fellowship. Thus, adjusting to graduate school proved extremely challenging and awkward. I found myself floundering in a new place, without the friends and familiar supportive atmosphere of my small college. At Park, most of my professors were always glad to see me, or at least seemed happy to see me when I visited them in their offices. However, at the University of Iowa, I felt as if I were in a foreign country—uncharted territory. Professors had office hours, but I somehow sensed that they didn't really want me to bother them. At first I didn't realize that I was detracting from their research time, which was very important to them. Indeed, publishing was imperative for history professors at

Iowa. All these experiences made beginning graduate school a disquieting experience. Moreover, in 1962, the history department was a formidable male bastion. No women professors, few female grad students. At Park, there had been more women professors and students. I wasn't such an anomaly.

My housing arrangements in Iowa City in 1962–63 were not very successful either. I tried sharing an apartment with women who were not students on three different occasions, but I finally realized that our interests were too different. I moved four times the first year of grad school before I found a cozy place to live. All the moving around was also unsettling. Luckily I could move easily by taxi because I could pack all my belongings into two suitcases and my antique grey trunk. Moving my stuff was easy. Adjusting to a large university of 29,000 students after having been at a college with only 350 was harder.

Classes at the University of Iowa

I found my history classes disconcerting because of the male dominance. I wasn't used to such an environment. The hordes of men, especially those from the East Coast, seemed awfully smart, aggressive, and competitive. I felt "out of my league." I soon realized that while lots of women went to college, not many went to graduate school in history. My salvation was meeting John in my historiography class. At our first class, I looked around the room at all the men, and three appealed to me. My future friend and husband stood out. I was definitely attracted to him, partly because of his good looks but also because he had a coherent worldview. He seemed to have it all together and was street smart from living in New York City—qualities that I lacked but admired. Although he had initially come to the University of Iowa to obtain a PhD in the humanities and was taking a course called Romantic Spirit, he was also taking the historiography course.

Sitting across the table from John, I talked to him a bit during the break in our three-hour class. We soon discovered a mutual interest in existentialism. My senior year in college I had read Søren Kierkegaard, and he Paul Tillich. I think we both were fascinated by the question of "authenticity." I was surprised that his spiritual journey had led him to Thomas Merton, Zen Buddhism, and existentialism. He had graduated from Fordham University, a Jesuit school in New York City, and I remember being impressed when he told me that he had to major in philosophy as well as history. Later I realized that this training had equipped him with a steel-trap mind. Apparently a medieval history course had piqued his interest in mysticism and asceticism. While his search for holiness was intellectual, ascetic, and aesthetic, mine centered on holiness found in joy, exuberance, and emotional expression of the psalms and hymns. Only years later did I realize his spiritual life and mine were worlds apart.

While recently reading a book on postmodernism, I saw how different John's and my intellectual approaches were. The book presented John's view as "logocentrism," based on the Platonic and Aristotelian philosophical systems prevalent in Western culture.[6] My approach wasn't identified, but I knew that I often understood my position on a subject only after I had written about it, a form of learning during the process. Writing revealed what I was thinking, whereas John thought everything out before writing. When he once tried to help me do some research, I realized that his approach was "top down" and mine "bottom up." His philosophy classes helped him develop a critical and rigorous mind, the pursuit of certainty via reason. John was fixated on clarity, and I on meaning, although I didn't know the words "structuralism" and "subliminal" then. Educated by Jesuits from junior high through college, he was influenced by logic and the Aristotelian-based St. Thomas Aquinas worldview. I lacked self-esteem and always thought that he had a "better mind" than I, since he was able to argue so forcefully and persuasively. It took me years to realize that our different ways of thinking and writing were both valid. Alas, he didn't share this view, and neither did I initially.

When I first began graduate school, I was involved in a discussion of existentialism at the Presbyterian church and invited John to come to our group. He didn't join it, but we remained interested in the topic and each other. I may have misinterpreted his interest in me as a friend for romantic interest. I was intrigued when he took me canoeing on Wednesday afternoons after our historiography class. I had never gone canoeing and that was romantic and whimsical to me. I had never known a man like him before. I had never dated much. I was impressed he could paddle the canoe to the Coralville dam and then back to the campus. John was good at doing this because he was strong as well as smart and handsome, a formidable combination. In the 1960s, it didn't cost anything to go canoeing. We simply showed our student IDs to the attendant at the canoe house, and he let us have a canoe and paddles for the afternoon. How John knew about the canoe house was a mystery to me, but he was an explorer and knew more about the campus than I did. Initially, our mode of playfulness in canoeing was similar. Only later did our senses of play diverge.

---

6. See Richard Appignanesi and Chris Garratt, *Introducing Postmodernism* (New York: Totem Books, 2005), 77–79.

Dilemmas

When I first met John, he was taking a course titled Romantic Spirit, which struck me as unusual. I'd never known anyone quite like him. He had traveled to Europe the summer before coming to graduate school, and I thought that exotic. After graduating from college, his family had given him one hundred dollars, and he had hitchhiked around Italy, France, and Germany. He could always survive on very little and had been content to live on bread and cheese in Europe. In many ways, he reminded me of my Park College history professor Ellery Hulbert. Both hailed from the East Coast and were suave, sophisticated, unconventional, and had a wry sense of humor. Both men impressed me. Traveling gave John a sense of braggadocio and confidence that I admired.

So, I fell in love. Little did I know then that when my world is falling apart, my need for connection is so great that I tend to seek out romance with a man or find a therapist. In Iowa City, I was unhappy in my housing situation and floundered in my studies. At that time, there were no women professors in the history department with whom I might have spoken to about my feelings, but I had heard there were psychologists at Student Health, so I went there to get help. Instead of consolation, the male psychiatrist told me, "If you are unhappy here, leave." That disturbed me even more. I thought: "What would I do? Where would I go? How would I survive?" I had a government fellowship to live on in Iowa City but no savings. I certainly didn't want to return home to my parents while I sorted out my life. Moreover, by then I was hopelessly in love with John and didn't want to leave him. The psychiatrist might have told me that graduate school was a big adjustment and that I was experiencing a lot of change, moving from being a "beloved student" at Park College to a cipher at the University of Iowa. He might have helped me work through my misery without telling me to quit school. But he didn't. Maybe this was his form of shock therapy. I don't know. All I remember was being unhappy and crying a lot.

I didn't know then that adjusting to graduate school was tough for men too, and a huge number left after the first year. Many never finished their master's or PhD degrees. However, this was not common knowledge to me as a new, lonesome graduate student. I only learned this years later when I was teaching as an assistant professor during the 1980s.

At times, my new friend John wasn't too helpful because the very things that made me uncomfortable at Iowa made him happy. He liked the anonymity of Iowa City and the university. He felt free, while I felt disconnected. He was a workaholic and loved being in the library until one in the morning, while I was a frustrated but shy extrovert and didn't feel so comfortable there my first

John, in coat and corduroys, with Martin, Iowa City, 1964

year since I didn't know anyone but John. Not being used to verbalizing my feelings, I probably didn't explain my situation to him very well. Still, I was glad to have him as a friend. That felt good. What I don't know even to this day is whether he also felt a little lost. He too had left his friends behind in New York City. He may have felt bereft too, but it wasn't manly to say so in those days. Moreover, I had already scripted him to be Prince Charming, so even if he had wanted to admit his fears to me, I probably didn't want to hear about them. He didn't ask me to idolize him, but I did. He was almost the only one who was kind, attentive, and attractive to me. How could I help falling in love with him? In those days, he looked so debonair in his corduroy jacket and Oxford blue button-down shirt. I was used to men more casually dressed. He told me that at Fordham all the men wore ties and jackets to class, so he was used to this dress, whereas at Park the fellows never wore jackets to class. Only our professors did that.

Little did I realize the repercussions of our different backgrounds. He was raised in a middle-class Catholic family on the East Coast and I in a working-class Protestant family in the Midwest. He was a charming, witty, introverted workaholic, and I was a shy, extroverted dilettante. While I was initially charmed by his accounts of hiking the Appalachian Trail alone in New York state and eating beans and tuna fish for two or more weeks, I had no idea what it would mean to live with an eccentric person. Initially, it seemed romantic, but it turned out to be problematic. Coming from such different backgrounds, it's no wonder we later had so many problems understanding and communicating with each other. Moreover, coming from my noncommunicative family, I wasn't prepared to express my feelings and ideas even to my husband. Later, I realized John's mother, being English, was also rather reserved, and I slowly learned that John himself was more reticent discussing his feelings than his adventures.

All my young life I had done my homework on time, but in graduate school I felt alienated and sloughed it off. I just didn't feel like studying. The work was more rigorous than I was used to and the competition more intense. I had a fellowship, which meant I could spend a lot of time in the library, but I felt so alone and scared that I did precious little research. History students who had teaching assistantships had more camaraderie. They shared offices near the History Department and interacted with each other more than I did, isolated in the library. John made friends with other history students more easily than I did. There was a gender and class barrier, and it was easier for him to pal around with male graduate students than it was for me. Many of the fellows were decent guys, but I lacked the skills and confidence to join their group.

I missed my girlfriends from Park, but I wasn't aware of it. I didn't meet another woman graduate student until my third year, when I was taking an American history course. There were more women studying American history, but none in Russian history. Initially, I was lonely, and it didn't feel good. I found my history lecture courses engaging, but I balked at studying the Russian language, even though my Russian teacher, Miriam Gelfand, was gentle and kind. Whereas I had loved mastering French grammar as a teenager, I was too depressed in grad school to be intellectually engaged or entranced by Russian grammar.

I was no longer the diligent student I had been. My heart wasn't into studying. I was tired from writing myriads of papers at Park. Though the term "burned out" was not in vogue in 1962, and although I knew something was wrong, I didn't know what. I couldn't identify my condition. I didn't have the language. Indeed, I hadn't finished a long paper required in my last semester in my history of economics class. It was the first time I failed to complete an assignment. I was probably already feeling worn out but didn't know it. The result was that I received a B instead of an A because I had gotten A's on all my other papers in the course. This was disappointing, but I think I was tired of studying after four years of fairly intense college work. I was also demoralized by that run-in with the president, and I probably needed a rest or a "gap year," as they say today. I had lived a "serious" life since the age of ten, when I began babysitting, and by graduate school I felt like playing and being a dilettante.

In Iowa City I just wanted to be in love. I wasn't very interested in reading classical historians like Herodotus who were assigned in our historiography class. But I did write a fascinating paper on Jacques Maritain's existential historical views. However, I wasn't careful enough in developing the transitions between ideas and paragraphs. I was writing in an innovative dialogue manner and didn't connect the main ideas as I needed to. I earned only an A– or B+ on that paper. I received B's the first semester, and unbeknownst to me that grade was a "kiss of death" in graduate school. Unlike me, John had studied hard and earned all A's.

Chapter IV

Unnerving Experiences in Grad School

The second semester in grad school, I took a seminar in Russian history, which proved a disaster. We met in Professor Alston's cozy office because there were only a handful of Russian history graduate students. We were all assigned a volume of Lenin's works to read and analyze. The students in the class were older married men, more advanced in their studies than I. They were also more competitive. I was used to the notion that in class we were a community of scholars gathered together looking for truth and that this was a joint effort. I was disabused of this notion when my paper was scathingly attacked one afternoon. I had compared Lenin with Calvin, arguing that both were hortatory in their writings. I thought it a valid interpretation. One of the fellows in the class took me to task saying I should have compared Lenin to Savonarola. I didn't even know who Savonarola was, so of course I didn't do this. I was so bewildered and overcome by the criticism that I broke down in tears. I tried not to cry, but I couldn't help it. I felt so hurt, angry, and conflicted that I didn't know what to do. I didn't know whether to stay in class with tears running down my face or to go to the ladies room and sob there. I had often found release in tears, but I had never cried in class before and couldn't control myself. I hated myself for crying as well as the fellow who had harshly attacked my paper. I just sat there feeling embarrassed, ashamed, and angry.

I felt conflicted because I loved Russian history, while the seminar was terribly painful. At the time, I didn't realize that men might resent women competing with them. I didn't feel like a competitor, but I guess I was. I had never encountered such behavior before. At Park, no one had ever attacked me in class. None of these men became my colleagues because I didn't trust them. My only colleagues were John, who was doing English history, and my friend Billie Jeanne, who was studying American history.

My Russian history professor and thesis advisor, Patrick Alston, was a kind and gentle person but not my confidant. As I was casting around for a thesis topic, he suggested that I write on "The Woman Question" in mid-nineteenth-century Russia. At first I balked at this idea and experienced an intellectual crisis. At Park, we had been taught to be scientific and impartial. I wondered, "How could I write about Russian women? Surely I would be biased." We had been taught to write in the third person singular and to weigh all the evidence carefully. We wrote only "it seemed" or "the evidence suggested," never "I thought the cause was" or "the women's situation interests me." We were not supposed to express our opinion or show prejudice or partiality. While historians were aware of having a Weltanschauung, or worldview, they tried to be aware of their presuppositions and remain impartial. I felt that just being a woman meant I couldn't do this sort of history dispassionately. I didn't understand how I could live up to the high standards of the profession if I wrote women's history. Surely I would be prejudiced, not just have presuppositions.

I didn't know who to talk to about these concerns. My friend Billie Jeanne was not writing women's history, nor was anyone else at Iowa at that time. I didn't know my advisor well enough to talk to him about my quandary. Moreover, my background of not discussing weaknesses made it psychologically impossible to ask him about my misgivings. Scientific, impartial history was what I had learned in college in the late 1950s and early '60s. This was before the development of postmodern social history—before historians were writing about workers, women, and the family. This was before historians admitted that we could have sympathetic views toward our subject matter, and we didn't have to be absolutely impartial.

When I was a graduate student, history was just shifting from the old traditional political history written from the top down to more inclusive social history viewed from the bottom up. The changing focus from political elites (men) to the lower orders—peasants, workers, and women—was just beginning. Although I was interested in it and had written about workers and trade unions in Europe at Park, I hadn't heard about this approach as a method for studying a period. I didn't know what postmodernism was. No one mentioned it to me. None of my Russian history seminars discussed this approach, nor did any of my readings. It certainly wasn't part of my European intellectual history course my second year in graduate school. No wonder I felt conflicted and confused. I just wanted to avoid my studies and fall in love with John. I remained a traditional woman adrift in an all-male world of academe, just vaguely aware of postmodern social history.

Bewitched by John

> Falling in love with love
> Is falling for make believe.
>
> Lyrics from *The Boys from Syracuse*, 1938

When I met John in 1962 not only was history being redefined but so were sexual relations. It was a time of social and sexual revolution, and we were part of it, although we were not very conscious of it at the time. In retrospect, it seems that part of our attraction for each other was that we were both inquisitive about sexuality. Neither of us had dated much, we were both pretty naïve, but we were safe people with whom to explore our romantic and sexual selves. Since I was a serious person most of the time, it is hard in retrospect to believe that I could be so foolish about sex. But curiosity, love, and lust can make even the most high-minded a little reckless. Listening to a John Denver song, "You Fill up my Senses," reminded me of how John thoroughly filled up my senses. I never encountered another man who did this as well as he did. Having grown up without sisters, and having attended a boys' grammar school and an all-male university, John didn't know much about women. Of course, I didn't know much about men either, aside from my dysfunctional, alcoholic father and my sterling, high-achieving brother.

In 1962, not much public information about birth control was available—at least not in Iowa City or at the University of Iowa Libraries. I found a couple of books about sex listed in the card catalogue, but they were not in the book stacks. They had to be obtained at the circulation desk and doing that seemed too public and embarrassing, so I didn't do it. Eventually, John and I became sexually involved with each other, and I just wanted to experience the grand passion I had read about in historical novels and seen in Hollywood movies like *Gone with the Wind* and *Duel in the Sun*. Having frozen my feelings since childhood, it was dangerous unleashing them in graduate school. In retrospect, I wonder if I was acting out the "life force" as described by George Bernard Shaw in his play *Man and Superman*.

I read this play in a philosophy course in college but didn't really believe Shaw's idea that women are overtaken by Nature's "life force" and desire to marry a man and bear a child.[7] I had no idea this could happen to me. But it did. While I was dazzled by John when I first met him, I didn't think I had set my cap to marry him. Now I think that may have been my unconscious desire. I simply wasn't aware of it, as women today speak of their biological clock running out. I have recently read studies that indicate women are attracted to men whom they think would be good fathers. However, I do remember looking around the room in the historiography seminar in September 1962 and thinking that three of the fellows looked promising. I just didn't know what that meant. According to Shaw, I was shopping for a husband. I had thought I was looking for someone to date or for intellectual companionship. How we deceive ourselves. As an adolescent I had heard people say that women went to college to

---

7. See George Bernard Shaw, *Man and Superman* (London: Constable and Company, 1952).

get a husband, but I didn't think that applied to me. I had loftier goals. I was going to be a missionary teacher. In graduate school, it seemed I wasn't so different from other young women.

Soon after John and I first made love, I became pregnant. I didn't want to believe it and didn't for seven months. Growing up in my alcoholic family, I knew about denial, had practiced it a great deal to protect myself from painful family and social relations, and was pretty good at it. When I finally acknowledged my situation to myself, I felt ashamed and ambiguous about being pregnant. Part of me felt I should wear a big D for Disgraced on my forehead, and part of me thought "So what?" Had I known in the 1960s that one third of Episcopal brides were pregnant at the time of their marriage in the diocese of Iowa, I might have felt a little less ashamed.

As I write these reminiscences, I realize that I now have a more compassionate attitude toward my youthful indiscretions. However, I had grown up at a time when the worst thing a young unmarried girl could do was to get pregnant. I felt emotionally torn for several months. Of course I didn't discuss any of these feelings with John. When I first met John, I felt sure God wanted me to have him as my boyfriend—even my lover. I had a simple "feel good" theology. If it felt good, God blessed my doing it. I was so enamored with John and the magic of being in love that I didn't want to analyze my behavior too carefully. We didn't tell our parents that I was pregnant until we were married and there wasn't much they could say. Once Martin was born, they were all happy to have a bonny grandson. So, once again, God brought goodness from foolishness and drew us together in a new and better way.

Thinking back over this period, I realize that I probably didn't really understand John when I first met him. When I gaze at pictures of him from that period, I can now see that he appeared more perplexed and disturbed than I realized. Maybe his charm and wit disguised his alienation. He was fun, suave, and alluring to be around, while I was shy and awkward. I was glad we both read existentialist writers, and I thought we had a lot in common being history graduate students. Little did I know that our upbringings were so different and that while we were both on a quest for holiness and authenticity, our ideas of encountering these differed profoundly.

Having been raised Roman Catholic, John sought the holy in mysticism, contemplation, and solitude. When I met him in graduate school, he spoke of Thomas Merton and some Buddhist scholars who wrote on contemplation. This was all foreign to me. Having been raised Protestant, I associated holiness with feeling an emotional high—joy in church, especially singing hymns, reading the psalms, and praying extemporaneously. I also linked it with my desire to be a teaching missionary. I thought it a holy vocation. I especially resonated with the psalms, which I read privately, but I didn't engage in contemplative or centering prayer at that time. I was still into Transcendentalism and the love of Nature with a capital N. That was my form of contemplation.

When we met, I didn't realize the implications of his more introverted and my more extroverted religious life. Decades later I began to appreciate contemplative prayer more, but I still prefer this sort of prayer in a quiet circle like Taizé worship or a contemplative prayer group. Presently, I do this sort of prayer with my icons at home in the mornings yet also enjoy the exuberance of singing and dancing during my devotions.

When I first met John, I had no idea that he had been so influenced by the Catholic Worker Movement and its emphasis on volunteer poverty and helping the poor. During our time together, he always subscribed to the movement's paper, the *Catholic Worker*, which cost only a penny per issue. The editor, Dorothy Day, agreed with Dostoevsky's character Father Zossima in his novel *The Brothers Karamazov*. Both espoused the idea that "love in action was a harsh and dreadful thing compared to love in dreams. Love in dreams was greedy for immediate action."

In retrospect, I must say I subscribed to the love of dreams that was greedy for immediate fulfillment. I always wanted to hold hands with John and sought "touchy, feely love," but he didn't like this. I thought there was something wrong with me for wanting physical connection and appreciation. I tried turning myself inside out to please him, but of course I never could. I too read Dostoevsky's novel, but I didn't remember those particular words of Father Zossima. I liked his characters Alyosha and Dmitri because they seemed real and authentically religious and sensual. Now I know that we resonate with different characters, words, and ideas. Who knows what I would notice were I to reread the novel. At the time, I thought Alyosha almost too good to be true and Ivan too inhibited to pursue the woman he loved. Dmitri seemed the most human.

Now, I can see that John and I were not well-matched partners in the dance of life. We didn't know how to cherish and honor each other. Indeed, we couldn't even utter the words "I love you" out loud. I remember one Valentine's Day when John had gone jogging with our Kansas City friend Al McDonald, and they had stopped at a health food store on the way home. Apparently Al had suggested that John buy me some "Love Tea." When he returned, John didn't say, "I was so happy to buy you this special tea." Instead, he said, "Al thought you might like this 'Love Tea' for Valentine's Day." He seemed incapable of saying "I love you" or "I bought you a Valentine's present." Maybe I was too. I think I said it to him sometimes, but now I'm not so sure. I surely wanted to love him, but he didn't make it easy. Maybe I didn't either. Since I suffered from low self-esteem, I may not have really wanted anyone to tell me he loved me. I sure didn't believe the men whom I met later when they told me they loved me. Deep down, I felt inadequate and unlovable before and after my divorce.

New York, Summer of 1963

After our first year of grad school, John went to Walla Walla, Washington, in the summer to work and earn money for his second year of graduate school. I went to New York City. I wasn't aware that I was pregnant, and I had made arrangements through my sister to work as a typist at *Christian Century* magazine. I had decided to work four days a week and spend three days in the New York Public Library finishing an incomplete grade in a medieval history course. I wanted to discover how peasants lived and what they thought in the Middle Ages, and I thought that maybe medieval mystery and miracle plays would give me a good idea. I didn't realize that I was interested in social history and thought these literary sources would reveal something of the peasant mentality. I was theoretically ahead of my time, but my Latin was not good enough for me to undertake the project I had set out for myself, so I didn't make the headway I expected.

When I arrived in New York City, it turned out that my sister wanted to live alone, so I ended up living with her roommate and my old college friend Marsia Alexander. Kathryn and Marsia had been living in the Village, but Kathryn moved to West 72nd Street, and Marsia and I to East 99th Street. Unbeknownst to me, we were living on the edge of Harlem. In 1962 it was not a problem, as it might have been later. Marsia and I rented a fifth-floor walk-up apartment—no elevator. Marsia had great plans for redecorating it, and I helped. We ripped up the many layers of linoleum from the floor and carried them downstairs in grocery bags. No small feat in the hot summer. It was June when we moved, so it wasn't the intense heat of August, but it was warm enough. Marsia painted the floor of our apartment, and she built a table. An artist, she had golden hands and could make almost anything. During the week, she worked part-time in a day care center where she constructed string puppets and other fascinating toys for the children.

Our apartment was a surprise. As was true for much of America during the 1960s, there was no air conditioning, so everyone left the windows open, and I could hear the neighbors when they argued. Just hearing them shout at each other at night unnerved me. I didn't like arguments, and that seemed to be all our neighbors did. The toilet was unique—a water closet, a small separate room. The bathtub was in the kitchen, next to the sink, probably to be near the hot water. We kept a large metal lid over the tub when not in use, and this served as a work area for cooking. Since we had no curtains, taking a bath meant arranging sheets between the kitchen and the living room, which had several large windows. All of this was a bit bohemian but endearing. It was OK for the three summer months I was there.

I wasn't as adventurous as Marsia, who enjoyed sitting out on the fire escape and gazing at the city. I found perching there scary and intimidating. Having grown up in Santiago, Chile, Marsia was not easily frightened or daunted. She wandered around Manhattan and told me about a Russian Orthodox church she had found in her ramblings. Later, she went with me to the church on Park Avenue, and I appreciated that. It was quite an experience, totally unlike any Protestant church I had ever attended. But it was nice to see how a service worked since I had read about them in Russian novels and history books. I was surprised to see so many icons in one room, to see people bow to the icons, even bowing to the floor to cross themselves. All this was strange and new to me. One woman was standing with a priest, and he had a black cloth over her head, presumably hearing her confession. The men in the congregation entered and left at will, going outside for cigarette breaks from time to time. That astounded me. I had never seen people walking in and out of an ongoing religious service. Moreover, I had never seen an iconostasis, a wall covered with icons separating laity and from the altar, and was surprised to see a priest in golden robes coming and going between these two parts of the sanctuary. The service lasted so long that we left before communion, so I didn't see how that was administered. Only years later in Oxford, England, while attending an Orthodox church with my mother-in-law, did I participate in an Orthodox communion service. Irony of ironies, the Oxford priest, Professor Zernov, had taught at the University of Iowa, where John had taken one of his courses in the 1960s.

While my sister had dreamed of living in New York City for years and was not frightened of it, I was. She was as thrilled to live there as John and Marsia were to roam around it. However, I was overwhelmed and unnerved by the huge city. My stop on the IRT subway was 96th Street and Lexington Avenue, and I practically ran all the way home to 99th Street after I got off the subway at night. Indeed, I was always relieved to see a policeman outside the 96th Street stop. His presence calmed me. I carried an umbrella with me the entire summer, thinking I would hit anyone who tried to hurt me. Luckily, I was never bothered and never had to see if I would have used my weapon. Maybe it frightened robbers and molesters away. I don't know. I also held my purse tightly under my arm to prevent theft. No doubt being tall was an advantage, but I wasn't aware of that at the time. One of my greatest fears was being robbed on pay day. I was paid in cash, and I could hardly get home quickly enough to hide my money in the apartment. I paid my rent in cash, so it wasn't in my possession very long!

While Kathryn and Marsia thrived in Manhattan, I remained fearful. I wanted them to show me around, to go with me on the subway a few more times when I first arrived. They did show me around a bit, but they had been living there a year before I came, so they had been to many places and were busy with their own lives. I wanted to go to the Bleecker Street Theater where they showed foreign films, but they didn't. I wanted to go to the Cloisters medieval museum but was afraid to go alone. I went only after John returned from working in Walla Walla. When his job ended, he and an Iowa City friend went to Mexico and hitchhiked around. He didn't have a proper address, so I couldn't write to him, and I missed him a lot.

I didn't get as much research done at the New York Public Library as I expected. I wasn't familiar with closed-stack libraries, and at New York Public, I had to fill in cards and wait for books to be delivered each day. This could take a while. While waiting, I went to the magazine room and looked at *Vogue* and the *New Yorker*. They were so unusual to me. I was attracted to the beautiful clothes, advertisements, and cartoons in those publications. I had never read them before. Growing up in La Porte, Indiana, I had never seen such elegance and beauty. I found these posh magazines fascinating. Of course, I spent too much time looking at them and not enough reading the mystery and miracle plays. I soon discovered that my knowledge of Latin was inadequate for reading and that was disappointing. I thought four years of high school Latin had equipped me for research, but it hadn't. Moreover, I couldn't find enough English translations of these plays to facilitate my research. Another case of my reach exceeding my grasp!

Although I had been very healthy during the summer and denied being pregnant to myself, sometimes my feet swelled. One Sunday at the library I took off my shoes while reading, and when I tried to put them on again, they wouldn't fit. This was so embarrassing. I didn't know what to do. I literally couldn't get my feet into my high heels. I suppose the scene was similar to Cinderella's sisters trying to jam their big feet into the small glass slipper. I pondered what to do and couldn't decide. Finally, I just decided to walk in my nylons and carry my shoes. I made it to the shuttle between Times Square and Grand Central station, and I think then I was able to put the shoes on before I took the IRT home. I'm sure I looked pretty funny, dressed in a nice navy summer suit, which I had worn to church, walking barefoot carrying my shoes. However, New York being the impersonal city that it is, no one laughed at me, at least to my face. I should have been grateful for the laissez-faire attitude that I encountered, but I wasn't. I wanted a little more caring that Midwestern cities provided. Recently reading E. B. White's book *Here Is New York*, some of his words struck me as very true. In one place he says, "but New Yorkers temperamentally do not crave comfort and convenience—if they did they would live somewhere else."[8] Now I can see how well that described John. I just didn't know it at the time. Nor did I know how much I craved a cozy, comfortable existence.

This was the summer of Martin Luther King's famous march on Washington, DC, and his "I Have a Dream" speech. I was politically ignorant then and didn't know much about efforts to desegregate the South. Marsia and I had no radio or TV, so I didn't hear or see coverage of the marches and struggles. We didn't subscribe to a newspaper, as my parents did at home. Yet I heard about the march and saw signs inviting people to go there, but I didn't know anyone who was going—certainly neither my sister nor Marsia. No one where I worked mentioned it, although there were some black typists who worked where I did. John was in Mexico, so I didn't have him to go with me. This was a missed opportunity in my young life. However, I was so politically unaware that I only vaguely felt that I was missing an important historic event. Recently I was able to participate in a "Black Lives Matter" rally in Lincoln, so I felt as if I was finally atoning somewhat for my earlier behavior.

One of my greatest solaces that summer was writing in a journal. I had never done that before, but I was pretty lonesome and miserable, so it was good to be able to write down my feelings and relieve them in that way. Now that I'm writing my reminiscences, I wonder what I did with the notebooks I filled that summer. It was the first time I had deliberately written to assuage my feelings, and it had worked. Decades later, I found it helpful writing in a journal while doing my devotions.

My second joy that summer was going to the medieval Cloisters museum with John when he returned to the city. Being used to Manhattan, he knew how to take the bus uptown through Harlem to get there. We went on a Sunday and saw lots of black women dressed in fresh white dresses getting on and off the bus, coming and going to church. I was a little afraid every time the bus stopped, but John wasn't, so that was reassuring. I had never been in a black neighborhood before. We had precious few black people in La Porte, at Park College, or at the University of Iowa, so I wasn't used to interacting with them. In contrast, John had grown up in Englewood, New Jersey, just across the Hudson River

---

8. E. B. White, *Here Is New York* (New York: Harper, 1949), 52.

from New York City, and he had gone to Fordham University for four years, so he was more used to interacting with many kinds of people on the subway. When we arrived at the Cloisters, we enjoyed looking around it. I was awed by its loveliness. It was a miniature slice of medieval life. We also enjoyed sitting in the gardens overlooking the Hudson River. John and I both enjoyed Nature with a capital N. It was a quiet bonding time.

In New York, John's idea of a good time was going on a book crawl, and it sounded romantic to me. However, when we did it, I found it rather tedious and boring. Probably today I'd find it worthwhile, but I didn't in the summer of 1963. Still, I was glad we went to a Russian used bookstore, where I bought a wonderful Smirnitsky Russian dictionary. The store owner was a Russian émigré, who looked about one hundred years old. He was so old-worldly that he kissed my hand as we left. I had never experienced anything like that before and was deeply touched.

When John returned to New York, I think I had finished my job, but I may have quit to have time with him. I also met some of his friends then. One of them told him she thought I was pregnant, and he told me this. Not being able to accept my pregnancy, I denied it. I still wasn't ready to face that fact. In late August or early September, I decided to go home to visit my parents before returning to the University of Iowa. Finally, even I had to admit that I was beginning "to show." My brother's wedding was coming up, and I didn't know what to do. Their ceremony was in the nearby town of Elkhart, so all my relations as well as those of my sister-in-law would be there, and I didn't want to face their scrutiny and possible condemnation. I wasn't sure I could I disguise my condition, and I didn't want all my relatives to notice me and embarrass me and my mom. My thought was "when in doubt hide," so I made up some excuse and didn't go to their wedding. Needless to say, I later regretted not attending their celebration (but I kept their wedding photo).

No doubt I was feeling hurt and bewildered. They were doing everything right, getting married before having a baby. I think I felt hurt that John had asked me if I was pregnant, but he hadn't asked me to marry him in New York when we had

Deana and Walt Hutton's wedding, Elkhart, Indiana, 1963

talked. Later, when I went to a doctor in Iowa City in October, I found out I was seven months pregnant. When I told John this, he asked me to marry him, but it seemed shallow somehow. Still, we began our life together wishing each other well and wanting to grow as a couple and as individuals. Deep down I think we echoed the hope of the writer Gail Godwin in her novel *Evensong*: "May their having each other make more of them both."[9]

Marriage

Early in our married life, there were some indications of our differences, but I initially thought them amusing. It's so easy to deceive ourselves when we're in love. As William M. Thackeray said, "Love makes fools of us all." This certainly happened to me. When I first met John, he lived in a boardinghouse with two other graduate students. They lived upstairs and had two bathrooms. John put his dirty dishes in one bathtub and washed them once a week. They used the other tub for bathing. I thought this pretty daring. Initially, I liked his rebellious, unorthodox behavior. John proved to be not only a romantic spirit but a rebel as well. His behavior seemed sportive and playful. I found this appealing because I was so inhibited and repressed. Girls in my circle didn't do those kinds of things. What I have learned in retrospect is that I am often attracted to people through whom I can rebel vicariously.

However, when we married and agreed that he would do the dishes and I would do the cooking, I got quite irritated when he would let the dishes pile up all week. When I would remind him on Friday night that we needed clean plates for supper, he would calmly reply in his jesuitical manner that all we really needed were two plates and then casually wash two. This wasn't my idea of doing dishes. In our household, when we washed the dishes, it included the pots and pans and also wiping off the table, stove, and refrigerator. So, it was one thing to admire his rebellious spirit from afar but quite another when I was affected by it. Moreover, I soon found myself over-functioning and John under-functioning in our marriage. When I took a semester's leave to be home with Martin in the spring of 1964, I began doing all the housework and cooking. Initially, I felt proud to be the happy housewife and mother. It was almost a playful time for me. I had grown up in the 1940s and '50s when the idea was that the woman should subordinate her ambition to the family, and I felt OK about this then.

9. Gail Godwin, *Evensong* (New York: Ballantine, 1999).

Years later, I realized that I was emulating my parents' marriage, in which my mother also over-functioned and my father under-functioned emotionally, financially, and practically. No one could have told me I would imitate my parents' behavior. I thought I was so smart marrying a man who didn't drink and who wasn't like my father, except he was a lot like my mother and father—somewhat stoical like my mom and a ranter and raver like my dad when political discussions arose. I certainly didn't realize I was marrying a man who didn't believe in presents: none for Valentine's Day, Mother's Day, my birthday, or Christmas. In retrospect, I don't suppose presents or endearments fit into his "harsh and dreadful love" philosophy.

During our second year in graduate school, when John and I married, I found it very different admiring him from a distance than living with him. He was a much freer spirit than I was. He liked to bathe sitting down on the shower floor with the lights out. It was a sensual/spiritual experience for him. Also, he listened to jazz, and I didn't. He had a record of Thelonious Monk, and he loved playing it, as well as his classical records, quite loudly. Again, I was too inhibited to turn up the music full blast like he did. In most ways he was more adventuresome than I. At night, he liked to walk by the art building and talk to the artists who were painting. I loved the somewhat cloistered, medieval architecture of the art building but thought it quite daring to walk inside and talk to the artists. Again, I was shyer and held myself back from doing things like that.

Second Year in Graduate School

While a lot of my life focused on John, I gradually met some other students and professors who improved my graduate school experience. In the fall of 1964, I took a course titled American Intellectual History and met a woman student in the class, Billie Jeanne Hackley. We spoke after class a few times and slowly became pals. This was the beginning of a long friendship. Through her I met a few other women grad students, but none of them were in European history. They were all Americanists, and we didn't share any courses together. Still, it was good to have a female friend. Once, Billie Jeanne told me that when she first came to Iowa to do her PhD, her major professor told her that there were no jobs for women historians. He didn't tell her she couldn't study with him but that the prospects for her were dim, and he didn't want to encourage her and give her false hopes.

The second year at Iowa, I also had two Russian language and culture classes, and these were satisfying. I felt comfortable with my Russian women professors who were Russian émigrés. They appreciated me, which was quite a change compared to my place in the all-male History Department. The competition in the Russian language courses wasn't so stiff. We all seemed to muddle through, looking up new vocabulary as we translated our assignments. The professor for my Russian culture class was charming and presented the material in a wonderful way. I felt the Slavic soul of both of them and felt so much at home.

Birth of Our Son, Martin

On December 31, 1963, during our second year in graduate school, our son Martin was born. He was a beautiful baby and possessed a wonderful disposition, so God smiled on us as new parents. The University of Iowa hospital gave me a US government publication about child rearing, and I bought a book by Dr. Benjamin Spock. Since we lived so far away from our parents—hundreds of miles away from mine in Indiana, and thousands of miles from John's in England—the books helped us rear our son. We didn't consult our siblings and friends because at that time none of them had children. Yet, we behaved as responsible parents once Martin was born, even if we had been a bit reckless about birth control before his birth. Below is a picture of us all at the hospital. I made the gown Martin is wearing and embroidered the little sheep. I had also knit Martin a bunting in which to bring him home from the hospital. Fortunately, Martin Eisenburg, a friend of John's and a fellow New Yorker and history graduate student, had brought us a basketful of flannel gowns that his landlady was discarding. She wasn't planning to have any more children and had put the basket of baby clothes on the porch of his rooming house where he had seen them. So, our son had several gowns to wear when he got home.

John, Marcelline, and Martin, University of Iowa hospital, December 1963

One of my fondest impressions upon seeing Martin in the hospital was that he looked like a tonsured monk. He had just a fringe of white blond hair encircling his head, and the gown the nurses dressed him in had little mittens attached to his hands, so he wouldn't scratch himself. All together, the hair and gown and covered hands made him look like a miniature monk.

The other early memory of Martin I have is of his beautiful white blonde hair and rosy cheeks. When I washed his hair, it stood up on end, and he resembled the Israeli Prime Minister David Ben-Gurion, who had white hair that seemed to stand out all over his head. Martin's rosy cheeks were really red when he awoke from his naps. He always looked so bonny. I felt blessed to have such a healthy and handsome baby.

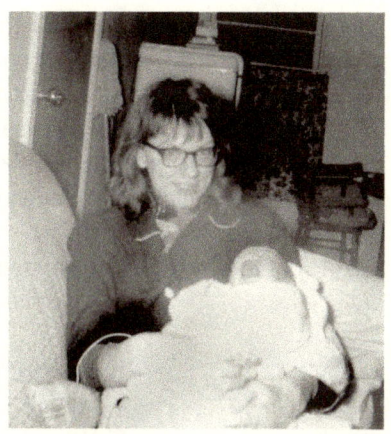

Marcelline and Martin, Iowa City, January 1964

I remember one amusing incident shortly after Martin's birth. I had gone to the grocery store, which was only a few blocks away. There I met Dr. Robert Kingdon, our Reformation history professor, and although I told him we lived very close by and I didn't need a ride home, he insisted on giving me a lift. So, I thought I should invite him in to see Martin. He was eager to do this. When we got to our apartment, John answered the door. As he opened the door, several glass ginger ale bottles, which had been lined up behind the door, fell over in a clatter. The noise was embarrassing. Then John said to the professor, "What an unpleasant surprise." Of course, he meant to say "What a pleasant surprise," but the visit was so unexpected that he made a Freudian slip. So, our early married life was not without some amusing incidents and surprises.

Another one occurred a few weeks later when I went to the head of the History Department to see if I could take a semester off from my NDEA grant to stay home to care for Martin. He said to me, "Are you pregnant?" and I said, "No, I just had a baby." I had thought my physical change obvious, but I guess it wasn't.

Looking back, I can see that Martin was a pretty easy baby to care for. He had no adverse reaction to the DPT shots he received and ate and slept well. After three months, he learned to sleep through the night. He thrived on the diet the University of Iowa hospital prescribed for him, and since he was a big baby he slept longer between feedings. At four months, he usually slept till six o'clock each morning. The only unusual event was one morning when he slept until nine, and I was frightened to go into his room. He had never slept so late, and I was afraid he had died. Perhaps it was a dark morning, I can't remember, but I don't think he ever slept so late again until he was five years old and we were living in England. That morning, we had all slept until eleven. It was most unusual for all of us. Martin was a very healthy baby until he started teething at six months, when he got some ear infections, but these were treatable.

Joyful Grandparents

The second semester when I was home with Martin, I discovered how much grandchildren mean to their grandparents. A few months after Martin's birth, my parents came to visit. They stayed at the Jefferson Hotel in downtown Iowa City. In those days, a room cost only about $3.50 per night. Moreover it was less than a mile away, and they didn't mind walking to our apartment. Martin was the first grandchild on both sides of the family, and both sets of grandparents adored him. He was a cheerful baby who was easy to love. Becoming grandparents was a marvelous experience for them. Still, nothing prepared me for the love and adoration they lavished on him. I was almost shocked because I did not remember such parental endearments. I didn't recall them playing with me or kissing me, so it was lovely to see them enjoying this with Martin. Seeing their behavior melted away some of the resentment I held at feeling so unloved as a child.

Since my mother was still working when Martin was born, my parents' visit was fairly short. Reading one of my devotionals one morning, I noticed the author saying that children bring some innate sense of the divine into the world, but the world soon seals it off.[10] I was musing that children are often the conduit of love. Babies are easy to love, and adults don't fear being rejected by them. Perhaps it's the channeling of divine love that makes grandchildren so attractive to their grandparents. In my own case, Martin certainly served as a new and more loving bond to my parents and to my in-laws.

In 1964, my parents could still take a train to visit us. The New York Central train ran from New York City to La Porte and then to Chicago, and from

---

10. See Nigel W. D. Mumford, *The Thirty-One Day Healing Devotional* (Virginia Beach, VA: By His Wounds, 2002), February 6.

there they took the Rock Island to Iowa City. At this time there were several trains each day each way. It took about a day, but it was worth it to them, and to me too when I later took Martin to visit them at Christmas and in the summertime. While I can't remember much of their whirlwind visit, I do recall afterward receiving a huge refrigerator-sized box full of baby clothes from one of my mother's friends. I couldn't imagine using so many dressy outfits for one child, especially since I usually dressed him in a gown. He literally couldn't wear all the clothes, so I gave some of them to an acquaintance who had a son a bit younger than Martin. Here is a picture of my father and Martin in our apartment in the spring of 1964.

Shortly after my parents' visit, my father-in-law came to see us in April 1964. He came from England, where he and his wife had retired. He was in the States to sell their home in Englewood, New Jersey. He too came by train and brought us an enormous wardrobe trunk full of presents—dishes, a toaster, and other household items that he was getting rid of since he was selling their house. He too fell in love with Martin. By this time, we had a baby buggy, and he loved taking his grandson for walks. The three of us walked uptown, around the university, and along the Iowa River, one of my favorite places because I found the water so soothing.

Dad and Martin, Iowa City, April 1964

John's father and Martin, Iowa City, April 1964

Chapter IV

Death of John's Father

While John and his father did not always get along, Martin pleased his grandfather and improved family relations. However, shortly after visiting us in Iowa City and returning to New Jersey, my father-in-law died of a heart attack. So, John had a lot of changes in his life in one year—marriage to me, the birth of our son, the death of his father, and the canceling of the PhD program in the humanities that had initially drawn him to the University of Iowa. Since John's mother was living in England when her husband died, John went to New Jersey to take care of his father's burial. It turned out that the extended family in Boston wanted his body shipped there to be buried alongside other family members. In Englewood, John stayed with some friends who sent presents for Martin and me and covered his expenses. I had taken a leave from my fellowship, so we were pretty poor that semester, and I remember we had to use an installment plan to pay for the overseas call to John's mother telling her of her husband's death. We were living on John's research assistantship, which paid our rent of eighty-five dollars per month and left a little for groceries. We just didn't have an extra thirty dollars to pay for a transatlantic phone call.

Yet, if I remember correctly, John returned from New York City with a beautiful red felt hat that he and his friend Paul had picked out for me at a Fifth Avenue department store. Apparently John and Paul had had a lot of fun trying on various hats, and John chose the red one. For me, it was an unfortunate choice. I was angry that he had spent money on such a frivolous thing, and angrier yet that he had gotten a red hat because I never wore red at that time and thought I didn't look good in it. It was the first of many misunderstandings in our marriage. In retrospect I realize that I was responding much as my mother had years earlier when she criticized my father for buying my sister and me dolls for Christmas when she needed the money for household expenses. I felt the same way. The result was the same: never another present from John, just as I had never received another present from my father.

Thinking of John's father's death, I can see in retrospect that God often brings good out of evil. The good that came of his death was that John's mother, Louie, invited us to come visit her in England in August 1964. It was helpful for her to have this family reunion because she had not come to the States for her husband's funeral. Traveling to England was pretty exciting for me. I'd never been abroad. First, we had to get a passport, and it was cheaper to add Martin to my new passport than to amend John's. To save money as poor graduate students, John took passport photos of me and Martin, but it worked.

We also tried to find the cheapest way to get to New York City and that turned out to be riding with a fellow from the University of Iowa who was driving there. Initially we stayed with my artist friend, Marsia Alexander, from Park College. She was living in Greenwich Village, and that seemed like a desirable place to spend some time before going to England. Unfortunately, Martin got sick on the way to New York City. He was teething then and had an ear infection. He'd been a very healthy baby, so we didn't quite know what to do. We took him to New York's Bellevue Charity Hospital, but they didn't diagnose his problem correctly. So, we went to stay in Englewood, where John used to live. We stayed with his friends the Lewins. The father was a famous plastic surgeon, and the mother, Mrs. Lewin, knew some pediatricians and arranged an appointment for us. This doctor made the correct diagnosis, and we soon had the right medicine for Martin and he began feeling better. Needless to say, as a handsome baby, Martin was a hit with this family. The teenage daughter, Barbara, especially enjoyed playing with Martin. I felt a bit out of place because I had never before visited an upper middle-class family that employed a maid, and I didn't quite know how to act. John had been friends with the family for years, so he was comfortable with them. The household revolved around the father, who commuted to work in New York City every day. The son, Bob, was an aspiring rock-and-roll star. His fascination with popular music mystified me. He had no musical training but wanted to become a rock star. He also had been in therapy for several years. Again, I had never known anyone who went to a therapist, especially for several years. People I knew neither aspired to become rock musicians nor had therapists. In contrast, the daughter seemed quite sweet and normal. I think John had had a crush on her before he knew me. If I hadn't come along, perhaps he would have married her. Who knows?

Visiting England

As previously mentioned, John's mother, Louie, paid for our trip to England. We found a cheap charter flight with the Irish Sligo football club, which was flying from New York to Shannon, Ireland. Then we flew to Dublin and on to Leeds, England, where Louie lived. I was so tired of traveling from all these flights I could hardly focus. However, since this was my first visit abroad, I did notice the picturesque fields and rock walls in Ireland and England as the planes made their ascents and descents. All this looked charming and quaint to me. Sharing it with John and Martin made it extra special. Although Leeds isn't as

Chapter IV

Martin and Grandma Louie, Leeds, England, August 1964

beautiful as places like Oxford, I found it captivating because it was my first visit to a foreign city. I went to church and a pub and did the grocery shopping for my mother-in-law. I didn't understand the currency, so I often had to stretch out my hand with some pound notes to let the butcher or grocer give me back the right change. All the people I encountered were incredibly honest—not one cheated me.

Despite some pitfalls, the visit proved a charming introduction to English life and some of John's relatives. We experienced whirlwind visits to various relatives, friends, and historic places, such as Scarborough, Harrogate, York Minster, and Hadden Hall. It was all enthralling to me. Some of Louie's friends invited us to afternoon tea, and that was fascinating. "Tea" meant a meal akin to lunch: a small meal with meat, sandwiches, and a variety of sweets as well as tea.

One afternoon, John's uncle Bernard was playing cricket, so we went to his cricket match, which was rather boring since I didn't understand it. John's elderly grandmother was also at the match, so it was good to meet her. I think she had dementia because it was difficult communicating with her. She had thought I was a Negro before we met. She knew that something was amiss, but no one had wanted to tell her that I was pregnant when John and I got married, so she knew there was some scandal but hadn't known what it was. She had sent us an impressive turn-of-the-century (1900) tea set with John's father, who had been in England before he came to visit us. So I was grateful to her for the lovely present. However, the entire cricket experience was a bit odd because when it was over Bernard went to a pub with his team, leaving Louie, her mother, me, and Martin waiting in the car. This was not nice but reflected the male-dominated atmosphere in England at the time. Women did not go into the main part of the pub where the men drank, and Bernard obviously wanted to celebrate with his teammates and not sit in the adjoining room where women could go. Yet Bernard had picked us up at the Leeds airport, and he did drive us around a few places, so I was thankful for those kindnesses.

I can only vaguely remember the bus trip from Leeds to Scarborough on a winding English road where the vehicles passed down the middle of the highway. It was a long trip and a bit trying since I was tired. We didn't have much time to gaze at the sea and that was a disappointment. Another day, we visited Harrogate and had a good time seeing the gardens there. What I remember most was seeing a young boy standing in a pool of cool water playing with a boat. He wore swimming trunks, while I wore a dress, sweater, and raincoat. I admired this hardy child. We had left the United States when it was the hot summer, and I had not brought warm clothes to wear in England, where it was much cooler. Luckily I had packed a raincoat and black mohair sweater. Both helped keep me comfortable. I even wore the sweater to bed to keep warm.

I can't quite recall all the circumstances of our visit to York Minster, but I can still remember walking up the very narrow stairway to the roof. We wanted to see the view from there, so we climbed up the narrow stairs. John carried Martin in a pack on his back, and I brought his baby bottle. I remember feeding Martin on the rooftop and enjoying the view. But I was terrified of descending the staircase, afraid of meeting others on their way up, with no railing to hold on to. Trembling, I resolved to myself: "Never again would I climb such a staircase." And I didn't.

Once, Louie and I attended evensong at York Minster. It was serene and impressive. The boys' choir was enchanting. The immensity of the cathedral amazed me. Having been brought up in a rather plain Presbyterian church, I was unprepared for cathedrals. Indeed, John had taken me in December 1962 to St. Patrick's Cathedral in New York City during our winter break, and I had been staggered by its size. I was overwhelmed by all the side altars but really touched when John lit a candle for me at one of them. Protestants didn't do things like that. This was another sign of how romantic I thought he was. It was a perfect moment in our courtship.

Our trip to visit John's mother lasted a few weeks, but eventually it was time to return to Shannon, Ireland, to get our plane home. Instead of flying to Ireland, Louie suggested we take the boat train from Liverpool to Dublin. We took a train from Leeds to Liverpool and then an overnight ferry from Liverpool to Dublin. Wanting to save her money, I suggested we go second class on the boat. It proved a foolish economy. We had no bed, and sitting up all night in a chair was exhausting. Years later when taking an overnight ferry from Klaipėda, Lithuania, to Sassnitz, Germany, I made sure to book a cabin with a bed.

In Dublin, we caught a train to Limerick, where we stayed overnight before going on to Shannon to catch the plane. It was like stepping back in time riding the train through the Irish countryside. We saw horse and donkey carts, and I was surprised how poor the countryside looked. In Limerick we stayed in a hotel that seemed right out of the 1940s. The print curtains and satin bedspreads seemed very old-fashioned. While we walked about the town, we saw six black horses pulling a black hearse. That was a powerful image. I had never seen anything like that in my life. Five decades later I was flabbergasted when people described Ireland as an economic tiger with a higher standard of living than England's. I simply couldn't understand it. I just couldn't believe that when the European Union invested in a country, it made that much of a difference, but it did.

When we left England, we felt a little guilty leaving Louie. However, we knew that Colette, the daughter of a French friend, was coming to Leeds to live with her. Colette thought Louie would be lonesome without her husband. Colette was not only very beautiful but a very thoughtful young woman. While living with Louie, she taught French conversation at Notre Dame grammar school, where Louie's sister taught history. I think Colette was studying English literature at the Sorbonne, so living in England probably helped her practice English. I'm sure she was a godsend to Louie. Her coming meant we didn't feel we were deserting Louie.

Back in Iowa City

After our return to Iowa City, John and I agreed that we would stagger our classes so that one of us would always be home to take care of Martin. John was always helpful in feeding and changing our son. Indeed, since he was a late night owl studying at the library until one in the morning, he often made Martin's formula, if I was too tired to do it at night. After our diaper service that a friend had given us ran out, John took the diapers to the Laundromat at night. He never begrudged doing those things. I felt caught between two worlds—that of the mother and the graduate student. At that time, few female graduate students were wives and mothers. Some male graduate students had children, but they also had wives who took care of the children.

Martin napping in our yard, Iowa City, summer 1964

Volunteer Poverty

As poor graduate students, John and I willingly adopted the volunteer poverty that Michael Harrington describes in *The Other America* (1962). He maintains that some groups, like black Americans and those living in Appalachia, did not escape poverty after the Depression, whereas mainstream America did. He also mentions students and how they often accept volunteer poverty while pursuing their degrees. While I initially considered this a temporary state, it lasted from 1963 to 1975, our many years spent in graduate school. Our family survived this poverty well partly because we were all remarkably healthy and had no medical expenses. The one time Martin had pneumonia he was treated at the University of Iowa hospital, and because he had been born there, no payment was required. Having recently read Alissa Quart's *Squeezed: Why Our Families Can't Afford America*, I realized how fortunate we were to have been so healthy. Quart shows how a child's illness can bankrupt a family today, especially a family with a single mother who is marginally employed.[11] Moreover, as graduate students John and I were able to obtain very cheap health insurance, and we could buy inexpensive accident insurance for Martin through the school system. Little did I realize that as a follower of *The Catholic Worker*, John intended to embrace the frugal lifestyle forever, even though I didn't quite share that view. In retrospect, I believe he was more influenced by Catholic asceticism and a "harsh and dreadful love" than I had realized.

Music as Therapy

Music was one of the things that helped me survive in graduate school and in my marriage. It offered a way to process my emotions. I was pleased that John didn't mind staying at home in the evenings, and I often went to free concerts at the university. Initially, symphonies were performed in the Union Ball Room. I remember hearing the Minneapolis Symphony Orchestra play there. The conductor at Iowa at that time was James Dixon. He included old favorites by Bach, Beethoven, Hayden, Mozart, Brahms, Tchaikovsky, and others, but he also introduced works of twentieth-century composers, so his concerts were educational as well as enjoyable. There were also free student recitals and performances as well as an Early Modern group called Collegium Musicum that often

---

11. Alissa Quart, *Squeezed: Why Our Families Can't Afford America* (New York: Harper Collins, 2018), 34–44.

gave concerts at the end of the semester and instructed the audience about medieval and early modern instruments. The university radio station WSUI played classical music during part of the day and at night. That too enhanced my life.

Friends

In Iowa City we didn't have a car, and we couldn't go to state parks by ourselves, so we appreciated it when someone took us. It was good to get out of town occasionally. Martin was so blond and winsome, all our friends loved him. Once a fellow graduate student, Abe, took us swimming at nearby Lake Macbride State Park. Coming home, Martin, who was then about three years old, casually asked Abe if he wanted to come in to have something to eat. We usually offered our friends food and drink, but I had nothing baked and was so embarrassed to have only graham crackers to offer. It surprised me that Martin understood hospitality at such an early age. He barely spoke at three, so I was astonished on several levels when he extended the invitation to Abe.

On Friday nights in Iowa City, friends sometimes stopped by, and we often had spaghetti. It was cheap, and we could feed several people. Our friend Larry Meisgeier often brought beer, and I always enjoyed that. We could never afford alcohol, so it was fun to imbibe occasionally. Since I had a fellowship, I was never a teaching assistant, and I missed the camaraderie of going to some of the local bars to drink after class with other grad students. When John became a teaching assistant, about the third year of our life together, he sometimes went drinking with the fellows after their meetings. I was never part of this culture though, partly because I was a woman, partly because I was a mother as well as a graduate student, and partly because I had a fellowship, not a teaching assistantship, and lacked daily interaction with other graduate students. Friends sometimes came to our apartment for coffee and dessert, and I loved making cakes. Our social life was simple at this time.

Martin as a bonny toddler, Iowa City, mid 1960s

At Christmas and in the summer, Martin and I often visited my folks in La Porte. My mother once had Martin get his hair cut there, and this is a picture of him looking dapper.

Escaping to England, 1968–1970

In 1966 John finished his MA thesis "'The Land' and the Death Duty Budget of 1894" in English history. I completed my thesis, "Three Russian Radicals and the 'Woman Question'" a year later. In the spring of 1968, John passed his five qualifying exams for his PhD. He had put

Martin, Iowa City, 1960s

so much energy into studying for several years and into preparing for those exams that passing them seemed an empty victory. He was very depressed afterward. I subsequently learned that when artists or writers have a great success, they are often unable to create for a long time. I didn't know much about psychology in the 1960s, but I knew John needed a change. So I proposed going to England, where his mother and brother lived, and where he could do some research on his dissertation. Initially, he toyed with the idea of writing on Edward Carpenter's bohemian attitudes toward sexuality, but I thought the things John suggested were a bit too risqué. John found Carpenter titillating, amusing, and fascinating. I was more prudish and didn't think these ideas quite right for history. Again, this was before social history had taken off and before such topics were popular. In retrospect, I'm sorry I dissuaded him from writing on these subjects since his heart was not really in reformatories of the mid nineteenth century, the topic he settled on. It turned out that he got a scholarship from the history department for one thousand dollars for dissertation research, and we thought we three could live on that money for a year in England. It turned out that we lived frugally in England for two years. That meant that we lived on about fifty dollars a month—more voluntary poverty.

Arriving in England in 1968, we discovered the cost of living in London was frightfully expensive, more costly than New York City. Fortunately we found a semidetached house in Southampton and rented it for two pounds, or five dollars per week. The two-story brick house was near a charming, red brick Victorian school, which Martin attended for two years. Children started school at age four in England, and he was just the right age.

Our Victorian House

The Victorian house we rented had three large bedrooms upstairs and a parlor, living room/dining room, and large kitchen downstairs. The toilet was a separate room located off the kitchen. It was a bit of a bother because we had to go out the kitchen door to use it. It was a vintage commode, and in the deep winter we had to keep a small kerosene lamp lit to keep the water in the toilet and pipes from freezing. Although our house did not have central heating or hot water, we didn't think that too important compared to the space and price. We could have one bedroom for Martin, one for us, and one for John's study.

Each room in our house had a fireplace, but we could afford to heat only one—the living room/dining room. We could afford wood, but a coal fire was warmer and cozier, yet more costly. Unfortunately, I was not adept at starting a coal fire, but John could. I tried and tried. I used the special fire starters soaked in kerosene, but even those didn't work for me. I tried folding newspapers in the accordion style my neighbor, Miss Lane, had shown me, but again I had no luck. One day I had washed my long, thick hair, and I was desperate to start a fire to dry it. So in desperation, I threw some kerosene on the coal and a huge whoosh threw me against the far wall. Never again did I try to start a fire with petrol. I just let John do it. I discovered that living in a foreign country was a learning experience. I couldn't do everything I wanted. Moreover, I observed that although we Americans and English speak the same language, our cultures and ways of life can be quite different. For example, English people valued their privacy because the country had a very dense population. The island was quite crowded, although I was never aware of it while living there.

Living in England did have its romantic aspects. We went to secondhand shops to buy furniture for our new home. We found a lovely carved wooden bed for a reasonable price along with some dressers and maple washstands with marble tops to use in various rooms. We bought a dining room table, and I refinished it to make it look nice. We also painted and wallpapered several of the rooms. But after a couple months of house beautification, we had had enough of that.

I also bought some wool curtains at a thrift shop. I soon learned as fall and winter approached that the windows did not fit very tightly, and curtains were necessary to help keep out the drafts. One of the greatest surprises to me was that the temperature was about the same inside and outside the house. My neighbor gave me a thermometer, and I was shocked to see that the temperature inside was only thirty-seven degrees in the winter—the same as outside. No wonder I suffered from the cold. John, however, had grown up with an English mother who didn't keep their house in America too warm. I remember visiting them in Englewood, New Jersey, one Christmas vacation and almost sitting in the fireplace to keep warm. At that time I didn't realize the significance of their chilly living room.

Entertainment

In England our entertainment consisted mainly of strolling around the town or walking several miles along the River Itchen to Winchester to see the cathedral. This long walk was a pleasant one. After about three miles, we came to a pub and could stop for a beer if we had the money. We took a frugal lunch of sandwiches, carrots, and apples with us. I was surprised to see that most of the English walkers we encountered also carried quite simple lunches. No picnic baskets or backpacks to be seen. It was refreshing that public footpaths existed all over the country, and they were kept open by people walking on them at least once a year. Years later, I read Bill Bryson's humorous book *Notes from a Small Island* (1995) about taking these public paths from southern England to northern Scotland. It's amazing that one can walk from one end of the United Kingdom to the other on these trails. His book showed what the system is like and how people worked to keep the paths open. Another captivating work about hiking these paths is *The Unlikely Pilgrimage of Harold Fry* by Rachel Joyce. It is more of a spiritual and psychological study. Recently, I read Bryson's *The Road to Little Dribbling*, also about walking the footpaths. While it contains funny passages, the book also laments the changes in English villages that have occurred since Bryson first walked those ways during the 1990s.

At Winchester Cathedral, I was surprised to see some folks making gravestone rubbings on the medieval tombs. We found Jane Austen's grave with a giant brass plaque on it, but I was almost afraid to walk on it because I felt so much reverence for the author. Martin was frightened by the sarcophaguses that seemed to be everywhere, and he ran out of the cathedral.

Once we took some friends visiting from Iowa City to see a building in Winchester that supposedly held King Arthur's round table on one wall. It turned out that the assizes court was meeting there, and a case involving the theft of cigarettes was being tried. We were all fascinated by the judges and lawyers in their wigs and the actual trial underway before our very eyes. This event preceded the TV show *Rumpole of the Bailey*, which revealed the workings of the English legal system. Years later, when I saw this humorous show, it reminded me of our experience in Winchester.

Another place we walked for entertainment was the downtown market. It amazed me that I could buy eggs from South Africa, Poland, or England. The South African eggs were the cheapest and the English the most expensive. So buying eggs became a political decision. I had to make similar decisions regarding grapefruit—Israeli or the cheaper South African? Irish or English butter? I hadn't faced these sorts of decisions at the A&P where I shopped in Iowa City and was almost dumbfounded by all the choices and political decisions. All kinds of goods were featured at the market, even an antique sewing machine from 1885, which I bought for two pounds—five dollars. I could also buy fabric and thread there.

One of my favorite booths at the downtown market was the bacon butcher. The first time I stopped there, I was astonished to see the size of the bacon. It was much thicker and wider than American bacon, almost like our pork steaks but without the bone. What really fascinated me about the bacon butcher was that when I came to buy some meat from him, he always recited a poem to me. Moreover, it was a different poem each time. I remembered this only recently while shopping at my local Whole Foods Market and remarking on it to the butcher there—and he burst into the recitation of a long poem for me. This surprised me too! Life can be full of unexpected happy events.

Visiting John's Mother in Sheffield

After her husband's and sister's deaths, John's mother moved to Sheffield to be closer to her elderly mother who lived there. It was also the city in which she had been raised. When visiting her in Sheffield in 1968, we enjoyed walking the public footpaths there too. Often, the paths skirted babbling brooks. Here, John and Martin would sail little paper boats down the stream. (Seeing the film *Goodbye Christopher Robin*, in which the father and son did something similar with sticks, made me remember our simple times and simple pleasures.) It touched me that people in Sheffield would drive to the edge of the city, park their cars, and then hike the footpaths or climb the moors. This was not so common in the States in the late 1960s, at least not in the Midwest. John's mother lived in Totley, Sheffield, and she walked a path through the moors to the grocer's. We walked it with her and then could do it ourselves to get the groceries for her. The moors are peculiar to Yorkshire and consist of rather low rugged hills with heather, sheep, and frolicking lambs in the springtime. In America they were made famous by Englishman James Herriot's books *All Creatures Great and Small* (1972) and *All Things Wise and Wonderful* (1976) as well as the TV shows about them. The TV series depicted a Yorkshire veterinarian prior to World War II and was quite popular. The episodes took place in North Yorkshire, mainly on farms in the moors where the winding roads and simple life were enduring and endearing. Herriot's books and shows had a tremendous influence on people; one of my friends in Germany became a veterinarian after reading his books.

Forty years after visiting my mother-in-law in Sheffield in 1969, I returned to visit a Ukrainian friend and her son who were living there. I stayed with them a week or so, and we went to Totley station by bus and then walked on the moors. My friend Irina loved hiking around the hills. I didn't have as much energy as she and her son, Vitaly, so I rested while they hiked. We saw small lambs frisking about in a field as we were passing by, and it was fun to see them escape their captivity and scamper down a lane. We tried to catch them to put them behind the fence, but they ran lickety-split and were too fast for us to capture. The moors reminded Irina of hiking in the Carpathians, which she did as a child since she was born and raised in western Ukraine. I also took Irina and Vitaly to York to see the cathedral and the city. They loved it. I was amazed that having lived several years in Sheffield that they hadn't been to either of those places, so I was glad I could introduce them to those sites. Of course it was odd for me to revisit places I had seen decades previously and to fondly remember Louie and John, both of whom had died. Visiting the Roman Catholic cathedral in downtown Sheffield, I thought of Louie worshipping there in the 1930s before coming to the States. Irina and I also visited the city art museum and enjoyed the Burne-Jones pieces there. Who doesn't love Pre-Raphaelite art?

One other incident stands out from our 1968 visit to Louie in Sheffield. One evening, she baked a whole chicken for supper. When she served it, Martin put down his knife and fork and didn't eat any of it. I was astonished. In Iowa City, I had often prepared one chicken breast and shared it among the three of us. Often I cut it up in small pieces to use in making rice pilaf, so it didn't look like a bird, as the baked chicken did. I remember being very surprised at Martin's behavior and didn't yet realize what a sensitive child he was. I hadn't liked seeing my grandmother Johnson kill a chicken when I was a kid. Nor when I was young did I like seeing my mother clean a whole chicken and take out the innards before cooking it for Sunday dinner. But I still ate chicken. I guess it's taken me a long time to realize how much more sensitive my son is than I am on many issues. Perhaps this is one reason he became a vegetarian as an adult.

Ordinary Life in England: Hard Slog

Back home, after our stay in Sheffield with my mother-in-law, we registered Martin at the nearby school. The first two days were difficult ones for Martin and me. Initially he screamed when I dropped him off for class, and I felt sad that he would have to learn to fight his own battles at school. I realized that I couldn't protect him anymore. That was a difficult realization for me. However, within a few days he became accustomed to school and loved it. He never missed a day. He developed the local Hampshire accent so the other children could understand him. I hadn't noticed the new accent, but when some friends from the University of Iowa came to London to study and visited us, they noticed it right away and pointed it out to me. Who would guess an outsider but not his mother would notice this about her own son?

In November 1968 we had invited two American couples to celebrate Thanksgiving with us. We borrowed some camp beds and thought our friends would each sleep in a narrow bed. However, they found our house so cold that they huddled together in one tiny camp bed instead. These beds were narrower than a single bed, and we could have given them Martin's bed to sleep in, had we known they would need to sleep together for warmth. Ah, the things we don't learn till later.

After our holiday dinner, we asked our guests if they wanted to walk to Winchester along the River Itchen to see the cathedral, but they refused. It was cold, and John had made such a big fire in the fireplace that none of our company wanted to leave the warmth of the living room. It was fun having them and a reminder of America at holiday time. At Christmas and some other times, my mother-in-law came from Sheffield to help celebrate, and she made the holidays festive.

At school, Martin loved the dinners and enjoyed the older students sitting at his table parceling out the food. I think they were proctors of some kind. They divided the pudding too, and Martin loved that. His favorite dinner was bangers and mash, that is, sausages and mashed potatoes. I didn't much care for English sausages because they seemed mushy, what with having so much bread in them, but they were popular among children. At first I didn't realize that my son was supposed to wear a uniform to school. Most of the boys wore grey short pants, a blue dress shirt, a blue and grey tie, grey knee socks, and brown sandals. The first few days I had sent him to school in red corduroys with a plaid flannel lining to keep him warm. He also had red socks. Americans often wear bright colors, but eventually I realized these were the wrong clothes for England. After a bit, he wore the school uniform and fit in pretty well.

In the first grade, Martin learned to read, and his father helped him with this. While I read stories to him at night, John made up stories about Wally Walrus that he told Martin while putting him to bed. Both of us played dominoes and cards with Martin, but John also taught him to play chess. It was a game they enjoyed for many years. Both of us played soccer with Martin and some of the neighborhood children in a nearby ravine called "the cut." The other boys thought it odd that I played too. In England in 1970, soccer was an exclusively male sport. They didn't seem to have any co-ed sports games besides tennis.

Once, we took Martin and my friend Maeve's eldest son to a professional soccer game. Everyone stood on the bleachers, watched the game, and drank beer. There was a festive air, yet people also sang hymns like "Abide with Me." In soccer, the fans are much closer to the field and to the players than they are at American football games. I was shocked years later to learn of the violence after some soccer games in England and Europe. That was not our experience, but at that time our city was not in the top tier of soccer clubs, where the competition was so keen.

In some ways, life in England was easier for me than for John. Upon our arrival, he discovered that the research topic and the papers he had expected to consult for his dissertation had been turned over to another scholar before his arrival. That was a blow. John had to find a new topic. No easy task in English history, about which so much had already been written. The other problem he encountered was that English male society was rather snobbish and aloof. I think he tried to make friends with some of the history professors at the university but was rebuffed. Maybe he was too left wing or looked too bohemian with his beard. It was easier for me. Female culture was more accessible to me. My female neighbors and the mothers of children at Martin's school were friendly and open to me. Indeed, one young English mother, whenever we met, always asked me to speak "American." I wondered if I represented America to her and others I met. If so, it was good for them to see that there were poor Americans as well as the wealthy ones in the movies. Still, I felt a little overwhelmed to be the only American these people might ever meet and wondered if I were a good example of the token American. What a responsibility! Needless to say, I tried not to think along these lines too much.

The pattern in our neighborhood was for mothers to walk their young children to school at nine, collect them for lunch, return them after a two-hour lunch break, and then escort them home at four. All the children and mothers walked to school. No one in our area, with the exception of our neighbor, Miss Lane, had a car. As a result of these daily walks, I became friends with two women along our road whose sons were also in Martin's class. It was fascinating getting to know them and their backgrounds. Both were working class, but one was from Ireland. The Irish woman, named Maeve, was married to an English engineer, and they lived in public housing down the street from us. He received four weeks of paid holiday a year, and this amazed me.

Few American workers I knew when I was growing up in the 1940s and '50s received paid holidays—certainly not a month's paid vacation. In England and Europe, this benefit resulted from Labour Party politics and high rates of trade union membership. It was one more reminder that despite our shared language, England and the United States have very different cultures. The British social safety net included monetary family allowances for children and universal government health care. These were much better than in the States.

Another woman on our street whom I got to know was bright and had been offered a scholarship to grammar school but had turned it down to work full-time at age fourteen. Upward mobility was not as important in English working-class life as it was in the States, where my siblings and I went to university, thereby becoming middle class. This friend was very bright and talented, but she cleaned houses for a living. I found this sad since she was so obviously smart and talented.

My Neighbor and Best Friend, Ivy Lane

My best friend in England turned out to be my next-door neighbor, Ivy Lane. She worked for IBM and loved the American bosses when they came to work in her office in England because they were more informal and easier to work with than her English supervisors. After she retired, Miss Lane often took us to tourist attractions in her car. Although she had a vehicle, she didn't have a telephone. Very few on our street had phones. One friend had to wait two years after applying for one to get it installed. Most of us used the famous red coin box a few blocks away. Miss Lane befriended Martin, John, and me. She liked all of us. We invited her to dinner—often meatloaf and baked potatoes or something similarly simple—and she was pleased to sup with us. Although she had lived next door for sixty years, she had never been in the house until we moved in. Miss Lane spoiled us, especially Martin. She made him dainty puddings and desserts in special small tins. She was like a grandmother to him since she lived right next door and saw him daily, whereas his actual grandmothers always lived far away—mine in Indiana and John's in Sheffield. Ivy also enjoyed talking to Martin in her garden.

Miss Lane often invited me to tea and to a warm place in her living room during the winter. She had a TV and invited me to watch *The Forsythe Saga* and *Upstairs, Downstairs* with her. It was delightful being in her warm living room and having tea with her fine china. What a pleasure it was being her neighbor! I appreciated her cordiality, hospitality, and cozy home.

A decade later I returned to England with my mother. We stayed at Miss Lane's for a few nights and had a grand time. It was March, and the weather was fine. There was green grass to enjoy instead of the mounds of snow that had engulfed my mother's house in La Porte since November. The incessant snow had made it easy to persuade mom to come to England with me. Getting a hundred-dollar round-trip flight from Chicago to London also made our trip attractive. Below is a picture of my friend Maeve, Miss Lane, Mother, and me in Miss Lane's garden.

Martin and Miss Lane, England, 1969

Left to right: Maeve, Marcelline, Madeline, and Miss Lane, 1977

Cooking, Knitting, and Studying Russian

In England, I was happy to be a housewife—for a while. I enjoyed shopping at the co-op grocery, buying meat from the local butcher at the bottom of our road, and finding a baker who made his delicious bread with a wood fire. I also liked making lemon tarts, knitting sweaters with special wool that I had ordered, and going to the immense downtown market on Saturdays. Maybe if we had had more money I would have been able to do more things and would have been less depressed. Hard to know.

I read a lot of English novels by George Eliot and books by Soviet writer Alexander Solzhenitsyn from our local public library. A friend told me about a Russian language class on the radio to which I could listen. A study booklet was also available. In addition to studying this one morning a week on the BBC, I also heard about a Russian class taught at a junior high school one evening a week. This was a fascinating entrée into English adult education. Our lessons were the same as for students who studied for the O-level exams in English grammar schools. The class represented a cross-section of society: a diligent, methodical civil engineer who studied his words each morning while shaving; a cavalier male civil servant who stopped to bet before coming to class; and some housewives like myself who were not quite so colorful. I don't know what prompted our teacher to offer the class and work with us older students, but I was glad she did. At this time I was almost thirty years old, and I occupied myself with studying a little Russian language and reading novels.

As I've said, in the winter our house could be thirty-seven degrees, the same temperature as inside a refrigerator. If I got under the feather comforter and held a hot-water bottle, I could stay warm while reading. Eventually, however, I became bored with reading novels and fell into depression. After a year and a half of job searching, I found employment with an agency that took one-third of my wages. Working as a clerk at the gas board got me out of the house and improved my mental outlook. It also paid me enough to occasionally go to London on Saturdays to see a ballet. That made the work worthwhile.

In England, I liked going to the secondhand shops to buy woolly undershirts to keep us warm. In one shop, I saw a strange phenomenon: a long row of pottery bottles standing on a shelf. I couldn't quite figure out what they were used for because they had a nozzle of some kind in the middle, not at the top. I knew they couldn't be used for pouring wine, but I couldn't figure out their function. Perplexed, I asked the women clerks what they were for, and they dissolved into laughter. I was dumbfounded because I didn't know what sort of faux pas I had committed. The English struck me as reserved, and for them to break into peals of laughter took me aback. They carried on quite a while, and then one finally told me that the ceramic containers were hot-water bottles made of stoneware. The clerks explained how they worked, and I bought one for a shilling, about twelve American cents. Eventually I bought two more because they were remarkably effective at warming up our beds at night. We had no fires in the upstairs bedrooms, so they were really cold. Changing clothes was excruciating in the winter. However, John and Martin never complained. They were more stalwart. (I brought one bottle home with me when we left England, and I still use it in Lincoln to keep warm while reading on a cold day.)

At night, I usually put a hot-water bottle on Martin's pillow to warm it up before he got into bed, and then I moved it down to keep his feet warm while I lay down to read him a story. But sometimes there was a mishap. We had two bottles in our bed to warm it up, and occasionally during the night one would slip out and hit the floor, sounding like a cannon going off. No harm done because they were sturdy and didn't break.

One night Martin was reluctant to turn in, and I finally ordered him to bed. Soon I heard him crying, but I didn't know what the matter was. I took him in my arms to quiet him, and then I saw blood streaming down his face. Since I had not gotten into bed with him to read him a story, when he jumped into bed, he hit his head on the sharp ceramic nozzle of the water bottle and cut his temple. I bundled him up and ran next door to Miss Lane's. She was always helpful. She gave me a shot of brandy to steady my nerves, and then she drove us to the emergency ward at the hospital where they stitched up his forehead. Eventually we came to know the head nurse there because her name was Mrs. Martin, and we made a few trips there after a couple other accidents. I loved the English medical system of national health care. Everyone who needed medical treatment received it. It wasn't rationed for those who had money, as in America. When I returned to the States in 1970, I vigorously praised this system to Americans I met, but few were interested. One aunt told me to return to England if I liked it so much. I replied that I wanted to improve America. It wasn't until forty-five years later that President Obama was able to get slightly similar health care extended to 20 million uninsured Americans. Then, of course, there have been complaints against it by conservative Republicans who have undermined it, even though another 10 million or so remain uninsured.

Baltic Cruise with Louie, Spring 1969

While writing these reminiscences, I have been intrigued to see how much I enjoyed my travels. I hadn't realized how blessed I have been to visit so many historical places. Looking back, I now realize how full and abundant my life has been.

My mother-in-law, Louie, was always full of surprises. In May 1969 she invited me to take a cruise on the Russian ship *Nadezhda Krupskaya*, named after Lenin's wife. The trip was inexpensive and lasted almost two weeks. It left from London's Tilbury port. After crossing the North Sea, we approached

Copenhagen and saw a castle—supposedly Kronborg castle in Elsinore, the setting for *Hamlet*. That was fascinating. Next we saw the statue *The Little Mermaid* in the harbor of Copenhagen. We docked and had a day to look around the city. Louie and I enjoyed that. Since we had eaten an immense breakfast on the boat, we didn't need to buy much for lunch.

On our short visit, Copenhagen struck me as an interesting but not exceptional city. The next day we were on the Baltic Sea heading to Stockholm. It seemed much larger than Copenhagen but reminded me of home in many ways. The department stores sold Libby's fruit cocktail and blue jeans. Not too quaint. However, seeing the renovation of the more than three-hundred-year-old ship named *Vasa* from the time of Gustav II Adolf and Tsar Michael I was enthralled. In the early decades of the 1600s, Sweden and Russia were at war, and it was fascinating to see the restoration of the antique ship. Climbing the steps in one building we saw some of the starkness that I'd seen in Ingmar Bergman's films. It was an "Aha!" moment. Now I understood him. One day wasn't enough to see Stockholm, of course, and we didn't get to see the Old Town or Skansen Park, but decades later I did see them. The next day we cruised to Helsinki.

Helsinki

This city was unique—quite unlike Copenhagen or Stockholm. As we approached Helsinki, we saw lots of small wooden houses, or dachas, along the coast. These were for summer or weekend visits, so people could experience nature since most residents lived in large city apartment houses. The dachas were a heartwarming sight. I had grown up in the Midwest, where we have many one-story wooden houses, so it was refreshing to see the small dachas. In England most houses were two stories and built of brick or stone. Unlike historic Copenhagen and Stockholm, Helsinki was a newer city that developed during the nineteenth century under Russian rule. It exhibited a combination of Russian and Nordic features, having a huge Russian cathedral looming on its skyline and a large square in the central city. We took a city tour and saw a striking sculpture commemorating the composer Sibelius, famous for his composition *Finlandia*. We also toured a folk park that featured simple nineteenth-century wooden houses. This tour was a charming outing, like stepping back in time. It restored our souls. More information about and pictures of this trip to Stockholm and Helsinki are contained in my travel memoir *Falling in Love with the Baltics*, published in 2009.

Leningrad

The next day our ship docked at Vasilyevsky Ostrov in Leningrad, as it was called from 1924 till 1985. It didn't retake its historic name St. Petersburg until the 1980s. My mother-in-law had booked this cruise partly because she knew my MA degree was in Russian history and that it would be a treat for me to see that historic city. While I found Copenhagen and Stockholm charming and Helsinki intriguing, Leningrad was absolutely fabulous, even in the drizzle. We saw the sadness of the empty parks and empty park benches, but it didn't dampen our spirits. We were determined to have a good time, and we did. It was fun traveling with Louie. Walking along famous Nevsky Prospect, which is featured in so many Russian novels, was delightful. Moreover, in 1969 there were not many cars, so the view was magnificent.

We took the trolley several places, and that was fun because we didn't have these at home or in England. On our first ride, several boisterous sailors boarded after us, and they were laughing and in a good mood, so we laughed too. They ogled us and laughed at us tourists. Somehow, they knew we were foreigners. The whole episode seemed good-natured. We didn't know the procedure for the trolley. We were supposed to pass a few kopeks forward to the conductor or driver, who then sent a ticket back to us. We didn't understand how the system worked at first, but we caught on and passed some money forward. We noticed, however, that the sailors didn't bother doing this, and somehow we found them as hilarious as they found us. So this was a good introduction to the city and people. Simple fun. No tragic misunderstandings. Although it was the Cold War, we all enjoyed each other immensely.

Perhaps because I had read so many novels by Dostoevsky, Tolstoy, and Gogol, the city felt familiar and beloved. I didn't feel afraid as I did in New York or Chicago. Growing up in a relatively small town of twenty-five thousand, big American cities frightened me with their threats of violence. Yet I never felt afraid in Leningrad or Paris, even though they are large cities. Perhaps their bridges, rivers, and historic landmarks make them romantic. I don't know. In Leningrad, the famous Falconet statue *Bronze Horseman* of Peter the Great, enormous St. Isaac's Cathedral, the splendid Hermitage palace and art museum, and Senate Square were all welcome sites to me because I had read about them in my Russian history books and novels, and had wanted to see them. The beautiful brightly painted stucco buildings were entrancing, often Art Nouveau in style. Indeed, the entire inner city appeared to be a lovely outdoor art museum because the architecture was so appealing and there were

Majestic St. Isaac's Cathedral, St. Petersburg (Leningrad)

so many historic buildings along Nevsky Prospect. It was an incredibly safe city with numerous soldiers walking around. Public parks were extremely safe, even at night.

Each interaction in Leningrad charmed me. Waiting at the trolley stop to catch our train back to the ship, a Russian fellow came up and asked me some questions in English. I was surprised he spoke English and that he knew where Iowa was when I told him where I was from. He further surprised me when I asked him if he had read Solzhenitsyn's banned book *The First Circle*. I had read it in an edition printed abroad, but he had read it in a clandestine, or samizdat, version which secretly circulated here. This made me realize that the intelligentsia was alive and well, even under Soviet rule. The late '60s were the end of "The Thaw" ushered in by Khrushchev. Writers had assumed that the relaxation of censorship would continue under Brezhnev, but instead it slowly came to an end. Censorship wasn't as draconian as under Stalin, but it was less open than during the late '50s and early '60s under Khrushchev. Russian writers often had to publish their works abroad "tamizdat," or illegally, in samizdat mimeographed copies. Ludmila Ulitskaya, a twenty-first-century Russian novelist, discusses the post-Stalinist period and some of these issues in her recent work *The Big Green Tent*.

No churches were open to us in 1969, even though we asked to see some. However, the foreign currency shops, or beryozka, were available, along with those in the famous department store Gostiny Dvor, which I had read about in all my Russian grammar books. The latter was a bit of a disappointment because its myriad small shops sold shoddy merchandise. The bathing suits looked faded and pathetic and the pianos looked as if they had been manufactured in the 1930s. They were humongous and would have taken up a lot of a room in any Soviet apartment. All I could find to buy was a small wooden toy for Martin. Still, Louie bought herself and me a Russian fur hat. I can't remember whether she got them in a foreign currency shop, from vendors selling them on Senate Square, or in a shop in Gostiny Dvor. Unfortunately, the picture of us modeling our hats is lost. We noticed that Kazan Cathedral, which we passed in a trolley, was serving as the Museum of Atheism in 1969. Fortunately, it had returned to a working cathedral by 2001, when I visited the city again.

We had only two days in Leningrad in 1969, but it was a magical time. Louie took a trip to Tsar Paul's palace in the countryside, which had been beautifully restored after having been badly bombed by the Germans in World War II. Because I knew a little Russian, some acquaintances from the cruise asked me to help them write and send a telegram from a Leningrad post office, so that took up my afternoon. Still it was fun to do something ordinary just to see how the Soviet system worked. Our cruise and trip to Leningrad was fulfilling and unforgettable. The food on the boat was outstanding. The oatmeal and ice cream were the most delicious I have ever eaten. The meals were extravagant with several courses, and it took us a few days to avoid ordering more than we could comfortably eat. I wasn't accustomed to consuming several courses at breakfast. Dinner seemed more manageable because we had a whole evening to digest it. Brandy and after-dinner coffee were new experiences for me. Louie introduced me to this custom because she was an experienced traveler, having made many transatlantic crossings from the United States to England and having taken cruises in the Mediterranean. She knew ship customs and etiquette.

Evening entertainment on the ship was quite pleasant. One evening our waitresses in Russian costume danced a lovely folk dance for us. They performed a handkerchief dance during which they moved slowly, stately, and serenely. They danced gracefully and impressively. Some evenings we had classical piano music. One evening, some English students offered the entertainment. They were dressed in drag, and while the Brits found it funny, the Soviets were shocked. The ship's captain complained and there was nearly an altercation. We felt very uncomfortable. However, that was the only misunderstanding on our voyage, and we usually had a good time. Most of the passengers were British since the cruise had begun in London. However, there was one young woman from Australia, an older woman from Scotland (who looked to be about eighty years old yet walked briskly round the deck each morning), and then me, an American. While we all spoke English, the dress and shoes of the Australian and me set us apart. Cultural cues are often small but discernable.

Return to England

We had had such a good time, Louie and I hated to say goodbye to each other in London. She had to take the train to Sheffield and I another one home to be with John and Martin. It turned out there had been a minor crisis while I was gone. The day after I left, Martin had gone to a friend's birthday party, and when he jumped over a galvanized metal fence, he cut three fingers on his right hand. He had to have fifty-seven stitches in his tiny fingers. When I got home, he still had an enormous white gauze bandage on his hand. It looked like a snow cone. I was horrified when I saw his little hand but soon realized that he was sleeping and recovering. Apparently John hadn't known what to do, whether to telegraph the ship to ask me to return from Copenhagen, or not. He eventually decided that he and Martin would cope, and they did. A week or so after my return, we took Martin to a surgeon. He told us that when Martin was older he would need surgery on one finger to restore a severed tendon. John was overcome by this news, and on our walk home he sat down on a bench and cried. It was only the second time I ever saw him cry. I had felt sad at our interview with the specialist, but I was obviously not as overcome as John. Indeed, the severed tendon did not alter Martin's life. He was left-handed, and he managed just fine without ever having the tendon surgery.

Usually our life in England was uneventful. We took long walks for entertainment, and John worked at the university library or in his upstairs study doing research for his dissertation. Martin went to school from nine till 4. I read and did the shopping, cooking, and cleaning. Since I wasn't a full-time student, as I had been in the States, I was sometimes bored.

I did learn more about drinking in England, partly because alcohol was cheaper and more available than in America. John seldom drank, but it turned out that I quite liked imbibing. Once, a friend gave us a gallon of Bristol cream sherry. During the course of several months, I drank the whole bottle. I don't remember John ever drinking any of it. Another time, an Anglo-Indian, who was an engineer working at a Ford auto plant and our roomer for a while, mentioned that in London there were special hard cider bars. I had never heard of hard cider, so I bought some to try. I liked it. Moreover, it was affordable. In England, people took their wine, beer, and cider bottles to the liquor store at the bottom of our road to have them filled. Doing that was cheaper yet, so I sometimes took my cider bottle to be refilled. Apparently today, many Americans who are gluten intolerant drink hard cider instead of beer, which has wheat and barley in it.

Occasionally, John and a friend went to the pub at the top of our road to have a pint of beer. Once I went with them, and I had a shandy—a lighter drink made of half beer and half lemonade. While I was away on the cruise, John, his brother, and Martin had gone to the pub. Children were permitted at the pub if they sat outside in the garden. Martin inadvertently left his coat there that evening, and the following fall I had a hard time finding it. I looked high and low, but it was nowhere to be found. Eventually, we found it at the pub. It amazed me that no one had taken it because we lived in a pretty modest neighborhood with some poor folk, and it had been there for several months. It wouldn't have mattered quite so much if someone had taken it, but my mother had sent money for the coat, so it had special sentimental value, and we didn't really have money to replace it. Here is a picture of Martin playing soccer in our backyard in his coat with the little fur collar.

Martin in coat from Grandma Hutton, England, 1969

Working in England

Substitute Servants, 1969

It's been almost fifty years since I lived in England during the years 1968–70, so I can't always exactly recall the sequence of events there. The other day I remembered working as a substitute servant in the posh Knightsbridge household of Simon Sainsbury's son in London one summer. Sainsbury's is a nationwide grocery chain in England, and the family was very wealthy. One day when John was returning home on the evening train from London after doing research at the British museum, he noticed an ad for substitute servants for a month or six weeks in the summer. When he told me about it, I thought, "Only in England do the servants get a month's holiday." Then I realized, "We could do that. We could be the substitute servants." What it really meant was that I could do the work while John went to do his research at the British Museum. I thought London would be captivating to explore, especially the gardens and museums. We applied for the job and got it.

It turned out the owner of the house was seldom home in the summer. He had houses elsewhere and jetted around Greece and other places, so there was not much work to do. Even when he was home, the duties were light—making a few beds and tidying up a couple of rooms. Mr. Sainsbury was an accomplished cook and did his own cooking, so I didn't have that responsibility. While we were in London, my mother-in-law came to visit, and we had such a good time. We went to the opera and messed about. She was always good fun, at least for me. Not so much for John, perhaps, because she scolded him a bit for not having a proper job and dilly-dallying on his PhD. I can't remember now if we received wages for our work or if we did it for the room and board we received. We had a nice apartment in the entry level of the house. There was a garden in the back, and Martin could play there and ride a scooter that his American grandmother had sent him. For a while, he also rode his scooter around nearby Thurloe Square park, to which Simon had a private key, which he gave us. Unfortunately, Martin lost the key, so we lost admittance to the park. But before losing the key, Martin met another little boy, and I met his mother. I invited her to tea, and it was enlightening getting to know her. Her greatest bane was not having a nanny for her boys. That was the greatest hardship she had ever experienced, and I was amazed but tried not to show it. Her husband worked for the Foreign Service, so I can see in retrospect that they were probably upper middle class. Growing up in America, I wasn't quite prepared for the intricacies of the British class system. That was part of my informal education in living there.

A Landlady

In the winter of 1969, I made some money as a landlady. Some of my neighbors took in roomers, and I decided to try it too. In retirement, my neighbor Ivy hosted student lodgers for a while, and it worked for her. She enjoyed cooking a large English breakfast for them. I didn't do that, but I cooked a nice evening meal instead. We had three large bedrooms upstairs, and I thought it would be OK to make some money and augment our budget, which remained at fifty dollars per month for the three of us.

One of my neighbors down the road recommended Jim, an engineer who worked at the Ford Motor plant and was an Anglo-Indian (one parent Indian and one British). He was fascinating to get to know. He taught me about Indian cooking and racism in India and England. He told us that in India people noticed his blue eyes and so did not fully accept him as an Indian; in England people noticed the color of his skin and did not see him as a full human being. They even pushed him off the sidewalk at times. That shocked me. I knew a little about racial discrimination in America but had never heard of anyone pushing someone off the sidewalk. Jim accompanied us to an Indian restaurant a couple of times and taught us about the food—the bread called papadum and which dishes to order. In those days Indian restaurants were cheaper than Chinese or English establishments. They were the only ones we could afford to patronize. Jim adored the pork and potato casseroles that I made with wine sauce and special herbs, and I was touched by his appreciation.

Clerking at the Southern Gas Board

Off and on during our stay in England, I had gone to employment agencies to try to get a job to help support us, but for a year and a half I had been unsuccessful. I finally learned not to record my higher education, and then I got a job. It turned out that the more education a person had, the higher the wages an employer in England would have to pay. When I recorded only a high school education, then I got a job working for an agency that contracted with the Southern Gas Board. The agency took one third of my wages, but I didn't mind too much. The job wasn't hard, and it was an entrée into English white-collar working life.

What surprised me most was seeing men and women doing the same job. I had never experienced this before. Now it is more common, but I had grown up in the sexually stratified society of the 1940s and '50s. At that time in La Porte, Indiana, the bank managers were men, and the tellers women. In offices, men were the bosses and women the secretaries. So, I was surprised to see both young and middle-aged men and women serving as clerks at the same job in a large office where people's gas bills were calculated. England was changing to the metric system and had just switched to British thermal units. This caused some consternation and confusion among the gas customers. We answered people's letters, recalculating their bills and explaining the process to them. Usually, I fit in, but in dictating my letters I sometimes made the mistake of saying "period" instead of the English equivalent "full stop." If I did this, the word "period" would be typed before the symbol for period at the end of the sentence. Another problem I had when calculating people's bills was to remember that while twenty shillings made one pound, I needed to carry one not two to the pound column. With twenty in my mind, it was hard to remember to add one instead of two.

At our office in the morning, a woman delivered tea and egg salad sandwiches to us at our desks at eleven o'clock. We had access to a full cafeteria at one o'clock for our dinner. Again, I was surprised at how different our eating habits were. When we had Indian curry with rice, some of the English workers also ordered French fries as well. I had never heard of eating rice and potatoes at the same meal. But, my neighbor Miss Lane sometimes served two kinds of potatoes at dinner—roasted as well as mashed potatoes. So, it's enchanting to live in another culture, even an English-speaking one, to discover how differently people live, work, and eat.

The hours of work at the Southern Gas Board lasted from nine to five, and this dovetailed with Martin's school, which ran from nine to four. I could walk him to school as I went to get my bus. Because John worked at home, he was usually there when Martin returned from school. Also, after a year and a half of school, Martin was acclimated and ate the school dinners, so he didn't come home for lunch anymore. They had good food, but his favorite remained bangers and mash.

Occasionally, Martin would go home with a friend to play after school, when his father was away. If he wasn't home when I got there, I would get frantic. Since no one in the neighborhood had a telephone, it wasn't easy to check up on him. Fortunately this didn't happen very often.

I was glad to work at the gas company, earn some money, and be able to go to London to see some ballets at Covent Garden. On Saturday afternoons, the balcony seats cost only ten shillings, a little more than a dollar. Covent Garden was enchanting. Little red lamps encircled the various tiers of seats and the rich red décor was posh and plush. I was able to go several times to see some of the famous ballets like *Swan Lake* and *Giselle*. This was the time of the duo Russian dancer Rudolf Nureyev and English grand dame Margot Fonteyn. I didn't get to see them because their performances were always sold out, but I did get to see some other famous Russian and English dancers, whose names I now forget. It was always a magnificent experience for me.

Once, I took one of the neighborhood girls to London with me to see the ballet. While no one living on our side of the street was impoverished, most people didn't have much money. No one had a car, except our neighbor Ivy Lane. Few spent money to go to London. I think it cost a pound, $2.40, to get a day return trip to London and back on the train. I knew Martin would not be interested in the ballet and that he wouldn't sit still for it, but I thought one of the little neighbor girls who was older than he might enjoy it, and she did. Her parents did not have money for such events. I think they did pay for her train fare, and I bought the ballet ticket. If John was doing research in London, I sometimes went and took Martin with me, and father and son would spend time together while I attended the ballet. At first, I was terrified to take the tube to Covent Garden by myself. But I did it because I really wanted to see the dancing. Sometimes our desires help us transcend our fears. I found this often happened when traveling.

Paris, Spring 1970

My time in England seems rather ordinary in some ways. What stands out in my memory are the two fantastic holidays on which my mother-in-law invited me: first to the Baltics in the spring of 1969 and then a year later to Paris. What helped me recall the Paris trip was listening to David McCullough's book *The Greater Journey: Americans in Paris*, which focuses on the nineteenth century. In the summer of 2015, I had cataract surgery, and while I was recovering, I listened to this fabulous book. His descriptions of the awe and joy of Americans coming to France and Paris during the 1830s reminded me of the wonder I felt when I first visited Paris with Louie and Martin.

Louie was a great traveler and benefited from a travel agent who lived in her apartment building in Sheffield and alerted Louie to good holiday buys. In the spring of 1970 Louie proposed that John, Martin, and I accompany her on a trip to Paris. I was delighted. John was less so because he had been there and really wanted to get on with his dissertation research. So we decided that Martin and I would join Louie on the trip. It was a short package deal but quite splendid to me. I made Martin a cute blue wool jacket out of an air force officer's suit I had bought at an English thrift store. Earlier, I had bought an old-fashioned sewing machine at the downtown market, and I was glad I could make a little jacket for my son for our travels. His school uniform consisted of grey shorts, blue shirt, and a grey and blue tie. The dark blue jacket was a nice addition and made him look very smart. He was a handsome boy, so it didn't really matter what he wore. He always looked attractive, but it was lovely having him nicely turned out for our trip.

On our travels, we went by bus from London through the picturesque Kent countryside to a small airport where we flew to Beauvais, France. There we took another bus to Paris. Needless to say I was excited. I had studied French in high school and college but never imagined I would actually go to France. So, I was delighted to be in our Parisian hotel, drink café au lait, and eat croissants with tasty French butter and jam in the morning, walk around the city, and go to the Louvre and to the opera to see Igor Stravinsky's ballet *Le Sacre du Printemps* (The Rite of Spring). Friends of Louie's even took us to see Versailles. I couldn't believe my good luck while standing alongside the Grand Canal, strolling through the Hall of Mirrors, and seeing Marie Antoinette's garden and palace. I can hardly explain how enchanting it all was. Having seen pictures of these places in my French books when I was in high school and having read stories of Louis XIV and his palace in my history texts, I never imagined that I would one day see them in person. Pretty amazing for a girl from La Porte, Indiana!

It was also enchanting to hear our host point out the "boules de neige," or snowball bushes. I was surprised that the terms were almost the same in French and English. It was gratifying when a Frenchman spoke and I understood. I had never dared imagine experiencing all this as a teenager learning French in high school. I had dreamed of visiting Montreal but not France!

In Paris, we also saw the daughters of old family friends of Louie's, Genevieve and Collette. They invited us to dinner one day. It was quite fascinating to see their family apartment and different parts of Paris as we went to visit them from our hotel. A few days later, Collette took us to a charming creperie in Paris. It was so tiny, I couldn't believe it was a restaurant. It was literally a hole in the wall. Still, the crepes were delicious and inexpensive. We would never have found such an authentic place without a native Parisian for a guide. We took Collette and Genevieve to see Stravinsky's ballet. I was overwhelmed by it. I felt repulsed by the dancers writhing on the stage to show the rejuvenation of life in the springtime. When I saw it forty years later in Vilnius, Lithuania, I wasn't horrified at all. Amazing how we change.

One day, Louie, Martin, and I went to the Louvre. I felt overwhelmed by the vast number of paintings. I couldn't take them all in. Martin somehow got separated from me, and he started crying before I found him. In retrospect, I think he was upset because we were taking him to sleep overnight with some Iowa City friends that evening while we went to the ballet. Apparently, he was frightened by that prospect—staying with a family he didn't know too well in a foreign country. It was all too much for him to process at five years of age. So, our visit to the Louvre was not a great success. Nor was my visit to the ballet that evening since I was revolted by the contortions on stage. So, while being in Paris was exciting, not all our experiences were as delightful as our trip to Versailles.

We went to Notre Dame to pray because it was Pentecost, but Martin took one look at the sarcophaguses and ran outside. I chased after him, so I didn't have much time to enjoy the ambience of the church. This was not unusual behavior for him because when we went to Winchester Cathedral in England, he didn't like the tombs there either, and he usually dashed outside when he saw them. I hadn't remembered this until we were inside Notre Dame. I had expected him to enjoy the cathedral as I did, but he didn't. I think he was bothered that both of his grandfathers were dead. As a first-time parent, I didn't understand what it meant for him to come to grips with their deaths. I had never gone into great detail about how they died, but he would ask me about it from time to time, I explained matter-of-factly that both his grandfathers had died, but he still had a great-grandfather (my grandfather) who was alive. I guess he was sometimes processing this more than I knew.

In Paris we went shopping in a grand department store. I didn't have much money, but I did enjoy seeing the goods and buying an inexpensive red purse and a sheer red blouse. I seldom wore red, but somehow these two objects attracted me and must have stood out as exceptionally pretty and affordable. Moreover, they went well with the grey and the turquoise suits that I had brought with me. I also remember buying some food at a French bakery. These two experiences charmed me immensely—walking into a French shop, ordering something in French, and paying with francs. I felt quite worldly and proud of myself for doing these transactions in French. All too soon, our Parisian holiday ended, and we returned to ordinary life in England and then the States.

After our trip to Paris with Louie and a few more months working at the Gas Board, it was time to return to Iowa City. This time John found a Greek ship that was making a repositioning voyage to New York City. It cost only sixty dollars per adult, and Martin went free as a child of six. There were many more children on this ship than there had been on the old *Queen Elizabeth*, so Martin had a better time on this voyage. The ship also had a special fenced-in place for children to play, which made the journey more relaxing for us as parents.

I wanted to take some of our beautiful antique furniture back to America with us, and although the shipping on the boat would have been free, we didn't have the money to ship it from New York to Iowa City. So, I gave it to a young friend at work who was getting married. We had enjoyed our furniture and dishes for two years, and now it was time to pass them on to others. The only souvenirs that we brought to the States were utilitarian: my antique sewing machine because it was small and had its own wooden carrying case with a handle; one of the crockery hot-water bottles, which still keeps me warm in the winter; and an unusual round wooden bread board that was a gift from a friend. It dated from around 1900 and has sheaves of wheat carved in the circumference. It is still quite useful in my kitchen, and I treasure it for its sentimental value of reminding me of friends and relations in England as well as earlier, happier times in my married life.

Life in Iowa City, 1970–1975

Before returning to Iowa City in the summer of 1970, John and I had agreed that I would find work to support us while he wrote his dissertation. Little did we know that it would take him five years to do this, and that it wouldn't be easy for me to get a job in Iowa City. Former university students often hung around after they graduated, and many wives were working to put their husbands through graduate school. Consequently, there were many well-educated applicants for each job. It was a depressing time while I looked for a position, which I couldn't find right away.

One day I was walking back home from the university hospital, where I had applied to teach young patients at the hospital. I realized after the interview that

I wasn't really qualified for the job, and that I wouldn't be getting it. I was so downhearted and depressed that I felt like throwing myself over the bridge as I stopped to ponder my situation at the Iowa River. It was the first time I had experienced such powerful negative feelings. Fortunately, I had Martin and John to go home to, and I slowly strolled down the long blocks trying to digest the sense of rejection. A few weeks later, I found a situation working as a secretary for the foreign student advisor and was very grateful for it. Moreover, it suited me. I enjoyed getting to know and help the foreign students, doctors, and writers who came into the office.

Working in the Foreign Student Office

I worked in that office from 1970 to 1972 and appreciated getting to know the foreign nationals who came to register their visas. As in college, I felt alert and alive when interacting with foreigners and really enjoyed my job. I was efficient in my work and liked it—all but the filing, which I found boring. In addition to the Writers' Workshop, the university also hosted the International Writing Program, and this drew people from diverse places.

In the fall of 1970, I met the famous Czech writer Arnošt Lustig. He had just come from Cuba and commented that Cuban communists had no sense of humor. That seemed like an odd remark to me, and I didn't quite understand it. When I first met him, I had no idea he was a Jewish Czechoslovakian who had been incarcerated in Theresienstadt, Auschwitz, and Buchenwald during the war. He was saved from Dachau by a bomb hitting the train engine as he was being transported. He was a delightful person, but I never read any of his writings until the 1980s when I used his book *A Prayer for Katerina Horovitzova* (1974) in a European women's history class I was teaching at the university during my second stint as a graduate student. When I read his book I was impressed by its authenticity but wondered how he knew about the prayers of a rabbi in a concentration camp. Reading much later about his life in several concentration camps, I began to understand him and his novel better. I hadn't known his background when I met him in the 1970s.

A year after I began working at the office, the foreign student advisor fell ill with lung cancer and retired abruptly. This left me with all the work but not the pay of the head of the office. The office had been situated in a house on the edge of campus, and the graduate college ordered me to carry out the policies in the Old Capital Building in the center of the campus. I assume they moved the office there so one of the deans could keep an eye on me. I never knew exactly. Eventually, I began to chafe at this procedure. I felt sorry for the students who came to tell me their woes and had to talk to me in a crowded office in front of several other secretaries. So, I threatened to quit and told my superior that I needed a private office to discuss personal issues with the students. He agreed to this and quickly found a private office for me in a nearby administration building.

Then the process of advertising for a new foreign student advisor began. I applied for the position but was passed over for a man. My previous boss didn't have a PhD, so I thought my MA was a sufficient credential. I also thought my experience working with the students stood me in good stead. I had a good personality for the job, and the students liked me. I liked them, and I displayed good administrative skills. However, I was not chosen, and I felt rejected and bitter. At this time, the university didn't have anyone to settle job grievances, and I had no feminist group to support me, so I applied to the federal Office of Equal Opportunity for redress of sexual discrimination in hiring. I asked for help, but the two investigators they sent were not too savvy, and I soon realized they were incompetent and would not help my case. They didn't, so I worked for the new foreign student advisor for only a few months before getting another job. It was no longer a joy to go to work. He wasn't a terrible person, just punctilious. Before leaving, my son and I enjoyed a wonderful trip to Disney World that the office sponsored.

Visiting Disney World with the Foreign Writers

In the spring of 1972, the Foreign Student Office accepted a proposal from a visiting Israeli writer at the International Writing Program to visit Disney World in Florida. He also wanted to visit the Smoky Mountains in North Carolina on our return to Iowa City. These were two places he wanted to see, and the foreign student advisor was agreeable to this plan. At that time, Martin was about nine years old, just the right age to enjoy Disney World.

Our trip took place during spring break, and we had so much fun. Martin and I relished Disney World—the rides, the ambience, the monorail, and the Polynesian village where we could lie in the sun and enjoy the water. It was wonderful, especially since it was snowing and miserable in Iowa City in late March. Martin seldom asked for anything, so it was delightful to do something special for him. Riding thirty-six hours in a bus one way was not a great experience, but my son was young enough to sleep a lot. I couldn't nap so well on the bus, but I was in my early thirties, and it didn't bother me too much. It rained during part of our trip, and sometimes it dripped in the tents, but everyone was pretty stoical about the difficulties. No one exaggerated them. We

Martin and our dog, Pokey, Iowa City, early 1970s

slept in tents to save money. We were all paying our own way, and no one wanted to spend money on hotels.

Some of the young workers in the office managed to stretch out in the overhead area above the seats and sleep there on the way home. I would never have thought of that and envied them a bit. But it was nice having Martin snuggled up on my lap. He was a big boy now, so he didn't sit on my lap much anymore. I was glad to have the chance to hold him a little as he slept on the bus. A few months after this trip I left the Foreign Student Office and took a part-time job in the Office of the State Archeologist, working there for two years during 1973 and 1974.

Raising Martin

Martin was a pretty easy child to raise. He had a slight impish streak, but he was well behaved. His father and I agreed on discipline, and John carried through on all his interactions with Martin, especially teaching him good sportsmanship. Martin never complained or asked for things we didn't have, such as color TV. However, he was more sensitive than I realized. Once I went into his bedroom and found him sleeping head to foot in his bed. When I asked him why he was situated this way, he said he liked to listen to the rain on the windows, and since the window in his room was toward the foot of his bed, he liked to lie that way. I was surprised but didn't yet understand how impressionable he was.

In this picture, Martin is reading one of his favorite books, which he traded around with his friends. For some reason, the public library did not carry the Hardy Boys books, and all the boys loved them. So, we usually bought him one from the

Martin reading, Iowa City, early 1970s

series for his birthday and one for Christmas. Then he exchanged them with his friends who had others. About this time, a friend told me that her son enjoyed C. S. Lewis's Narnia books, so I bought some of them for Martin. He would get up at six in the morning to read them, they captivated him so much. If he had a good book or a friend to play with he was happy.

In fifth grade, Martin got a university paper route like his friend Brian's. Martin would look out the window across the alley to see if a light was on in his friend's room, which meant that Brian was up and going to deliver his papers. When Martin first got his paper route with the *Daily Iowan*, I went with him so he could learn which apartment complexes were his customers. It was a pretty simple route a few blocks from our house. Often he left many papers at the same building. It was a good kind of job to have because the paper came with university tuition, and he didn't have to collect money, as the *Iowa City Press Citizen* carriers did. In addition, the paper was delivered only Monday through Friday, so he had weekends free as well as the holidays and university vacations.

Martin and Marcelline, Iowa City, 1970s

Martin opened a savings account, and he always put his entire check into his account. This rather surprised me. I think most kids would have spent some or most of their money on candy or movies, but he didn't. He was amazingly easy to bring up.

Even if he didn't want to do something, like go swimming at the community pool down the street, he would do it. His English grandmother often visited during the summer, and she enjoyed swimming. So, she, John, and Martin often did so. When we went to my mother's in La Porte, he was always agreeable about walking to the beach with me—no small feat since it was a couple of miles away. He never complained. If some visiting cousins were around, they would all play in the water. Most of them were about eight or ten years old, and none of them swam. I was blessed to have such a son, but I didn't quite realize it because I took him for granted. Occasionally, my uncle Lloyd took Martin, Mother, and me to the huge sand dunes near Lake Michigan, and we played in the waves. We didn't really swim because the current was too strong.

Martin and Marcelline, Iowa City, 1970s

Martin was so well behaved that I never heard about any of his pranks until years later. But the same was true of my brother. I had never known about any of his until he recently told me of one—putting a frog under a hat on the French teacher's desk when he was in high school. Only the wildest kids in La Porte or Iowa City got into serious trouble or continually played pranks.

We lived a rather simple life in Iowa City in the early 1970s. I usually put Martin to bed at seven on week nights. Since he was tall for his age, I thought he needed lots of sleep. Again, he didn't complain too much. He once mentioned that his friends got to stay up later, but I explained to him that he was growing so fast, I thought he needed extra sleep. He didn't question his bedtime again.

Since I had to be at work at 8:00 a.m. at the Foreign Student Office, I usually went to bed at 9:30 p.m. to read for a while. I awoke around 6:00 a.m. to the strains of Antonín Dvořák's "New World Symphony" on the radio and walked our dog at 6:30. Listening to this symphony the other day, I remembered how much I loved it and how much I relished waking up to it. I still had the clock radio that my parents had given me when I went to college, and in Iowa City the university station WSUI played the opening bars of the "New World Symphony" when it came on the air every morning.

One of the reasons the university station played this piece is because Dvořák lived in Spillville, Iowa, the summer of 1893, and there he composed part of this symphony *From the New World*. It debuted in December in New York City, where he was the director of the National Conservatory of Music of America. Iowans liked to claim that he composed the symphony while living in the state, but he may have only worked on it there. He did complete two chamber pieces while living in Spillville. He may have chosen Spillville because it was a small town with a sizeable Czech community and a Czech Catholic church, St. Wenceslaus, built in 1860.

Pilgrimage to Spillville, Iowa

One summer in the early 1970s, John worked as a historical consultant for a state agency that assessed the historical and archeological significance of areas before a highway was widened or constructed. He did the historical part of the environmental impact statement that allowed a highway to be built. John had gone to Spillville for this work, and there he observed the Czech heritage. He saw the unusual Czech crosses in the cemetery as well as the house where Dvořák had lived. So a few weeks later, our friend and neighbor, Chuck Miller, who loved classical music as much as we did, and who had a car, suggested that we make a pilgrimage to Spillville to see Dvořák's house. John and I didn't have a car, so it was always fun to get out of town and see something new.

We arranged our trip so we could see the town and also nearby Backbone State Park. I too was impressed by the Czech grave markers but not so much by Dvořák's simple house, where the downstairs had been turned into a clock museum. The upstairs was kept as it had been in the late nineteenth century, but the clock museum was jarring. It distracted from our pilgrimage to Dvořák's home but didn't ruin it. Since Martin was pretty young, he wasn't too interested in historical houses, but he did like the state park, which was located nearby. It was a pretty summer day, hot but bearable. We brought a picnic lunch or snacks with us so we didn't have to spend any money for food. At the park were incredible rocks cut by the Maquoketa River, and I remember sitting on one for a while before I noticed a huge snake coiled up nearby. That was unnerving, but after looking at it, we slowly moved away. Going to these two places meant we were pretty tired going home, but it was delightful to have had an "outing."

My Routine

My routine in Iowa City after waking up to lovely classical music included taking our black lab, Pokey, for a morning walk. When I came home, I made breakfast for Martin and me. John seldom ate breakfast because he usually worked late at the library and preferred sleeping in. Martin and I had pancakes or oatmeal. I cooked nutritious, inexpensive meals and don't think I ever consulted Martin about what he'd like. I just assumed he'd like what we ate. Most of the time he did. Once after a visit to my brother's in Oregon, however, he asked for the kind of eggs his uncle ate. I didn't know what kind that was, and he didn't know the name of them. I tried various methods, thinking my brother might still eat poached eggs as he did when he used to play basketball in high school, but those were not the right kind. Eventually it turned out that Martin wanted a fried egg. Because John couldn't digest fried food, I had never made Martin a fried egg. After his return from Oregon, he often made himself a fried egg when he came home from school in the afternoon. This amazed me because I thought most kids would have wanted a candy bar or a piece of cake. Our children often surprise us—sometimes teaching us lessons we need to learn, and especially forgiving us wrongs we do them.

Since we lived on a meager budget, I never bought sugar-sweetened dry cereals because they cost too much and had little nutritional value. However, on holidays when we visited my mother in La Porte, she often bought the miniature boxes of dry cereals that were sweetened—like Corn Pops. She spoiled Martin a little. I was grateful he got to eat the sugar-sweetened cereals occasionally because I thought it wrong to completely deprive children of popular things that all their friends enjoyed. Still, Martin ate everything John and I did. Sometimes John would go on a health food kick of some kind, and we just went along. Once, John thought we should give up sugar entirely, so I learned to cook with honey instead. My cakes, breads, and pancakes turned out all right using honey instead of sugar. At times John substituted Pero for coffee or honey for sugar, but most of the time he was content eating ordinary food.

Since John's parents had suffered from ulcers, his family never ate fried food. I didn't realize that John couldn't digest fried food, so I cooked him sausage and eggs only once. He got so sick and messed up the bathroom so badly vomiting all over that I never made that mistake again. While John could easily have been a vegetarian, I couldn't. I always wanted some sort of meat for supper.

When we were first married in the early 1960s, bacon, hot dogs, ground sausage, and hamburger all cost thirty-nine cents per pound. So I cooked one of them each night with boiled or baked potatoes and vegetables and served them with lettuce salad. I could have skipped the vegetables, but John liked them, so we always had some for supper. I remember beets being cheap at the nearby A&P grocery—two cans for twenty-five cents—so we had them occasionally. I hadn't grown up eating beets, but I learned to eat them since they were nutritious and a good source of iron.

On Sundays, I usually made a more elaborate dinner, as my mother had. I felt we deserved to have a special meal of meat loaf, roast beef, or pork with baked potatoes and acorn squash. It was easy to prepare such meals because everything took about an hour in the oven and was ready at the same time. In the 1970s, when I was working full-time as a secretary at the Foreign Student Office, John often made the supper, and it was always the same: baked potatoes and hamburgers. Sometimes I grumbled about eating the same thing every night, but usually I was tired by five thirty and was glad to have dinner ready when I got home. None of us complained much about food. As an adult, Martin became a connoisseur, and he pays considerable attention to food and drink. I appreciate it especially when he and his wife come to visit me in Lincoln and take me to fine restaurants.

This of me in 1974 shows me in an old fur coat I bought from the wife of the foreign student advisor. It had belonged to her mother and was quite large and incredibly warm. I treasured it during the deep Iowa winters. I remember wondering once as I walked to work in 1970, decked out in my fur hat and coat and a red mohair scarf draped around my neck, what I would wear to keep warm when I would be old, since I needed so much when I was still in my early thirties. Needless to say, this was a time before furs became politically incorrect, so I didn't feel guilty wearing it. I have this picture because I had gone to a shop to buy some film, and the shopkeeper took this picture of me to see if my secondhand camera worked. Thankfully it did.

Marcelline in fur coat and mohair scarf, Iowa City, 1974

Culture in Iowa City

After we returned from England in 1970, I was delighted to see that the university had built Hancher Auditorium for the performing arts. I was fortunate to attend many inexpensive ballets and concerts there. I remember finally seeing the Russian dancer Rudolf Nureyev there one winter. He danced an entire weekend—Friday and Saturday nights and Sunday afternoon. I was blessed to attend all these performances. It had cost too much to see him and Margot Fonteyn dance in London, but at Hancher it cost university students only fifty cents to go to his performances. Because my husband was a graduate student, I used his ID to buy my tickets. I felt as if I were in heaven. I remember seeing Nureyev dance in *Sleeping Beauty* on Friday night, some modern pieces on Saturday night, and in *Swan Lake* on Sunday.

I could get two tickets for each performance with John's student ID, so I invited my friend Elizabeth to attend the ballets with me. She worked in the historic preservation office at the university, and when I was working at the Office of State Archeologist she drove me around to many of the old towns in Iowa to put buildings on the National Register of Historic Places. Because she had taken me around so much, I was eager to do a favor for her. I also invited her to dinner the Friday evening before the ballet performance, and we had wine with our meal, which I seldom did. Since I had worked all week, I was tired, and the drink made me drowsy during the ballet. Later I was angry at myself for dozing during *Sleeping Beauty*. I remember having trouble keeping my eyes open and thinking the ballet was well named.

Hancher Auditorium also staged operas, but the first opera I saw in Iowa was *Madame Butterfly*, performed at MacBride Auditorium. The presentation was magnificent. Indeed, when I saw it professionally sung in London a decade later, I realized that the university production had been innovative in its staging and costumes. I also recall a friend taking me to hear Luciano Pavarotti sing at Hancher. I was reluctant to go because I couldn't imagine a solitary singer would be enthralling, but he was so expressive I was mesmerized and glad I went. Living in a university town offered affordable concerts and other musical performances. In 1970 I realized again how much music enhanced my life.

The theater was also well done at Iowa (even though I wasn't as enthralled by it as I was by music). Plays could be avant-garde or traditional. They were always well staged. I remember seeing the musical *Man of La Mancha* being well performed there. One summer when my mother-in-law was visiting, we went to see the repertory company perform several witty Noël Coward plays. They were superb. The next summer, we saw some plays by Jean Genet that were also stunning but much darker. As previously mentioned, Louie was good company and a bit more culturally adventuresome than I. Once when visiting, she heard that the movie *Jesus Christ Superstar* was playing and wanted to see it. I wasn't particularly attracted to it, thinking it sounded a bit blasphemous. However, Louie insisted, and she, Martin, and I went to see it. We found it fabulous. Her taste was good, as usual.

The only unfortunate event I remember is that I once took Martin to see a high school production of *Fiddler on the Roof*. I thought he would like it, but he was very disturbed by the massacre scene. I hadn't realized this would upset him. Having studied Russian history, I was prepared for it, whereas he wasn't. He didn't know the story of the Russian pogroms against the Jews. He tolerated violence on TV better than I did, so I was surprised that he was so upset by the mock violence in the musical. Oh, the problems of motherhood!

One other time I thought he'd enjoy a Gustav Mahler program that the university symphony and choir were performing at Hancher. I wanted him to see and hear all the classical musical instruments on the stage. The evening was connected to the opening of the auditorium, and I thought he should experience it. Much to my chagrin, he wasn't impressed by the stage full of instruments. In fact, he fell asleep during the Mahler piece; when the audience began applauding, he awoke, clapped his hands, and then promptly fell asleep again. I guess the message is "Don't make children do things they aren't interested in." It was several years later that we took him to a ballet and play in Kansas City. He wasn't wildly enthusiastic, but this time he didn't nod off. As an adult, he likes both classical and popular music and culture.

Once John graduated with his PhD in 1975, having completed his dissertation titled "Social Policy and Juvenile Delinquency in England and Wales, 1815–1875," I was hoping he would get the "big job," and we would finally escape poverty. Alas, it never happened. He got a normal-paying job at the University of Missouri–Kansas City and earned much more than when he had been a teaching assistant, but he was more wedded to the minimalist life than I realized. It took several years for me to come to grips with this. Eventually, I decided his view of life wasn't for me.

CHAPTER V

Married Life in Kansas City, 1976–1979

From Dreams to Struggles and Nightmares

When I finally wrote my dissertation, I used the words "Dreams, Struggles, and Nightmares" to describe some aspects of Russian and Soviet women's lives during the nineteenth and early twentieth centuries. However, I could have been describing my wedded life. Like most young women, I married with dreams of family happiness. But I slowly experienced my dream dissolving into struggles and eventually nightmares in Kansas City. Our marriage began to deteriorate into misunderstandings and became an emotional wasteland for me. I became distraught and disconsolate.

In August 1975, I remember feeling very hurt when I asked John why he was bothering to go for the job interview at the University of Missouri–Kansas City when he didn't really seem interested in it. He said he needed professional employment so he could pay into Social Security for retirement. I was shocked and hurt at his response. I had expected him to say that he wanted to provide for Martin and me, but he didn't. I internalized my anger at his reply for a while.

So, when he got the job in Kansas City, I argued that Martin and I wouldn't move with him because Martin was just going into sixth grade, and if we moved to Kansas City in August, he would have to attend a new school there for one year, and then change the next year when he would go into junior high. I knew that John wouldn't have much time for us, and I didn't want to feel jealous of his work. I was also probably angry and wanted to punish him.

The irony was that he died at age fifty-seven, before he ever collected his Social Security. Instead, it fell to me as a widow's pension at the age of sixty, when I went to teach at Lithuania Christian College in Klaipėda, Lithuania, in 2000. There his Social Security provided well for me since the American dollar was quite valuable. It enabled me to attend concerts and go to restaurants and take holidays in Eastern Europe.

In 1976, with the help of some friends, Martin and I did move to Kansas City, and all seemed to go well as we settled into a cozy house that we rented near the campus and near a Catholic school. Our house had two bedrooms downstairs and a large area for John's study upstairs. Somehow, I never had a study, or a room of my own, as Virginia Woolf would say. I guess it shows that I didn't take my dissertation work very seriously.

Fortunately, Martin adjusted well to the nearby Catholic school, and soon he had several school chums who lived in the neighborhood and became his pals. In the summer, they all liked playing pickup games of baseball. Sometimes John, Martin, and I went to a Kansas City Royals game. With a beer it was enjoyable, or at least bearable, in the intense summer heat. Once, John gave Martin an enormous baseball encyclopedia, and Martin just about memorized it.

How he loved baseball when he was twelve! At first he wanted to be a baseball player, and he spent hours organizing imaginary teams of brothers playing on them. It was probably his form of fantasy sports—the sort of thing people play today on computers. Slowly the dream of being a baseball player faded. Then he fancied being a sportswriter. By high school, he was covering sports for his school paper, and he was playing soccer for his school team. Slowly, his passion for baseball faded away.

In our rented house, Martin's room overlooked part of our back garden. He loved watching and listening to the birds, often sleeping head to foot in his bed. This showed me again how sensitive he was—more so than I realized.

Soon after our move to Kansas City, I realized John felt very antagonistic about his situation in the history department at the university. I offered to make dinners and invite his colleagues to our home, hoping to promote his position in the history department, but he didn't want me to do this. I thought it odd, but after a few attempts to convince him, I didn't insist. I only slowly realized that we didn't celebrate life the same way. He wanted to do well but by working on his lectures and writing articles, not by influencing his colleagues through social means.

We enjoyed doing some companionable things together. We often walked a few miles to the Plaza for coffee or to the Nelson Art Gallery café for lunch and to see new exhibits. But gradually we argued more, laughed less, and experienced less joy. I kept wanting him to admire Martin, to pat him on the head as he did our dog, Pokey. I also wanted him to cherish me, but he didn't like being affectionate with us, only with the dog. Life seemed bleak.

For years, I drove myself crazy wanting John to appreciate me. Since I idolized him, I thought he was the perfect man, and thought he could and would cherish me more if I were just prettier or more intelligent. I tried turning myself inside out to please him but to no avail. When we first married, I thought him like the character Ashley Wilkes in *Gone with the Wind*, but over time I realized he was tougher and more like Rhett Butler, and eventually I found him to be like the contemporary curmudgeon Doc Martin on TV.

Once, our friend Al McDonald asked John to write a letter of recommendation for him for a teaching position overseas. John told Al that he wasn't very good at composing such letters but said: "If you write the letter, I'll sign it." At the time I thought this a bit odd and only now realize how incapable John was of showing approval, even to one of his good friends.

Instead of seeing how difficult it was for John to show affection and approval for our friend, I drew the wrong conclusion, thinking I just didn't deserve his affection. I kept worrying there was something wrong with me that John didn't express any love for me. But, I wanted affection from someone who had little to give. It was bewildering!

In retrospect, I realize that I was the classic codependent—trying to control his behavior—and that I was driving myself crazy trying to get him to do something he didn't want or couldn't do. More shocking was John's remark to me two years after our divorce when he told me he really had loved me. I didn't know what to say, so I only said I wished he had told me this when we were married. It would have meant the world to me then. Indeed, only later did I think of the perfect retort—that it didn't feel much like love. It felt too "harsh and dreadful." Of course, I was touched that he told me he had loved me. It melted some of my resentment.

In retrospect, I suspect that John suffered from low self-esteem as much as I did, only he covered it up better. I remember being surprised and sad when his English history professor at the University of Iowa, Henry Horowitz, offered to publish a paper with him in the mid-1960s, but John refused. "It seems odd to pass up such an opportunity," I told him. But he adamantly refused to do it. He was just not ready for this experience. I've heard it said that people of like dispositions attract each other, and I can see now that John and I both lacked self-confidence but in different ways. While he often said "Everyone has at least one book in them," he never published one. He suffered terribly from writer's block and thought each sentence he wrote had to be perfect. I always felt when reading his papers that even the "the's" had weight. Nothing was superfluous, unlike my garrulous prose. Neither of us would have imagined that decades later I would publish five books.

In Kansas City, I slowly realized that John did not share my dream of a modest middle-class life. I gradually discovered that I was living under false expectations. I hadn't minded going to thrift shops to buy clothes because I was frugal. But I did want to buy some used stuffed chairs or a couch to make our home cozier and was shocked when John absolutely rejected the idea. A minimalist, he thought the few wooden chairs we had brought from Iowa City were sufficient. I thought now that he had a good position, we would have a normal household with decent furniture. Boy, was I wrong! We had a terrific argument when I spent forty-five dollars on a secondhand stuffed chair for our living room. I thought his mother deserved a comfortable chair to sit in when she came to visit for a few months at a time. John didn't agree.

It was probably then that I could no longer "suffer and be still," as the English historian Martha Vicinus put it in her book of that title on English women in the nineteenth century. I was just surprised to find myself engaging in such behavior in the second half of the twentieth century! While we had been settling in, I had been busy painting the walls and making curtains. I was glad to subordinate myself to John's career, but after a few years, it became harder to do. Besides, when I wanted to bitch, moan, and complain about my life, who wanted to listen? Not my husband. Nor our male friends. I found it pretty alienating being a housewife in the mid-1970s. Yet, I found it equally hard to throw myself into completing my PhD, which I needed to do. Perhaps some of my unhappiness was caused by my own anxiety and fear of writing my dissertation. When Martin started high school and wanted to buy new shirts, John again refused, and I was horrified. I hadn't realized that John had internalized his father's parsimonious attitude toward money. He had told me that his father reluctantly shelled out five dollars each Sunday night for his meals at Fordham. But I had no idea that he would repeat his father's behavior with our son. I guess none of us knows how deeply influenced we are by our parents.

Martin had asked for very little over the years, and I had often bought him nice shirts and dress pants at the thrift shops. But in high school, I thought he should be able to dress like his friends. That means a lot to teenagers. When John refused to let Martin buy new shirts to "fit in," I realized that his "ways" and mine were radically different. I remember my mother saying years earlier: "I like everybody, but I don't always like their ways." I began to realize that I didn't like John's ways, his commitment to voluntary poverty, and his lack of affection for me. Indeed, I didn't like him very much anymore. He had never explained how much he believed in the ascetic life, at least not in a way I understood. This misunderstanding became more pronounced, and I became more disenchanted.

John's mother recognized this trait in him long before I did. To my astonishment, she often said, "He should have been a hermit." Eventually, I realized why she said this, but I didn't quite get it at the time. However, I gradually accepted that our marriage had become pretty joyless and loveless, and something needed to be done.

Whenever I suggested we attend a marriage workshop or get some marriage counseling, he adamantly refused. I didn't know what to do. I suppose one of the confusing things was that John's mother, who sometimes came to live near us in Iowa City or Kansas City, was a very cultured, bourgeois woman. I had expected that we would have a life like hers. Indeed, she was an unusual person. She had been a teacher before her marriage, so she was an educated woman, which was unusual during the 1930s. She was very open to change, whether it was change in the Roman Catholic church when it replaced the Latin mass with the vernacular or in modern music. I remember John disliking the change in the church's liturgy. This surprised me because he was so much younger than his mother, seldom went to church, and was also more leftist politically. I just didn't understand his conservatism in that area.

Louie and I were cultural pals, or "culture vultures," as John dubbed us, going to concerts and operas together in London and in Kansas City. Once we went to an unusual concert by Ravel in a theater on the Plaza. The piece was the "Piano Concerto in G" that had been influenced by his time in New Orleans with American jazz and spirituals. It was quite a surprising blend of sounds and moods. Louie wasn't put off by the modernism but was quite open to it. In contrast, my mother was from a small town and culturally conservative. As a worker, she had not had the opportunities for education and travel that Louie did. Only late in life did my mother get to travel—first to England to visit John, Martin, and me in 1969, and then again with me in 1977 to England and Holland. She also occasionally visited my brother and sister-in-law in California and Oregon and my sister in New York City. She lived her life in La Porte, Indiana, not often crossing the ocean as often as Louie did.

John, Louie, and Martin celebrating Louie's birthday, Kansas City, 1976

While going to concerts, yoga classes, and lectures with Louie enriched my life in Kansas City, it couldn't disguise the slow disintegration of my marriage and my feeling like a neglected housewife. Here is a picture of John, Louie, and Martin celebrating Louie's birthday one February. I had asked her what sort of cake she would like, and she answered: "A layer cake with mashed bananas between the layers, frosted with whipped cream." I thought I could do that, and she was very touched and appreciative when I made it.

John spent increasing amounts of time preparing lectures for his classes, leaving me more and more in charge of the work of family living—riding our bike to do the grocery shopping and cooking, cleaning, and ironing. Although I was supposedly working on my PhD exams, I was dispirited. Our ideas of celebration clashed again when I did pass my PhD exams. I returned from Iowa City feeling triumphant at doing well, but he dismissed my success, saying "They just praised you because you're a woman."

John didn't honor my work and derided women's history. He would say things like, "History of the family has a future but not women's history." This hurt my feelings because my dissertation topic focused on Russian and Soviet women's history. The message I got was I was supposed to honor his work, his intellectual life, and especially the English Marxist historians E. P. Thompson, Eric Hobsbawm, and Gareth Stedman Jones, but my world view was unimportant. I should know the "big" names in English history, but when I mentioned Russian economists like Evgeny Preobrazhensky and Nikolai Bukharin of the 1920s, he accused me of name dropping.

Initially, I had wondered if marriage could support two strong egos, and at first I repressed mine. However, I eventually wanted to express myself intellectually too. Moreover, many other women had this idea in the 1970s as feminism spread. More and more were dropping out of painful, unfulfilling marriages. So when John continually refused to go to marriage counseling, divorce proved the only way out. I didn't know it at the time, but feminism and divorce were parts of postmodernism in the 1970s, not simply experiences in my private world.

For years I had been angry at John for refusing to go to marriage counseling with me, but now I can see that I should have gone for myself and then perhaps I would have understood John and myself better. However, my meeting with a psychiatrist at the university's student health center in 1962 had not been a helpful one, so I didn't pursue my own emotional development as I might have.

Moreover, I was reading radical feminist works for my dissertation, especially those by Alexandra Kollontai. No doubt reading about her idea of the "New Woman" in her *Autobiography of a Sexually Emancipated Communist Woman* produced even more conflict within me. While I wanted to be a traditional helpmeet to my husband and subordinate my work to his, I was reading her modern ideas that were just the opposite. In her autobiography, she says that the new woman does not recognize any power over herself. She does not belong to a man like an object, giving him her whole will, heart, and understanding. Nor does she gear all her energies to the beloved's well-being. Instead, the new woman is a working, thinking, woman–human being.[12]

Likewise, feminism was in the air. The ERA—the Equal Rights Amendment—had passed both houses of Congress with overwhelming approval by 1972 and was on its way to being confirmed by the states. Republicans and Democrats had both endorsed it, and thirty-five of the necessary thirty-eight states had passed it by 1980 when President Reagan disavowed it and the Republican National Convention dropped it from its platform. I remember agitating for the ERA in Missouri when I lived in Kansas City. Indeed, the Supreme Court endorsed women's right to abortion in its *Roe vs. Wade* decision in 1973. However, cold warrior Phyllis Schlafly convinced women of the religious right that the ERA would undermine married women's way of life. She undermined support for equal rights and by 1977 split the women's movement into pro- and anti-abortion camps, which has continued until the present day.[13] Initially, I had not anticipated that securing my equal rights would lead to divorce, but it did.

End of My Dreams

At some point in the 1970s, I began having trouble with my eyes, so I stopped taking the birth control pill. I had read the pill could cause thrombosis and eye problems. Little did I know the consequences of this decision. Indeed, it's only in writing these memoirs that I have entertained the notion that my giving up the birth control pill, and John's reluctance to ever buy condoms or take responsibility for our sexual life may have been linked to his distancing himself from me by staying upstairs in his study until late at night. I don't know what his thinking and feeling about these matters were because he didn't share them with me. Nor did I know how to broach this subject with him. So, slowly, the joy drained out of our relationship. I remember feeling quite perplexed. I wondered if "just putting up with it," as Dolly Obolenskaia remarked in Tolstoy's

---

12. Alexandra Kollontai, "New Woman," in *The Autobiography of a Sexually Emancipated Communist Woman*, trans. Salvator Attanasio, ed. Irving Fletcher (New York: Schocken Books, 1975), 62.
13. For a good review of this issue, see Linda Greenhouse, "Who Killed the ERA?" *New York Review of Books*, October 12, 2017, 6–10.

novel *Anna Karenina*, was all there was to marriage. It wasn't a very satisfying answer in the late 1970s.

Failures of Appreciation

While it's easy to fault John for not appreciating me, in retrospect I can see that I didn't honor the hard work he did each night preparing thoughtful, entertaining lectures. I didn't realize how demanding it was preparing for so many courses. Yet, once I became a teacher, I discovered that it could be intoxicating too. Perhaps this is what kept him slaving away. I was surprised when he came downstairs to ask me about a joke or story he was using in his lecture. He organized all these quips and asides very carefully. Until I became a professor myself, I didn't appreciate all the *work* that his presentations required.

Actually, my philosophy of history was not very well developed until I started teaching. It was then I decided gender and class were the two most helpful categories of analysis for me. I realized that the Hegelian dialectic was also a useful tool for interpreting complicated episodes of history and used it when appropriate. However, I did not subscribe to the Marxian variant to which John adhered.

I remember one of John's favorite put-downs of me at this time was "You have the personality of the artist but none of the talent." What could I say? How could I defend myself? I wasn't as quick-witted as he. Other times he would quote Paul Tillich, saying: "God is for men, religion is for women"—implying women's inferiority. Sometimes he would remark that men went for the jugular, but women didn't. I thought that was a good thing, but he thought it showed women's weakness. I felt under attack. Unlike John, I wasn't good at quips or comebacks, and I internalized my hurt feelings, which intensified my low self-esteem and simmering anger. I felt approved of and supported by others only when working for a friend's political campaign, attending a Slavic conference, or conducting research at the Summer Research Lab at the University of Illinois, where I was accepted as a scholar and person. In those situations, I felt valuable and good. To his credit, John also often repeated the phrase, "Everyone has at least one book in them." Years later, I reminded myself of this as I finished my first book.

Bleakness

Eventually, I began to feel immense bleakness in my "harsh and dreadful marriage." Martin was still a joy, but he had become a teenager and had his own friends, which was as it should be. He didn't need me the way he had when he was younger. I just felt incredibly alone. My dream of family happiness slowly ebbed away. Years later, I recognized that John and I interpreted life differently, but I hadn't picked up on this. A friend took a photo of me during this time, and in it I appeared to be brooding and thoughtful. I never liked the picture because I liked those that show me as happy and carefree. In contrast, John liked this portrait. He accepted the brooding part of my nature much more than I did. Perhaps he accepted our many-faceted selves more than I did.

Sometimes I wish John were still alive so I could ask him some of these questions. After we had divorced, I remember being surprised at how angry he was when I cut up that unhappy picture of me when I was staying in the house with Martin one time and he was away. I told him that he disliked my taking photos of him, that he never gave me anything of himself, so I didn't think he should have anything of me. It was probably one of the most honest exchanges we ever had. It was too bad it took divorce to make me speak up to him.

Slowly, John began to drop out of my life. In Iowa City, I had been a helpmate to him, typing his papers for his classes and helping him memorize German for his PhD German test. However, in Kansas City, he had a departmental secretary to type his letters and papers, and I didn't feel needed. Eventually, we developed separate sets of friends—mine from church and political causes, his among graduate students whom he enjoyed being around. I became very active at St. George's Episcopal Church, serving on the vestry, singing in the choir, and going to prayer groups. I also participated in an intercessory prayer group at St. Luke's hospital, taught by a medical doctor who was so convinced of the efficacy of prayer that he became an Episcopal priest. At this time, I suffered from false consciousness. I prayed for others but never asked them to pray for me. My marriage was miserable, but I lived in denial that I needed prayer.

New Social Life

While my marriage fell apart, my social life filled up, providing some consolation. I didn't yet let myself admit that I didn't find marriage and family life completely fulfilling. That was the value I had grown up with in my traditional working-class life in La Porte. What I hadn't realized was that it didn't fit me as a college-educated woman living in the post-modern 1970s. Only in writing my memoirs have I realized that I wanted some fulfillment of my own apart from my husband and son and that I would have to struggle to get it.

Church

"I am the Resurrection and the Life . . ."

In Kansas City, I came into contact with praise music like "I Am the Resurrection and the Life." It was very affirmative. My best friend in Kansas City was Sandie Colbert. We shared common interests such as choir at St. George's Episcopal Church and enjoyed the Kansas City Lyric Opera. Our sons, who were close in age, played together. All these things drew us together. Sandie had a car, so she always gave Martin and me a ride to our integrated church, which was located in a somewhat dangerous neighborhood, east of Troost Avenue, the dividing line between the black and white areas in Kansas City.

One summer shortly after I moved to Kansas City, Sandie and I attended the International Charismatic Church Conference held at the Royals' stadium and other venues around Kansas City. It was so exciting. We sang songs like "I Am the Resurrection and the Life" in a stadium filled with thousands of people. I loved hearing some people speaking in tongues and others interpreting the prophesies. Ruth Carter Stapleton was one of the leaders, and she prayed for the healing of memories of several hundred of us gathered at the old Kansas City airport. When she led us in a guided meditation to heal hurt feelings about family members, I felt some release from my anger at my father. As I followed her guidance, I imagined going home and seeing my dad and me in our living room along with Jesus. Then I spoke to my dad, telling him what I felt mad and hurt about. Then I saw Jesus laying his hand on each of us and forgiving us. Remembering this recently made me imagine my former husband and me in our living room in Kansas City and visualize Jesus with us, helping us express our feelings and forgiving each other. This felt good. I cried both times while doing this spiritual exercise.

At St. George's, Sandie and I also sang in the choir. Sandie had an outstanding soprano voice, and our young organist, Kevin, composed special pieces to showcase her talent. In addition, he composed music for the synthesizer. I was reminded of this the other evening when I attended an organ concert in Lincoln which featured organ, synthesizer, and cello. Until then, I had forgotten about my music experiences in Kansas City. Once Kevin composed an entire synthesizer Easter mass for our church. He was an amazing young man and made singing in the choir enchanting. In addition, the choir had a strong young alto, Carol Vandenberg, and she helped me with the alto part. Fortunately, our music was rather simple. Because I loved singing, I was glad to participate in a choir again, even in our small one of six or seven members. Our organist also composed music for two young black children who lived in the neighborhood. He produced drum music for the young boy and a charming vocal piece called "Come on Down, Come on Down, Lord Let Your Holy Spirit Come on Down" for the young girl. When they performed together, it was always very touching. Moreover, this was the sort of experience that our priest, Father George, supported.

At St. George's, I also volunteered typing the weekly bulletins and became active in a prayer group. One evening at the manse, where we were meeting, we were robbed. That was scary. Two young boys accosted us as we were leaving. They had guns and grabbed our purses and beat up the fellow in our group. Then they ran away. I was so stunned that I couldn't remember whether they had grabbed my purse or whether I gave it to them. It all happened so fast and furiously.

One day when I had gone to church to type the bulletin, my bicycle tire exploded. I always rode my bike to church unless Sandie gave me a ride. Being on the move was safer than walking in that neighborhood. That day it was cold outside but warm inside. I parked my bike near a radiator in the church, and the heat from the radiator made the tire explode. At first we thought it was a shot, since there were robberies at our church and in the neighborhood. Our priest called the police, but when they came to investigate, they found that it was my tire that had caused the noise. We felt very foolish. This story shows how on edge we all were at church.

The 1970s was an active time at St. George's. We prayed at the Bishop's Office for the ordination of women, which was not a popular item with our bishop or many of the Episcopal clergy in those days. Our priest's wife, Katrina, had privately prepared for ordination and belonged to a group of women "irregularly" ordained. Our bishop did not accept her ordination, so she couldn't officiate at our church or in Kansas City. Eventually they moved to New Jersey, where they could both serve as priests.

We also had a prayer vigil at the Bishop's Office for permission to use our manse to house nonviolent women sentenced to prison. We sought permission for them to live a "supervised" life at St. George's instead of being sent to prison, which was poorly run in the state of Missouri. Getting to know some of the women, I was astonished to discover that they drank vanilla and other flavoring extracts for the alcohol since they were not supposed to have alcohol or drugs while at St. George's. Learning how manipulative some of the women were was an education. Getting books for them from the library was easy, but it was harder getting the women to return them to me to take back to the library.

Political Life

In Kansas City, it was also easy to get involved in local politics. We lived in an area called the 39–63 Coalition. This referred to the area bounded by Troost Avenue from 39th to 63rd Street. Troost was the dividing line between the black and white neighborhoods in our area, and the coalition was an effort to promote greater social justice and neighborhood involvement. One woman named Dottie Doll was very active in this coalition. She lived near us, and I became involved in the coalition through her and then later in her political campaign when she ran for the Missouri House of Representatives. It was fascinating going to fundraisers for her in Kansas City. Some were held in palatial homes, and that opened my eyes to the wealth in the city. She won the election, but it turned out to be a hollow victory because legislators get embroiled in a lot of pork barrel legislation, which violated her idealistic teacher ethics. She didn't stay long in the legislature, but by then I was divorced and had gone to live in Iowa City to resume my graduate school studies.

Marriage Disintegration

This is the way the world ends
This is the way the world ends
This is the way the world ends
Not with a bang but a whimper.
T. S. Eliot, "The Hollow Men"

This stanza from Eliot is sort of the way my marriage ended. It felt like a whimper. In the late 1970s, John and I still walked down to the Plaza in Kansas City on Friday mornings for a cinnamon roll and coffee and talked about his relief at finishing teaching for the week. On holidays we got together with some of his nonhistory university colleagues to have potluck dinners (not the weekly events these had been in Iowa City). Sometimes we had lunch at the Plaza at an elegant restaurant that we couldn't afford to patronize in the evening. At lunch toward the end of our marriage, I realized we didn't laugh together much anymore, and I had very little to share with him. Our lives had gone in different directions. He was willing to lend a thousand dollars to a friend but not to buy Martin and me anything like a modern washing machine to replace the 1932-vintage model that a friend had given us, and which had a broken wringer, so we had to wring all the clothes, including the heavy towels and jeans, by hand. John was the professor, busily preparing lectures, working late every night, and ignoring me. Once, when I asked to have a cleaning lady, he refused, saying he wouldn't want to exploit anyone by paying her low wages to clean our home—yet somehow he thought I should do the housework for free.

Most nights he came to bed after I had already gone to sleep. I usually arose earlier than John because I took our dog for a walk at six thirty and made Martin's breakfast before he went to school. I felt sexually and emotionally abandoned. Early in the marriage he had made it clear that he detested holding hands or any show of physical affection. He also insisted that we have no more children, even though I sometimes wanted to. So this may have been one reason he avoided me sexually. I really don't know. What I can see now is that for different reasons, my mother and my husband were sex avoidant.

At the same time, John seemed attracted to one of his female students, and that bothered me. He spoke of her fondly and enjoyed being with her and other students, whom he invited to our house and garden. He seemed on the same wavelength with them but not with me. It broke my heart to see him lavishing his students with kindness, conviviality, and joy when I wanted that for myself. I felt ignored and increasingly jealous. I didn't want to live my life like that. I hated myself for being jealous and had never experienced that emotion before. I didn't know how to deal with it. I was in such pain; all I could think of was running away. I tried confronting John about these issues, but he refused to talk about them.

Finally, I made up an excuse that I needed to go to Iowa City to do some research and lived there one academic year. Of course that didn't solve my problem, but it removed me from it. Life was more bearable, although I missed Martin and John a lot. But Martin was a teenager and busy with school and his friends. I had taught Martin to cook, but I don't know that he did it while I was away or whether his father cooked. In Iowa City, I supported myself by renting a cheap room and getting some financial aid from the history department. My professor was always helpful in getting me money to live on. He took care of me in a kindly way.

When I returned to Kansas City in the spring, I told John that I thought we needed marriage counseling. I had suggested this several times before, but he had always rejected the idea. I didn't know then that he didn't want anything changed in our relationship since he held the power in it. Finally I threw down the gauntlet and told him that we either had to go to marriage counseling or get a divorce. I was devastated when he said we'd get a divorce. I just didn't believe him. But he got a lawyer and divorced me. I didn't have a lawyer. We had no property or money, so I didn't really need one. The summer of 1979 proved a very painful time. John's mother was dying of ovarian cancer in England, and Martin didn't want to go to England. He and I needed new passports, and I didn't have the emotional strength to convince Martin to go when I had mixed feelings myself. I knew I would feel very awkward saying goodbye to Louie and trying to explain to her why John and I were getting divorced. However, it turns out that her friend Mary Louise had noticed John in company with his student B. and had written to Louie about this situation, so Louie already knew some of our problems. She had always been good to me, and I just couldn't face her. It was excruciating telling our friends that John and I were divorcing. As an intellectual, I smoothed over the pain by blithely saying we didn't have a healthy relationship anymore. This was true but not the whole truth. Thankfully, no one asked for details.

Recently, while reading passages of Evelyn Waugh's *Brideshead Revisited* on the winding down of a relationship, I saw some remarkable similarities in the spouses he described and my own life:

> I was aghast to realize that something within me, long sickening, had quietly died, and felt as a husband might feel, who, in the fourth year of his marriage, suddenly knew that he had no longer any desire, or tenderness, or esteem, for a once-beloved wife, no pleasure in her company, no wish to please, no curiosity about anything she might ever do or say or think; no hope of setting things right, no self-reproach for the disaster. I knew it all, the whole drab compass of marital disillusion; we had been through it together.[14]

I felt guilty for leaving my son in Kansas City, but he wanted to stay there with his high school friends. After John got a lawyer and we divorced, I felt angry and devastated. By the 1990s, we had friendly phone conversations about our son and university life when I was teaching Russian history in El Paso, and he was teaching English history in Kansas City. Indeed, it proved much easier being his friend than his wife. Maybe I had fewer expectations. Who knows? It was fifteen years after our divorce when the rancor ebbed away. I was enraged at the time of our divorce. As William Congreve expressed (only more poetically), "Hell hath no fury like a woman scorned." I was mad as hell for a couple of years. Only now, some decades later, do I realize that the dream of happy, middle-class life that I treasured and sought was not John's dream, and

---

14. Evelyn Waugh, *Brideshead Revisited* (Boston: Little, Brown and Company, 1945), Prologue, 5–6.

that mine had turned into a nightmare. It took several years for me to work through my sense of moral failure, my anger and disappointment in John and myself. But I began to do this with the grace of God, help from my friends, and a new more realistic and feminist theology. Underneath my rage and anger, however, was the fear of my own validity. I had been afraid to be who I was for years and had lived vicariously through John. Now I had to live my own life, no small task.

During the 1970s, I had not been very aware of the resentment building up inside me as John ignored me and my needs. In the end, I became enraged. Although I had asked him to go to a marriage counselor or get divorced, perhaps in my heart of hearts I wanted out of a very painful relationship. And although I felt shocked when he said he'd rather get divorced than work on our relationship, perhaps he too knew it was really over and past the stage of repair. Part of it was that he did not want to renegotiate his position of power in our relationship, and I did. He didn't acknowledge this to me until after our divorce. I hadn't realized that he was so wed to power, but he was. He knew it, but I hadn't been conscious of it.

At some point in our marriage, John eschewed Roman Catholicism and the intellectual framework of St. Thomas and became a Marxist. He told me that only Marxism offered the intellectual structure that Thomism had previously provided him. John seemed to admire Marxism's "faith that history with a capital H had a discernible logic."[15] I hadn't grown up with such a systematic theology and didn't crave one, as he did. I certainly didn't know how to critique John's views. Recently, my priest in Lincoln spoke of being suspicious of systems that define God too narrowly. He indicated that God is full of surprises, and I agreed. However, I hadn't known how to say any of this to John.

John contemptuously looked down on bourgeois life. For a long time I didn't realize that we didn't share the same dream of family happiness. Slowly I became disillusioned with our marriage, but I didn't know what to do. Raised in the 1940s and '50s, I believed that marriage and a nice house went together. I thought that John as an intelligent, talented man would provide this for me and Martin. I hadn't realized this was not his dream. He hadn't asked me to idolize him, but I did. I thought he was my passport to the bourgeois life. I had worked four years to provide for us in Iowa City while he finished his PhD after our return from Europe in 1970, and I thought he would fulfill my dreams when he got "the big job" after graduating with his PhD.

15. See Michael Ignatieff, "Messianic America: Can He Explain It?" *New York Review of Books,* November 19, 2015, 29.

In retrospect, I realize that as long as I played by his rules and never asked for anything, for Martin, the house, or for myself, life proceeded smoothly. When I asked for furniture for the house, new clothes for Martin, or affection for me, however, he balked. I eventually realized how stubborn he was. Indeed, he was more tough-minded and power-oriented than I reckoned. Years after our marriage, I realized that I had seriously misjudged him.

After our divorce, he told me that he thought relationships were built on power, and he hadn't wanted to change our dynamics. That dismayed me. I remembered that when he and his friend Paul played chess that it resembled a clash of titans, but I hadn't realized that he thought our relationship was based on his holding power over me. Sad. Yet, at some level I fed into this system because I initially thought him strong enough to love and save me, when I didn't feel I could love myself. It took me years to understand that he didn't love himself very much, and he certainly didn't have extra love to save me. It took even longer for me to recognize that I too needed to learn to love myself.

I was fortunate in having Jaroslaw Pelenski as my Russian history professor in the 1970s and '80s. He was a gracious East European, a Ukrainian Pole. His field was medieval and early modern Russian history, but he was open-minded and didn't mind my doing Russian and Soviet women's history. He was encouraging and always helped me get money for tuition and teaching assistantships. Although I was a bit of a dilettante about working on my PhD exams and my dissertation, he was never harsh or critical of me. Maybe he realized that I had psychological struggles. I'm not sure. He always treated me with courtesy, and I appreciated that. He never complained that I was taking too long or accused me of being a loafer. He was always kind, a real gentleman. He never made me feel intellectually inferior, as John did. So Russian history remained a solace for me.

Before John divorced me in the summer of 1979, I didn't think that John may have wanted his inheritance from his mother and may not have wanted to share it with me. When I heard of his inheritance, I assumed he would use it for Martin's education, but he didn't. Instead he bought a house with his new partner, Stephanie. Again, this confounded me since he had never wanted to buy a house while we were married. The summer I psychologically prepared to leave, I had known for a while that his "ways" were not mine, but it took years for me to comprehend that my dream of a cozy life was not his. I had to achieve my dream myself. This proved to be hard and lonely.

Chapter VI

Divorce: Finding My Own Voice in Graduate School

> For I know the plans I have for you, declares the Lord,
> plans to prosper you and not to harm you,
> plans to give you hope and a future.
>
> Jeremiah 29:11

> God heals the brokenhearted and binds up their wounds.
>
> Psalm 147:3

I wasn't very aware of the scriptures from Jeremiah 29:11 and Psalm 147:3 when I first got divorced, but I value them now. Although I was feeling brokenhearted, wounded, and defeated when I returned to graduate school, God healed me. I had no idea if I could or would complete my PhD and become a professor, but I did. I had wanted to become a teacher since high school, but my fears had inhibited me from doing so. Now, as a penniless divorcée, I had to earn my own living, and I thought I would try my hand at teaching. I knew if I didn't succeed, I would have to do something else. Little did I know the plans that God had in mind for me—to heal me and prosper me, not to harm me.

In writing these memoirs, I now see that my personal crises took place within a wider postmodern context. Social mores were changing, and no-fault divorce was popular. I wasn't the only one getting divorced. Feminism was challenging the patriarchal order and becoming a national movement. I wasn't the only feminist. Finally, Protestant theology and the Episcopal Church, in particular, were redefining themselves. While traditionally the Russian Orthodox Church expressed the feminine element in the Mother of God, and the Roman Catholic in the Virgin Mary, Protestants were beginning to redefine the Godhead and express the feminine element in God the Creator and the Holy Spirit. In 1979 the Episcopal Church revised its Book of Common Prayer using more inclusive language and ordained women priests. Both these signaled seismic change. While I was reluctant to reinvent myself, it was a little easier living in the midst of such events. While I had felt very guilty about leaving my son in the care of his father after our divorce in the summer of 1979, he didn't seem to suffer too much. He was a junior in high school and didn't want to leave his friends and buddies to come live with me in Iowa City, which was less glamorous than Kansas City, where he had the Royals baseball team, the Chiefs football team, and many other attractions for a young person. I knew his father was no cook, but I had taught Martin to cook when he was twelve, so I knew he could at least cook a little and wouldn't starve.

While John and I had divorced each other, I hadn't divorced my son. That was some consolation. I cried from my sense of guilt for several months, but I continued loving Martin the same way I always had, but from a distance. I had realized when he was baptized that I was offering him up to God, and that he belonged to God, who entrusted him to me to raise. I knew he wasn't mine alone, much as I loved him. It was much more complex and emotionally wrenching to detach myself from John, with whom I was intellectually and emotionally enmeshed.

Martin and Mother, Thanksgiving, Iowa City, 1979

Martin and his father stayed in the same house, so he had some stability in his life. Martin and I had holidays together. Usually he and I met at my mother's in Indiana for Christmas vacation. Sometimes he came to visit me in Iowa City, and sometimes I returned to Kansas City to see him. Still, I missed him tremendously and felt great remorse about having left him.

If I knew John was going to be away from Kansas City, then I took a bus there and stayed in the house with Martin. I was glad when I could be with my son. He was still the light of my life. He graduated from Bishop O'Hare High School and then went to the University of Missouri to study. He did well there

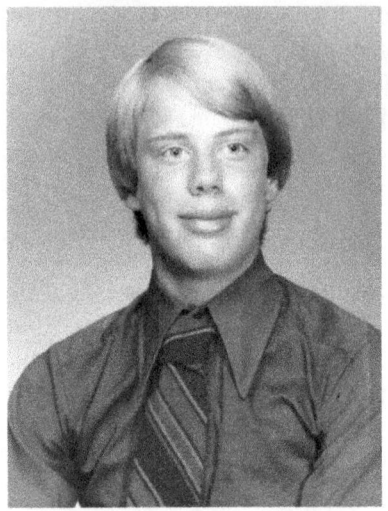

Martin's high school graduation picture, 1980

but returned to Kansas City to finish his BA degree in economics at UMKC, where his father taught.

During our sixteen years of marriage, I had become so enmeshed in John's life and personality that it was extremely difficult to extricate myself. It was hard to live my own life instead of his. I didn't know how to be me and accept that I was enough. I had always thought of John as more exalted than me. That was another reason that I didn't mind so much leaving Martin with John. I thought John was a better person than I was. He was smarter and more accomplished. I still discounted myself at this time. Getting divorced and considering John's "seriously flawed behavior" were exhausting and enervating. Only years later did I examine my own flawed behavior. While I could easily see John's inability to love me, it took decades before I realized that I hadn't known how to love him very well either. Returning to graduate school at age thirty-nine, I was frightened of being a teaching assistant but decided I had to try to see if I was any good at it. If not, I would have to find another way to support myself.

In the fall of 1979, I was a more serious student than I had been in the 1960s. Still, I encountered greater difficulty writing my dissertation than I expected. My mind drifted into interior monologues, working over questions like "What if I had done such and such, would John and I still be married?" "What if I had been a better wife, would we have gotten divorced?" "If only I had been prettier, smarter, more thoughtful ... would we still be married?" I was so miserable and lonesome. I suffered from insomnia and feared I'd die if I fell asleep. I read books about sleep and others about divorce. The best pamphlet I read about divorce said, "The only thing you need to tell anyone about why you got divorced is that we are all seriously flawed." That helped the most. Then I could accept that John and I were not perfect but had hurt each other. I cried a lot the first year after my divorce—almost all the time except when I was teaching, so I was grateful to have a teaching assistantship to keep me busy. Some of the highlights of my second stint in graduate school after dealing with my identity crisis were "falling in love" with teaching, falling in love with a fellow graduate student, writing my dissertation, meeting other women historians, visiting the Soviet Union in 1985, and discovering feminist theology.

Identity Crisis

> It was hard to know which to fault more—the dream or the reality.
>
> Milovan Đilas

I can relate to the quote by Yugoslav communist Milovan Đilas, who became disenchanted with communism as an ideology in the 1950s, because I felt the same about the death of my marriage. Which should I blame more: my unrealistic dream and expectations? or the reality and unpleasantness of our situation? I found solace one Sunday about two years after I had been divorced when I heard a psychologist assert that it was more painful to lose a spouse in divorce than in death. That surprised me, but I certainly agreed with this idea. He argued that when a spouse dies, the survivor can continue to think well of the deceased and not have a change of opinion. But, when a couple divorces, each survivor has to reevaluate his or her relationship to the beloved, which is a more painful process. Losing one's dream is also part of postmodernism.

New Theology

As I began the new semester at the university as a teaching assistant in August 1979, I slowly realized that I was entering a new life and needed to develop a new world view and theology because the old ones weren't helping me work through my grief and fashion a new life. Doing this took time. Psychologically, I had an identity crisis. For sixteen years I had vicariously lived through my husband. Now, I no longer could. I had subordinated myself to John, to his needs and his intellectual prowess, and it was hard becoming me, accepting all my inadequacy and self-loathing. I couldn't idealize myself, as I did him. I knew I needed to become a new person, but I didn't realize how much effort this would take. All I knew was that I was crying a lot, eating little, and feeling miserable. At night, I was terrified of going to sleep, afraid of dying. Having been married for many years, I wasn't used to living and sleeping alone. It was alienating and frightening. I read the psalms seeking solace for my loneliness and anger, especially Psalm 69:

Chapter VI

> Save me, O God, for the waters have risen up to my neck.
> I am sinking in deep mire, there is no firm ground for my feet.
> . . .
> Reproach has broken my heart, and it cannot be healed;
> I looked for sympathy, but there was none,
> For comforters, but I could find no one.

In my misery, I also turned to Psalm 22, the opening words that Jesus exclaimed from the cross:

> "My God, my God, why have you forsaken me?

Needless to say, I searched the psalms for the sad and miserable ones. Reading them comforted me. I felt as if the psalmists understood my pain. I tried praying before going to bed, but sleep still eluded me. I listened to music every night, especially Vivaldi's *The Four Seasons*; I tried drinking some brandy before bed to relax; all to no avail. I lit candles and hugged an icon to my chest to comfort myself, but still it was difficult to nod off. I didn't think of going to a doctor to get sleeping pills. I had never known anyone who did this, nor had I ever had trouble sleeping before. I was unprepared for this reaction. Later, I read the poet John Donne's *Devotions upon Emergent Occasions*. They were beautiful and comforting. He wrote them one time when he thought he was dying, and they are a testament to the human psyche. In retrospect, I can see that my old self was dying and a new one was being born.

I remember saying to myself as I walked down the street in Iowa City the fall after my divorce: "I'm no longer Mrs. John ——, so who am I?" I answered: "I can be just plain Marcelline, or Dr. Marcelline Hutton, if I need a title." I also recalled asking myself: "Where is your home now that you don't live with Martin and John?" I replied: "My home is wherever I am." These words satisfied me. They still do.

When I returned to Iowa City in the fall of 1979, I didn't realize that giving up my old self and becoming a new person would be a long, complicated, drawn-out process, but it was. I was hoping for a cataclysmic event to suddenly transform my life. Of course that didn't happen. Fortunately for me, Trinity Episcopal Church had a very savvy priest named Anne Baker, and talking with her and participating in her feminist theology group helped me integrate my new self. During the day, I taught my classes at the university, and this was helpful. I was fully engaged while teaching, and I liked the students and the material in the history classes. Unlike Dostoevsky, who felt that in writing he was "being most of all," I felt this way about teaching. However, holding up a false front all day, appearing as if everything was fine in front of my students and colleagues, left me drained at night.

I was renting an upstairs room that our old family friend Larry Meisgeier had told me about, and I didn't have any neighbors. Living alone meant I didn't have anyone nearby to commiserate with. Eventually I found some friends at church who had also been divorced, and sharing with them helped. An evening Bible study group at Trinity also assuaged some of my pain and provided friends for my new spiritual journey. Attending Communion services there several times a week also helped, especially the healing service on Tuesday mornings at six thirty. Several of the folks who went for healing were also hurting. I even had a friend who used the phrase "the walking wounded" to describe us, but I was still in denial that I was wounded and didn't want it applied to me. The behavior I learned growing up in my alcoholic family taught me to deny pain, not to acknowledge or deal with it.

Eventually I realized that I had a lot of false, patriarchal, and oppressive religious ideas that were hurting me, and I needed to replace them. The angry, punitive patriarch of the Old Testament that I had grown up with was no longer helpful. I realized that I had been trying to earn God's love rather than accept it. I had tried to make sure I was one of God's favorites, but since my divorce I wasn't anymore. Our feminist priest, Anne, urged me to give up the idea of being "Lady Bountiful" and formulate a more inclusive and loving theology. She encouraged me to think of the Trinity in terms of Creator, Redeemer, and Sustainer, and to use words for God from the Medieval mystics such as "Fountain of Wisdom" and "Cloud of Unknowing" as well as other neutral nouns instead of the old patriarchal, androcentric language.

The late 1970s and '80s were a time of postmodern ideas, although I didn't know that term then. Feminist scholars were challenging the old order, especially in psychology, theology, and history. These writers were a godsend to me and represented a postmodern view of the world, one in which the traditional patriarchal forms no longer dominated. I especially remember a psychological study emphasizing intuition in *Women's Ways of Knowing*, and of course I read a lot of pop psychology including *Our Many Selves*; *Life Is Goodbye, Life Is Hello*; and others. Impressive theologians I read included Carol P. Christ and her book *Diving Deep and Surfacing: Women Writers on Spiritual Quest* (1980), Rosemary Reuther's *Women of Spirit*, and Phyllis Trible's *Texts of Terror*. These works helped me create a new feminist framework for interpreting women's experience. It was a revelation hearing God defined not as a noun but as a verb: godding. Finding new feminist religious language and symbols was liberating yet wrenching too in surrendering my old ideas, more postmodernism. Rediscovering and valuing the feminine element within, the emotional and intuitive aspects of myself, provoked an awakening not only for me but for many women in the Midwest at that time. Conferences on feminist theology were held in Lincoln, Nebraska; Mankato, Minnesota; Iowa City and Des Moines, Iowa; St. Louis and Kansas City, Missouri. Learning new names for God was important, and I remember attending a weekend conference in Des Moines focusing on "Sophia, Goddess of Wisdom."

At the same time, I was also reading Matthew Fox's *The Coming of the Cosmic Christ* (1988) as well as several by the Dutch Jesuit Henri Nouwen. His books spoke to me and still do. Some of his most memorable are *Out of Solitude* and *Behold the Beauty of the Lord: Praying with Icons*. It was Gretchen Bingea, the head of Christus Community, who introduced me to his works. Nouwen led me to incorporate Russian icons into my religious life in the 1980s and 1990s, and research for my books *Remarkable Russian Women* and *Resilient Russian Women* deepened my understanding and appreciation of Mary the Mother of God in the Russian Orthodox tradition. Andrei Rublev's icon *The Trinity* and the *Mother of God of Vladimir* have comforted me. Somewhere in my readings and discussions, I encountered two new notions: "We are all icons (images) of God" and "I am a child of God." These were new concepts that helped me but took years to digest.

In addition to feminist theology, new history books and political critiques also affected me, particularly Julia O'Faolain's *Not in God's Image* and Kate Millett's *Sexual Politics*. Both offered illuminating critiques of patriarchy. Their books, along with Gerda Lerner's articles on the significance of gender as a category of analysis for understanding history, shaped my understanding and teaching of women's history at Iowa.

Two years after my divorce, I moved to Christus House, a religious community for students. By then I was no longer quite so distraught. I had begun reconstructing myself psychologically, theologically, and professionally in women's history. In Christus community, I learned some new theology and behavior. I learned about being on a religious journey. I didn't like this term because it implied time-consuming work. Part of me still wanted immediate gratification and cataclysmic healing from my pain. I desired sudden change, not the hard slog of daily work. Ridding myself of old patriarchal ideas was not easy or fast. It was slow, steady progress in building a new worldview. It took a while to shed old ideas and develop more appropriate ones. I finally learned that God provides and heals but not always instantaneously. I learned God does not excuse me from pain but goes through it with me, which was quite a change from my earlier simplistic belief that God wanted me to have the good life and whatever I wanted.

I still believe that God intends the abundant life for us, but it's not necessarily pain-free. Gradually, I learned to read the scriptures with new eyes. I saw that God wasn't just the judge of the Old Testament but also the loving shepherd in Psalm 23. I realized that our Creator made each of us a beloved child but more flawed than I had originally thought. Still, I had never before felt like I was a child of God, so that was a new development in my religious life. Of course, I didn't accept this notion easily. I struggled a long time to incorporate it into my fundamental belief system. I still struggle and sometimes forget and judge myself and others too harshly.

After I first returned to Iowa City, I met a woman my age who had recently gotten divorced, and we commiserated with each other. She was doing her graduate work in the religion department and had her sad story, just as I had mine. In talking with her I no longer felt so alienated and alone. Indeed, her situation was bleaker than mine because one of her daughters reacted to her mother's divorce by committing a crime and landing in jail. The other daughter did something antisocial too, so I felt blessed that my son was not reacting violently. This woman and I shared our pain and in doing so helped each other heal. Initially, I rejected my mother's platitude that "time heals all wounds." But eventually I realized that it did take time for God to work in my life, slowly restoring me by bringing new and helpful friends into my life. I'm sorry to say I wasn't very conscious of this process, just grateful for the acceptance of new friends.

Christus Community

While most members of the Christus community were more integrated than I was, many of them had their own minor crises. Some were adapting to graduate school, some to a new country, and some had to do both. During the two years I lived there, we had three women from Taiwan, one from Indonesia, and a fellow from Thailand. Life was not so easy for them either.

Shortly after returning to Iowa City in August 1979, I recall going to a movie and thinking that I knew exactly how John would analyze it but not knowing how I would. It was then I began to realize I needed to find myself, my voice, and my own worldview. A little later I read an article about Virginia Woolf titled "Killing the Angel in the House." I thought the imagery rather savage. But I suppose it's always a struggle to assert ourselves and become who we are.

Christus community: Marcelline (second row, left) and Gretchen Bingea (second row, right), Iowa City, 1980s

Certainly it had been difficult for me to claim my intellectual self as an academic and writer. Growing up in the Midwest in the 1940s and '50s, a woman's place was definitely in the home, caring for her husband and children—being the angel in the house. It was probably all right for a woman to be a nurse or a high school teacher, being an angel in society, but to be a professor was a challenge to the social and economic structure. I didn't set out to overtly challenge society, but I somehow read my way to a PhD in Russian history. I didn't initially set out to subvert my husband's authority and position nor society's assumptions, but I did. It has been a difficult but worthwhile struggle. It still is.

Upon retirement, I decided to continue writing historical books and that too has been a challenge. Now I realize that writing is a form of reification. It makes me feel real. Having lived much of my life among people who don't honor intellectual work, it's been hard to assert my intellectual pursuits in retirement. Maybe it's because part of me doesn't completely honor the intellectual life. Yet respect for intellectual life was one gift, besides our son, that my husband gave me. He honored this pursuit a great deal—sometimes to the exclusion of me from his life. Marrying him and divorcing him were part of my journey to find myself and my own intellectual life. It is hard to acknowledge this, but now I can.

When I was growing up, it was OK for a man to be an ambitious, achieving person but not OK for a woman. Society viewed such women as stepping outside their "place." Somehow it's not always clear what our "place" is, especially for those of us from the working class. This book is an effort to redeem my "place" in society, my family, and my religion. Sometimes it's an upsetting and unsettling journey. Sometimes it's inspiring.

Teaching at the University of Iowa

In the fall of 1979 when I returned to the History Department, it was a different place from 1962. Two outstanding women history professors, Linda Kerber and Sarah Hanley, had been hired, and more women graduate students were enrolled. It was fascinating getting to know them all. I was older, wiser, and better prepared for graduate work than I had been earlier. Moreover, by 1979 I realized I could no longer avoid my own shortcomings and poor performance by concentrating on John's achievements. I realized that it was OK for women to be achievers too. This idea was a change in American cultural attitudes from the 1950s and '60s, a part of postmodernism.

I found the graduate students different from those of the 1960s. The men were less aggressive, competitive, and antireligious and more cooperative. It was a pleasure working with them, and I loved teaching the special social history courses History of the Family, European Women's History, and Reformation and Revivalism. It was delightful having small classes of twenty to twenty-five students. I felt relaxed in this atmosphere, even though I had never taken classes in such subjects. It felt good to integrate some of the historical material I had been accumulating much of my life.

I was surprised to learn that teaching could be so engaging and endearing. I soon realized that behavior I had learned in various church groups could help me facilitate my classes. I had learned about inclusiveness and community where everyone sat in a group and shared their ideas before commenting on others' interpretations. When I taught freshman classes of twenty students at the University of Iowa, we sat in a circle and shared our ideas about the books we were reading or the papers the students were writing. This format helped even shy students participate in class. I preferred these more participatory forms of class structure. I liked our sitting in circles instead of my lecturing from a podium, which I felt was patriarchal and intimidating. Speaking with a friend much later on about this preference, he suggested that this too was part of postmodernism since it represented a feminist approach to teaching instead of the established lecture method. I hadn't thought of this before. I preferred the feminist bottom up to the top down patriarchal approach.

I remember several students well. Once in the History of the Family class, an Indian woman shared that in her culture, mothers still swaddled their babies. Since she had blondish hair, I was surprised she was an American Indian. I appreciated her revealing this information with the class. Later, when teaching Western civilization one summer, another woman, a Muslim from Malaysia, told me that her bride price had been a Koran. That was what she requested, and it was a common request. She had come to talk to me because she had been absent one day while being with a friend in the hospital. It was in my office that she shared about Muslim wedding customs. I asked her if she would feel free talking about this to the class, and she said she would. Her revelations were fascinating to the other students.

I also remember two male students who surprised me by their observations. One was a basketball player who had to drop out of my class because Iowa ended up playing in the March Madness tournament and advancing further than he had anticipated. He said he had to practice a lot and couldn't do the readings. I was sorry because one day he had asked, "Why was Daniel Defoe a protofeminist?" We were reading something by Defoe in our book *Not in God's Image*, and the student was perplexed that a man in the seventeenth or eighteenth century had such modern views. I didn't really have an answer for him but remembered his insightful question. Later, another basketball player asked me who had written our Western civilization book. He wondered because he found the focus on one war after another distressing. This was a thoughtful observation, and I was impressed by him too.

I learned a lot from my students at Iowa, and I appreciated their preparing for class and taking my courses seriously. Since I had never taken courses in the history of the family or European women, I asked them to submit essay questions for our final exam. I read them all and culled the best ones to use for our test. I didn't have this problem with teaching Russian or Soviet history because I knew some of the standard questions in those courses. However, I kept this exercise and often added some of the student questions on those exams too. I also asked the students to evaluate the books we used. Normally we read five books in the social history classes, and they wrote essays on some topic in each book. I didn't know until tabulating the results which books the students preferred and found helpful. This information helped me decide which books to keep.

Occasionally, I found humor in teaching and grading exams. Once a group in my Russian history class was presenting a play by Gogol, and one fellow dressed up in a black academic grown to represent the judge. Students found this cute. Another time one of the play groups had only men in it. So one of the fellows borrowed my red felt hat from my office and wore balloons for a bosom in portraying a female character in the play. His outfit was so outlandish, we all laughed. I soon learned that laughter was an excellent bonding experience for a class. I wasn't very good at repeating jokes in class, but I somehow got the class to laugh. Grading papers could be another occasion for humor. When writing about the Middle Ages, students often confused the word peasant with pheasant, with which they were more familiar. Likewise, some wrote the word smurfs for serfs for similar reasons—they had heard of smurfs but not serfs. We teaching assistants sometimes had a good chuckle when grading our students' papers.

Later, as an assistant professor, I taught some very large classes in Russian and Soviet history for Dr. Pelenski when he was away. Teaching a Soviet history class of 103 students in an auditorium of the engineering building across the street from Schaeffer Hall, where most history classes were taught, was not so cozy. Indeed, I found I had to lecture from a podium to this large class. It was stimulating and a little intimidating, but I did well enough. I loved communicating what I admired about Russian and Soviet history. In addition to midterm and final exams, I assigned the students a project of writing fifteen entries in a journal, as I had in my freshman classes. I had no idea how long it would take to privately discuss the journals of 103 students. I spent a lot of time that semester in office hours. Still, I was glad to get to know the students and discover why they were taking the course. Many had grown up in conservative environments and just wanted to check out a Soviet history class to make up their own minds about it. This was great. Who wouldn't be happy teaching open-minded students?

As an instructor in Russian and Soviet history courses, I had a chance to observe differences in the students between the two. Russian history seemed to attract those from the humanities, while Soviet history brought in more polemical, political science majors. The first group delighted in Russian culture and was interested in Russian literature, music, ballet, and so forth. The class members were cooperative in performing Russian plays as part of group participation. One student was a Russian language minor and he recited in Russian some of Griboyedov's couplets from the play *Woe from Wit*. The class was polite and appreciated his sharing. Another student made some very sensitive comments about one of our texts, *The Family in Imperial Russia* by David Ransel. In one of the chapters, the author described how Russian mothers used guilt to control their sons, and this student said his mother was doing the same thing one hundred years later. Again, I was surprised by the student's observation. I was also surprised at the animated discussion stirred by Nadezhda

Durova's memoir *The Cavalry Maiden: Journals of a Russian Officer in the Napoleonic Wars*. Several of the fellows in the class were intrigued by this reading. They contributed a lot to our class discussion that day. I had expected women, not men, to be fascinated.

When teaching Russian history at Iowa, I decided to include plays in my classes for a variety of reasons—they provided cultural history and helped students understand people's lives, feelings, and a historical period in ways that textbooks do not. They also enabled students to think about specific issues in history. For example, the Russian playwright Griboyedov's play *Woe from Wit* illustrated a good example of the alienated Russian intellectual. Others by Gogol, Ostrovsky, Chekhov, and Tolstoy highlighted issues of class, gender, patriarchy, and politics in nineteenth-century Russia. At Iowa I also thought that working in a small group on a play presentation provided students an occasion to get to know a few others in a large class. Acting out scenes from a play proved to be a bonding experience. My hope was that after being in a small group, students would feel more like participating in large-group discussions. It also offered an opportunity for cooperative rather than competitive learning, which was one of my feminist ideas.

Soviet history classes cast a very different tone. More students expressed extreme views, both left and right wing. Discussions of Stalinism and other subjects sometimes got very intense. I had to remind a class that while we might not agree with everyone's opinions, we respected everyone's right to express it. One student wrote in her journal: "I don't know how you can keep from throwing that student out of the window." That shocked me. Some students were very savvy. Once, I assigned a group the topic "Does art reflect reality?" This was the contention of many Russian radical literary critics of the 1860s. However, one student maintained that art didn't *reflect* reality, it *was* reality. What a profound insight. The same student may have been the one who made the astute observation "Russian avant-garde art preceded revolution, in 1905 and 1917." Her comments made me notice that artists in Russian history often presaged wider social and political events. The literary and artistic avant-garde of the Silver Age preceded the 1905 revolution, and Acmeist poetry and primitive and cubist art the 1917 political revolutions. Likewise, Soviet censorship often forced writers to put innovative pieces into their "desk drawer" in the 1930s and '40s, and they were able to publish them only during Khrushchev's "Thaw" in the late 1950s and early 1960s.

Teaching a course titled European Women's History from 1750 to 1950 for Dr. Sarah Hanley the next year proved equally exciting and challenging. In her and Dr. Pelenski's classes, I loved the subject matter but felt greater responsibility as an assistant professor than I had as a teaching assistant. I had expected the process to be the same, but it wasn't. Somehow the stakes were a little higher with older, more advanced students. Moreover, the method I had developed in teaching small freshmen classes didn't apply to the larger upper-level courses. I settled into lecturing, having some class discussion, and asking the students to work in small groups for the plays or discussion of special topics. Lecturing was a pretty patriarchal structure, but I felt forced into it because of the larger class size. I still wanted students to get to know each other and get to like the course. Working in small groups promoted this. Two refreshing things about teaching were using my creativity as well as my intellect. I really enjoyed learning from the students' journal entries and their presentations.

Marcelline in Dr. Hanley's office, Schaeffer Hall, University of Iowa, summer 1986

Teaching also had some sobering aspects. When I was replacing a professor at Iowa, which I did on three occasions, I was also expected to attend and participate in faculty meetings. It was unsettling being treated as an equal by my former professors. Yet it was fascinating to see how faculty lined up on different issues and to see their radically different positions. This was a surprise. They were not all alike, or like-minded on all points. Yet the chair of the department was always able to let people talk until a consensus was reached.

Research at Russian Lab, Urbana, Illinois

In addition to teaching in the 1980s, it was a gift to do research and meet fascinating Slavic scholars at a special summer laboratory sponsored by the Slavic and East European Center at the University of Illinois. The center director,

Ralph Fisher, obtained a special grant each year to bring professors and graduate students together to participate in this event. Special topics of discussion included Soviet drama in the 1930s taught by a renowned Slavic expert and many other similar literary and historical subjects. I found meeting other Slavic scholars, especially women who were working on social topics like mine in literature and history, to be humbling and exhilarating. I especially remember meeting and becoming friends with Birgitta Ingemanson, who taught Russian language and literature at Washington State University; Olga Owerla, who each year presented a newly translated poem from a Belorussian writer to us; and Mary Zirin, who was translating the biography of Nadezhda Durova, the fascinating woman soldier who fought in the Napoleonic Wars. (Mary later published the Durova biography and called it *Calvary Maiden: Journals of a Russian Officer in the Napoleonic Wars*, which I used when I taught Russian history, and students were captivated by it.) Other significant women scholars I met included Toby Clyman, Diana Greene, and Eve Levin. Of course there were many others—whose names I have now forgotten—who were doing important research.

After my first year at Urbana, I decided we could have a program at the lab on Slavic women, and we did. Mary Zirin and I initially organized it, but it soon became a standard feature, and I learned so much through the papers presented and the scholars who were doing research in Russian women's literature, history, and art. Most of the scholars were women, and this topic gave us a tremendous bonding experience. David Ransel ans a few other men participated in our seminars on Slavic women. I also gave a paper each summer. Doing this was always scary but gratifying. I was always afraid of making some sort of mistake, but writing a paper also advanced my thinking and writing about a given topic in my dissertation. I always appreciated the constructive criticism. Giving these papers prepared me to later give papers at Slavic conferences after I became a professor.

While our summer grant included free housing and use of the marvelous Slavic library at the University of Illinois for our research, we usually took our meals in local restaurants. At supper, we had the opportunity to meet and talk informally with other Slavic scholars. Doing this was an education in itself. University of Illinois historians told us about local bookstores that sold new and used Russian books. These bookstores proved a godsend. When my friend Birgitta mentioned that she posted her books home in a box and didn't take them in her suitcase, that was a helpful hint; I started doing the same. When I first attended the laboratory, I didn't have a car or know how to drive, so I usually took a bus to Chicago and then the train from Chicago to Champaign-Urbana.

Sometimes my graduate student friend Janusz Duzinkiewicz also came, and we traveled together. This time at Illinois was one of the highlights of my second graduate school career.

I can't neglect to say that it was Pat Brodsky, who taught with John at UMKC, who first took me to the program at Urbana. Pat taught Russian and German language, and she as well as her husband, David, participated in the lab. Every year they went there to do research and renew old friendships. It's strange how connections develop and continue. After I left Kansas City and moved to Iowa City, I saw this couple only in Urbana, and it was nice to keep in touch this way. Pat always jokingly referred to our lab as "summer camp for Slavicists." We all did serious work during the day and then enjoyed dinner and sometimes Russian films in the evenings. I remember once discussing a film and realizing that all the PhD experts disagreed about the meaning of the film. That was enlightening.

Falling in Love Again

I also fell in love again with a history student during my second graduate school career. One day I was surprised to come to my desk in the TA room and find a flower there for me. This was pretty romantic. I guess that's how relationships begin—with romance. It turned out the fellow who left me the flower had been married and divorced twice before, so he knew what pain was. I was surprised that he chose me because I was older than he was. Since he was a little bald, people didn't think he was seven years younger. This helped. With this man I too lived as a graduate student in "volunteer poverty," but at least it wasn't so "harsh and dreadful." He had a car and soft furniture in his living room, and he loved refinishing old cars—quite different interests from those of my former husband. Initially he shared an old thirteen-room farmhouse with several relations—a cousin, his younger brother, a childhood friend, and his son. I found this setup a bit difficult, but eventually they all moved out and left him, his son, his dog (Ginger), and me alone. Eventually, I even bought an old car from his friend and learned to drive. My partner was pretty witty and remarked, "You are the only person I know who owned a car before learning to drive."

It took a couple of years for me to feel comfortable driving. I had taken a driver's education class in high school years earlier, but I had never had the opportunity to practice driving because my family had no car. In those days, people didn't lend their cars to young people for practice. After three attempts, I finally passed the driver's test in Iowa City. But I was a cautious driver and drove only from our place in the country to the university or to church on Sunday. I never drove around for pleasure. I was too scared. With my partner's help, I mastered the art of driving and parking. He helped me learn to angle park by lining up ripe zucchini in rows so I could learn to back out between them. If I ran over one, it didn't matter! It proved helpful knowing how to drive when I later got jobs at Hamilton College and the University of Texas at El Paso. We lived happily in the countryside from 1983 to 1987, until we each got a job in different places. (This story is short because this fellow is still alive, but I have been unable to contact him to ask him to read my autobiography and suggest changes or omissions. It didn't seem right to say too much about our time together since it was a good but not long-lasting relationship.)

Women Historians at Iowa, 1980s

Another life-changing event in the 1980s was meeting other women historians at the University of Iowa. The most influential was Linda Kerber. She had a tremendous positive influence on my career and life. She was the second reader for my dissertation and was diligent and helpful to me in that capacity. She also broadened my social network. Linda was an incredible facilitator, and she organized countless lunches to introduce women graduate students to each other and to visiting women historians teaching at Iowa. When faculty members took sabbaticals, a surprisingly high number of women served as their replacements. I remember a Japanese expert especially. She normally taught in Chicago, and she was so delighted with the Iowa students. She was impressed by their high SAT scores and their participation in the classroom. She found teaching to be a pleasure at Iowa, and I did too. It was good to have my experience echoed by someone else.

French historian Sarah Hanley also mentored me, helping me develop intellectually and socially. Before going on a sabbatical, she arranged for me to teach one of her courses in women's history. Since I had taught a course in European women's history for several years, she knew I was experienced in this field. Still, teaching the course at a higher level was a challenge.

Another woman historian at Iowa who mentored me was English historian Carole Levin. She replaced Henry Horowitz for two years, and I learned a lot about teaching from her. My friend Lee worked as her grader, and he told me about some of Carole's assignments for her students. She had them write journals, reflecting on their readings, and this was innovative at that time. I adopted this format in my classes and found it a helpful way to teach students how to write about historical topics. Carole also became a friend of Lee's and mine, and through Carole I met Elaine Kruse, who was writing her dissertation in French history.

All four of these women enhanced my understanding and teaching of European women's history. Linda Kerber's letters of recommendation helped me secure my first two teaching positions. Linda was highly esteemed in American history circles and was one of the founders of American women's history. She was greatly respected, as were her letters on my behalf. A historian at Hamilton College told me in 1987 that he was not going to interview me but changed his mind when he received Linda's letter of recommendation for me. Later, a colleague mentioned that he would have voted for me for tenure at the University of Texas at El Paso if only I had had a letter from Linda in my file. I hadn't known to request it, so I didn't ask her to write on my behalf. I'm sure she would have done so. What we don't know can hurt us! Friendship with Sarah, Carole, and Elaine also enhanced my scholarship and life. Fortunately, in retirement I reconnected with both Elaine and Carole. Elaine taught at Nebraska Wesleyan University in Lincoln for twenty-five years, and Carole still teaches English and women's history and heads the Department of Renaissance Studies at the University of Nebraska–Lincoln. Her dedication to scholarship and publishing many books on Queen Elizabeth have inspired me in my writing about Russian women. It has been a privilege to know and teach with such remarkable women.

Trip to Moscow and Leningrad, 1985

Another highlight of my second graduate career at Iowa was taking a ten-day trip to the Soviet Union in the winter of 1985. I had received a flyer announcing a trip from New York to Helsinki, Moscow, and Leningrad for five hundred dollars available to Slavic specialists. The tour included airfare to Helsinki and back, all the trains and buses while in the Soviet Union, and the hotels and meals. Amazing. All for five hundred dollars. At first I didn't think I could go. I didn't have the money on a teaching assistant's salary. However, since the IRS under Reagan was auditing graduate students who filed their returns as tax exempt, it had sent me a bill for eight hundred dollars for back taxes. I wondered how I would pay for this. I was pretty angry about it because medical interns claimed their stipends as tax free and got away with it, whereas we mere history grads didn't. The university paid no Social Security taxes for us, so we wondered how we could be counted as regular employees for tax purposes. The whole situation was unpleasant. Apparently, the Reagan Administration went after small fry like us teaching assistants and let the big corporations enjoy enormous loopholes in the tax code. I smarted a while at the injustice of it all, but a friend in the geography department told me that lawyers cost five hundred dollars an hour, and there was no guarantee I could win a suit against the IRS. So, I finally decided to take out a student loan for two thousand dollars—eight hundred dollars for the IRS and five hundred dollars for the Russian trip. This was my first and only student loan. I had always received tuition scholarships while in college and grad school, so I hadn't racked up college debt. Since I was about halfway through my dissertation, a modest loan seemed worthwhile. I was delighted to be taking a trip to Russia since I hadn't been there since 1970 and had never seen Moscow.

On this trip, we had several days each in Helsinki, Moscow, and Leningrad—enough time to see the sights and enjoy many cultural events. In Helsinki, we enjoyed a fantastic Scandinavian smorgasbord one evening, following by gambling. I had never gambled before, but one of the fellows invited me to join him, and I thought "Why not?" However, my natural frugality put a two-dollar limit to my evening's spending. Still, it was fun to have done it. I never needed to do it again. The next day it was bitterly cold, so some of us went to the splendid Stockmann department store to shop, look around, and keep warm. It was a magnificent place with several floors, like Macy's in New York City. It had everything from plants to clothes to ice cream cones. I was happy to explore it. Iowa City had no such place. I bought some yarn and a charming miniature weaving loom. I had taken a course in weaving once and had always wanted to do more of it. I knew my friend Lee would figure out how to thread the loom for me. He was a mechanical genius. Sad to say, I never used it and gave it to a neighbor in the country when I left Iowa City.

From Helsinki, we took an overnight train to Moscow. This was fun. It provided my first glimpse of the enormous Russian padushka, or square pillow. They were so comfortable, as was our berth in our little compartment. Riding along, looking out the train window at the falling snow, I felt as if I were in a scene from *Dr. Zhivago*. When we went to a dining car for supper, we noticed a New Year's tree and that cheered us up. (We would call it a Christmas tree, but since the Russians didn't celebrate Christmas, they called it a New Year's tree.) We enjoyed our evening meal immensely before retiring. Our sleeper came with a small adjoining room with an antique nineteenth-century sink and lamp. There were only two of us in each sleeping compartment, so it was quite luxurious. However, I suffered from jet lag, had a hard time falling asleep, and then the next morning could barely get up when we arrived at the station. I was so groggy I could barely dress and depart from the train. It always takes me a few days to adjust to a transatlantic flight, and I could hardly function when we pulled into Moscow station. Each day it became a little easier to get up because we had so many exciting things to see and places to go.

We found Moscow transformed by the snow, as cities often are. We went to the Tretyakov Gallery art museum and saw one room with life-size portraits of the three grandsons of Catherine the Great: Tsar Alexander I, Constantine, and Tsar Nicholas I. They were all so blond and handsome; I was overcome looking at them. I had read so much about them but had no idea they were such handsome, dashing figures. The portraits of Russia's finest poet, Pushkin, and the writer Gogol also thrilled me. I had no idea Pushkin was so bonny with beautiful curly hair, and that Gogol was so comely. I was surprised that such young men had written such influential literature. It was like meeting two of one's beloveds.

In Moscow we also went to some ballets at the Bolshoi Opera, and they were splendid. The dancing and music were exquisite. One ballet was *Spartacus*. I had never heard of it. I thought, "Only the Soviets would create a ballet about a Roman slave revolt." Apparently it is also in the Western repertoire, but I hadn't been aware of it before this trip. While the ballet was magnificent, it was equally fascinating watching young Muscovites promenading during the intermission. Young women wore their finest frocks and shawls, parading around in a circle, inspecting everyone. No doubt they were as intrigued by us foreigners as we were with them.

Another day we took an excursion to the monastery Trinity Lavra of St. Sergius, about fifty miles away. It surprised me that a religious complex was on our itinerary since in 1970 our guide had forbidden us to go to any churches in Leningrad. But Moscow in 1985 was a different world because of Gorbachev's perestroika reforms. At Trinity I saw some unusual sights. In one small chapel, a priest was washing his face in the spigot, splashing himself with holy water. After he had finished, an old lady took a bottle labeled "Pepsi Cola" in Cyrillic script and filled it with holy water to take home. That was unique! We toured some of the famous churches, saw a copy of Rublev's famous icon *The Trinity*, and then were led to a splendid gift shop. This astonished me. We looked around and bought whatever we wanted. I bought a medium-sized picture of the monastery done by wood burning. I also bought some small enamel crosses for friends.

One fellow in our group bought a censor, the sort the priest uses on holy days to bless the congregation with incense. As our bus was leaving the area and waiting for an enormously long train to cross in front of us, he came down the aisle of the bus waving the censor, pretending to be a priest. We all thought it quite funny, but the bus driver didn't. We were glad, however, that we were soon able to cross the tracks before another one came along. It all seemed a miracle.

Some of our cultural forays were more successful than others. Once, we joined a Soviet friendship group to discuss international affairs in a giant auditorium, but it was a rather stilted affair, and we felt a bit confused by it. One evening we attended an entertainment program put on for some workers, and the performance was poor. However, it was enchanting looking around at the people attending the show to see what sort of clothes they wore, their hairdos, and their responses to the program. This was an exercise in social observation, and it was fun.

Because the Russian Orthodox Church follows the Gregorian calendar and celebrates Christmas and Easter about two weeks after we do in the West, we were able to attend a Christmas Eve service in Moscow when we were there in early January. I realized right away that I had forgotten that women wear a head covering in that church, and the only scarf I had was an enormous mohair one I wore to keep my face covered in the subzero temperatures. It was much too warm in the crowded church to wear the hood of my down coat or my mohair scarf, but I knew enough to drape my head with my scarf despite the discomfort. When the ushers passed an offering plate around, I was startled to see that it had a plastic cover with a slot, so one could put in rubles but not take any out. Since it was late at night, and I was still suffering from jet lag, I didn't get as much from the service as I had hoped. It wasn't the spiritual high I had expected. Maybe I was just too hot and too tired. I don't know. Maybe we didn't stay long enough to experience the beauty of the service. They are unusually long, and we finally left before communion. We took a taxi there and back at little cost.

Other fascinating trips included Peter the Great's Moscow retreat Kolomenskoye, several palaces, and even a peace museum for the victims of World War II. The day we visited the charming wooden village of Kolomenskoye, the strangest part was seeing a corpse in a little church. No one had expected that and we were all astonished at the display. Apparently, a funeral was to take place later.

The ballet we saw in Leningrad was based on a Soviet Georgian story about a young girl's refusal to honor her father's betrothal of her to a fellow tribesman. She wanted to go to the university instead. It was a bittersweet ballet. In one scene, the dancers brought out an enormous Persian carpet, and when they unrolled it, there inside was a TV for a wedding gift. This was the unexpected, funny part. The ending, when the father kills his daughter for disobeying him, was the saddest scene of the dance. I later spoke to a professor of Russian literature in our group, and she knew the Georgian writer and story on which the ballet was based.

Another excursion took us to the restored palace of Catherine the Great at Peterhof. It was magnificent. Most of us were enjoying our visit to the splendid place when one fellow in our group asked our guide if Lenin would have approved of spending such huge sums of money to restore the Tsarist building that had been shelled during World War II. He wondered if Lenin wouldn't have preferred spending money on housing for the workers. This temporarily flustered our guide. She recovered her wits, but I can't remember what she said in return. In fact, Lenin did preserve historic buildings, so the fellow obviously did not know much about Soviet history.

One of the most touching incidents I had in Leningrad was walking through a World War II memorial to the 2 million Leningrad victims who died during the war. As I walked along, an old man brushed past me, saying quietly in Russian, "Mir" (peace). I was deeply touched. Except for the Civil War, I don't think the United States ever lost a million soldiers in war. All together, the Soviets lost a staggering 25 million in World War II, so I understood why he said "peace." The winter of 1985–86 was bitterly cold in Russia and western Europe, and we were often happy to just ride around Leningrad in our bus, viewing from our warm seats the famous churches and buildings we had read about in our history and literature books.

Recently reading a review of four books about the siege of Leningrad, I noticed that scholars now find that more than eight hundred thousand civilians died during the "Season of Death" in the winter of 1941–42. All together, 1.6 million to 2 million Soviet citizens perished during the German Blockade. That was more than all the war losses in the United States from 1776 to 1975.[16] And Leningrad was just one place in Russia that suffered during World War II. Some cities, like Stalingrad, were totally obliterated.

In Moscow, we stayed at a posh hotel built for the winter Olympics. It was far from the metro, so we were dependent on our tour bus to take us everywhere. In Leningrad, we stayed at the luxurious Pribaltiyskaya hotel built by the Finns. From it we could get to a city bus and the metro. In both places, we saw some very drunk American students as well as Finnish tourists. Once, the elevator opened and a drunken tourist fell out face first onto the floor. That dumfounded us. Apparently the Finns brought blue jeans to Leningrad to sell or

---

16. See Anthony Beevor, "The Unmentionable Season of Death," *New York Review of Books,* January 18, 2018, 43–44. Beevor reviews fours works: A. Peri, *The War Within: Diaries from the Siege of Leningrad;* S. Yarov, *Leningrad 1941–1942: Morality in a City under Siege;* P. Barskova, *Besieged Leningrad: Aesthetic Responses to Urban Disaster;* and P. Barskova (ed.), *Written in the Dark: Five Poets in the Siege of Leningrad.*

exchange for vodka, which they drank on their drunken sprees. We saw more of these men on the train home from Leningrad to Helsinki as we left. A few times Russians approached me, asking to buy my tennis shoes or the down coat I was wearing. I was unprepared for this. Had I been thinking, I probably could have traded my down coat for a Russian fur coat, but I was too stunned to reply. All I could think was "What would I wear if I sold my coat?" Also, we had been warned not to engage in black market deals. The only thing I did was buy some beautiful Russian stamps when I was leaving. I had a lot of rubles left, and I couldn't take them with me out of the country since at that time it was a nonconvertible currency. I had tried to buy my son a hand-carved chess set but saw only plastic ones. Indeed, I didn't buy many souvenirs besides those from the Trinity monastery. I had taken a pair of jeans, but I left them and my flannel nightgown for the cleaning lady at our hotel. They were the most appropriate things I could think of to give as gifts.

Receiving my PhD degree, University of Iowa, 1986

The food and drink on our trip were included and were quite good. In Moscow, we had a vegetable beef borscht that was the best I have ever eaten. Delicious bread accompanied all our meals. Apparently the recipe had not been changed since the time of Stalin. Some of our group complained about the lack of salad, but I didn't miss it since I prefer cooked food. We sometimes drank tasty Russian beer and occasionally light Georgian wine or champagne. We never had Pepsi or vodka, and I was glad because vodka does not agree with me.

Soon it was time to return to the university to resume ordinary life again. Eventually, I finished my seven-hundred-page PhD thesis on Russian and Soviet women from 1860 to 1939. I even won the prestigious D. C. Spriestersbach Dissertation Prize for the best dissertation in the social sciences in 1986, with a cash prize. That was an honor, but a rather overwhelming one with a party at the president's house to celebrate. No matter what honors I received, I never thought I deserved them. I did attend the PhD graduation ceremony, and this picture shows the president of the university congratulating me in 1987.

Iowa City Support Groups in the 1980s

Reading one of my devotional books one morning reminded me how going to Adult Children of Alcoholics (ACOA) meetings changed my life in the late 1980s. A church friend in Iowa City had told me about the program earlier, but I had thought, "That's a good program for her, but I don't need it." However, after finishing my PhD and going on several job interviews and not getting any offers, despite good recommendations from my professors, I began to suspect something was "wrong" with me. I didn't know what it was, but I knew something was amiss.

I didn't realize I was suffering from low self-esteem, and this came across in my job interviews. Consciously I wanted a position, but subconsciously I thought I didn't deserve it and was sabotaging myself. I didn't yet fathom the huge role that denial played in my life. It had protected me when I was growing up in my alcoholic family, and it protected me in much of my marriage, but it was undermining my ability to get a teaching situation.

Going to ACOA meetings helped me accept myself, my fears, and my foibles. Talking with others who had experienced the childhood trauma of an alcoholic household was truly liberating. I felt less fearful. Eventually, I was able to accept and approve of myself enough to get a one-year job at Hamilton College in New York state and then a tenure-track position at the University of Texas at El Paso. After living in Texas for a while, my priest there suggested I might want to investigate the support group for codependents (CODA). At first I thought, "Oh, no. I'm just healing from the impact of my father's alcoholism, and now I have to deal with my own issues." But, his advice proved correct, and I found the CODA groups very helpful.

In her book *The Language of Letting Go*, Melody Beattie, author of *Codependent No More* and *Beyond Codependency*, writes about denial in ways that reminded me of my youth. She writes:

> When I was a child, I used denial to protect myself and my family. I protected myself from seeing things too painful to see and feelings too overwhelming to feel. . . . The negative aspect of using denial was that I lost touch with myself and my feelings. I became able to participate in harmful situations without even knowing I was hurting. I was able to tolerate a great deal of pain and abuse without the foggiest notion it was abnormal.[17]

---

17. Melody Beattie, *The Language of Letting Go* (Center City, MN: Hazelden, 1990), 249–51.

I too learned to participate in my own abuse. I did this in marriage. I continually told myself that if I were just prettier or more intelligent, then my husband would love me. I thought it was my fault that he didn't show any love for me. I didn't understand then that neither of us was capable of showing much affection. In the same passage, Beattie goes on to say:

> Denial protected me from pain, but it also rendered me blind to my feelings, my needs, and myself. . . .
>
> Eventually, I began to recover. I had a glimpse of awareness about my pain, my feelings, and my behaviors. I began to see myself, the world, as we were.
>
> Life participated in this process with me. It is a gentle teacher. . . .
>
> It's an exciting process this journey called recovery, but I understand I sometimes use denial to help me get through the rough spots. I'm also aware that denial is a friend, and an enemy. . . .

She ends the section with a prayer:

> *Help me strive for awareness and acceptance, but also help me practice gentleness and compassion for myself—and others—for those times I have used denial.*[18]

---

18. Beattie, *The Language of Letting Go*, 249–51.

Chapter VII

Teaching, 1980s and 1990s

Hamilton College

After teaching at the University of Iowa for several years as a teaching assistant and then as an assistant professor in Soviet and European women's history, I was hired to teach Russian and Soviet history as well as Western civilization for one year at Hamilton College in Clinton, New York. It was my first real job, so I was pretty excited. My friend Lee Anderson helped me move. He was teaching that year at Nebraska Wesleyan University in Lincoln, Nebraska, so it was a break between us, and I was pretty lonesome. However, I was busy teaching several courses each semester, plus a new class in Soviet cultural history during the January term, so I didn't have too much time to whine and moan.

The History Department at Hamilton had made it very clear to me that theirs was a one-year appointment, and that I needed to go on job interviews. They financed every Slavic and history conference I attended, and I was grateful for that. They paid my way to the American Slavic Association conference in Boston that fall. It was good to see some old friends like Birgitta Ingemanson there, and my cousin Lester Hutton, who also taught Russian and Soviet history in Massachusetts. I seldom saw him, so that was a treat. Teaching interviews were few at this conference, but there were several at the American Historical Association conference in Washington, DC, that December, and there I chaired a session as well as interviewed for positions. I had gone on one seemingly successful interview to Ursinus College in Pennsylvania before the AHA meeting, so I felt fairly confident about getting a position when leaving Hamilton.

I found teaching at Hamilton College disconcerting. The students were more introverted and less cooperative than those at Iowa. They wrote papers quite well, but I had a hard time engaging them in class discussion. I didn't know that college students vary. It was frustrating adjusting my teaching techniques to this introverted group. The first semester I taught Russian history, I asked the students to sign up to prepare part of a play to present to the class. Imagine my dismay one day to find the students refusing to cooperate and unprepared for their play performance. I was dumbfounded. Nothing like this had happened before, and I didn't know what to do when they boldly declared they were not doing the play. I didn't know how to fill in the remaining class hour. I felt betrayed and angry. I can't remember now what I did, except go to confession at church to discuss my anger with the priest.

Still, when I taught a short course in Soviet cultural history in January, students who signed up for the play presentation were cooperative and performed well. One fellow even wore a woman's wig to make his presentation of a female character more convincing. Maybe it was the students in the two classes, or perhaps I was more explicit in the second class. I was shocked when the young women asked to sit in a separate circle from the fellows when we were discussing Gladkov's 1920s novel *Cement*. I guess they did not feel comfortable disagreeing with the guys about the role of the liberated communist heroine, Dasha Chumalova. The fellows generally argued that Dasha was inconsiderate of her husband's feelings. In the book, Dasha tells her husband, Gleb, that she knew he had had other women when he was away fighting in the Civil War, and didn't he think she was equally entitled to a lover during this time? The men in the class found Dasha crass, while the women sympathized with her. This was a learning experience for me. At Iowa, I think the young women would have been able to hold their own in a classroom argument, but maybe since Hamilton was a small, liberal arts college, the students knew each other too well, and the girls didn't want to be tagged as feminists. I never knew for sure why they behaved the way they did. Very few students ever came to my office to talk about the class or their problems. This was a disappointment. I had expected Hamilton to be more like Park College, with close student-faculty relations, but it wasn't, at least not for me.

One of the highlights during my time at Hamilton was participating in a feminist study group with other faculty members. I thoroughly enjoyed this group and got to know one of the French language professors well. I followed her advice and used Marguerite de Navarre's sixteenth-century novel *The Heptameron* in my Western civilization course when teaching the next year at the University of Texas at El Paso. There are not many books by women to use in the first semester of Western civilization, so I was glad to have this one. Moreover, I thought her work showed the corruption in the Catholic church, especially among the friars and monks in France, just as well as in Rabelais's novel *Gargantua*, and I was happy to use it.

Another good experience was facilitating a feminist theology study group at the local Episcopal church, with the approval of the priest. Some of the women in the college feminist group also belonged to that church, so we read some female theologians I had studied earlier in Iowa City. We also incorporated some of the feminist writings I had used in my European women's history courses, like Rosemary Ruether's *Women of Spirit*.

The church in Clinton was very welcoming and provided me a "shepherd" to include me in the foyer dinners and other church programs. My church life was rich and full, and I was grateful for that. Some of the people at church helped me understand the conservatism and racism in upstate New York. I had expected the entire state to be liberal like Manhattan, but that was a mistake. It was a lesson in how different rural and urban environments are.

I must admit that when I attended a couple of sessions of ACOA at Hamilton, the students were very welcoming and kind. I didn't want to put any of them on the spot and soon found another ACOA group in a nearby town. Still, I had been shocked that so many of the intelligent, beautiful, handsome, rich, and talented students came from alcoholic, dysfunctional families and that they had to be the mature ones in their families since their parents were not.

Indeed, one student missed a few weeks of class the second semester because when he went home for the semester break, he was afraid to leave his mother and siblings at the mercy of his alcoholic father. He developed a terrible infection in his arm and couldn't return to class on time. He told me all this when he explained why he had missed so many sessions. My heart ached for him. What a quandary he lived in.

At Iowa, too, I had had a male student come to see me about finishing my class because he had missed so many weeks of school. He confessed that he had become an alcoholic at eighteen years of age. That astounded me, but we made arrangements for him to make up the work he had missed.

One of the final consolations at Hamilton was the local FM National Public Radio station, which served Clinton, New York, and Kingston, Ontario. It played classical music all night long, and since I wasn't sleeping so well while living there, it was a godsend. Initially, my teaching didn't go so well; I missed my partner, Lee; I had the pressure of getting a job for the next year; and I had conferences to attend and interviews to prepare for. I had a lot to keep me awake. My only complaint about the music station was that they played Ralph Vaughn Williams's "The Lark Ascending" too often. It's a lovely piece but a bit much night after night. Yet the classical music was a boon during my sleepless nights.

Another good fortune was having my son visit me while I was teaching there. He was attending Johns Hopkins University, studying economics, and I was delighted by having him come on Valentine's weekend. We had planned to visit a brewery in nearby Utica, but it snowed so much—about three feet outside my living room window—that we were unable to go. Even though the city managed to keep the roads pretty clear, I was afraid to drive in such huge piles of snow.

Life in El Paso

Teaching at the University of Texas at El Paso

While I initially thought I would take a position at a small liberal arts college in Pennsylvania after my good interview with them, that school delayed offering me a contract, so I decided to explore a situation at the University of Texas at El Paso (UTEP). At the American historical conference, I had been convinced that I didn't want to go to El Paso, Texas—it was just too far away from major cities and good Slavic libraries. The historians I met were nice enough, but after living on the East Coast, El Paso seemed like the end of the earth. However, going to the interview there in February, when it was cold and snowy in New York, made El Paso more attractive. As I was heading off to my interview at UTEP, the head of the history department at Ursinus College called me and was quite nasty, even swearing at me, over the telephone. So I thought, "Why not give UTEP a chance?" A dean at Hamilton told me that I owed it to myself to check out UTEP. I had never heard that phrase before—that I owed it to myself to check out something. It seemed like a good one, and I've used it on other occasions when facing a dilemma.

When I got to El Paso and interacted with the members of the department, we all clicked, and I took the position there teaching Russian/Soviet history and Western civilization. While I liked and respected my colleagues at UTEP, I soon realized they were more high-powered than I was. I wanted to publish my dissertation, and indeed had several offers to do so, but I lacked the self-confidence to do so right away. They were enthusiastic about publishing, while I experienced a failure of nerve to publish my dissertation quickly.

When I tried once to talk to one of my colleagues about dreams, he was horrified, and I realized that emotionally and spiritually we were on different planets. We also had some fundamental differences in our teaching. I felt a great responsibility to teach my students to write, while most of my colleagues taught huge American history classes, had teaching assistants, and just gave multiple-choice exams. In contrast, I had my students write journals about the readings in the course and gave only essay exams. So I spent a lot more time teaching and grading than my colleagues did. Reading the student papers, I also got to know them, which I appreciated. I felt uneasy when some of my colleagues disparaged the students at UTEP. Only later at Lithuania Christian College did I understand the frustrations they experienced teaching first-year students. At UTEP I was fortunate to have upper-class students, who were usually diligent and hard-working, so I never needed to complain about them.

Many of my UTEP students liked performing in the plays I assigned in each course, and they gained new insights into cultural history. This was gratifying. Sometimes they surprised me, especially my students in Western civilization. One April first, the class presenting Ibsen's *A Doll's House* reversed the gender roles, with men playing the women's roles, and women playing the men's. This was very humorous yet impressive. Seeing a woman behave condescendingly to her husband was thought-provoking. One play group made puppets to enact a play by García Lorca. Again, this was innovative and fun. Another student was impressed with John Osborne's play *Luther*, which he and two others presented. It was the highlight of the semester for him. I especially remember one Vietnam veteran student who said to me after the presentation of Aristophanes's anti-war play *Lysistrata* that now he understood why civilians said "Make love, not war" when he returned to the States. A woman in the same class was also touched by the play but for different reasons. Because the play centers on Greek women's sex strike to get their husbands to return from a long war, she was shocked at the language. She told me the translators must have made some mistakes because of the theme and language. It was then I discovered that youth sometimes think they are the only ones who care about sex. So this young woman was able to make a new connection with Classical Greek women from hundreds of years earlier. Many students wrote in their journals about how good it felt to connect with other students when presenting their group project. That was my aim, and I felt satisfied when this assignment worked in a number of different ways—intellectually, politically, emotionally, and socially.

Generally, I found my students well prepared and disciplined in their studies, so they were a pleasure to teach. Occasionally, they didn't get the point of a book. Once I used a book about British cultural imperialism in Egypt, but only one student, a philosophy major, got the point. I had thought that since many of the students were Latinos they would pick up on cultural imperialism, but they didn't.

Gradually, I began to feel like an outsider at UTEP. Maybe I made myself one, I don't know. At the end of the semester, I remember feeling sad and crying when my classes ended because together the students and I had created something special. My colleagues didn't share this view or understand my reaction. The history department secretary comprehended, and said she too cried at the end of the semester when she was a student. So I was on the same emotional wavelength with her but not with my colleagues. In retrospect I can see that I fell into the same pattern that my husband had. I felt more at ease socializing with my older students than with my colleagues. This wasn't a conscious decision on my part, it just happened.

Another issue was feeling uncomfortable with my colleagues drinking together at a bar on Friday afternoons. No one got drunk, and I should have felt safe, but I didn't. One colleague always teased me about my not having tenure and that made me uneasy. It was mainly one fellow who did this, never my female colleagues. Maybe it was because my colleagues mostly taught American history and I didn't. Who knows? We just didn't seem to have a lot in common except when we participated in some January seminars.

One colleague was good at grant writing, and she often obtained grants and speakers for special programs on Southwestern and Indian history. I enjoyed taking part in these study groups. They were challenging, and I still loved learning, but they had nothing to do with my work in Russian history. Three colleagues at UTEP seemed interested in my research. One was a fellow in political science named Tony Krushevsky. He was a Polish émigré, and he found my work worthwhile. However, he wasn't part of my daily or weekly life. Two other colleagues, who taught European history, shared more of my interests. Several colleagues were kind but were busy teaching, writing books, and serving on university committees.

At UTEP, I served on several master's committees—some in the English department, a few in the political science department, and two in the history department. I enjoyed getting to know my German history colleague, with whom I directed the MA students' research: one on the Evian Conference in France during the Interwar period and one an oral history of a Holocaust survivor. The latter was particularly poignant.

I was so impressed by the use of oral history that I later assigned my Lithuanian history students an oral history project. At Lithuania Christian College we were situated in eastern Europe on one of the crossroads of World War II, so I asked the students to interview their grandparents and then write an oral history of their lives as civilians during the war. These were always the best papers the students wrote, captivating but painful to read.

At UTEP, I also enjoyed participating in the history and Russian language clubs. I especially liked getting to know students through these informal venues. Overall, I can say I enjoyed my time with students there because the students were cooperative and usually diligent in doing their work.

Struggles in Research and Writing at UTEP

While teaching at UTEP, I continued attending the summer Slavic lab at Illinois, but I was criticized for doing so. The head of the department once accused me of wasting my time going there. His remarks hurt my feelings, and it was hard for me to explain to him the acceptance and support for my research and writing that I experienced there. Now I realize how poorly I communicated with my colleagues.

In the summer of 1992, I received a grant from the Woodrow Wilson Institute. It enabled me to consult nineteenth- and twentieth-century women's diaries, memoirs, and biographies at the Library of Congress that had not been available to me elsewhere. My grant provided enough for me to rent a room while doing my research. In the evenings I had time to have dinner with my friend Rosemary, the rare books librarian at the Library of Congress.

Rosemary showed me the tsar's collection the library possessed, and I was interested to see that the tsar and tsarina read books in English to their children, since that was their common language. His native language was Russian and hers German, but they both knew English. Some of the other books were also unexpected. One was a Roman Catholic priest's manual that indicated the penance imposed for various sins at confession. For decades, the Russian Orthodox Church had fought the influence of the Roman Catholic Church, and I was certainly surprised to see this manual, which I had read about in one of the French historian Flandrin's books when teaching History of the Family at Iowa during the 1980s.

While teaching at UTEP, I wrote a variety of book reviews and conference papers. I reviewed Jo Burr Margadant's book *Madame le Professeur* for *History of Education Quarterly*, and it appeared in the Spring 1992 issue. This was the first book review I had written, and I knew I was supposed to find some minor or major flaw in the book, but I couldn't find any. It was excellent. Margadant's book covered the lives of French women teachers around 1900, and the only flaw I could see was that she didn't say anything about nuns as educators, and many upper-class French girls attended convent schools. Still, this was a picky criticism. The book became a prize winner and was well received in the profession. No wonder I couldn't find much to criticize. Myself, I was able to use some of her information about married French women teachers in comparing them with Russian women who were also more likely to be married than their English or German counterparts in the 1890s and 1920s.

Later, I reviewed Anna Horsborough-Porter's collection of interviews titled *Memories of Revolution: Russian Women Remember* for *Slavic Review* (1996).

Horsborough-Porter's work covered Russian girls' school experiences following the 1917 October Revolution. It was based on interviews with Russian émigrés who had moved to England. The discussions occurred decades after the revolutions when many of the interviewees were in their nineties, but their memories remained clear and their stories adventurous. They charmingly revealed an aspect of the revolution seldom seen, the viewpoint of children. I ended up using quotations from some of them years later in my work *Remarkable Russian Women*.

While at UTEP, I wrote several papers for various conferences. My misgiving was that the papers wouldn't be "good enough." Although I was an authority on the topics, it was still unsettling to present a paper. One paper was titled "A Class and Party Analysis of Soviet Female Purge Victims in the 1930s," which I presented at a women's history conference in Austin, Texas, in the early 1990s. Although a fellow in the audience challenged me about the schema of my work, it wasn't a scathing criticism, and I defended my analysis. Another paper made me uneasy because I couldn't get a handle on the existential language for discussing the dilemmas of the Russian Communist Alexandra Kollontai and the English writer Virginia Woolf. Both came from upper-class families and grappled with feminist concerns about authenticity, alienation, anxiety, consciousness, and woman's construction of the self in patriarchal societies. Both were beautiful women and married, but both rejected becoming "trophy wives." Both wanted to be "subjects," not objects, especially "sex objects," as Simone de Beauvoir later phrased it. Kollontai wrote about the necessity to leave her lover when she no longer felt respected in their relationship in her *Autobiography of a Sexually Emancipated Communist Woman*. Woolf wrote about the problems feminists faced in some of her novels and her diaries.

I thought the term "feminist existentialist" applied to them both, although I had a hard time expressing my ideas as clearly as I wanted. Both needed courage to be feminists: Kollontai faced ridicule and condescension from male Bolsheviks like Lenin and Trotsky, and Woolf outlined the problems English women faced in her work *Three Guineas*. The title of my paper was "The Courage to Be: Two Feminist Existentialist Writers in the 1920s: Alexandra Kollontai and Virginia Woolf," and I presented it at the Western Social Science Association conference in April 1993. I never published it because I thought it lacked clarity. An easier paper to write was one titled "Russian and German Female Students in the 1930s: Paramilitary Training," and I presented it at the Western Social Science Association conference in April 1996.

Publications that emerged from some of my conference papers included "Soviet Dual-Career Marriages in the 1920s: A Literary and Class Analysis" in *Proceedings of the Second International Conference on Women in Higher Education*, San Diego, 1989, and "Voices of Struggle: Soviet Women in the 1920s: A Study of Gender, Class, and Literature," first given at the AAASS Slavic Conference in Hawaii in 1990 and then published in *Feminist Issues*, Fall 1991.

I also published a chapter titled "Women in Russian Society from the Tsars to Yeltsin" in the book *Russian Women in Politics and Society* in 1996. This chapter arose from meeting political scientist Norma Noonan at the conference in Hawaii. She was editing a book and asked me to participate. Indeed, she asked me to write the introduction to the book but didn't like my interpretation and kept changing it. My understanding of Soviet history was too liberal for her.

Social Life

Feeling isolated and alone in El Paso in the early 1990s, I remember asking God to provide a dog or a male friend for companionship. Much to my surprise I soon met a fellow at the Wednesday noon communion service at the Episcopal Cathedral. I had nervously asked the priest there to bless a manuscript I was submitting to a journal, and he agreed but wanted to read it first. We were talking about the manuscript at the end of the service one day when a guy named Dick heard me talking about emancipated women and my need for a man in my life. He was impressed and called me for a date. That was the beginning of our romance, which lasted until I brought my mother to live with me several years later. Then he just disappeared. He was a Southern gentleman, an elementary school teacher, and had a great sense of humor. Although he sometimes asked me to marry him, I couldn't feature it since he was politically so much more conservative than I was. Still, we had fun and shared companionship while our relationship lasted.

Taking Care of My Mother

Whether it was wise or not, I brought my mother to live with me in El Paso after she had recovered from an operation. She wasn't able to return to her own home, and she was unhappy in the nursing home in La Porte. Initially, I didn't realize she was suffering from Parkinson's disease and dementia. She hadn't been diagnosed with either of those ailments when I decided to take care of her. Since she had recovered enough to dress and feed herself, I thought the least I could do was make her last years pleasant. At first, I didn't know what caring for someone with health problems entailed. It turned out she fell down every night, and it was hard for me to get her back to bed. While she easily returned to sleep, I did not. I'd be anxious, worrying that she might fall again, and too keyed up to relax and doze off. Eventually, I realized that caring for my mother was a distraction to finishing my book, but it had seemed the right thing to do at the time. I can't blame her for not finishing my book more quickly. It was my own lack of self-confidence that kept me from completing it in a timely manner instead of expanding it.

I found a Lutheran adult day care center that mother could attend from nine till three, but that didn't leave me much time for teaching, writing lectures, and editing my manuscript. Of course, I met some helpful people while caring for my mother. Her neurologist kindly helped me understand her disease and manage her medicine by writing her prescription to M. Hutton (Madeline for her, but Marcelline for me), so I could cover it on my insurance. Mother's Social Security was only $232 per month, and initially that covered only the $100 per month for her Parkinson's medication and part of her care at the Lutheran day care establishment. It didn't provide for food or nonprescription drugs like Tylenol and other over-the-counter medicines that she needed. It stretched my budget caring for her, but we managed.

Knowing Mother as an Adult

Getting to know you, getting to know all about you.

Mother lived with me during the mid-1990s, and I was privileged to learn a lot about her and to appreciate her as a person, not just my mother. She told me stories of her childhood that I'd never heard before. I had never known why she had false teeth, and it turned out that my aunt Gladys was driving a small vehicle when she had an accident in which Mother lost her front tooth. Eventually mother had to have all her top teeth pulled and get false teeth. Nor had I ever heard the story of my Swedish grandfather's participation in a Ku Klux Klan parade in downtown La Porte in the 1920s. Mother told me that once when they went to town, they had to get down on the floor of the wagon because men in white robes with torches were marching down the street, and she wasn't supposed to look at them.

After this revelation, I asked a friend of mother's, who was a librarian, about the role of the Klan in La Porte, and she sent me some intriguing material on it. Apparently, the Klan in La Porte County was mainly engaged in anti-Catholic behavior, like burning a cross on land across from a farmer whose son had married a Catholic. However, it must have been racist as well because La Porte had very few black people for a city its size, especially compared to nearby South Bend, Michigan City, or Gary, which had sizeable black populations. According to the article, the Klan declined after a Catholic was shot on a train going to South Bend. It seems to have been the Klan's influence that "blacks did not stay overnight in La Porte," as my father once explained to me.

Here are two pictures of my mother in El Paso. The first shows Mother with my friend Helmi in the front of my house on Whitaker Lane. Helmi was a middle-aged friend who had been my student at UTEP. Later we became good friends. She was married to a man in the army, and they had a beautiful home in the suburbs. They had a swimming pool, and I loved visiting them and playing in the water. Helmi was very kind to my mother, and I was surprised that she and my mother bonded because Helmi's flamboyant personality and my mother's conservative nature were so different. Who can account for the chemistry between people? I was grateful that Helmi not only came to visit my mother when she lived with me but also saw her in the nursing home when Mother's health deteriorated.

Mother (left) and friend Helmi at my home in El Paso

Mother (in eyeglasses) at Helmi's daughter's wedding dinner, El Paso, 1990s

My Home in El Paso

I appreciated my home in El Paso because it was surrounded by trees in the front: two enormous pecan trees, some evergreens, and others whose names I've forgotten. My house had three bedrooms and three baths—enough room to care for my mom and to house visitors and later on French and Japanese students. Although the house had trees in front, and large cactuses too, it had no grass to cut, which was a boon. I had to have my gardener, Gilbert, trim the trees twice a year, but I could take care of the bushes in the front of the house. Not so those in the back—they were too tall. In the back garden there were geraniums and rose bushes, including one that bore lavender flowers. Looking out my kitchen window while doing dishes I could take in this beauty. When I felt playful, I wore a rose in my hair to class.

El Paso border culture was more colorful and expressive than the repressed Nordic culture in which I had been raised. In El Paso, I felt comfortable wearing dangly earrings and flowers in my hair. This would have been considered too flirty in La Porte or Iowa City, but in El Paso, it was OK.

I was probably a decade older than my colleagues at UTEP, so they didn't understand what it was like to be a caregiver for one's parent. While children grow up and require less care, the elderly require more help. As a single woman, I found mother's care a responsibility and a burden. My siblings who lived in Santa Fe and Tucson had not wanted me to move mother from the nursing home in La Porte, and they were unwilling to help. I was alienated and alone taking care of her. After two years of sleep deprivation because of mother's nightly falls, I was also angry. I sought help from a therapist, and I also went to the YMCA twice a week to kick the water since I surely didn't want to kick my mother working out my anger.

Caring for my mom, I did get to know her as a person instead of just my parent, but it was a bittersweet experience. My neighbors were a big help. One neighbor would come to help me get my mother up when she fell during the day, if I couldn't lift her. Many afternoons my mother and I made apple walnut cake and served that with ice cream to these neighbors. Usually mother peeled the apples and diced the nuts while sitting at a table. Doing this gave her something useful to do. We all enjoyed each other's company, and it made the afternoons go faster having company.

Another neighbor, Frank Oppenheimer, who lived a couple blocks away in Kern Place, understood my situation in caring for my mom. He always invited both of us to his Saturday night soirees. He served wonderful chocolates, which my mom enjoyed, and great Scotch, which I fancied. He was always so gentlemanly helping my mother out of the car and into his home. Frank was a German Jew who had escaped Hitler. He was a fabulous raconteur, and we all loved listening to his stories of living in Germany in the 1920s, and in Belgium and France in the 1930s. His accounts of being drafted into the French army made us laugh uproariously.

Frank also aided me in the research for my book. I had a lot of data from German sources, and I couldn't always translate it. He had studied law in Bern,

Switzerland, so he could help me with legal phrases I couldn't quite fathom even with a dictionary. Sometimes I also asked him to read some French sources and let me know if he thought them pertinent to my study, and if I should read them myself. His knowledge of languages and his intellectual demeanor made him a wonderful friend. He and my mom were the same age, and I often thought he would have been a wonderful father. Frank was so urbane and suave, very gentlemanly and courteous—so unlike my boorish, alcoholic father. Yet I discovered that he had been a demanding taskmaster to his own children. Odd, how we interact with each other!

After caring for my mother for a few years, I realized I couldn't do it anymore. It was a dreadful discovery. Mother could no longer go to the toilet alone, and I feared hurting my back lifting her. I had to be in good health to work and provide for myself, so I made the decision to place her in a nursing home. It was the hardest decision I ever made. Harder than getting divorced. I felt so guilty. So sad. I tried some intermediate situations first, but none of those caregivers could cope since Mother required care day and night.

Fortunately I was able to find a nursing home that was near my home and the university. That way I could frequently stop to see her. At first, I fed her lunch and supper but eventually her health declined further and she needed a feeding tube. This happened one summer when I was in New York attending a Slavic program at Columbia University. I had gone to this program partly to learn more about Russian imperial history and partly to collect the three-thousand-dollar stipend it offered. This was the summer my income from UTEP ended, and I didn't have employment for the fall, so I was worried about money. By living frugally in New York I was able to save about two thousand dollars to tide me over that summer and fall.

My sister lived in Santa Fe, so she came down to El Paso when the doctor put the feeding tube in mother. When I returned home from New York, I could see that mother had declined, and that saddened me. At the nursing home, it was hard visiting mother because I had to pass many and crippled people to get to her room. For strength to do this, I learned to pray for God's help on my way up the elevator. I found it emotionally overwhelming. My mother never looked so bad physically, but many of the other patients did. Once they put a woman who was dying in my mother's room, and I asked the nurse how long it took someone to die. She answered, "Three days." They apparently gave the person sedatives during this time but no food or drink. That was sobering to learn. In the nursing home I did find some consolation. Other children also came to feed their parents during meal times, and I got to know some of them. We were almost a community.

Occasionally there was humor. Once I had taken mother to the dining room for lunch, and after she had eaten, she leaned over to me and whispered, "I think I am pregnant." I could hardly keep from laughing out loud. I didn't want to hurt her feelings, so I only smiled inwardly and thought, "Pregnant at eighty-five? I don't think so." But the exchange was poignant.

As mother's dementia worsened, she began to call me her sister. I didn't mind because she knew that someone had come to see her. At this time my friend Helmi also visited her, but Helmi always came late in the evening when she cruised around town. It was good of her to do this, and I appreciated it. Mother did too. I knew that the more visitors she had, the better her treatment. My brother and his wife came occasionally, and when they did, Mother brightened up. I always wanted them to come more often, but it wasn't their pattern.

Once, while mother was still living with me, my sister came at Christmas. That was wonderful. Mother was so glad to see her, and so was I. I was happy my sister could help Mom at night, and I could sleep a few nights without the interruption of getting up when mother fell. How restorative sleep is when we haven't had it for many months! Also, we called Kathryn's son in New York, and Mom was glad to talk to her grandson and her great-granddaughter.

The first year Mother was in the nursing home, she could still use a wheelchair, and I could take her to church and for rides. Once, the nursing home staff arranged for a bus to take her and other patients to Target to buy Christmas presents for their grandchildren. I drove there separately and helped Mom choose a nice doll for her great-granddaughter in New York. Staying in the nursing home took most of Mother's Social Security, but she was allowed twenty-five dollars per month for personal expenses, and she was so happy to buy some Christmas presents with her money. She even bought a new outfit for church. Sad to say, the laundry personnel ruined her new outfit, even though I had carefully explained to them to leave her special clothes for me to launder. The lowly paid aides changed so frequently that although I explained about her laundry and also covering her ears when bathing her to one group, soon others took over and didn't know my instructions. All that change in mother's care saddened me. Aging and dying are difficult processes in the United States. By the time we understand the system, our loved one may be dead.

Recently I read a book called *Being Mortal*, and it has helped me begin to come to grips with my own mortality. A follow-up book by Mary Earle called *Beginning Again: Benedictine Wisdom for Living with Illness* has also been very helpful in dealing with illness and death. Fortunately, I have more money than my mother had, so I hope I will be able to afford care from Home Instead Senior Care or an organization like that for a short time when I become infirm.

However, at thirty dollars per hour or seven hundred dollars a week, I wouldn't be able to afford too many months of this sort of help. Yet, there are more alternatives to nursing homes today. Of course, we don't always just become infirm—we may have a stroke that necessitates assisted living. But laws are changing so that even nursing homes have to listen more to patient requests. This is an improvement.

In 1997, when mother died at the age of eighty-five, it was a bad year for deaths. Two of my good friends, Betty Wetlaufer and Frank Oppenheimer, also eighty-five, died. My former husband died at age fifty-seven; my gardener, Gilbert, at seventy-two; my next-door neighbor at eighty-five; my aunt Gladys at eighty-six; my uncle Lloyd at ninety-three; and my UTEP colleague, Ellery, at about sixty. It was a heavy time.

It was even sadder when my good friend Helmi stopped coming to see me. When I asked her why she remarked, "You attract death." That was a blow. What could I say? It wasn't as though I was purposely causing peoples' deaths. I guess in her mind I was somehow contaminated by these deaths.

John's Strange Farewell

While my mother had been slowly dying since she had entered the nursing home, and her death therefore had not been unexpected, John's death was quite sudden. He had fallen ill a day after moving to Washington, DC, in May 1997. He had a blood clot that traveled to his heart. It was hard to believe. He drank very little coffee or alcohol and jogged every day, and yet he died so young. My son called to tell me about his father's serious condition, so I went to a midweek communion and healing service at our church in El Paso to pray for him. I lit a candle for John's healing before the service, and when the service ended, I noticed the flame had gone out. I had never seen anything like that happen before. Usually the candles burn themselves out after the service. I was shocked and depressed and must have looked dreadful because the husband of a friend sat down next to me and asked what the matter was. I told him about John's dire situation. Kind and comforting, he said, "Maybe this is John's way of saying goodbye to you." Pretty mystical and disquieting! Yet it proved true. John died the same morning we were praying for him and the candle went out. I learned of his death later and thanked God for this omen.

Since I never saw John dead, it took a long time for me to really believe it. Even years later I would find myself pondering a historical question and thinking "What would John say about that?" Then I would remember that he had died. I had the same experience with my mother. I often wanted to ask her about something and then would realize that she too was dead. It seems to take a few years to process death, especially of those close to me. Sometimes I would talk to them anyway. It was a sort of prayer-talk and was comforting. I'm not sure what happens in the afterlife, but it seems OK to talk to our beloveds and imagine their answer.

Losing My Job at UTEP

In the midst of caring for my mother, I came up for tenure at UTEP, and I didn't pass muster. I was two-thirds done with my comparative history of Russian and European women, but that wasn't good enough for the department. They demanded a completed book and signed contract. Even though my editor, Susan McEachern at Rowman & Littlefield, wanted my manuscript, this didn't satisfy them. It seemed sad but not tragic at the time. I was sure I would easily get another position.

But I was mistaken. A miscalculation on my part! I was a decade older than when I had come to UTEP, and after the fall of the Berlin Wall, departments nationwide were cutting back on Russian history and language professors in the 1990s. I underestimated the dire situation of Slavic specialists in America, and the discrimination against older job applicants. Sad to say, I never got another full-time position in my field.

To its credit, the UTEP History Department gave me a grace period of two years, 1994–96, to find another situation, and I was sure I could since I had had several employment offers in 1989. But this didn't happen. Maybe I was too depressed. Losing my job, caring for my mother, and trying to finish my book were all overwhelming experiences.

In retrospect, I can see that when I went on interviews, I wasn't ready for a new situation. At one interview in Reno, Nevada, I came close to getting a job. However, when one of the professors asked me if I felt comfortable organizing a national history conference there, I wasn't sure and was evasive. This was the moment I lost the offer. If I could have bluffed my way through that, I would have gotten the teaching position. But, alas, that didn't happen. I still lacked the self-confidence to tackle a challenging situation.

A lifetime of denying my feelings enabled me to mask my disappointment, and I didn't really let myself experience my job loss until a decade later during the Great Recession of 2008 when I heard unemployed workers voice their dejection and pain in interviews on National Public Radio. Then I let myself feel bad and began to unblock my frozen feelings of hurt and sadness.

In 1996, I wasn't able to share my pain with my former colleagues, neighbors, siblings, or church friends. I could have gone to see my priest and talked with him, but I was too ashamed to do so. It's a blessing of old age that in retirement I now have some friends with whom I can share my feelings, even the dark and hard ones.

Another sadness is that when I brought my mother to live with me, my boyfriend, Dick, dropped out of my life and disappeared. When I desperately needed some moral support, he wasn't there. He helped me bring her to my house from the airport, and then I never saw him again. He didn't say anything—he just stopped calling, stopped coming to see me, and stopped attending church with me. He vanished from my life. So there I was, single at a very hard time. Luckily, my church friends did not desert me. And I didn't feel as if God had rejected me. Still, there was upheaval in my religious life too because our handsome, talented, devout, intelligent priest, Al Holland, left our parish, and our new priest did not fill his shoes. After a few years, the parish also faded away.

Substitute School Teaching in El Paso

After losing my teaching position at UTEP, I substitute taught one year in various public schools. Some of the classes were good, some were horrible. Once, a third grader made me cry. I didn't cry in front of him but waited until I got into my car after school. I hadn't realized children that young could be so mean, but some of them are. At the end of the miserable teaching days, I drove to my friend Molly's for tea and sympathy. Hers came in the form of homemade chicken soup, which she always kept in her refrigerator. Sitting in her cozy kitchen with her was a safe place to cry and complain. She helped me get though some of the hard times that year. Doesn't God provide the friends we need when we are down and out?

I found some pupils who were endearing. I often substituted for the physical education teachers, and they did the same exercises in the various schools and grades, so it wasn't hard. The elementary school children called me "coach." Most of the pupils liked having PE. In sunny, warm El Paso, we usually had our classes outside, even in winter. Once, I was teaching a junior high class with two male coaches, who insisted I rest. They took care of all the classes. I didn't know if it was male superiority or just their good nature. It didn't really matter. I was relieved of teaching for an hour, and it was a gift I accepted. I wasn't used to being called "coach" by students, and it was rather endearing and made me chuckle inside. I was used to titles like "professor" or "Dr. Hutton" but not "coach." Who knows what life has in store?

Indeed, I encountered several redeeming classes. I remember quite fondly one junior high school where I taught English to minority students, and they were very cooperative and hard working. One young Hispanic boy was reading Tolstoy's *War and Peace*. When I talked to him about why he was reading such a big book, he told me about his great plans to be a doctor. That impressed me. I was also fortunate at this school because one of my former UTEP students taught history across the hall from my class. So, he told them to behave, and they did. It was a wonderful experience working there. It turned out that the teacher of this good class was sometimes absent attending conferences, so I got to teach his remarkable class several times.

A sixth-grade class near Fort Bliss Army Base also had some winsome, innovative students. Instead of going outside for recess, a few boys stayed inside to work on their design for a golf course on an enormous roll of paper. Their creativity and diligence impressed me. They were also the students who calculated their math problems in their heads and didn't use calculators. It was gratifying to see students willing and happy to use their brains. Needless to say, I left this teacher a note saying I would happily substitute for her class, and I did so several times when she had doctor's appointments and other commitments.

Providence often provided meaningful work, even as a substitute teacher. While I was happy to have meaningful work and delighted by some of the classes, I was dismayed at the number of substitute teachers students have today compared to when I went to school. El Paso employed hundreds if not thousands of substitute teachers each day. This was quite different from the 1940s and '50s when I was growing up. Then, it was extremely unusual for a teacher to be absent. Today students often lack the educational continuity and stability that we experienced decades earlier.

Renting Rooms during Unemployment

After I had lost my job and Mother was in a nursing home, I needed income, and one of my history colleagues at UTEP, Ellery Schalk, arranged for some visiting French students to each rent a room from me. This was very kind of him. Ellery later succumbed to cancer and died quickly. He died the same year as my mother and eight other relatives and friends. I would sometimes walk by their home, which I had rented the first two years I was teaching at UTEP, and would stop to commiserate with his wife, Ninon. I was usually on my way to the drugstore at the end of our road, and if I saw Ninon outside, we would give each other a hug and shed a tear or two. It was a hard time for both of us. It was more tragic for her because her husband was not yet sixty, whereas my mother was eighty-five and lived a long, full life. Moreover, Ninon had a young son still living at home. It was hard for her to be a single mother to four boys, the eldest ones in college.

Later, I rented rooms to Japanese students who were studying English at a private institute in El Paso. These students helped me both financially and psychologically. It was good to have the rent money while I was only substitute teaching in the city schools and later teaching English part-time at El Paso Community College. It was also helpful having their company when I felt depressed after the deaths of my mother, friends, and other relations.

One Christmas, the parents of my French student Nadege Bray also came to stay a few days. They arrived from New Orleans, which they had toured, and it was lovely having them as guests. I remember making pancakes and serving syrup and pecans with the breakfast, and they had never had pecans before. I was glad I could give them a few pounds to take back to France with them. We also had a good time driving to La Mesilla in nearby New Mexico. It is a charming town and enchants tourists with its art galleries, ethnic restaurants, and boutiques. It is like a miniature Santa Fe.

A Japanese graduate student named Hadji, who was studying linguistics, also invited his family to come to visit. His father, mother, and sister came, and we also drove to La Mesilla. The Eagle was such a charming place with its enormous skylight, fountains, small tables, and bougainvillea twining around the

Hadji's family and me at the Eagle restaurant in La Mesilla, New Mexico, 1998

ceiling. It was a delightful place to dine. I also remember taking my son and my mother there.

Several students came to stay with me while my mother was in the nursing home and after she had died. I was living on the surface of life at this time, trying not to feel so depressed and sad. Having other people around was a blessing. I remember when Princess Diana died in August 1997, and Nadege and I watched the funeral. I cried and cried. At first I didn't understand it, and then I realized that my tears were partly for my former husband who had died. I had always loved him—thought him invincible—and was shocked at his death.

I remember feeling survivor guilt. I wondered why I was left alive when I hadn't gotten tenure, while he possessed such a superb intellect and was an award-winning teacher. I felt like such a failure and wondered why I was alive. Even writing this makes me cry, years after the event. Life is so unfair. And I have seldom been grateful enough for all the good in my life—for life itself, for good health and friends, for a wonderful son and daughter-in-law, and for many, many blessings.

One advantage of having my large house in El Paso was that I could invite friends to stay, even friends and their families. Once, while still teaching at UTEP, I met Fred Schmidt from East Berlin, who had given a paper on politics in East Germany for the political science department. It turned out he needed a place to stay, and I invited him to my place since I had two extra bedrooms and baths. I thought it would be for a few days, but it turned out to be a few weeks.

The next year he came and brought his wife, Inge. The first year or two they stayed with me, she did not speak much English, but by the third year she did speak a little. Eventually, they brought their family—one daughter, a son-in-law, and two grandchildren. It was good having the three bedrooms and two large couches in the living room where the grandsons could sleep. Who would imagine that years later I would teach in Lithuania, and they would invite me to East Berlin to spend Christmas and New Year's with them? Life is full of surprises!

My Maid Josefina

When I first came to El Paso, I hurt my back moving heavy boxes of books into my house. The result was that it was painful to vacuum the carpets in my house, so I asked my neighbor if her Mexican maid could help me temporarily. Her name was Josefina, and she had a green card, so she worked legally. She proved a godsend. I soon discovered that when I hired Josefina, I had entered an unwritten social contract that wasn't easy to break. Her poverty made me realize that I needed to employ her long-term. Moreover, it was helpful to have her clean the house, change sheets, do laundry, and iron clothes. I never had a house husband, so I had never appreciated someone doing all those chores for me. Indeed, I never had a maid who did all those things so well again, and I've had several in the past twenty-five years.

During the years she worked for me, we became friends. My Spanish was limited to asking her how she and her family were and similar short phrases. Still, we communicated well enough. I paid her wages above the norm, so I wasn't exploiting her. I helped her get work with some of my UTEP colleagues, and she earned extra money from that. I sometimes tried to clean alongside her, but she was like a tornado, moving fast and furiously. I certainly couldn't keep up and ran out of energy after an hour or so. How she was able to work all day, from nine in the morning until three in the afternoon, was a mystery to me. She was a godsend when I had mother and the college students living with me. She kept my large house neat and clean, washed and ironed my clothes, changed my sheets and tablecloths, and was always cheerful and diligent. Sometimes I would give her clothes and towels that she would distribute to others less well off than she was.

I discovered she was a neighborhood leader, distributing favors and goods to others in Juarez. That was nice to learn. After I lost my university job, I sometimes had to pay her in goods instead of money since I was so strapped for cash. I once gave her my mother's new washing machine because I had my own in the maid's annex. This worked out to our mutual benefit.

Josefina often astounded me. She was illiterate yet she could take the right bus to my house and also find the streets and houses of my colleagues when I found her other jobs in Kern Place. How she did that without knowing how to read amazed me. Occasionally I noticed that when she dusted my books, she sometimes replaced them upside down. That reminded me that she didn't understand writing but still coped with life well. I learned a lot from Josefina and appreciated her very much. She was loyal and a joy in my life as I experienced the loss of my job and my mother. She understood my fractured Spanish, and we had fun communicating about her children and grandchildren. She was another example of how Providence provides.

Teaching at El Paso Community College

After a year as a substitute teacher, I obtained a part-time situation at El Paso Community College teaching English as a Second Language. The students were endearing and I enjoyed teaching there. My colleagues were kind and supportive. I was even allowed to take a Spanish course that involved a trip to Mexico to see Copper Canyon, and another course in wellness in Las Vegas, New Mexico.

The perks of being a part-time teacher were substantial. When I first started teaching English, I audited a couple of linguistics courses at UTEP. I pondered whether to take a degree in linguistics and pursue a career teaching English as a Second Language (ESOL) but decided against it. I would have been sixty years old when I finished my study and wondered if I would be too old to find employment to repay a significant student loan. Later, I discovered that I might have acquired a job teaching English abroad, but I didn't know that then. As a friend once remarked, "We make the best decisions we can, given the circumstances."

I was glad my work at the community college lasted two years while I recovered from losing my position at UTEP. I was still visiting my mother at the nursing home and working on my book on Russian women. It was a busy and heavy time, yet God provided for me in many marvelous ways. I earned enough to pay my mortgage and slowly regained some self-esteem so that I was able to get a one-year job at Radford University in Virginia.

Life in El Paso

Music played an important part in my life in El Paso, where I lived and taught from 1989 to 1999. My music buddy was Molly Shapiro. She had three sons who were violinists, and she was a classical music aficionada. Through her I came to know some of the local musical groups, especially chamber music ensembles. She introduced me to the El Paso Symphony, which she supported. The popularity of Latin American music was unique to El Paso. It was new, enticing, and enjoyable. The university also had a music department, and I often attended concerts. However, it was a much smaller department than the one at Iowa and had fewer concerts. Musical theater was almost as good as in Iowa City, and I enjoyed several dinner theater presentations at UTEP.

Madeline Park, El Paso

The house that I rented and the one I owned in El Paso were located in Kern Place, an enclave north of the university near the mountains and Madeline Park. It was a charming area. The houses were all refreshingly different, and the park was centrally located, circular in design with lovely grass and trees—a real oasis in the desert. I usually walked around it each morning around six thirty. This is where I met my friend Molly. She too lived in Kern Place and walked. Soon we were walking buddies, then music buddies as well. She was Jewish and an unreconstructed Brooklyn socialist from the 1930s. Outspoken and well read, she was fun to be around. She introduced me to Frank Oppenheimer, who was so delightful and helpful, and his wife, Birdie, who also lived in Kern Place. Birdie sometimes walked with Molly and me in the early morning. Colleagues as well as other intelligent, charming people like Molly and Frank lived in the neighborhood.

Several years ago, I thought of writing a piece about Madeline Park from the point of view of the park. But I never got around to it. Madeline Park was such an usual place—not only beautiful but functional. It had incredibly high usage. Walkers circled it in the morning, as did dog owners who strolled around in the mornings and evenings. Maids, who came to clean the middle-class houses surrounding the park, disembarked from buses and rested there in the shade in the afternoons waiting for their return buses to take them downtown and then to Juarez. Neighborhood children played there in the afternoons, and lovers sometimes met there in the evenings. On the weekends, people from other areas, even Juarez, flocked there to have picnics and watch their children play. It was a quiet, peaceful, delightful park—one of the nicest I've known. Fortunately, the neighborhood association keeps the park looking good. Each decade, some flowers or good additions are made.

Teaching at Radford University, 1999–2000

After teaching at the El Paso Community College for a couple years, the hurt of losing my job at UTEP lessened, and I felt better about myself. There was a magic about teaching—even a subject like English as a second language—that redeemed me. One summer, I applied for a temporary position in Russian and world history at Radford University in southwestern Virginia. This time, I was successful, and I was glad to be teaching history again.

It turned out to be a mixed experience. Some of the students were lazy and lacked motivation, which made teaching and grading difficult. I didn't quite know how to make learning more attractive to them. Many wanted to slide by, and I didn't know how to challenge them. Some had come to Radford because of its reputation as a party school, and it was quite different teaching there than at the University of Iowa, where the students were highly qualified and willing to work, or at UTEP, where most of my students were older army wives or retired military—diligent, hard-working, and ambitious. So while my previous teaching experiences had been quite positive, I was unprepared for my lack of fulfillment at Radford. Moreover, I had a heavy teaching load, four courses per semester.

Given my difficult situation, it was a boon encountering a former acquaintance from the University of Iowa. Her name was Kay, and she taught in the Religion and Philosophy Department. Her specialties were Indian religions and philosophy, and she often taught a course in Buddhism. Since I needed brushing up on that topic for the world history course I was teaching there, I was grateful for the helpful information about Buddhism that she shared.

During the academic year, Kay and I became pals. She insisted my chief duty was to finish my book, and I did it. She also introduced me to her editor, Mary Holliman, who owned Pocahontas Press. Mary lived in nearby Blacksburg, Virginia. The publisher for my book on Russian and European women wanted my book presented to them in "camera ready" condition. I lacked the computer skills to do this, so I paid Mary to do it. Her services cost something like two thousand or three thousand dollars. Still, it was worth it to finish the book and get it published.

Kay had lived and taught at Radford for several years, so she knew the local sites and enjoyed showing me around on Saturday mornings. We often drove to Roanoke to shop at the local farmer's market, which was located near a fashionable Indian restaurant and a fabulous French bakery. She also drove me along the Blue Ridge Parkway with its spectacular views of the Appalachian Mountains and the Chateau restaurant and winery. This proved a popular place to take my friends. The year I was at Radford, four sets of visitors came: my sister from Santa Fe, Rosemary from Washington, DC, Terry from Atlanta, and Larry from Milwaukee. They all enjoyed the drive along the Blue Ridge Parkway, the vistas, and the meals at the Chateau winery.

Kay really took me under her wing. She invited me to ride along with her when she went to conferences in Richmond, Virginia, and Washington, DC. I had an old Park College friend, Rosemary, the rare books librarian at the Library of Congress, and she was available to hobnob with me the weekend I was in DC with Kay. Rosemary lived in Alexandria, Virginia, and I had stayed with her many times when doing research at the Library of Congress. She was always a wonderful hostess. On this trip, she was equally helpful. While Kay attended her conference, Rosemary took me to a program at a Russian Orthodox church. On another visit, Rosemary had taken me to a Russian museum named Hillwood, which is located just outside of the capital.

Konstantin Makovsky, *A Boyar Wedding Feast* (1883)

Hillwood Estate, Museum & Gardens is a small gem built by Marjorie Meriwether Post Hutton Davies. Her third husband, Davies, had been the US ambassador to the Soviet Union in the 1930s, and with her Post family fortune she had bought many Russian objects during their stay in Moscow when the Soviets needed foreign currency for their industrialization. Since Rosemary had a car and free time on the weekends, she happily squired me around, and I appreciated it. At the museum, I found all sorts of tsarist treasures, but the one I liked best was Konstantin Makovsky's 1883 enormous painting titled *A Boyar Wedding Feast*. It depicts an elaborate aristocratic Russian wedding in the seventeenth century and was unknown to me. Thoroughly captivated by it, I bought a print and had it framed.

On another occasion I rode along with Kay when she attended a conference in Richmond, Virginia. There I was free to walk around and explore the city. I thoroughly enjoyed the historic district with its red brick houses and tree-lined streets but was disconcerted at finding a large boulevard lined with statues of Confederate soldiers. I hadn't expected this. Of course, in the South the Civil War is still not over. Growing up in northern Indiana, I never heard it discussed. Indeed, only one great-grandfather on my father's side of the family participated in it. My mother's relatives all emigrated to the United States after that war.

In Richmond, I discovered a small museum featuring Fabergé eggs from Tsar Nicholas II's collection. What an unexpected find! I had read about these treasures in many Russian novels and history books, so it was enchanting to see the priceless jeweled objects. It was fabulous being able to enjoy some Russian culture since I had never lived in an area in America where this was possible.

I had other heartening experiences outside the classroom at Radford, mainly intellectual. At a spring conference, I read a paper about Soviet women prisoners in the Gulag. It documented women's supporting each other in food, community, and protection. During the discussion afterward, one of the Radford professors mentioned that in American prisons it is common for women to form surrogate families who encourage each other and help each other survive. This gave me a new insight into Soviet women's experience in the 1930s in Siberia. I began to see that it was not only their individual grit and intellectual and spiritual resilience that helped them survive but also their solidarity that helped them endure years, even decades, of mistreatment, degradation, and short rations.

Like other universities, Radford had a musical and intellectual culture with concerts and speakers. Some professors were going to China on a university-sponsored tour, and it sponsored presentations on Chinese culture, which fascinated me. Sometimes I walked to the university at seven thirty in the morning to teach my three Monday, Wednesday, and Friday classes and didn't return home until ten at night after listening to a lecture. I remember once thinking that I had put in a twelve-hour day. That surprised but pleased me. I felt fulfilled from the teaching and learning. I was "being most of all," to paraphrase Dostoevsky.

Nestled near the Blue Ridge Mountains, Radford basked in great natural beauty, including being right on the New River. Walking to my classes, I could see the mountains, amble through a woods collecting raspberries on the way home in the summer, and enjoy snow in the winter. Having lived ten years in snowless El Paso, it was fun playing in it again, as this picture indicates.

Marcelline with a colleague's dog, Radford, Virginia, winter 1999–2000

My one-year job at Radford meant I was busy looking for a full-time position. I liked the small town of Radford and the people at the local Episcopal church where I worshipped, so I thought I wanted to move only if I could find something full-time. Moving every year was too wrenching emotionally. There were not many options during the winter of 1999–2000, and I didn't have many interviews at the American historical convention or get any job offers. By January, I was depressed. I was thinking of working for the federal government analyzing census data when I noticed a teaching position advertised in the *Chronicle of Higher Education* for a history professor at Lithuania Christian College in Klaipėda, Lithuania.

I had never heard of this small international college, but I applied for the situation, and the dean contacted me. He was in Virginia recruiting faculty, and he interviewed me on the telephone. The job was a volunteer one. No pay. I didn't know what to make of that, but I was going to turn sixty in November 2000, and I could draw widow's benefits of $770 a month from my former husband's Social Security. This would finance my life in Lithuania. It was an answer to prayer as well as an adventure. That summer, my son and daughter-in-law met me in Washington, DC, to say goodbye. Here is a picture of Martin and me with the Lonely Planet guide to the Baltic states that he had thoughtfully bought for me.

Marcelline and Martin, Washington, DC, summer 2000

Chapter VIII

Life in Lithuania

When I first resolved to go to Lithuania to teach, I assumed I would be there for just a few years. But it turned out that I lived there for almost ten. I have briefly written about my life, teaching, and traveling in *Falling in Love with the Baltics*. In this memoir, I dwell in greater detail about living in Klaipėda and teaching at Lithuania Christian College, or LCC as it was called. We had a major break each semester as well as holidays at Christmas and in the summer, so I was able to travel in Eastern Europe as well as Germany, France, and Russia (St. Petersburg), and I describe that. While Klaipėda was the third largest Lithuanian city with 240,000 people, the picture below shows the picturesque Danė River in the downtown.

Danė River, Old Town Klaipėda, Lithuania, summer 2003

Teaching at Lithuania Christian College

In hindsight, my teaching at LCC partly dates back to when I was a teenager in high school in the 1950s—when I felt called to serve as a missionary. As a teen I had vowed to teach in Africa, yet it was decades later in Lithuania that I was able to fulfill that vow, but in a different venue. While I initially thought of LCC as just another place to teach, when I told someone in Radford about it, she said, "Oh, you're going to be a teacher missionary." I hadn't thought of it that way, but then I realized that she was partly right. So, forty years after I had expected to go somewhere in Africa to teach, I ended up serving in Lithuania instead.

In retrospect, I can see how God works in mysterious ways. Although I had seen my dream of being a teacher missionary die when I was a junior in college, it later came true at LCC. Below is a picture of me in the doorway of a colleague's office around 2005.

At LCC I mainly taught Western civilization to freshmen students. Although the students all knew how to read, write, and speak English, teaching there proved challenging because of cultural differences. Once, after finishing a lecture about Charlemagne, one of my best students came up to ask me if this was the same person they called Carlos Magnus. I felt so frustrated. Why hadn't she asked me this during class? I felt as if I had wasted the entire period since she, and maybe most of the class, hadn't understood the basis of the lecture. I only later learned that many students read the text the week of the test, not each class period, as the syllabus indicated, and as I had expected. Perhaps this was why she hadn't known the name Charlemagne. She hadn't read the text and seen it in its English format.

Marcelline at a colleague's office, Lithuania Christian College, 2005

Most upsetting in teaching at LCC, however, was that some students chattered to their friends while I was lecturing, and I had never encountered this before. I found it rude and distracting when I was trying to concentrate on communicating. Moreover, I never discovered a good way to curtail this whispering.

Having always taught rather well-behaved American university students, I was unprepared for some disruptive Lithuanian, Russian, and Central Asian students. Fellow LCC teachers, who had taught mainly in high school, possessed better disciplinary methods than I did as a college professor. However, a Canadian dean had similar problems, and he was equally frustrated. Neither of us ever solved our dilemma.

Still, most of the students were bright and attentive. It was only a minority that bothered me or challenged my authority. Sometimes I taught Western civilization to a lecture class of one hundred students. Then, I had them write a paper in class on Fridays about one of the documents in our text, and I had one hundred papers to grade each Saturday afternoon. Usually, I enjoyed reading these papers, especially those by the best students. However, toward the end of my time at LCC, grading became a drudge. Even papers by the best students no longer captivated me. Then I knew it was time to retire. Still, I had some unbelievably good classes.

My favorite teaching experience was presenting Baltic history to small classes of American and Canadian study-abroad students. They were well behaved and studious. The course wasn't a specialty of mine, but I knew something about it from my study of Russian and Soviet history. At LCC, I learned about it from the perspective of Poles, Swedes, and Baltic peoples.

In Klaipėda, it was fascinating to see remnants of Nazi and Soviet rule from during and after World War II. In the forest opposite my apartment were many Nazi bunkers dug into earthworks left over from the war. Along the beach were also some enormous bunkers left by the German Army. When I took my Baltic history class on an excursion to the beach to see the underground defenses and the fortresses above the ground, I was amazed that the salt from the sea had not destroyed these remnants of the war. The iron ladders leading down into the bunkers and the concrete buildings remained in excellent shape.

Apparently the Germans anticipated an attack from the sea, but it didn't turn out quite as they expected. In Latvia, the Soviet Army circled around the German enclave in Courland and marched westward. Only six people remained in the city when the Soviet Army arrived. All the Germans had left. Historically, Klaipėda had belonged to East Prussia, and the Germans called it Memel. Another legacy of German occupation was the German soldiers' cemetery across from the forest and the block where I lived. Whenever new graves of German soldiers were found in Lithuania, they were brought to Klaipėda to be buried in that cemetery. I also heard that some German youth came each summer to weed and care for the beautifully tended burial ground.

After the war, the Soviets occupied Klaipėda and built a massive World War II monument to commemorate the Soviet soldiers who had died in the battles on the Eastern Front. I had been to the sculpture park many times before I saw this enormous, rather touching sculpture. Most of the park is occupied by huge statues in Socialist Realist format. Other reminders of Soviet rule are found in buildings that were used by the KGB. Once I went to nearby Telšiai and was surprised to see two different buildings in the same city with plaques indicating the KGB had been housed there. These reminders of Nazi and Soviet occupation enriched my understanding of Baltic history.

The Soviets deported tens of thousands of Lithuanians both before and after World War II. In 1940, a year after the division of Poland and Eastern Europe between Germany and the Soviet Union, the Soviets deported many Lithuanian intellectuals, whom they thought might resist their rule. After the war, they deported many groups, including the Forest Brothers, who resisted by fighting in rural areas. I met one of them through my artist friend Tatjana Simonaitienė. Her father-in-law had fought Soviet domination as a young Forest Brother after World War II but had been captured and deported to the Soviet Union to work in a mine. Upon his release, he was allowed to attend a university and become an engineer. He eventually became head of a factory near Kaunas, and after the Soviets left, he became deputy defense minister of Lithuania. He exemplifies Lithuanian toughness.

This strength and endurance pervaded Lithuanian culture. For example, the father of my Lithuanian teacher at LCC, Dr. Kęstutis Vaišvila, had been deported to the Soviet Union prior to the war when he was a six-year-old child. His whole family was taken—his grandparents, parents, and three siblings. It was astonishing that although they had to live and work in a prison camp above the Arctic Circle, his family survived, except for his father, who died from harsh work in a lumber camp. In the far, far north, his older brother was assigned to catch fish for the Soviets. If he exceeded his norm, he could trade his surplus for other food. During the war, Lend-Lease Act products sent by the United State government—carrots, dehydrated milk, and potatoes—could be exchanged for fish by the prisoners. These vegetables helped his family stay alive. Also, his mother later worked as a nurse in a school, so when the children attended school they received lunch, which helped them survive. At sixteen, Kęstutis began to study medicine in Siberia.

In the late 1950s, Soviet leader Nikita Khrushchev released many of the exiled minorities like the Lithuanians. Members of the Vaišvila family were allowed to return one by one to Kaunas where Kęstutis continued his medical studies and became a doctor. Much to my amazement, despite his time in the Gulag, he has an attractive, sunny, and resilient disposition.

One May, a group of graduating LCC seniors, who had been freshmen in my Western civilization class four years earlier, took my Baltic history course. Even as freshmen, several of them had been outstanding students who wrote beautifully, even about a grandparent banished to the Gulag. It was delightful having them as seniors and seeing the intellectual progress they had made. I seldom had that experience since Western civilization was an introductory course, and there were no advanced history classes, except for Baltic history.

That summer, these marvelous students redeemed some of my earlier unhappy teaching experiences. This seemed to be the theme of my life in Lithuania: some hard times interspersed with unexpected delight in individuals and classes. Indeed, life seemed to be about improvising and appreciating the good when it came.

Research and Writing at LCC

When writing the history of my time at LCC, I initially forgot to mention that my first book, *Russian and West European Women, 1860–1939: Dreams, Struggles, and Nightmares*, was published during the first year I was there. Later, I wrote two book reports and an article for Dr. Pelenski, for my mentor's Festschrift, a collection of articles written by former students and colleagues in his honor. One of the book reports was about the education of young people at the time of the revolution. It was a review of Lisa Kirshenbaum's *Small Comrades: Revolutionizing Childhood in Soviet Russia, 1917–1932*, published in the *Slavic Review*, October 2002. I have forgotten the name of the second book I reviewed for the *Slavic Review*, but I do remember the title of my piece in the Festschrift. It was called "Surviving Imprisonment in the 1930s: Social and Religious Experiences of Soviet Female Prisoners," in Jaroslaw Pelenski's *States, Societies, Cultures: East and West: Essays in Honor of Jaroslaw Pelenski* (New York: Ross Publishing, 2004). Initially, writing and publishing were not much encouraged at LCC, but eventually the administration realized their significance for accreditation, and more colleagues began to publish.

I had no one to discuss my writings with there but was glad to have some connection to Russian history. I had been surprised but pleased when one of the editors of *Slavic Review* approached me about writing book reviews. I felt honored and did them with gusto.

Living in Lithuania

When I first arrived in Lithuania in August 2000, it was sunny and bright. The late summer and early fall beguiled me with their sunshine, warm temperatures, balmy beaches, and colorful trees. In contrast, late fall and winter could be dreary and cold. The country's name in Lithuanian, Lietuva, literally means "rain," and it could rain for six weeks at a time. Then it seemed as though the sun never shone except in summer. To deal with depression, many Lithuanians walked along the beach, even in winter. Some women wore their winter boots, fur coats, and hats to keep warm. The summer was the light of my life, walking along the beach enjoying the sun, sand, and sea.

Baltic Sea at the Klaipėda beach, 2003

When I first arrived in Lithuania, it was wracked by high unemployment following the Soviets' departure as well as high rates of alcoholism and suicide. Many of the families I met had several members who were alcoholics. I had known that Russian society suffered from alcoholism but hadn't realized that Eastern European society also did. I hadn't known that the governments sold vodka at low prices to keep the population quiescent. People could drink a lot for very little money. I also didn't know that vodka was served at most social occasions, and for several years I served only tea and cake to my visitors.

Finally, a Lithuanian friend clued me in, and then I served brandy to my older Lithuanian and Russian friends to add to their tea. None of my Mennonite LCC friends served vodka or brandy when entertaining, and they had never mentioned it to me as being part of the culture.

LCC was not exempt from the high rate of Lithuanian suicide, and we experienced this the second semester I taught there. During spring break, a male student, who had been dismissed for not attending his classes or doing his work, returned to the dorm and took his life. Then a week later, his younger brother, who was a high school student and a drug addict, killed himself. This was tragic for their parents and for all of us at LCC. We felt guilty for the suicides, and it took a while to digest this experience.

Making Friends at LCC and in Klaipėda

Despite the harshness of Lithuanian weather and society, I found that God provided even in that challenging situation. Although it usually takes some time to make a friend, life at LCC sped up this process. Many of my colleagues were helpful and friendly, and I initially identified with them. We taught together, ate our lunch together, and went to restaurants, concerts, and even on holidays together. I made friends with ordinary Lithuanians and Russians more slowly.

In my eleven-story apartment building, I was rather lonely before becoming acquainted with two families. I became a sort of "surrogate grandmother" to two teenage boys. I first met Viktoras when he was sixteen. He had studied English at school, so he translated for his mother and me when we first met. He even wrote poems and short stories in English. He went on to become a student at LCC, graduated, and then went to live and work in Dublin, Ireland.

During one spring break, Viktor and I went to visit our German friends Mecki and Helmut Grimm in Bad Camberg, Germany. It's near Frankfort, so we flew from nearby Palanga to Hamburg and then took a train to Frankfort. They hosted us in grand fashion, taking us to nearby historic sites and cities like Mainz, home to Gutenberg's famous press.

In Mainz we also saw beautiful blue stained glass in St. Steven's Cathedral made by Chagall when he was ninety-three years old. I was astounded that a Jewish artist would come to Germany to make stained glass after World War II. What a lesson in forgiveness.

As in Klaipėda, the Grimms wined and dined us with incredible largesse. Here we are at their well-laden breakfast table. Later we had sumptuous midday and evening meals there. Each was a culinary delight, a feast for the eyes as well as the palate.

The Klaipėda apartments where Viktoras, his family, and I lived, 2000–2010

Left to right: Marcelline, Mecki, and Viktor at the well-laden breakfast table, Bad Camberg, Germany

Chapter VIII

Grocery Shopping in Klaipėda

Because the large apartment complex where I lived was the size of two American city blocks, three grocery stores were nearby. So it was fairly easy obtaining the things I needed for ordinary life—bread, butter, cereal, milk, juice, ice cream, cookies, fruits, vegetables, and beer because they were clearly displayed and I could pick them up easily to take to the checkout counter. It was more daunting to decide which of the many kinds of bread or beer to buy—the choices were much greater than in an American store of similar size. What was most difficult was buying meat, salads, and small things like baking powder or cinnamon to make cakes. Spices were not visible to a shopper walking around a Lithuanian grocery store.

Like other European countries, Lithuania uses the metric system, which meant that prices were for a kilogram—2.2 pounds. Since I knew the word "half"—*polovina* in Russian—I could request half a kilogram, or a pound, of ground beef by pointing to it. I didn't know the Russian or Lithuanian for the cuts of meat but found pointing effective. Unfortunately, I didn't think of looking up the word "half" in my Lithuanian dictionary but continued using the Russian word for several years.

Initially, many older Lithuanians spoke Russian because of the fifty years of Soviet domination, and they didn't seem to mind my speaking Russian. Slowly, many learned English and avoided Russian. Some insisted on speaking only Lithuanian, so it became harder to use my Russian. While it was easy to obtain half a kilo of an item, it was harder at the delicatessen section to ask for a small amount of salad or cake because these were sold in quantities of one hundred or two hundred grams. I didn't know how to pronounce those numbers. Eventually, I learned the Lithuanian word for "small" and used that to indicate the amount I wanted to buy.

Grocery shopping was often an anthropological experience. Some of the supermarkets had small cafés, and it was captivating buying a cup of coffee and a sweet roll, taking a seat, and watching the other customers. Of course, it took a while for me to feel comfortable doing this. I had enough money to eat in cafés and restaurants in Klaipėda because they were so much cheaper than in the States, but I wasn't used to doing this alone.

Once I had gone to a café with friends, then I didn't mind returning there to eat by myself. A few times I went to the Radisson Hotel with friends from LCC to celebrate someone's birthday, and then I began to feel comfortable going there alone. I liked going there because I could read newspapers such as the British *Financial Times*, which was informative but otherwise pricey. At the

Radisson, I often bought coffee or a beer and snacks, and then read the free papers. The price of a beer was much less than the cost of a paper. The *International Herald Tribune* and the *Financial Times* cost more than 20Lt (litai, about $5.00) and the *Baltic Times* 5Lt ($1.25), while beer cost only 3Lt ($0.75).

Restaurants and Cafés

Learning to read a Lithuanian menu could be challenging. One LCC couple told us the story of when they first lived in Klaipėda and went to a restaurant. They simply pointed to an item on the menu and then later discovered they had ordered pig's ear. That was a shock. Fortunately, this never happened to me because some of the restaurants I went to had the menu in Russian and German as well as Lithuanian. Through the other languages I learned what chicken or pork was on the menu.

Our Lithuanian colleagues at LCC didn't go to restaurants very often, so we North American expats were the blind leading the blind. Sometimes LCC old timers clued us in. Our Canadian colleagues always ordered tea instead of coffee because tea was much cheaper. In 2000 the American dollar was stronger than the Canadian currency, so American retirees did not have to watch their pennies quite as closely as the Canadians did. Also, the coffee was either instant or made with boiling water poured over grounds in the bottom of the cup. This made it less appealing after stirring sugar or milk into it. Having coffee could be an unpleasant surprise the first time or two.

Going to concerts and dining out were favorite pastimes for most of us. These were cheap ways to get together and enjoy each other's company. From 2000 to 2004, before Lithuania joined the European Union, the cafés and restaurants were incredibly cheap for Americans. A nice dinner of meat, potatoes, vegetable, and garnish was often three to five dollars. Beer, coke, and mineral water each cost seventy-five cents. Guess which one I usually chose? Klaipėda produced an internationally famous beer called Švyturys. It had been brewed in Klaipėda since 1784 by German brewers and was the oldest brewery in Lithuania.

I met the British brewmeister and his family at the English-speaking church we all attended, and once he gave me and my Baltic history class students a tour of the brewery. He worked for the Danish brewery Carlsberg, which had taken over Švyturys. After the fall of the old Soviet Union, the Danes took over many East European breweries. Carlsberg bought the Lithuanian workers' shares in Švyturys that they had been given when the Soviet Union collapsed, and Carlsberg allowed them to continue working at the brewery or retire with their new wealth.

Švyturys was the only case I heard of in which workers profited from privatization. Usually, it was Communist party hacks and apparatchiks who took over the former Soviet enterprises. One of the Švyturys workers used his windfall to build a beautiful mansion near LCC. It was so grandiose that initially I thought it belonged to the Russian mafia, but I was mistaken, as the brewmeister pointed out.

The British brewmeister lived in Klaipėda for a few years and then moved to Vilnius, and then on to Ukraine and other places. I first met him at the English-speaking church in Klaipėda, which he, his wife, and their darling three-year-old twin boys attended. Getting to know them all was delightful. I especially treasured a time I spent with them one holiday when I was in Vilnius.

Visit by Cousins in Klaipėda

It was delightful having some cousins come to visit me in Klaipėda in April 2002. I had grown up in La Porte with my cousin Jean Breese Bruce, and I was so happy when her family came to visit me. She and her husband, Cliff, were on holiday in Germany, where they were visiting their son Bob, who lived with his partner in Kiel. It was a treat to have relatives from home come to see me. We had good times, and they were happy to include Victor in our sorties. He was an excellent guide to local sites and enjoyed the dinners at the restaurants.

Klaipėda Bookstores

Klaipėda was a city of 240,000 people with one university and two colleges, and it supported a goodly number of bookstores. One of my delights was going on

Left to right: Viktor, Cliff, and Marcelline at Winter Garden restaurant, April 2002

Left to right: Ingrid, Bob, Marcelline, Cliff, and Viktor at a small café near my apartment, 2002

Left to right: Cliff, Jean, Marcelline, Viktor, and Bob having tea in my living room, 2002

a book crawl. Several bookstores were scattered around the downtown. Some were large, rather general stores, and some were more specialized, catering to students and the books they needed in grade school, grammar school, and university. I liked browsing in them all to check out the history books assigned to students in various grades.

It fascinated me that Lithuanian high school students studied classical Greek and Roman art. Having taught classical Greek and Roman history in Western civilization for several years, I was happy to see that Lithuanian pupils studied this subject. I enjoyed looking at the books available at Klaipėda University bookstore.

Chapter VIII

I never visited the Pedagogical Institute where French, English, German, and other languages were taught. Two of my friends taught there: Laurent Gontier, a French expat, taught French, and Helmut Grimm was paid by the German government to teach German there and at one of the high schools. His wife, Mecki, taught German at LCC as a volunteer. Since our offices were next to each other, we became friends.

Mecki and Helmut entertained on a lavish scale, and it was an honor being invited to their lovely apartment for dinner, to imbibe the luscious aperitifs, and to sample the hors d'oeuvres. We especially enjoyed the beautifully decorated table Mecki provided. It cheered us up. She arranged it with candles, rose petals, chocolates, colorful streamers, shiny silverware, and lovely china. We were satiated by several succulent courses including salad and soup as well as the main course and dessert.

It was at one of their dinners that I met the Frenchman Laurent Gontier. He was married to a Lithuanian woman named Kristina, but during my first two years at LCC, she was often away working on a degree in English in Vilnius, so he was alone a great deal. He was such a sensitive soul and so charming that he was a fascinating dinner guest to get to know. Indeed, Helmut and Mecki often invited the "orphans" of LCC, that is, the single professors who were a little lost, like me.

She also invited our philosophy professor, Daryl Culp, and it was a boon getting to know him. His office was next to mine, and I had to rely on his computer expertise for several months until I understood the system. I had been using WordPerfect in the States, and at LCC we had only Microsoft Word, so that was an adjustment. Daryl was also a music and art aficionado, and it was through him that I learned about the many concert venues. The concerts were a godsend to me!

Daryl introduced me to some of the bookstores in Klaipėda. He lived in a different section of the city, so in his daily life he often passed bookstores and libraries that I didn't. That difference proved helpful in finding a bookstore that he knew of near the corner of Donelaičio and Manto Streets that featured Lithuanian dictionaries, maps, and additional historical material, which helped me in teaching Baltic history. Since Germany had dominated Prussia, the area east of Lithuania, from 1200 till 1945 and had controlled the city of Klaipėda, which it called Memel, some of the historical sections in the bookstores focused on Baltic and Prussian history. Another bookstore named Akademia, pictured below, sold very large beautiful maps of medieval Lithuania and Prussia. It was delightful browsing there.

One of the book stores featuring student books was on the main street, Manto. My friend Viktor first took me there. Lithuania was just emerging from

Soviet dominance, and lack of advertising made these shops difficult to find. I either stumbled upon them while wandering around the city or someone showed them to me.

Another large bookshop existed on Manto Street, toward the downtown market. It featured serious works on history and philosophy as well as a large collection of popular novels by Steven King and John Grisham along with American pop psychology translated into Lithuanian. Since it sold books on Baltic history, it also provided resources for teaching my course. In addition, it sold some T-shirts, cards, and newspapers like the *Baltic Times*, and I stopped there about once a week to buy this small, but informative paper that carries English news about Latvia, Estonia, and Lithuania. It was good to read it as well as *Riga, Tallinn,* and *Vilnius in Your Pocket* pamphlets before traveling to those places on a holiday. Together, they provided good updates on social, cultural, and political events.

Akademia bookshop, Donelaičio Street, Klaipėda, 2003

My artist friend Tania introduced me to some used bookshops in the Old Town. These were wonderful sources for art books. The Soviets produced lavish art books filled with reproductions of major artists like Rembrandt. I especially loved a book of Rembrandt's pictures that contained an anachronistic painting of Mary holding a small book in one hand as she rocked baby Jesus' cradle. The light and themes were exquisite! The art books were always in immaculate condition and reasonably priced. I just loved them all, bought several, but couldn't bring them back to America because of their weight. I was able to distribute them to artist friends like Tania and Viktoras's sisters Loreta and Kristina, who both graduated with art degrees from Klaipėda University.

Sad to say, all these bookstores were economically threatened when a megastore named Maxima opened some distance from the city center. It resembled our Wal-Mart, and it featured books at discount prices. By the end of my stay in Klaipėda, some of the regular and used bookstores had gone out of business because of this store's competition. Maxima also sold clothes and groceries, so some of the downtown clothing stores also closed. Eventually, an entire shopping mall called Akropolis grew up around Maxima. It now contains an ice skating rink, movie theaters, restaurants, and shops. It's tremendously popular with all age groups but especially among young people.

Thrift Shops

Some of the faculty at LCC shopped at the thrift shops. My friend Dottie West and I especially enjoyed doing this. Some of the shops featured lovely items from Germany—suits, coats, suede jackets, formals, and scarves. Had I known about these great thrift shops, I wouldn't have brought so many of my clothes from the United States. Once, I bought a pretty orange suede jacket, two nice cashmere sweaters, other warm clothing for the damp climate, and some for the sunny weather too. I had brought enough suits and skirts from America for teaching, but it was always fun to buy something elegant and extravagant to wear to a concert or other dressy occasion. Shopping could also be an anthropological excursion, checking out the Lithuanians who patronized the shops, and seeing the low prices for most items except baby and children's clothing. Children's things always cost more than I expected.

I often toyed with the idea of buying a used fur coat because I wanted the comfort and warmth it offered, and furs were acceptable in Lithuanian society. But I never did. New Lithuanian dresses and clothes were inexpensive compared to American prices, so we bought a few linen outfits at the markets in Klaipėda and in Vilnius. Later, we found some wonderful linen outlet stores in Plungė and had outfits custom made for us by a tailor in Klaipėda.

Handicrafts in Plungė and Klaipėda

Our friend Janice Turner had a car because her husband worked at the oil company in Mazeikiai, and she often drove us out of town to visit some of the linen manufacturers and artisans. The nearby town of Plungė hosted many handicraft workers. One we came to know well was a woman who carved wooden angels in her kitchen with a hatchet. It's difficult to describe the appeal of her art. Her unique angels were one to two feet tall, and she painted them, giving each a personality. Some were named after various saints, and a friend bought an expensive one named St. Barbara for several hundred litai. I had a small one that cost about fifty litai, or fifteen dollars. It reminded me of my mother, and I treasured it. Unfortunately, I left it in Florida by mistake when I moved from there to Nebraska. This Plungė artist was so talented that she eventually moved to Germany, where she found a lucrative market for her work.

Another artisan that we visited in Plungė made beautiful bowls, vases, and furniture from burl wood. Again, it's hard to describe his work except to say that each bowl was exquisite. His large urns were impressive, smooth, and elegant. His furniture was a little weird since he sometimes put deer antlers on the chairs of the dining room sets he made. His tables made from the burl wood were extraordinary. Each piece was special and unique. I guess that's why his creations attracted customers from far away to his shop.

Klaipėda also had craftspeople and a special amber market, where lovely rings, necklaces, and broaches were very cheaply available. However, as the tourist trade increased, the cost of amber jewelry increased. Still, compared to home it was an excellent buy and I often brought special pieces back to the States with me as presents for friends. Whenever someone admired a piece I was wearing, I would give them the necklace or broach. Eventually, as the cost of amber increased and the value of the dollar decreased, I had to stop buying some of the striking original pieces I had earlier enjoyed.

Not far from LCC was an elderly woman weaver who made very special linen tablecloths. Her work was attractive because it was one of a kind and had character. Maybe she wove some of her soul into her work. It's hard to say why it was so special. Her weavings were not cheap because it took her a long time to make a large tablecloth from natural Lithuanian linen. Other handicraftsmen sold their wares at the Saturday market downtown. I loved seeing the children's toys and wooden bowls and spoons. I especially appreciated the hand-knit stockings. I bought them to wear around my apartment instead of house shoes because they were warm and comfortable. Most Lithuanians took off their shoes in the entry and wore slippers or knitted booties indoors, and I adopted this practice.

The handicraft items at the markets in the larger cities like Vilnius, Riga, and Tallinn were often of higher quality and price than those in Klaipėda. I bought some devastatingly beautiful red wool knee-high stockings with a brilliant pattern in Tallinn and still have them even though the toes have worn out and I have darned them several times. These socks have a beautiful pattern in the leg, and are dear to me. I first saw them in a handicraft collective in Tallinn and thought them too expensive, so I didn't buy them on that visit. When I saw them again a year later, I just had to have them. They were so exquisite and lovely.

A Rumšiškės wood sculptor and one of his ironic pieces, 2001

Visiting an artisan village like Rumšiškės near Kaunas or any handicraft shop is akin to going to an art museum. The quality of the work is high. Sometimes it's the blown glass, sometimes the hand-knit stockings, scarves, or sweaters at the sweater wall in Tallinn. The attraction is a little hard to explain, but perhaps it's one of the reasons we travel—to see things that are beautiful and different. We don't have to buy them all, just admire them. That's enough.

Pickpockets, Professional and Local

Because Klaipėda hosts many art and music festivals, and its beach attracted many tourists, pickpockets flocked there in summer and at holiday time. These same pickpockets, or their friends, also ply their trade in major cities like Riga and Tallinn where festivals and tourists also come together. Some of the professors at LCC and two of my visiting American friends had their credit cards stolen at the downtown Klaipėda market and at the Riga bus stop. I had escaped this insult until one summer when I was accosted three times by pickpockets and fell victim to one at the market. This is how it happened.

I had gotten off the bus at the downtown market one Saturday and was going to buy some vegetables and have a look around the handicraft booths, when I saw an elderly woman begging. I stopped, took my coin purse out of my backpack, and gave her some money. Instead of returning my purse to my backpack, I slipped it into my nylon jacket pocket. Unbeknownst to me, a professional thief was watching, noticed where I put my purse, and later stole it. It was only after I had gone into one of the secondhand shops at the market and had accumulated several items to buy that I realized I couldn't pay for my purchases because someone had stolen my coin purse. I was really angry. Not so much because I had lots of money in the bag but because I really liked the little leather purse, and because I had earlier stood in line at the post office to buy ten international stamps, and they had cost me both money and effort. So, I was feeling downcast and bothered. Finally, I realized that I could go to my nearby travel agency to borrow coins for the bus fare home. Compared to many others, I had gotten off lightly. I wasn't carrying any documents, credit cards, or large bills in my purse.

Two separate summers I experienced an attempted robbery. I had been downtown at an arts festival and had taken out my purse to buy a lavender crocheted sweater, and again a thief noticed where I put my coin purse. All of a sudden I realized something was wrong and touched my jacket pocket, noticing that my purse was gone. I turned around, shook my finger and stupidly shouted in English to a fellow: "Did you take my purse?" I doubt he knew English, but he dropped it at my feet and ran into the crowd. I should have been glad, but I just felt deflated. I wandered over to my friend Tania, who was selling some of her artwork, but I just couldn't get back into the ebullient mood of the festival. Dejected, I went home.

Another attempted robbery occurred at the beach. I loved going to the beach because it cheered me up. I usually went on Tuesday and Thursday mornings during the semester because I didn't teach until the afternoon on those days. Since I always prepared my lectures the night before, I was then free to go to the beach in the morning. When the weather was grey and miserable and I felt depressed or alienated, it felt good to go walk along the water, or walk in it if it was warm enough. During the winter and early spring, the beach was often deserted, but I never felt afraid. No one ever bothered me there.

One morning I had finished a nice walk, and it was sunny and warm as I waited at the bus stop. Some local people had come to the nearby forest to gather mushrooms and had basketsful to take home. I retrieved my bus money from my shorts pocket and was climbing onto the bus when an old man reached into my pocket to steal my coin purse. I was flabbergasted. I hit his hands with mine and said, "Stop that." Then to my astonishment he boarded the bus behind me and proceeded to sit opposite me on the ride to town. I felt so insulted. He didn't try to hide or take a later bus. He seemed to feel no shame, and I certainly couldn't scream at him in Lithuanian to shame him. I didn't have the language for that. So I just sat there feeling upset and put upon.

Since I suffered only three minor robberies in ten years, I was remarkably fortunate. I wasn't aware of being protected by my guardian angel, but I guess I was. I never lost any large amounts of money, never had my bank card or passport stolen, nor suffered any financial difficulty. I was blessed. On the other hand, I had heard of the problems with pickpockets when I first arrived, and I never walked around with any of my documents. When I had to pay my eight hundred litai in rent, I went to a nearby ATM kiosk to get the money during the daytime and then returned straightaway to my apartment. It always made me nervous to carry large amounts of money.

When traveling in foreign cities, I carried only a photocopy of my passport in my purse and always left the original in my suitcase in my hotel. I stayed in some pretty cheap hotels but was never robbed by the cleaning personnel. This system worked for me. In contrast to my experience, members of the Tarvydas family suffered both assaults and robberies. Once I gave Kristina some money so she could take an exit exam in high school. Some students ganged up on her and stole not only her money but her backpack as well. Another time her mother, Adolfina, was beaten up and given a black eye early one Sunday morning as she was walking her bike across the railroad tracks returning to her apartment from her garden. An LCC colleague was also attacked one night as he was walking across the bridge over the railroad tracks, and thieves stole his backpack with his computer.

So, in writing this account, I count myself blessed not to have ever been accosted. Maybe it was because I was an American and hence off-limits, or maybe it was because I was tall and intimidating. I didn't think about it when I lived there. I knew I could hide neither feature—my nationality or my height. All the locals took me for either a German or an American. They knew I wasn't one of them. When I asked Viktor how they knew, he said, "You swing your arms when you walk. Lithuanians don't do that." That surprised me. I guess there's always a clue that we don't pick up, but that local people do.

Winter

While Klaipėda charmed me with its summer sunshine, the rains soon set in with cooler fall weather. September was often not so cold, but October could be cold and damp. It turned out that the legacy of Soviet rule hung heavy in the city. Large apartment houses like mine were connected to a central heating system, and the heat for the entire city was not turned on until November. Apartment dwellers had no thermostat. I hadn't dealt with this problem since living in England during 1968–70, when we had no central heating, only fireplaces.

In Klaipėda, we had no fireplaces in our apartments, nor woolly underwear, so I kept warm as well as I could. When writing my lectures for Baltic history during the first semester, I warmed my hands using my ceramic teapot for a hot water bottle. I put it in my lap and placed my hands on it intermittently to warm up my fingers as I read, made notes, and wrote my lectures. Later, I boiled hot water in two tall soup pots, which produced steam and warmth for the kitchen as I worked at night. Since the kitchen was a fairly small room, if I shut the door, the steam heated up the room. I lived in this fashion for a few years before I discovered that I could buy a modern, rubber hot-water bottle at the pharmacy. My friend Viktor lent me his sister's hot-water bottle, and it was then that I found I could purchase a new one. That made my life more comfortable since it was portable and cozy.

In the bedroom, I initially coped with the cold by burying myself under two feather comforters. I could read in bed under the warm comforters. Usually I read from seven till eleven at night. Of course, the problem was how to stay awake when so cozy.

As I read more Baltic history, I became acquainted with the late nineteenth-century Polish writer Henryk Sienkiewicz. His long novels were intriguing, and I fell in love with several of them, especially *The Teutonic Knights*, set in medieval Poland and Prussia. I really appreciated this book because it helped me understand the medieval concept of knights and their love of fighting and code of honor, which I had never really understood before. His other novels also helped me comprehend Polish history. These included his trilogy of the seventeenth-century Polish commonwealth: *With Fire and Sword, The Deluge,* and *Fire in the Steppe.* My University of Iowa graduate school friend Janusz Duzinkiewicz gave me a video of his novel *With Fire and Sword*, and I showed parts of it to my Baltic history classes at LCC. It was such a long film we could never watch the whole thing, but it revealed the flavor of the period: the historical figures, the costumes, the ambience, and the warfare.

While history books tell us what happened, literature and films show us what it felt like. Scenes showing the armies of the Poles, Ukrainians, and Tartars were stunning. Sienkiewicz is more famous in the United States for his book and the 1951 Hollywood film *Quo Vadis* set in Nero's Rome. I had read this book and seen the film when I was in high school but didn't notice that the writer was Polish. He received the Nobel Prize in 1905 for his writings, but, sad to say, translation and copyright problems prevented him from becoming well-to-do.

After finishing my book on Russian and European women in 2001, I felt as if I could indulge myself and even began reading mysteries, a genre which I had heretofore avoided. The LCC library had many of them, and I soon devoured all the Dorothy Sayers, P. D. James, Agatha Christie, Jeffrey Archer, and other detective writers that the library possessed. Often faculty traveling to LCC would read a mystery on the plane and then donate it to the library, which is why there were so many of them.

I visited several of the downtown Klaipėda libraries, but their holdings in English were skimpy. Even so, I got a library card. One card enabled me to use all the libraries in Klaipėda, and for a few extra litai I could buy one allowing me to use all the libraries in the country! That astounded me. I used my card at the art library when looking for a picture for the cover of my book, but I never used the music library, although I often looked in its windows since it was located downtown near the Danė River. Later, I even did some research at Vilnius University Library, but no papers evolved from that research. I couldn't find sufficient resources to make meaningful comparisons about Lithuanian women in the 1930s and later census periods.

An LCC colleague who had a PhD in German history and I visited the head of the History Department of Klaipėda University. He was also the head of the

Baltic History Institute located downtown. At this institute, I found a few books in English—two very good ones about the Teutonic Knights and their organization and function during the twelfth to the fourteenth centuries. These were helpful in understanding how the Teutonic Knights invaded the Baltic areas after the Crusades ended. These knights even invaded parts of Russia, like Pskov and Novgorod, which were Orthodox but not Catholic. These events are well portrayed by Sergei Eisenstein in his film *Alexander Nevsky*. The knights conquered and converted parts of Latvia and Prussia but were unable to dominate pagan Lithuania, which only became Roman Catholic two centuries later when the Grand Duke of Lithuania Jogaila married Jadwiga, the Catholic Queen of Poland, in 1385.

In the fall of 2000, I was finishing my book *Russian and West European Women, 1860–1939*, when my editor asked me to provide a picture for the cover. She also wanted the book publishers' names in the bibliography. I had included only the place and date of publication to save space in my long book. These two requests led me to unforeseen experiences: one in Berlin and one in Klaipėda.

Christmas in Berlin

My first Christmas in Klaipėda was looking pretty bleak because most of my colleagues at LCC had returned to North America for the holidays. I was feeling lonely when I got an invitation from my East German friends Fred and Inge Schmidt to stay with them for Christmas and New Year's. This was an answer to an unspoken prayer. Moreover, with the aid of the internet I had been able to find all the publishers for my bibliography except those in German. Going to Germany presented an opportunity to obtain those.

I had met Fred Schmidt when he came to give a lecture at the University of Texas at El Paso in the 1990s. I had been designated to give Fred a ride, and when I asked him where to take him, he hesitated and then confessed he needed hospitality for a few days. So Fred stayed at my house for a couple of weeks. In subsequent years, I hosted him and his extended family. It was good that my house in El Paso had extra bedrooms and baths to accommodate guests. Little did I know then that I would one day be teaching in Lithuania, and that they would return my hospitality.

The Christmas of 2000, I took a ferry from Klaipėda to Sassnitz, East Germany, to visit them. It was an adventure, but since some Canadian colleagues from LCC had done this over our fall break, it seemed OK. Still, everything was new. I hadn't taken a ferry since 1963, when I was traveling with my husband and son. It was a bit unnerving traveling alone. After a long, long, long taxi ride to the port, I found and boarded the boat. I ate supper and slept well. The next morning, however, I was mystified at how to get off the boat. Everyone else was driving off in cars or trucks. There didn't seem to be any foot passengers except me. I finally exited the boat after wandering around for a while. I hurried to a bus stop to go to the train station and hadn't seen the passport control officials in my haste to catch the train. I didn't get my passport stamped, and this later caused me problems when trying to leave.

According to Fred's instructions, I needed to get a train in Sassnitz, then change for Berlin. I was a little apprehensive doing all this alone, but at the bus stop I was aided by a Bosnian refugee and her son, who had just gotten off a ferry from Sweden. They too had to change trains. The young boy spoke German as well as English and he not only helped me find my second train but also carried my suitcase for me. What a boon he was! Traveling has taught me that God hears our desperate prayers and provides in amazing ways. When I arrived in Berlin, Fred and Inge were waiting for me at the station—another blessing.

Although they had a car, we took the metro to their spacious apartment, where I met Inge's aged mother who was living with them and occupying the guest room. This meant that I would be staying in a downstairs apartment of some friends of theirs. The student who lived there was away on holiday, so his apartment was free for me to use. I think I may have eaten breakfast there, but I ate my other meals with Fred and Inge. I was astonished that Fred was such an excellent cook. He and Inge took turns showing me the sights of Berlin, but he always cooked the huge midday meal. Since it was the holidays, Inge was busy making various cakes and strudels. It was fun to watch her in their large kitchen. She used cooked potatoes with flour and eggs as the dough for one dessert. Then she added apples and baked or fried them. These were a delicacy from her childhood in Czechoslovakia. I had never eaten anything quite like them. They were scrumptious. On Christmas day, I attended a nearby historic German church for the service, but neither they nor their children did. Many Germans and Europeans are rather secular. They are not anti-Christian, just not very religious.

In the afternoon, their families and friends arrived, and we ate an enormous Christmas dinner, drank wine and liqueurs, ate dessert with coffee and tea, and then drank more wine and liqueurs. I was in agony by the evening. My family never ate and drank so much rich food in one day.

The next day I mentioned to Fred that I needed to go to a university to do some research for my book. He had studied philosophy at Humboldt University, in East Berlin, so he called and discovered that the university library was open only one day during the holidays, and that was the following day. He took me there, and I met the reference librarian. It turned out that all the information I needed about the German censuses and other sources was located in his office. What a relief. Since all the publication material was in one place, I could quickly add the publishers' names for my bibliography.

After I finished my work, Fred showed me around the university, and it was fascinating seeing a German university classroom, and learning that Inge's brother had been his philosophy professor in Marxism/Leninism when he was a young worker in Berlin after World War II. The connections in our work and friendships can be astounding. I was reminded of this incident while reading an article about the German philosopher Alexander von Humboldt in the October 26, 2015, *New Yorker*. Seeing the name Humboldt triggered the memory of our visit to the university.

After our visit to the university, Fred took me to a historic Berlin synagogue. It is a huge, awe-inspiring Moorish-style building, not reconstructed from its bombing during World War II. It had been a liberal synagogue with an organ, and a woman rabbi had been ordained there in 1935. Who would have guessed they had women rabbis then? There was also a small gift shop and an impressive art display. It was sad to see an armed guard at the entrance to prevent an anti-Semitic attack.

In addition to the synagogue, Fred took me to a nearby park that had been a Jewish cemetery. Now it contains only the marker for Moses Mendelssohn's grave. He was such an important figure in the German Enlightenment that even the Nazis left his stone untouched. I discovered that in Lithuania the Soviets also destroyed cemeteries to create parks. This occurred in downtown Klaipėda Sculpture Park and Kaunas Peace Park, both of which had been famous cemeteries.

Another day, Inge took me to the Berlin Pergamum Museum. It contains artifacts from the ancient Babylonians, Greeks, Romans, and Arabs. The Gates of Pergamum are enormous structures with dazzling decorative tiles. The Greek and Roman temple columns were equally awesome. Rows and rows of Greek military helmets and red and black funeral vases made me wonder if the German archeologists had left any treasures in Greece. On this visit, the Islamic section of the museum was not open. It took several years for it to be renovated, so I saw it later.

New Year's Eve

Soon, it was time to celebrate New Year's Eve, or Sylvester as the Germans call it. For this holiday, we went to friends of Fred's. They lived in a beautiful fifth-floor Mansard-roofed walk-up apartment overlooking Charlottenburg. That night we were able to see the fireworks from their windows. Again, I was unprepared for such a holiday feast. In the late afternoon, we were treated to a very rich cake, coffee, and cream. We talked a while, and then had a sumptuous dinner beginning with creamy pumpkin soup, several courses of meat, potatoes, and vegetables, wine and liquors. The dessert was chocolate mousse, and when I praised it to our hostess, she served me another portion. I ate it and then was in misery. At nine o'clock I had to lie down on the couch because my stomach was groaning from all the unaccustomed rich food and drink. I was a little embarrassed to lie down in a stranger's living room, but I was in such agony I could no longer sit up.

At midnight, we all went to the windows to watch the fireworks. Then we drank and ate more: herring that Inge had made and chips and guacamole that Fred had prepared. We also engaged in some traditional games, which were new to me. We each had a cup of boiling water into which our hostess poured melted lead. Then we deciphered what the lead images indicated for the New Year! Our host was a retired Protestant pastor, and I was surprised he and his wife participated in such a custom.

The pastor and Fred had met when they were working on a peace project. The pastor later escorted me around the famous Dome Cathedral in Berlin. He took me by elevator to the loft where I saw the immense organ that occupied an entire wall. Descending to the main floor, we attended the German noonday service. It was so touching reciting the "Our Father" in German and singing German hymns too. The printed bulletin contained the words, so visitors like me could participate in the worship service even though I didn't know much of the language. Something similar happened a few years later when I attended a Swedish worship service and was able to join in because the words of the Lord's Prayer and hymns were presented in Swedish for us to follow along. This service was equally endearing.

Friends in Klaipėda

In the winter of 2000, I told my colleague Daryl Culp about needing a picture for the cover of my book, and he suggested that I go to the art library on Donelaičio Street for help. I did and met a charming artist/librarian, Tatjana Simonaitienė, who helped me find some Russian art books. I checked out a few and asked Daryl his opinion of several of the paintings. He was an artist as well as a philosophy professor and very perceptive. He suggested that I choose one that showed a frontal view where the woman was looking at the viewer. He said this would draw the reader in. Finally, I chose Valentin Serov's *Portrait of Nadezhda Derviz with Her Child* (1888). It is an arresting picture and appropriate to the subject of my book.

Since I went to this library several times, I got to know Tatjana. She had some of her art on display at the library, and I found it captivating. That spring, my sister came to visit, and since she is an art therapist, I thought she might enjoy seeing some of Tatjana's work. So, Tania (short form of Tatjana) arranged a showing for us at her little apartment, which still had a coal-burning stove for heat. Much to my surprise, Tania had painted in many styles. While she trained as a watercolorist in Telšiai, she later learned to paint oil on canvas. After this visit, I bought several of her paintings, which cost only about one hundred dollars each, about four hundred litai at that time.

In the spring of 2001, the exchange rate was quite good, four litai for one dollar. During the latter part of Bush's presidency, it fell to 3Lt and finally 2.5Lt. So while my rent cost me 800Lt, it was only about two hundred dollars the first few years, but then almost four hundred dollars per month plus utilities the last few years. Part of the rate change was because Lithuanians pegged their currency to the euro rather than the dollar after they joined the European Union. Part of the decline was the fall in the value of the dollar under President Bush.

Tania's Garden

Over the years, I became friends with Tania, and she took me to her country garden where she and her mother grew flowers and vegetables. They also had fruit trees. We shared simple meals of bread, cheese, cake, tea, and perhaps an apple from one of her trees. She eventually built herself a lovely two-story summer home there. Her garden and dwelling were many miles from downtown Klaipėda, but buses often went there in summer. Below is a picture of Tania's mother and me in their garden having tea.

The Lithuanian bus system was a two-tier affair. One could take a large, old, cheap public bus, or the more modern, slightly more costly minivan. It was hard for me to believe that a litas difference in price was significant because I had enough money to live on. However, for artists like Tania and pensioners like her mother, who lived very close to the margin, each litas made a difference. Poorer Lithuanians seldom took the minivans. They almost always took the large, old buses or even walked long distances when they were short of money.

Amina and Marcelline in the garden, outskirts of Klaipėda, 2005

My friend Viktoras told me the origin of the Lithuanian buses. He said they usually came from Germany or the Scandinavian countries. When these countries replaced their buses, they sold the old ones cheaply to Poland and Lithuania. They looked like 1940 vintage to me.

At the bus stops, I usually took whichever bus arrived first. The routes were the same, but the large buses stopped only at designated stops, whereas the minivans would stop anywhere along the route. All one had to say was the Lithuanian word "Sostokite!" So the LCC faculty learned this command right away. This two-tier system also worked for traveling long distance. We could take a big old bus or a minivan to Kaunas, Vilnius, or the neighboring towns of Kretinga or Plungė. When traveling longer distances, the minivans were often faster, but the seats on the big buses were larger, more comfortable, and less crowded. Although the big buses were old, I only once took one that broke down. It was after a twenty-hour trip from Cyprus to Warsaw to Vilnius. It happened going from Vilnius to Klaipėda, and I was very, very tired and deprived of sleep. But our only option was to wait for a replacement bus to come, so we did. That was a lesson in patience, which travelers need.

Tania's Paintings

While I had been tremendously influenced by music most of my adult life, I hadn't been as touched by art until I met Tania. At LCC, I arranged various shows of her work, both the watercolors and oil on canvas. In the summer, Americans who came to teach at the English Language Institute were grateful to buy her watercolors. She charged only 40Lt, or ten to twenty dollars. What buys! An original watercolor for less than one would pay for a print in the United States.

One Mennonite teacher bought ten watercolors and repainted her living room to accommodate them. LCC friends Janet Turner and Alexa Maples, whose husbands worked at the oil refinery in Lithuania and who had high-paying positions, also bought canvases from Tania. My German friends Mecki and Helmut Grimm also bought several of Tania's paintings. Still, there were many galleries and markets in Klaipėda and Vilnius, so people bought art in lots of different venues. Tania took me to some of these galleries, especially those off the beaten path in the old towns of Klaipėda, Kaunas, and Vilnius. It was fascinating to see the beautiful ceramics, oil on canvas, glassware, jewelry, leatherwork, and so forth. The Klaipėda city art museum featured paintings but also displayed enormous woven textiles, leather work, and other arts and crafts by local artists and artisans.

Below are Tania and me with two of her paintings in her apartment. I am holding one called *Georgian Still Life*, meaning Georgia in the former Soviet Union. Tania is holding one that is an icon of Jesus with Russian Orthodox cupolas in the foreground.

Slowly, Tania and I became friends, and I began inviting her to tea at my apartment. She also came to the Anglican English-speaking church on Sunday nights. Our church met on Sunday nights at a Lutheran church downtown. Some people, like Tania and her friend Irina Petrochenko, were Russian Orthodox and taught me a keener appreciation of Russian icons. They came to our church partly for company and partly to practice their English. Others did the same, but I never got to know all the local people who came.

On Friday afternoons, I would often serve tea and cake to Tania, Irina, and my LCC friends Dottie and Roxanne. We all practiced English with Tania and Irina, prayed a bit, and enjoyed tea, fruit, cake,

Marcelline and Tania with Georgian Still Life and icon, Klaipėda, 2002

Left to right: Irina Petrochenko, Viktor, and Kristina Tarvydas, birthday party, Adolfina's place, 2003

and socializing. In the United States I was used to entertaining by serving tea and cake, and I kept this custom in Lithuania. As I noted earlier, it was only years later that I discovered some of my Lithuanian friends were disappointed that I served tea instead of vodka. During the Soviet period, vodka was the universal drink and very cheap. Apparently everyone served it to company. I just hadn't realized that was the custom since none of my Mennonite friends or Lithuanian colleagues mentioned this. It's not always easy learning the customs of other cultures. Sometimes people are hesitant to tell you what is polite or rude.

Holiday in Kaunas with Tania

Over the years, I got to know Tania pretty well. One spring break I didn't have much money for a long-distance holiday, so I asked Tania to be my guide on a trip to Kaunas. I knew she'd studied and lived there, so she could guide me around the city, especially the restaurants, museums, and art galleries that were off the beaten path. Our arrangement was that I would pay for our transportation there and back on the train and buy our food and she would help us find some reasonably priced lodging. I was quite surprised when she asked her former in-laws to put us up. They lived in the nearby town of Janova, and we took a minibus from there in the mornings and back again in the evenings. Apparently when Tania was married, she had been very good to her mother-in-law. She had helped her when she had bad asthma attacks and was hospitalized. This was why we were welcome to stay with her in-laws even though she was divorced from their eldest son.

Her father-in-law had been a Forest Brother, one who resisted Soviet rule by living in the forest and engaging in guerilla warfare for a few years after World War II. Like others, he was eventually captured, taken to the Gulag, and made to work in the mines. When he had completed his sentence, he was allowed to study in Leningrad/St. Petersburg but not to study journalism—his heart's desire. Instead, he had to study engineering.

He eventually worked at a factory in Janova, outside of Kaunas. A clever, ambitious man, he eventually became head of the factory, and when the Soviets left, he became deputy minister of defense in the new Lithuanian government. Since he had enjoyed an important position at the factory, he and his wife and three sons occupied an apartment with three bedrooms. It was spacious by Soviet standards, and I never saw another like it.

Since they were fond of Tania and had extra space, they put us up during our holiday in Kaunas. At breakfast they served something that looked like uncooked bacon, which they all ate with great gusto with bread. I just couldn't quite choke it down and was quite embarrassed that I couldn't eat it. I did, however, eat the bread and drink the coffee they offered.

This trip revealed other examples of how God provides. Even though I hadn't had enough money to take a noteworthy vacation to Cyprus or Tunisia, as some of my colleagues did that spring, I had a delightful time with Tania. We visited some unusual places like the Museum of Musical Instruments. It was fascinating because Lithuanian folk music requires a variety of instruments I had never seen. It was fun learning about them. She also took me to an art gallery where the creations of the local university art students were sold. Their works were innovative and reasonably priced. Later, I went there several times by myself, but I seldom bought anything. Still, I enjoyed looking at the striking creations. She also showed me some enchanting restaurants on the edge of the Old Town that served traditional Lithuanian meals, and she showed me some exquisite churches I had never seen before.

We also toured a restored Jewish synagogue in Kaunas. The Nazis had stored furniture in it during the war, so it hadn't been destroyed. It is near the Old Town and the Čiurlionis National Art Museum. Sad to say, hardly any

Lithuanian Jews survived the Holocaust. Most who worship there today are Russian Jews from the former Soviet Union. Behind the synagogue is a memorial to those Jews who died at Ninth Fort during World War II. It was odd experiencing Jewish culture devoid of Jews. Once Tania asked me if I was Jewish since I was interested in Jewish culture. I had to explain that Americans take the Holocaust seriously.

The most charming event of our Kaunas trip was our visit to Pažaislis Monastery on the outskirts of the city. This was a convent with only a few nuns because the Soviets had closed the monasteries and convents in Lithuania during their rule, 1946–1990. Only a few women surreptitiously lived a monastic life, working as teachers, so this was not a flourishing place. We met one of the nuns, and she graciously offered us hot tea and cookies on that cold snowy day. She belonged to the Congregation of the Sisters of St. Casimir.

Imposing renovated synagogue in Kaunas, 2006

We took a special bus to get there, but Tania knew how to do it. On our way to the convent, I remember falling into deep snow on the rugged path we walked. Luckily I didn't hurt myself in the fall, and I didn't get too wet either. Still, for March it was a very cold, snowy day.

Pažaislis Convent, Kaunas, 2006

Most of my LCC colleagues went south during our holidays. Some went to sunny Cyprus, Egypt, or Tunisia. They often got together to share their pictures and held a potluck dinner to talk over their experiences. I envied them their good times but have to admit that my experience at Pažaislis and in Kaunas was so special that I could only thank God for bringing so much joy from so little money.

Marcelline with LCC friends and buddies Ann and David Wollman, 2001

LCC Friends

The first year I arrived in Lithuania, I had a buddy named Jackie from LCC who showed me around. The second year I became a buddy to the Wollmans, Ann and David. We became good friends partly because David also taught history at LCC, and we went on trips together. One fall break, the Wollmans, Dottie, Marg, my friend Rosemary (from Washington, DC), and I went on a sightseeing tour of Latvia and Estonia. We rented a van and hired a driver, who happened to be one of Dottie and Marg's students.

Having an experienced guide, we were able to go to some out-of-the-way places like the Palace of the Duke of Courland, which is located outside of Riga. This majestic mansion was built by Rastrelli, the same Italian architect who built the Hermitage in St. Petersburg. Like Versailles, it was designed to impress visitors, and it does. Forty of its one hundred rooms had been restored, and the white grand ballroom was splendid. The windows and light were incredible. In Riga and Tallinn we were able to stay in pleasant but inexpensive hotels because our driver's parents owned a travel agency and provided well for us. In Riga we bought tickets to a lively ballet, which was held at the historic and impressive Opera House. That evening was a real treat. We had excellent seats for very reasonable prices. The next day, we went to two castles in Sigulda, Latvia, dating from the time of the Teutonic and Livonian Knights. One was not restored and laying in ruins but was haunting in the mist and rain. The other had been renovated and was quite impressive.

The next day we drove to Estonia, stopping in the little Hanseatic town of Parnu. It was utterly charming. I always meant to return to see more of it but never did, mostly because public transportation only goes from Riga to Tallinn and doesn't stop in Parnu. Pushing on to Tallinn, we viewed the magnificent walled city, which is often called the "Pearl of the North." Again, we saw many lovely old churches, and I went to another ballet.

Everyone else went to eat a large meal in the Old Town, but I figured I could always have a good meal but not always see an exquisite ballet. Besides, I knew I could get a candy bar or something during intermission if I was really hungry. The performance hall was rather nondescript and fairly modern, rather like the one in Vilnius, not nearly as grand and distinguished as the nineteenth-century Riga Opera House. The more imposing building in Tallinn is Kadriorg Palace and Art Museum. It is sumptuous and worth seeing. In the palace's museum, I saw an oil painting by the Russian artist Anna Ostroumova Lebedeva, whose work I had only seen reproduced in books. I had discussed her life and art in my book *Russian and West European Women* and was impressed to see her rather Socialist Realist painting of a Baku oil rig. However, it was nothing like the more romantic etchings of Italian and Russian landscapes I had seen in pictures.

After all our sightseeing, we returned to LCC refreshed and ready to finish our semester. Since living in Klaipėda was challenging, we LCC teachers often bonded and then remained friends after returning to the States. Some of my friends and I have visited each other during our retirement. Dottie West and her husband, Harold Mondal, have invited me to their home in Lansing, Michigan, several times. We have even met up in Florida. Others, like Richard Hansgen of Columbus, Ohio, and Barbara Hoffman of St. Joseph, Missouri, have visited me in Lincoln, and I have stayed with them. These friendships were and remain an unexpected bonus of living and teaching in Lithuania.

Klaipėda Wedding Palace

At the end of my first year at LCC, our chief librarian got married at the Wedding Palace. I was anxious to see the ceremony but also the building since I had read many Soviet novels that mentioned such places. The one in Klaipėda was a modern red-brick building that was rather nondescript on the outside. On the inside, though, it was captivating. A lovely mosaic mural covered one wall, and an organ provided traditional wedding music. On Saturdays, many couples dressed in traditional white wedding gowns and black suits patiently waited in the parking lot to enter the building to get married. Everyone had to have this civil ceremony to be legally wed.

The couple from LCC was unusual in that they had a church ceremony afterward as well. A church ceremony alone would not have been legally binding. During the Soviet period and even during independence, people had to go to the Wedding Palace to be properly wed.

The newly married had fascinating customs. They would go downtown, where the groom carried his bride over seven bridges. They also put a lock on one of the bridges to symbolize their union. In Russia, brides usually took their wedding bouquets to the local Tomb of the Unknown Soldier as a form of homage. I had seen this ceremony in both Moscow and Leningrad during the winter of 1985. The Soviets lost millions in World War II, so soldiers were honored as a form of patriotic remembrance. Whether Russians in Lithuania followed this custom, I don't know.

Music in Klaipėda

Another godsend in Lithuania were the professional classical music concerts held several times a week. They were extremely affordable, often costing only a few litai, sometimes not even a dollar. Klaipėda being a sizeable city, it had four concert halls, with live, usually classical, music available several nights a week. Many concerts began at six in the evening, but the operas and symphonies at the main concert hall began at seven or eight. *Fiddler on the Roof* and *Threepenny Opera*, performed in Lithuanian, were two of the most memorable performances I saw. Among the outstanding concerts, I remember Ravel's *Bolero*, a Tchaikovsky piano concerto with orchestra, the Vilnius Kanga Drummers, a fascinating harp concert, Stravinsky's poignant *Ballad of a Soldier*, and a memorable Chopin concert played on two grand pianos in a newly renovated concert hall. Ballets like *Tango in Fa* were choreographed and performed by famous Lithuanian dancers.

Music was important to me because I was sometimes lonesome, depressed, or upset. Music heals, restores, and refreshes us. I surprised myself by listening to American jazz while preparing supper at night. I had never enjoyed jazz, but it was available in the evenings on a Lithuanian radio station. It made me feel connected to home. Even though I wasn't aware of being homesick or patriotic, obviously on occasion I was. After a while I even went to some of the free International Jazz Festivals that were held each June in Klaipėda. I hesitated to ask my friends about going to the jazz performances with them, but eventually I began feeling more comfortable about this. One Sunday evening after church, I remember going to the festival and hearing a Russian jazz band play a haunting, enticing piece with a Central Asian melody.

One of the most unusual experiences I had in Klaipėda was taking my neighbor Adolfina to an accordion concert one Saturday afternoon. I had seen the concert advertised in the paper and thought it would be folk music that we would enjoy. But surprisingly, it was classical accordion music. They played pieces by Bach with violin accompaniment. In some ways the bellows of the accordion resemble an organ, and this was the effect the group created. The ensemble even played a new classical composition by a local composer. He was in the audience, as were many of the pupils of the performers, so it made the entire afternoon a memorable one but different from what I had anticipated. At the concert, former pupils lavishly bestowed flowers on the performers and composer.

The presentation of flowers was one of the most touching aspects of any concert in Klaipėda. It always amazed me. Lithuania was such a poor country, and yet people presented flowers to performers, even to their accordion teachers. It was so bittersweet. America is such a rich country, but we don't have this custom, at least not to the same extent. Only occasionally do we give flowers to our performers. It's not standard practice in the Midwest where I live. However, flowers are a significant part of Lithuanian culture. People usually give their friends flowers or candy for their birthday. Also, children march to school in the fall carrying a flower to present to their teacher at the beginning of the school year. Alas, this custom did not extend to university professors, and I didn't receive any flowers from my students. Another fascinating aspect of flower culture was that grocery stores had a corner with a flower arranger who made striking displays. The prices were not exorbitant. Two dollars could buy a splendid arrangement. The aesthetic sense was very highly developed there—whether in the stunning presentation of flowers or the artistic arrangement of food in a café or restaurant.

Church in Klaipėda

In Lithuania, I witnessed how international the church is. Our priest, Roy Ball, was an Englishman. His wife, Joke, was Dutch. The worshipers were Americans, Lithuanians, Ukrainians, Russians, Armenians, Ghanaians, and even a few Muslim converts from Albania and Central Asia. One of my American friends was a Baptist from Oklahoma, and her home church provided shoes and winter coats to children at the orphanages in Klaipėda and Palanga. They even gave me 100Lt (about twenty-five dollars) one Christmas to buy my friend Viktor a new winter coat and trousers. When I asked him what size pants he wore, he didn't know, he'd never had new ones. He had always worn clothes from the thrift shops. I was dumbfounded.

Here's a picture of our priest, Roy Ball, administering communion with a friend and me in the background assisting. Since Roy was an Anglican and I was an Episcopalian, he asked me to help distribute the bread and wine. I was deeply touched to do this. Religion was intertwined with life at LCC. We had Roman Catholic and Russian Orthodox students but few Protestants, except for the faculty. One of our professors, David Shenk, was a Mennonite missionary, and when he went to places like Albania, Macedonia, Kyrgyzstan, Uzbekistan or Ukraine to evangelize, we soon had students from those countries at the college.

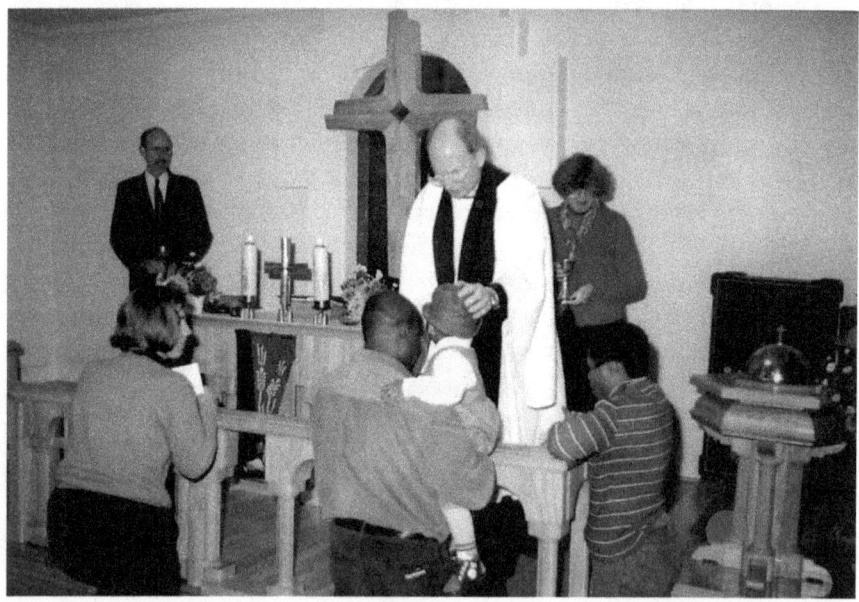

Communion at church, with a Ghanaian family at the altar and Marcelline in the back right, 2001

Once, LCC faculty and staff were invited to meet with the Dalai Lama in Vilnius for a discussion. I really looked forward to this, thinking it would be a small group. However, it turned out that we were not the only ones involved, and it was less intimate than I had expected.

The best part of the trip to Vilnius was that Alexa Maples and I decided to stay at a convent near Kaunas that a colleague had visited. We thought it would be cheaper than staying in Vilnius and a captivating experience too. The nuns at the convent were so welcoming, especially the night we arrived after driving around for several hours to find the place. They prayed for us and served us tea and cookies when we finally arrived at eleven. The abbess was of Lithuanian ancestry but had grown up in Scotland, so she knew both English and Lithuanian. We were blessed that she knew English and we could communicate. I think we stayed two nights, and we had a refreshing time walking near the Nemunas River. I love being near water, so I enjoyed strolling there one evening. We worshiped with the nuns in the morning, received their food and hospitality quite willingly, and vowed to return but never did. Above is a picture of me and two of the nuns the night we arrived. My friend Alexa was an avid photographer, and I'm indebted to her for some of the photos included in my memoir.

Marcelline and nuns at the Carmelite convent Paštuva, Kaunas, 2006

Travel in Lithuania and Eastern Europe

Churches

Travel in Eastern Europe and Russia often included a spiritual dimension. Stunningly restored churches grace all the major cities. Vilnius, Kraków, Riga, Tallinn, and Prague all oozed Old World charm and beauty. It was impossible to decide which was the most splendid and remarkable. Each has many breathtaking churches in addition to a main cathedral. Vilnius, Kraków, and Prague were not bombed during World War II, so they have an enormous number of beautiful medieval and Baroque church structures.

Russian influence is also felt in the ornate Russian Orthodox churches in Riga, Tallinn, Kaunas, and Vilnius. There are even some lavish Reformation churches where worship services are offered in German or English. Travelers can make a pilgrimage to visit the elegant churches in each city. This was often my favorite way to see a city—going from one exquisite house of God to another to offer a prayer and bask in the beauty and holiness.

In Eastern Europe, most of these impressive structures were in the old towns. Since many of these cities had been under Soviet rule, the architecture outside the old towns is often nondescript, while the old towns shine with beautiful Baroque churches and brilliant Art Nouveau buildings from the nineteenth century. They envelop the visitor in splendor and expectation.

Another fascinating aspect to these churches was that during the Soviet period many served as venues for concerts, and they still offer marvelous music today, especially on high holy days such as All Saints' Day, Christmas, Good Friday, and Easter. Indeed, in Prague, tourists can enjoy concerts every day during the summer in its exquisite Baroque churches. At times, music literally drew me into a church. The first All Saints' Day that I was in Vilnius, I just kept following the music I was hearing on the street until I found the source.

Walking with a friend one night, we came upon a wonderful concert at St. John's Church, which belonged to the university in the Old Town. You can only imagine our pleasure in sitting in such a beautiful venue listening to equally spectacular music. Later that same weekend, we came upon a group of young

St. John's Baroque R. C. church, Vilnius (Olga1969, Wikimedia)

musicians playing at St. Bernardino Convent, raising money for its restoration. The next summer, when my son, daughter-in-law, and sister were visiting me, we also visited this desecrated place, as the picture below shows.

Nothing compares to the thrilling experience of my first magnificent organ concert at the medieval Dome Cathedral in Riga or Tallinn. The dome in Tallinn also serves as a showplace for art, and the display of the Danse Macabre is overwhelming, almost frightening. It's reminiscent of Ingmar Bergman's film *The Seventh Seal*, set in the Middle Ages. Another time when visiting Tallinn, some friends and I went to see Charles's Church and listened to a remarkable choir that was visiting from an Orthodox monastery. When they sang the Russian national anthem, everyone in the church rose to their feet. I recognized the Tchaikovsky melody but hadn't known it was used for the Russian anthem.

Martin at the unrestored St. Bernardino Convent, Vilnius, 2001

Most surprising to me was that many smaller towns in Eastern Europe also possessed elegant churches. Plungė, Lithuania, boasts an impressive church that has been restored to its original splendor. Likewise, the small Latvian city of Liepāja has three magnificent churches with amazing wood sculptures and decoration, and one has an enormous organ. This organ was the second largest in Europe before World War I. Some LCC colleagues were blessed to hear this organ, but the Sunday I was there, the organist was absent, so I didn't get to hear it.

Other international church experiences that I know are possible are staying at the Baptist seminary in Prague, the Lutheran study center in Tallinn, and the Christian University Conference Center in St. Petersburg. One Lutheran colleague from LCC stayed at the center in Tallinn, and some other colleagues stayed at the Baptist seminary while attending a conference in Prague. Several times toward the end of my time teaching in Lithuania I stayed at the St. Petersburg Christian University Conference Center. Meeting Christians there from Canada, Belarus, and Russia was heartwarming and endearing.

Travel to St. Petersburg, March 2001

One of my first trips outside Lithuania was going to St. Petersburg in March 2001. A Park College friend, Kathy Hilt, had inquired about my sister, and I ended up corresponding with her by email and then staying with her during my spring break. Kathy was teaching American literature on a Fulbright Scholarship in St. Petersburg, and since her teaching load was fairly light, she took time to be a splendid hostess to me. From her apartment in Pushkin Square near Nevsky Prospect, we walked to many of the major historical and cultural sites. I was grateful to have her show me around because it had been almost thirty years since I had walked around the city, and I didn't remember where everything was. We strolled along Nevsky Prospect to famous places like the immense department store Gostiny Dvor and the Saltykov-Shchedrin Library, where I did some research for a few days. The library's impressive medieval, nineteenth-century, and early twentieth-century holdings were magnificent.

Saltykov-Shchedrin Library, St. Petersburg, 2001

We also took in the Russian State Art Museum, which I had never heard of before, as well as a concert hall called the Capella. Having not been to the Russian museum, I found it refreshing to discover several rooms overflowing with breathtaking icons. Many of them were immense and brightly colored. Some, like one memorable painting of St. Paul, were the work of famous icon painter Andrei Rublev. Otherwise, the early modern Russian art of the sixteenth to the eighteenth centuries was not so impressive.

I especially enjoyed seeing the work of famous Russian artists Natalia Goncharova, Mikhail Vrubel, Vasily Perov, and Vasily Surikov. Portraits of famous Russians by Ilya Repin, Vladimir Serov, and Nathan Altman were superb. Pictures by the Constructivists in the Soviet period were also outstanding. Later in the week, we heard an enchanting concert at the Capella hall. One of the perquisites Kathy enjoyed was a special card that enabled her to attend Russian cultural events at Russian instead of inflated tourist prices. This meant that going to the ballet was not expensive for her. However, even the tourist prices at the Capella were modest. Walking down Nevsky Prospect with a college friend from forty years ago was so refreshing. I had known no one in Lithuania when I came to teach at LCC, so it felt good to renew an old American acquaintanceship.

Before going to St. Petersburg, I had heard of a cheap flight from Kaliningrad and was delighted to pay only one hundred dollars in American money for a roundtrip flight. Kaliningrad was very close to Klaipėda, and I could take a bus there for about ten dollars. I found out about this deal from some Mennonite colleagues at LCC. They often knew inexpensive ways to travel and cheap places to stay. At the Saltykov-Shchedrin Library, I did some research on Russian women in Civil Defense in the 1930s. It was fascinating to use a Russian library since I had read so much about them in various novels. I had taken a letter of introduction signed by President Menninger of LCC. The rules and regulations reminded me of everything I had read about the old Soviet bureaucratic system.

After I found some Soviet periodicals that I wanted to use and had identified some helpful articles, I asked to photocopy some pages. I soon discovered how complex this process was. First I had to pay to have a journal from the 1930s copied because it was considered fragile. Then I had to go to a separate floor and stand in line again to pay to have the pages copied. Finally, I had to join a line to pick up the work when it was finished. All this was enthralling. It was Soviet bureaucracy exactly as I had read about it. Sorry to say, it remained unchanged in modern Russia. Gorbachev's restructuring reforms had not made it to the library.

However, I did meet a charming young woman from Uzbekistan when I went to the lunchroom to wait for my copying. I enjoyed talking with her but was flabbergasted that she spoke English but not Uzbek. She was of Russian heritage, and many of these people did not bother to learn the language of the people in the countries where they lived. This was true of Russians I met in Latvia too. They were Great Russian Chauvinists. They thought Russian language and culture superior to those of the various republics where they lived. I also met many students who held these views when I taught at LCC.

I discussed ethnocentrism in my Western civilization course when teaching about the conquistadores in Mexico and Europeans during nineteenth-century Imperialism, but the Russian students did not "get" it. Needless to say, the Lithuanians were not charmed by this behavior and resented the fact that Russian was often the lingua franca in the dormitories because there were so many students of Russian heritage.

In St. Petersburg, Kathy and I decided to make a pilgrimage to Dostoevsky's grave in the Alexander Nevsky Monastery cemetery. Unfortunately, it was a rather bleak, icy day. Entering the monastery, I was shocked that they charged a fee for admission and a second fee to walk around the graveyard. We didn't find Dostoevsky's grave but Tchaikovsky's, and we were able to pay our respects to him as well as the famous Russian composers Mussorgsky, Borodin, Rimsky-Korsakov, and Cui who were buried nearby.

Marcelline at Tchaikovsky's grave, Alexander Nevsky cemetery, 2001

At right (top) is a picture of Dostoevsky's grave that I was able to see the next year when it was warmer and we had more time to look around the Alexander Nevsky Monastery. Below that is the stunning statue of Catherine II with her lovers arranged below her. It is located opposite the Saltykov-Shchedrin Library on Nevsky Prospect, so I got to see it each day I walked to the library to do my research. I was always impressed by the statue's size and theme.

Second Trip to St. Petersburg, 2002

The next year, a Canadian couple at LCC, Bert and Leonora Suss, asked me to accompany them to St. Petersburg as a guide. Leonora was a fan of Catherine because Catherine had offered asylum and land to Mennonites to come to Russia in the late eighteenth century. She was one of the few monarchs to do this. She gave them free land and freedom from military service. As pacifists, they appreciated this. We stayed at an inexpensive hostel that my American friend Larry Meisgeier had told me about. We noticed a trolley ran near the hostel, then onto Nevsky Prospect, where many of the cultural sites were located, and to imposing St. Isaac's Cathedral.

The trolleys cost only a few kopecks, or pennies, and were convenient and fun to ride. I tried to take trolleys in the East European cities I visited, since we don't have them in the States. They're usually an inexpensive and good way to see city environs and observe the local population. My friend Dottie West also came on this trip, so we booked an entire sleeping car on the Riga–St. Petersburg train. We didn't get much sleep,

Dostoevsky's grave, viewed on a later and warmer visit to St. Petersburg, 2002

Statue of Catherine II and her lovers, Nevsky Prospect, St. Petersburg, 2001

despite the comfortable beds, because in the middle of the night the Latvian border guards woke us up to stamp our passports, and then a bit later the Russians did the same thing. After two interruptions, we couldn't get back to sleep. Maybe we were too excited, or too worried. Who knows? During their inspection, the Russians persistently demanded something, but we didn't know what. We had our visas in our passports, but they were looking for an additional document showing that we had permission to stay in St. Petersburg. The only problem was the Lithuanian travel agent hadn't given us this paper. Finally to get rid of them, Bert Suss repeated loudly, several times: "Professor, Professor," and then they let us alone.

When we got to our hostel the next morning, the receptionist explained the form and why we needed it. The hostel sold the document only when a traveler was booking with them outside the country. Since we hadn't done that, they couldn't sell us one. Another traveler at breakfast told us the next day that we could buy it nearby for five hundred rubles, about twenty dollars each. The form was for the police in case they stopped you and wanted to know where you were staying. I hadn't known about this form the first time I went to St. Petersburg, and I wasn't stopped by the police, so I hadn't needed it. However, I then remembered my hostess Kathy Hilt asking me about it before I came, and I hadn't known what she was referring to. It turned out some friends of hers in England had been unable to obtain it and so hadn't been able to visit her while she was teaching on her Fulbright scholarship.

In St. Petersburg, my LCC colleagues and I did many of the usual tourist things—strolled along Nevsky Prospect, visited the Hermitage Museum, viewed the holdings of the Russian State Art Museum, enjoyed the Museum of Ethnography, and took a canal cruise around the city. We also did something a little unusual—we took a public bus and a tram to Peterhof, Catherine the Great's Palace, with its marvelous fountains built by Peter the Great. Leonora was anxious to see the "Amber Room" in Catherine's palace. She knew a lot about Catherine, and this surprised me since many people only know about her sex life.

This trip was endearing to me not only because we got to see the exquisite fountains, Catherine's fashionable palace, and Peter's modest summer house but also because we could see what life was like in the suburbs. Few Russians lived in apartments near Nevsky Prospect, as my friend Kathy Hilt did. The acres of decrepit suburban apartments were pretty depressing. While most of them were not so old, having been built after World War II, after so much of St. Petersburg was destroyed by the Nazis, they looked aged and worn. It was sad seeing how most people lived. It was a good antidote to the beautiful, brightly painted, former gentry-class stucco houses that dotted Nevsky

Prospect. Without this trip to Peterhof, I wouldn't have known how and where ordinary Russians lived.

Third Trip to St. Petersburg

The third time I went to St. Petersburg was when a high school friend, Karen Piper, from La Porte, came to visit me in Klaipėda. In retirement, she had taken up watercolor painting and was eager to see some particular pictures at the Hermitage. We took the bus to Riga and then the overnight train to St. Petersburg. This was in the spring of 2007. By this time, I had heard of another inexpensive place to stay. One LCC couple had stayed at St. Petersburg Christian University Conference Center. Since they were missionaries to LCC, they received a special rate and lived there quite cheaply. Through the internet, I connected with SPCU and made arrangements for Karen and me to stay there.

It was a long way from Nevsky Prospect to Narvskaya metro stop and then to SPCU. We took a cab but still had a hard time finding it; although its address was 13 Narvskaya Prospect, it was hidden away in a courtyard and difficult for our taxi driver to find. It was a Spartan place, in a neighborhood where ordinary Russians lived. There was a fruit stand, grocery store, and other shops nearby. While I usually cooked my own food in Klaipėda, we didn't do much cooking in St. Petersburg since part of the charm of traveling is eating out. On this trip, we often ate at the nearby McDonald's because Karen couldn't eat anything with onions or garlic, and she was leery of Russian restaurants. This was OK with me because it gave me an opportunity to see how the Russian breakfast and dinner menus compared with American menus and also to observe what sort of Russians patronized the place. This McDonald's was always packed, mostly with young people. The food was cheap by American standards, but I don't know if it was so cheap for Russians because I hadn't yet been to local restaurants to check prices for meals there.

I had read in the *St. Petersburg in Your Pocket* travel booklet that the Hermitage had free admission one Thursday per month. We were fortunate to be visiting that particular Thursday and so we went then. I again visited the Rembrandt section to see his painting *The Prodigal Son*. As in previous visits, I was deeply touched—certainly a spiritual high. I bought some calendars with the picture for friends at LCC who had read Henri Nouwen's book *The Prodigal Son*. He wrote it after gazing at Rembrandt's painting for several days.

Karen had a few favorite artists whose work she wanted to see at the Hermitage, and we were able to see them. She also bought some captivating art pieces at an outdoor market on Nevsky Prospect. She purchased some porcelain figurines at the Russian Imperial porcelain factory stores, while I bought some special gold-rimmed white plates that would go with my blue and gold Catherine the Great tea service. During our week there, we had a good time. The weather was warm but not hot, and we thoroughly enjoyed ourselves as typical tourists.

Catherine II tea service, St. Petersburg Imperial Porcelain Company

Fourth Trip to St. Petersburg

The next year I returned to St. Petersburg again but by overnight bus from Riga, and again I stayed at the SPCU conference center. Somehow I didn't mind the long-distance buses in Europe. Long distance usually meant overnight—ten to twelve hours—whether from Kraków to Klaipėda or Riga to St. Petersburg. Missing one night's sleep wasn't so awful. And of course I did rest and doze a bit.

In contrast, long-distance buses in the States often mean twenty-four hours or more. When I was married, we sometimes took the bus from New York City to Iowa City, a total of twenty-three hours. The trip was tedious and not so picturesque. On the overnight bus from Riga to St. Petersburg, we stopped in Pskov, and in the moonlight this historic city looked attractive and thrilling. In contrast, stopping at stations in Cleveland, Ohio, and other American cities along Interstate 80 at night was not such a historic or enchanting experience. On the contrary, these stops struck me as unpleasant and dangerous in the middle of the night. Another difference was the attitude of the passengers.

In Eastern Europe, travelers often had a sense of conviviality on the overnight buses. Maybe they were more used to making the best of life. Traveling at night usually seemed more of a lark and not threatening. The passengers were never drunk or boisterous, just good natured. They usually brought their own food to save money. Often it was older folks or students, mainly middle-class people, who were on the bus, so I always felt comfortable in their midst.

By my fourth visit to St. Petersburg, I knew where to buy my bus ticket as well as to arrange my visa with a Russian travel agent in Klaipėda. Moreover, I was familiar with one of the directors of the St. Petersburg Christian University

Center. He spoke English, was a fount of information about modern Russian life, and was approachable.

Much to my surprise, he didn't seem to mind the petty corruption that existed and that I had inquired about. He told me that when he was stopped by a policeman for a traffic violation, he could either spend a lot of time going to the station to sort out the problem and pay his fine, or just bribe the police officer and drive away. He didn't mind the bribe. It saved him time and energy. For him, the issue was money versus time, and he preferred to pay in coin.

I also asked him about the treatment of Muslims in St. Petersburg. A Kirgiz student at LCC had told me he was treated better there than in Moscow, and I asked the director of the center about this. I had noticed that the drivers of the minivans in our neighborhood were mostly Central Asian. Some of them also shopped at the nearby grocery, and I didn't see anyone harassing them. He said that nobody in St. Petersburg discriminated against Muslims. This rather surprised me because I had observed quite a bit of racism in Klaipėda and knew from several sources that in Moscow thugs beat up Central Asians. St. Petersburg seemed a more tolerant city.

On this visit, I met some Belorussian women. We were on the same floor at the seminary, and they were endearing. I tried my fractured Russian on them, and they graciously responded. They even shared their food and some of their religious experiences with me. This was a very tender time. I knew most Belorussians were poor, so I felt guilty when they shared their precious food with me. But I didn't want to insult them by not eating with them. It's always touching to break bread with Christians in foreign countries. On this trip I was going most days to the St. Petersburg film and photo archive to do research for my new book *Remarkable Russian Women*, and I usually took the minivan from Narvsky Prospect to Tavricheskaya Ulitsa, near beautiful Smolny Convent.

Taking the minibus each day, I noticed the Central Asian van drivers. I could have taken the underground, but I was fearful of the steep escalators. The metro had been built as a bomb shelter, and the escalators frightened me. Also, by taking the minivans and trolleys I could see the buildings of the city, like the Mariinsky Theater, St. Isaac's Cathedral, and those occupied by assorted shops, on my way to and from Nevsky Prospect. The view of the city depended on the route of the minivan, of course. It changed from one year to another, and this was all right since I could see different parts of the city. Traffic jams near Nevsky Prospect in the late afternoon showed me how the city had changed since I'd first seen it in 1970. There were lots of cars in 2009 and not enough bridges over the canals to accommodate the traffic. It was congested, unlike the deserted Nevsky Prospect I had seen in 1970.

It was on this trip that I met Esther Wiens, a Canadian woman with whom I had taught at LCC in the year 2000. She was staying at SPCU with a Canadian group and teaching English to Russian English teachers. One afternoon, I was astonished to meet her walking near the Narvskaya Metro. I hadn't expected to see anyone I knew in a foreign city of five million people. We were so busy talking that I wasn't paying attention and stumbled and fell on the trolley tracks. My knees hurt so much from the impact of hitting the metal tracks that I thought I had broken both knee caps. After a few minutes rest, I could barely stand up. Fortunately, I hadn't done any permanent damage, and the next day I could do my usual exercises.

It was only later that I learned to look where I was going and not turn my head to speak to the person next to me. It took several more falls before I remembered to look straight ahead or down instead of to the side at my walking partner. It was so refreshing meeting Esther in St. Petersburg. She proved doubly helpful because she had tried some of the local restaurants and recommended several. We had dinner a few times, which was delightful. Traveling by myself I got pretty lonely, so it was nice to meet a friend in St. Petersburg.

It was after I met her and several other Canadians that I took the metro with them to attend the Anglican Church. Although I never took the metro by myself, I decided that if I kept in the middle of the group, I wouldn't feel so overwhelmed on the escalators. And I didn't. I was touched when young people on the underground got up to give us older ladies a seat. Their politeness was an unexpected kindness because this seldom happened in Klaipėda on the bus. There, I often had to motion to a youngster to give his seat to an old person. At the time, I didn't think of myself as old since I was in my early sixties and capable of standing, but I often thought that older ladies weighed down with bags of groceries deserved a seat.

In St. Petersburg, it was uplifting to attend an Anglican Church service with communion. After several years, the Anglican priest in Klaipėda had left, and without him we had no weekly communion. The Mennonites at LCC didn't celebrate communion very often. Instead, we had sermons and hymn singing, and I missed the weekly Eucharist to which I was accustomed.

The Anglican Church in St. Petersburg was located just off Nevsky Prospect in a rather decrepit building. It was a meeting place for visiting American tourists and choirs. I heard one choir on a Saturday night in the Capella concert hall, then the same choir the next day at the Anglican Church. This was a pleasant surprise. The church also had a coffee hour, and it was gratifying to see one of the Russian students from the SPCU classes at church. I had spoken to her a couple of times, so I recognized her at the social hour and enjoyed speaking with her again. She told me about helping some old friends in their gardens in the summer. I felt comfortable with her and asked her about the role of culture in the city. Seeing huge advertisements for rock-and-roll concerts, I wondered if the present-day generation of young people still memorized the poetry of Pushkin and Akhmatova as previous generations had. She told me that in some families they did, but not in all.

Looking back, I can see that LCC friends in Klaipėda helped me meet church friends in St. Petersburg by telling me of the SPCU Center. This reminded me of how international and connected the church is. On a later visit, I was astonished upon turning around to exchange the peace at the Anglican Church to see two former LCC colleagues, Jannecke and Rueben. It was so unexpected to find them with their two babes, and ever so lovely being invited to their apartment to have lunch, talk, and catch up on their lives. They had returned to the United States and were studying law and linguistics in North Carolina. Rueben had won a scholarship to study Russian language that summer, and the entire family was there in St. Petersburg for part of the time. How amazing it was seeing them again, especially in that city.

While my stays in St. Petersburg were without unpleasant incidents, and I was grateful for that, it surprised me that the Russians charged tourists higher prices for concerts, ballets, museums, and taxis than they did ordinary citizens. If someone from SPCU called a taxi to take me to the train station, the price was usually one third the cost than when I engaged one myself at the station to come to the conference center. The most difficult part was that the St. Petersburg film and photo archive charged me twenty-five dollars (625 rubles) for each historical photo I bought, while the price for Russians was negligible. I would have liked to have bought more photos that fit my research topic of Russian women in the nineteenth and twentieth centuries, but I couldn't afford very many.

On this trip, when I inquired at the Russian Art Museum how much they would charge to use one of their paintings in a book, they told me thirty-five euros. Years later, my editor found that copies of most paintings were free on the internet. Likewise Prokudin-Gorskii's photos of pre–World War I Russia were also free to use from the Library of Congress.

Shopping in St. Petersburg

I shouldn't complain about shopping in St. Petersburg since the exchange ratio was usually twenty to thirty rubles to one dollar. Most items were affordable, so I couldn't be unhappy. Many of the items, such as a malachite ring and earrings that I bought at a Russian shop, were very cheap. Some of the nicest presents I bought came from the shops at the Hermitage or Museum of Ethnography. As in the United States, a visitor could go to the café or the museum shop without having to buy an admission ticket to the museum. Several times I bought beautiful quilted velvet tea cozies with pictures of a church with a cupola, a river, and the moon appliquéd on them. These made wonderful gifts. Once I bought a lovely turquoise brooch at the Hermitage gift shop. I usually ended up giving the tea cozies and other souvenirs as gifts to my Russian friends. Another time when I was shopping near Narvskaya Metro I saw some cute pot holders in a shop and decided to buy them. Then I noticed that despite the samovar motif and Russian look, they had been made in China. This seemed sad to me. I couldn't quite figure out how the Chinese could supply the world with goods, but the Russians couldn't even produce their own potholders. The exchange ratio was so favorable to Americans that my housing, food, and transportation around the city were very affordable. Once, I bought some special tea cups for a friend at the Russian Imperial Porcelain factory outlet store for a fraction of what they cost in the United States or in a china shop in Klaipėda.

Travel in Eastern Europe: Lithuania

Falling in love with the Baltics is easy to do. As the song says: "Falling in love with love is falling for make-believe," and this is definitely true in East European old towns. One willingly suspends disbelief in walking around these impressive historic cities. Relatively few people live in the historic districts of Riga, Tallinn, Vilnius, Kaunas, or Kraków, but they are all so alluring that one cannot help falling in love with them and preferring them to the outskirts, which are greyer and dingier. Indeed, I always felt livelier and like flirting with life in the old towns. While Baroque churches in the old towns were entrancing, some of the medieval churches and monasteries were equally moving. I had endearing experiences praying in the Bernardino monastery in Vilnius and touring the ruins of the Dominican monastery in Tallinn and seeing a medieval grammar book on display.

I was so pleased that Martin; his wife, Donna; my sister Kathryn; and my friend Elaine Kruse all came to visit me at the end of my first year of teaching in Lithuania. My friend Elaine had been on sabbatical in Paris doing research, and she came to visit me in May. With her I visited Kaunas and the nearby Lithuanian ethnographic village of Rumšiškės. This is a place where old houses from historic villages had been brought and reassembled. The Lithuanians did this during the Khrushchev period, and the Soviets didn't like this feature of Lithuanian nationalism, but they tolerated it. There were also workshops for a weaver, a sculptor, and a jeweler. I bought some headscarves from the weaver. I wanted to buy a beautiful hand-carved chess set for my son, but he said he didn't play chess anymore. I thought of buying an exquisite five-inch knight for myself, but I didn't. I wondered where I would have put it.

After Elaine's visit, Martin and Donna came in early June, and then Kathryn in mid-June, so their visits overlapped. They all got to know my adopted Lithuanian family: Viktor; his mother, Adolfina; and his sisters, Loreta and Kristina. Everyone loved Viktor, and we included him on our walks around town and visits to local restaurants. He was a helpful guide, and it was delightful seeing him and Martin walking and talking together while Donna and I trailed behind. In Klaipėda we frequented the usual Old Town haunts: cafés, amber shops, and the market. We also visited nearby towns like Kretinga and Palanga. My favorite graveyard was in Kretinga, and I didn't feel too weird showing it to Martin and Donna because they told me they had a favorite cemetery in Paris.

During my sister's visit, we went to Kaunas and saw some captivating sites. She had read about a "devil's museum" and wanted to visit it. I wasn't too excited about doing this, but I humored her, and it turned out to be a rewarding experience. There were all kinds of wooden animal sculptures showing the devil

Lovingly tended graves in my favorite cemetery in Kretinga, Lithuania, 2001

as a goat with cloven hooves dancing and playing the violin. These were quite remarkable. Many of the sculptures depicted millers and water mills, with the miller depicted as the devil with a cloven hoof, presumably because he extorted the peasants when grinding their grain. Many of the sculptures were historic, but one set of dishes depicting a devil were quite modern. One set had been designed by a Latvian artist.

My sister noticed other unusual items in her guidebook, and we visited some old, almost dilapidated churches that I had not seen. She also wanted to patronize different kinds of restaurants than I normally did, so her visit enlarged my appreciation of Kaunas. Once I realized that she liked unusual places, I took her to an unusual sculpture park called Hill of Witches on the nearby peninsula of Nida. It contained weird tree sculptures of different motifs. Carved in 1979, the tree sculptures reflected Lithuanian nationalism and folklore. It is a somewhat macabre Lithuanian Disneyland.

Kathryn and I enjoyed walking along the Kaunas pedestrian walkway called Freedom Alley. It had many shops, restaurants, and bookstores. The bookstore pictured below had quite a few modern books in English, both fiction and nonfiction, which made it delightful for browsing. Note the window boxes with flowers and nicely painted façade on the second floor.

Because Kaunas was the capital of Lithuania between the World Wars, it had a lot of art deco architecture; many government buildings; a small, attractive opera house; lots of restaurants; and many good bookstores. It was easy to take the bus or train to Kaunas for the day or weekend because it was not far from Klaipėda. When going to Poland, I caught the overnight train to Warsaw from Kaunas because it left an hour later than in Vilnius.

Street-level Kaunas bookshop on Laisvės Alėja, 2006

Some historical sites in Kaunas were quite somber. I had

Ninth Fort sculpture and killing wall, Kaunas, 2002

heard of the Ninth Fort outside of Kaunas, but at first I couldn't fathom why people were talking about it. In the late nineteenth century it had been an old tsarist fort. After World War I, the Lithuanians used it as a jail. When the Nazis invaded Lithuania and came to Kaunas in the summer of 1941, they forced all the Jews into a ghetto. Then they took them in small groups to Ninth Fort, where they shot them. As the war was ending, they decided to try to cover up the slaughter by using Jewish prisoners to dig up and burn the dead bodies, thus destroying the evidence of their dastardly deeds. A few Jews escaped from Ninth Fort, and one, Alex Faitelson, wrote a fascinating memoir, *Escape from the IX Fort* (1998), that describes these events.

One spring, the father of one of my Baltic history students drove his daughter, Svetlana, Dottie West, and me to the fort. He stayed in his car during the three hours we toured the place because he had been before and didn't want to see it again. A sculpture, pictured above, by a Lithuanian artist depicts writhing bodies and souls ascending to heaven. It shows the power of art to transform the pain and suffering of the Jews and communists killed there by the Nazis.

A group of us from LCC sometimes hired a student to drive us around to Lithuanian towns, and once we stopped at Švėkšna, one of the ninety-nine places where Lithuanians, not Nazis, massacred Jews. Before Lithuania could become a member of the European Union, it had to make an effort to come to grips with its past treatment of the Jews. Part of the effort involved identifying all ninety-nine places and putting plaques at each one.

Švėkšna, a rural site where Lithuanian Jews were killed during World War II, 2004

My friend Tatjana, the painter, studied to be a guide in Klaipėda, and she told me that before World War II there had been fourteen synagogues in the city; after the war, only one. I used to take my Baltic history students to visit it but was surprised to find that the rabbi was Russian, as were most of the members. The situation resembled that of the Kaunas synagogue where all the men were Russian, not Lithuanian. A German acquaintance told me that her aunt had bought furniture on credit from a Jewish merchant in Klaipėda before the war, and after the war she sent money to the state of Israel to finish paying for the furniture and to atone for the loss of Jews in Lithuania and Germany.

Good books I have read about the situation of Jews in Lithuania include the following: Rachel Kostanian-Danzig's *Spiritual Resistance in the Vilna Ghetto* (2002), about the work of the Jewish intelligentsia to keep everyone sane and healthy in the Vilnius Ghetto; Solly Ganor's *Light One Candle* (1995), about a boy who survived the massacres in Kaunas and various Holocaust camps; and Balys Sruoga's *The Forest of the Gods* (1996), a memoir of a Lithuanian professor incarcerated in Stutthof concentration camp in Poland from 1943 to 1945. Author Solly Ganor was also featured in a very moving 1997 PBS film *Kovno Ghetto*, which I showed to my Western civilization classes. Likewise, a film was made from Sruoga's book by Algimantas Puipa. He created a marvelous adaptation of the novel. I had wondered how he could possibly convey Sruoga's sense of irony, but he did it very well. Indeed, it was so horrific and overwhelming that I had to leave before the end.

On a trip to Kaunas when I was photographing some of its art deco buildings, I came upon a mosque I had read about. It was in Peace Park and had been built during the interwar years. When Kaunas was the capital of Lithuania during the 1920s and '30s, many striking art deco buildings were constructed: the post office, Čiurlionis National Art Museum, banks, businesses, and houses near Peace Park.

Historic Plungė

Small mosque built in the 1930s, Kaunas Peace Park, 2006

Decorated cemetery in Plungė, 2006

While living in Klaipėda, we often visited Plungė to enjoy its cathedral and historic ambience and to buy artifacts from the local artisans. A lovely gentry-class estate had hosted the famous Lithuanian painter and composer Čiurlionis. I had been to Plungė several times with American friends, but it was only when my friend Tania took me that we visited this lovely home and park.

Plungė was also the only place we visited that had a cafeteria, and we all enjoyed seeing our food before buying it. Sometimes we got a ride there with Janis Turner, but often we walked from the bus stop to a special linen factory outlet where we could buy yard goods at reasonable prices. This shop also sold a few finished goods: placemats, napkins, book bags, and aprons. Once, I bought ten yards of lavender linen and employed my seamstress in Klaipėda to make me a matching sundress, skirt, jacket, and purse. Later, I bought other colors of linen and had other outfits made, particularly skirts with pockets so I could carry my office key to class and not have to take my purse with me. I have worn the lavender items more than fifteen years. The lavender linen skirt has pleased me more than any others I had made, and it has worn well. On the street to the linen shop we often stopped at a souvenir store filled with wooden toys, hand-knit sweaters, and other handicraft items. We also lingered at the beautiful cemetery as we strolled from the city center to the linen shop.

Seeing the cemeteries made me reflect on my life, teaching, and travels in Lithuania. Sometimes I realize that not only does Providence provide new, challenging, and good experiences for us but arranges our lives so we can fulfill the vows of our youth. God does not offer us pain-free lives but is with us in the difficult times. I learned that God shepherds us through the hard times, and often provides dear friends on our journey.

Travel in Estonia and Latvia

Lithuania is one of the Baltic states, so my colleagues and I often visited nearby Riga and Tallinn. One summer, my friend Alexa Maples and I explored the Old Town of Tallinn and had a great time seeing the historic churches. Both cities possess splendid cathedrals which also served as concert venues during the Soviet times. They were not allowed to function as houses of worship, but they were not always destroyed. We heard stunning organ concerts in the Riga and Tallinn Dome Cathedrals. We also listened to magnificent choirs in the churches in the old towns. We loved eating in restaurants with historic themes, like the Medieval Café.

Left to right: Alexa, our waitress, and Marcelline at Medieval Café, Tallinn, 2003

Alexa and I packed a lot into our three days in Tallinn. We visited Kadriorg Palace, saw a Baroque musical production there, visited most of the historic churches, checked out the numerous art galleries, and walked around the Old Town until we dropped.

In the summer of 2007, my friend Ninon Schalk from El Paso, who lives in Versailles in the summer, came to visit me in Klaipėda. Ninon is French, and she had studied Russian language in Paris in her youth. She had even visited Moscow and St. Petersburg while a student. She came to America to study at the University of Wisconsin, and there met her husband, Ellery, who later became a colleague of mine at the University of Texas at El Paso. As I mentioned earlier, Ellery died the same year as my mother, and our grief brought Ninon and me together.

Ninon periodically invited me to visit her in Versailles in the summer, and these visits refreshed me. Living in Lithuania was a bit of a hardship, and going to her lovely apartment in Versailles renewed my spirit. Everything was comfortable, especially the view of the trees from her living room. So, when she

Alexa and Marcelline at the Church of the Holy Spirit, Tallinn, 2003

Ninon and Marcelline in Riga at the Pankūkas (pancake) café, 2007

came to visit me in Klaipėda toward the end of my time there, I wanted to show her a good time.

We had planned to go to St. Petersburg, but we ended up going to Riga and Tallinn instead. Getting a visa to Russia was not so easy for Ninon in Paris, whereas we didn't need one to travel in the Baltic states since they were part of the European Union. Ninon brought a guide to the Baltics, and she was eager to see the sites. She wasn't disappointed. I thought she might be since St. Petersburg is so spectacular, but the Art Nouveau buildings in Riga's Old Town are stunning while the medieval walls of Tallinn are splendid.

Ninon and Marcelline in Ninon's lovely Versailles apartment, 2010

Travel in Poland

I repeatedly visited Kraków because it is so charming. The first two times I went with a University of Iowa friend, Laura Julier, who presently teaches at Michigan State University in Lansing. I was finally shamed by my LCC students into going to Auschwitz. Some of my North American Baltic history students went to Kraków on their holidays and visited Auschwitz. Having seen the film *Schindler's List*, they also visited his factory, which still exists and is featured in some guidebooks. I had avoided Auschwitz on my first visit with Laura, but on our second trip we paid our respects to the Jews who died there.

Each time I visited Kraków, I went to the bookstores, especially the ones in the Kazimierz section, to buy books about Jews who had survived the Holocaust and written their memoirs. I read these tomes and used them as resources in my Baltic history classes. On my first visit, I remember buying and reading Władysław Szpilman's *The Pianist*. It was the moving account of one Jewish man's survival during World War II in Warsaw. The film based on the book is equally touching. Of course, there were many other tragic memoirs. Several of them were written by children who had miraculously survived and told of their experiences. Other books about the Holocaust in Poland I read were Thomas Keneally's *Schindler's List*, James Michener's *Poland*, and Diane Ackerman's *The Zookeeper's Wife*.

We stayed at a university dormitory, which was inexpensive and just a few stops on the trolley from the Old Town. On our second visit, we discovered that the dorm arranged excursions, and we took two: one to

Marcelline and Laura Julier in Kraków near Kazimierz Jewish section, summer 2004

the pope's hometown and the other to Auschwitz. It was helpful to have the dormitory's van taking us to these places because coming home public transportation could be crowded. We visited Pope John XXIII's hometown on August 15, the Feast of the Assumption. We hadn't realized the significance of this holiday in Poland, and it was unbelievably crowded but also colorful and exciting. Young people in national dress paraded around, and young children were all dressed up in their first communion clothes. However, as the day wore on, it became more and more crowded, and we were glad we had a ride back to Kraków and didn't have to take public transportation.

While the excursion to the pope's hometown was upbeat, the one to Auschwitz was somber. There is a train that still stops in Auschwitz, but it was handy taking the van from the dorm. Few of the buildings in the camp have survived, but the chimneys of the barracks where the Jews were confined are still there and remind us of what happened. Also, some of the less destructible items, such as the brick ovens, remain. One of the saddest buildings we saw was one containing the hair of the victims who died there, their old battered suitcases, and the little leather children's shoes. These items were unforgettable. Because the camp is disintegrating, there is discussion about preserving the remaining evidence—whether to build a glass bubble over the entire complex or let it all disappear.

On my third trip to Kraków, I met my son who was in transit to India, but was breaking up his trip to see me and Kraków for a few days. It was wonderful touring the city with him. It was a very different experience because he was especially interested in beer and klezmer music. With him, I went to some cafés at night and saw students drinking from a huge container called a sleeve. I had never heard of or seen this before. Since my son researches beer

Marcelline (far left, bowed head, with umbrella) at Auschwitz, Poland.

production and consumption, he engaged the various bar and restaurant owners in conversation.

Martin also went jogging in the early morning, so he saw parts of the city and Old Town I had never seen. He was also keen to see the salt mines in Wieliczka, a nearby town to which we took a minivan. We climbed down the 380 steps to the mines. Walking this way, we could see the handiwork of the miners in their carvings of salt-sculpture chapels and chandeliers as well as Mary, Joseph, and Jesus in Egypt. They even had a salt sculpture of the German poet and engineer Goethe, who had visited the mines. I've been pondering returning to the salt mines for treatment for my lungs.

Cyprus Holiday

One of my best friends in Europe is British expat Brenda Goodwin. She's an enchanting person who sold her house in England and wanders around various cities enjoying life. She often settles temporarily where there is an Anglican Church, and I got to know her in Klaipėda at the Anglican Church there. Our priest, Roy Ball, introduced us when Brenda was there one summer. He and his wife, Joke, invited us to dinner because we both write. Having some common interests, we became friends and travel buddies. Twice I met Brenda in Riga and stayed with her for a few days, learning a lot about Riga I'd never known. Since she lived in Riga a month or so each summer, she knew the city well—much better than I did because my stays were limited to a few days visiting the Art Nouveau buildings and historic churches in the Old Town. She always shopped at the markets in the places where she lived, so I enjoyed going around the market with her. The Riga market is in three airplane hangars that were built for zeppelins in the 1930s. They are huge structures with rounded roofs.

We always went to the Riga Anglican Church, and there I got to know the kindly priest who had been born in Canada but returned to Latvia to serve after independence. He was a theology professor as well as a priest and taught at the university in Riga. His church ministered to the poor, and it was touching to see the outreach they did in the capital.

One summer, Brenda and I met in Liepāja, Latvia, which is between Klaipėda and Riga. Our bus from Klaipėda to Riga always stopped in Liepāja for a rest, and I wanted to take the tram that ran next to the bus station. I always wondered where it went. The summer we stayed there, I used the tram to see the town and suburbs. We stayed in an art school dorm in Liepāja that

Marcelline (far left) and Brenda (far right), Anglican Church courtyard, Cyprus, 2005

Tania had told us about. It was empty during the summer and offered inexpensive rooms. It was near the center of the city—convenient as well as light and cheery. In Liepāja, we visited the beach, which is beautiful but polluted from radioactive waste left during the Soviet period. We couldn't really sunbathe on the beach, so we toured various enormous nineteenth-century churches that contained beautiful wooden altar carvings and magnificent organs. Liepāja has a very small historic district, and we enjoyed strolling through it. We went to a couple of museums, ate in some great cafés, and enjoyed buying fresh fruit from the central market, which was close to our rooms.

In the fall and winter, Brenda often lived in Warsaw, Poland, where I stayed with her on my way to Kraków. In Warsaw, Brenda usually stayed in a boat hotel on the Vistula River. It was cheap and romantic. What a combination! There was also a tram stop nearby, so she could walk or take a tram downtown.

One spring, I decided to visit Brenda in Cyprus, where she often wintered. It was warmer than most of Europe but not as warm as I expected it to be in March. I hadn't taken warm enough clothes so had to wear several layers to keep warm. Brenda usually stays at an American Fulbright center that has rooms to let in the winter but not in summer when archeological digs occur. I stayed there with her during my visit. It was a charming place, not far from the center of Nicosia. We visited some of the historic museums and churches, and even the market one morning at five. Brenda liked to buy eggs there. Having jet lag the first few days, I did not appreciate going to the market so early in the morning, but the beautiful produce, neatly arranged was a feast for the eyes. It made the American farmers' markets look anemic. Of course, the Cypriots have had centuries instead of decades to develop their wares, and it showed.

When Brenda came to Klaipėda, she and I often attended concerts, along with summer LCC language teachers, as this picture shows.

Left to right: Marcelline, Brenda, and two LCC teachers, Klaipėda, 2009

Chapter IX

Blessed Assurance:
Retirement and Old Age

Therefore do not lose heart. Though outwardly we are wasting away,
yet inwardly we are being renewed day by day.
2 Corinthians 4:16

As I was finishing teaching at Lithuania Christian College (LCC), I wasn't thinking much about how I was being renewed day by day. Instead, I was feeling apprehensive about where and how to retire. Indeed, I wondered who I would be and what I would do then. Would I have a purpose? I didn't feel "blessed assurance" yet. Instead of making plans, however, I drifted along as usual, scaring myself with thoughts of the unknown. I knew I would like to live in a university town but couldn't identify which one. I didn't imagine that I would have a new career as a writer, gain new friends, feel at home with my own values, realize that appearance didn't matter so much anymore, and enjoy a new life teaching adults in Lincoln, Nebraska. So that's why I titled this section "Blessed Assurance." God kept on blessing me in old age, providing both financial and social serenity.

Toward the end of my stay in Klaipėda, my friend Dottie West's husband, Harold Mondal, told me about a place in St. Petersburg, Florida, where he thought I might like to live during retirement. It was a government-subsidized apartment building but run by the Presbyterian church. It seemed worth a look, so I wrote for their application, was accepted, and checked it out when I returned to the States. The place was a massive fifteen-story building, close to the water. It was near the downtown bus center and opposite a beautifully restored Italianate hotel built in the 1920s. So the setting was attractive. However, I was unprepared for the impact of so many elderly people crammed into one space. Moreover, I had some reservations about living in Florida and what that would feel like.

I decided to think about the place and take a bus to visit my 103-year-old aunt Ethel, who lived in Port St. Lucie on the other side of the state. There I had a good time chatting with her about old times and going to church and dinner with her son, Harry. They lived in a single-family dwelling, and it felt fine being with them. I didn't feel quite as depressed as I had in St. Petersburg.

It was then I recollected a graduate school friend, Janusz Duzinkiewicz, who had inherited a house in Ft. Lauderdale. At some point, I called Janusz to ask if I could stay in his house part of the winter to see what it felt like living in Florida. It turned out that Janusz was teaching up north in La Porte County, where I grew up, and that he seldom occupied the house in the winter since his mother had died. So, after retiring from LCC, I flew to Ft. Lauderdale and began staying in Janusz's house for several winters from 2007 to 2012. Initially, I was very lonely because I soon realized that I couldn't live at the beach. It was too hot in the middle of the day. Fine for the morning but not so healthy in large doses. Eventually I discovered some programs at a nearby Presbyterian church and occupied myself going to their senior exercise classes on Mondays, Wednesdays, and Fridays and attending a musical program, dinner, and movie on Thursdays. Those activities plus services at All Saints Episcopal Church on Sundays and Wednesdays, and concerts on some Fridays and Saturdays provided some structure to my life.

Marcelline at Janusz's home in Ft. Lauderdale, 2012

For five winters I had the pleasure of staying at Janusz's house in Fort Lauderdale. Although it was quite an adjustment living in glitzy Fort Lauderdale, I made some good church friends at All Saints Episcopal Church and appreciated wintering there. Two of my best friends at All Saints were Gail Cote and Sally Wolinsky. Besides attending Sunday services, we also attended the healing service on Wednesdays, where we got to know each other better.

We often went to lunch together after the service, and sometimes I invited them to Janusz's place for egg salad sandwiches, cake, and tea. I really liked these two women, but they were not daily friends. I only met them on Wednesdays and Sundays. The other days of the week I was still pretty lonesome.

During the winters of 2007 and 2008, I lived in Fort Lauderdale and worked on my book *Falling in Love with the Baltics* at the public library. Working on this book gave direction and meaning to my life. Janusz had left me his library card, and I used it for several years because I could not get one in my own name. I even tried bribery—offering them copies of my books *Russian and West European Women* and eventually *Falling in Love with the Baltics*—but to no avail. Without a Florida driver's license or a utility bill paid in my name, it was impossible to get a card. I just didn't qualify, but I hated having to pass myself off as someone else at the checkout and in the computer room where I worked.

The beach was always a great retreat from my work and my life, as the following picture shows.

Ft. Lauderdale Beach, 2009

I seldom walked to the beach from Janusz's house because it took more than forty minutes. I usually took the city bus or a special trolley that ran on the weekend and cost only fifty cents (compared to one dollar for the city bus). Once there, walking along the water's edge, lying in the sand, and enjoying the sun, sand, and sea were so restorative. Except for the palm trees and major highway, this beach reminded me of the Baltic Sea in Klaipėda and Lake Michigan near my hometown of La Porte.

For a few years, I alternated winter in Florida at Janusz's, spring living with my Aunt Marce in La Porte, and then returning to LCC for the summer months and teaching the fall semester. Eventually I realized that I needed my own place, and I contacted my friend Elaine Kruse, whom I had known in Iowa City. I had stayed with her at various times in Lincoln, Nebraska, during the 1990s and 2000s and she had told me about an inexpensive place to live called Pioneer House, a housing cooperative. She got me the number of the place, and I contacted one of the owners who was selling a unit, and after checking on the library holdings and its proximity to an Episcopal church, I decided to move to Lincoln. It met my guidelines as a university town and had two old friends from the University of Iowa from the 1980s: Elaine Kruse and Carole Levin. That's how I came to live in Lincoln, Nebraska, and winter in Florida at Janusz's.

Life in Florida, 2012

When I flew to Florida, I always felt as if I were going to a foreign country, and in many ways I was. Its climate and flora are tropical, not at all like the Midwest where I grew up and lived most of my life. Sometimes I forget how different Florida is. However, events occur when I'm in Florida to remind me of how southern, tropical, and coastal the state is. One day after our dinner at the Presbyterian church, we saw a movie called *Dolphin Tale 2*. It was about an area where people rescue injured turtles and dolphins, mend them, and return them to the ocean. It was a heartwarming tale of adults and adolescents working together, reminding me that not everyone wants to raise animals to kill them, as happens on Midwest farms.

Nebraska and Iowa raise cattle as well as chickens and hogs, and several cities have slaughterhouses. This makes me aware of the profit motive in American farming. Watching *Dolphin Tale 2* was refreshing because it showed Americans working for the good of Creation—not destroying the water with phosphates and nitrates or polluting the air with chemicals, as happens in a lot of the

Midwest these days when farms are gigantic and chemicals overused to increase profits and production. Central Florida has a large cattle-raising business, but living on the coast, I wasn't so aware of it.

Sitting in the church theater, I was wishing that the United States sent more of these kinds of movies abroad instead of our sexualized, violent Hollywood blockbusters. But guess where the profit is? In sex and violence! I was sad to see that these were the kinds of films that were shown in Lithuania when I lived there from 2000 to 2009.

Life in Florida sometimes resembled Shangri-la. I was retired and writing but not teaching. Life was lazier, filled with visits to the beach and trips to art museums and galleries, unlike my former, ordinary life which also involved much more work. However, I was often depressed and lonesome, especially during the Thanksgiving and Christmas holidays when I had no one to celebrate with.

But, the winter of 2012 was different. I was revising a manuscript, and work can be a good antidote to depression. Also, we had several wonderful concerts by the Delray String Quartet and the Seraphic Fire Choir at All Saints Episcopal Church, and these fed my soul. I went to two fascinating art exhibits. The first one was an exhibition of Toulouse-Lautrec and other impressionists at the Coral Springs Museum of Art. A church friend, Monte, drove me there, and we enjoyed viewing the exhibit and discussing it on the way home. He's an amateur artist himself and didn't mind taking me to the museum. If I had taken the bus, it would have taken three and a half hours one way, and that hadn't seemed feasible.

At the Toulouse-Lautrec exhibit, I especially liked some attractive pen and ink drawings by Whistler that were also featured. I had no idea he had done that sort of work. My friend Halimah took me to a private showing of watercolors by an artist named Liora. They were brightly colored and different from my friend Tania's. That winter I enjoyed ballets, concerts, and other museum visits with Halimah. She's one of my intellectual and cultural friends there.

Again, I had exercise at First Presbyterian Church with other middle-aged women (aged 55 to 103). Our instructor, Elle, was full of fun but firm about working all our muscles. I almost lived at that church in the winter. On occasion, they let me use my computer to do my email in one of their empty offices. I appreciated the staff, especially Tricia, who supervised the programs for seniors and was supportive to us. That year I got to know Lyn Dubransky. She lent me discs of various books and provided me with homemade soup and cheer. She and her father, Craig, were real blessings at the Presbyterian church programs. I attended All Saints on Sundays, where the liturgy, sermons, and music are so impressive. The Episcopal church also offered a healing and communion service on Wednesdays, and Friday night choral and chamber music concerts.

After I completed some technical changes to my manuscript, I slackened off in my research and writing. I had brought a few photocopies of Russian poetry to read and translate, but after a month and a half I had done the easy work. I never got around to completely translating the Russian poems. Before her untimely death, Janusz's sister, Therese Baker, read my work and suggested a few changes. Her chief criticism was making four chapters out of the long first chapter of 225 pages. I realized she was right and divided the prewar period into four chapters—

one about women in religion, the second about marriage, the third their employment, and the final chapter on women in politics. I had already decided to add quotations to the various sections and subsections to break up the text. All this involved some reorganization but nothing drastic. It was more technical than analytical work. Later, those four chapters became my book *Remarkable Russian Women in Pictures, Prose and Poetry*, which was published online and in paperback in 2013.

At the end of February, I felt like I could do some things for fun, like taking the Tri-Rail train from Ft. Lauderdale to the University of Miami to use its library. This proved more of an adventure than I anticipated. I was a bit afraid of going by myself, so I asked an Irish bloke I met named Jon Joe to accompany me. I had met him at the nearby canal where he fished each day. It seemed odd to me that an Irishman like him came to America to visit family and fish, while Americans went to Ireland to fish! One Saturday, we began our trip to Miami at nine in the morning, walking from 12th Street to 3rd Avenue to catch a bus to the airport. There we got a free shuttle bus to the Tri-Rail station. A round-trip ticket to Miami cost only five dollars, a reasonable price. When we arrived at the Metro Center stop in Miami, we got a ticket for the Metro. It cost four dollars round trip, and it stopped at the university. Making the trip in these stages took five hours one way. We were so tired and hungry when we arrived at the school, we went directly to the rathskeller in the student union, which we found on our way to the library. We had a beer, hamburger, and fries while looking out on an enormous swimming pool with many sunbathing co-eds. I wondered how anyone did any studying there. Apparently many don't.

When we finally got to the library, the young woman at the entrance said it cost five dollars to use the library. I said it had taken us five hours just to get there, and I only had one hour to do some research, so she let us in free. This was the second time I ever heard of paying to use a university library. At the University of Miami library, I found some great poems by Russian writers but didn't have enough time to photocopy them all. We knew we had to allow several hours for our homeward journey, so we couldn't really savor our library experience.

Another time I was requested to pay to enter a library was in Dublin when I went to Trinity College. There it cost ten euros to go into the library. I didn't especially want to see the Book of Kells, which was included in the cost, because I already had a facsimile copy. I yearned to soak up the ambience of the magnificent library, but the admission fee seemed too steep. I had only gotten fifty euros at the airport ATM and found that it would cost thirty euros to return by taxi the next morning, so I really didn't have much left for food or library visits. It was a disappointment, but I was able to buy a picture of the impressive library at the bookstore.

At the end of my winter 2012 stay in Florida, I decided to visit two LCC colleagues, Dennis Erikson and Richard Hansgen, on my return to Lincoln. I flew to Durham, North Carolina, where I was able to spend some time with Dennis, who has subsequently died. I told him I was interested in seeing the Thomas Wolfe papers at the University of North Carolina, and he called the archivist and arranged for us to go there the afternoon I arrived. Driving through historic Raleigh and walking around the university was a real high. History oozed from the antebellum houses along the avenues, the arboretum, and the university library. Dennis had done his PhD at North Carolina, so he knew the campus well. It was nice having a guide, and I thought about including this library in a proposed study on libraries.

The Wolfe papers were not available for viewing because of the installation of some sprinklers, but the archivists were very helpful and gave us each two lovely booklets about Wolfe to make up for it. They also spent some time trying to answer my questions, but they didn't know the answers. I wondered what happened to Thea Volker, a woman Wolfe had lived with in the mid-1930s when he was traveling in Germany. Another question was whether Wolfe knew Langston Hughes. They were both born in 1900 and lived in New York City at the same time. Finally, what was the influence of editor Max Perkins on Wolfe's work? It was frustrating that the archivists had no answers.

Our LCC friend, Richard, had invited Dennis and me to come watch March Madness basketball in Columbus at his home, and we joined the fun. It turned out that the next weekend the Midwest Slavic Conference met in Columbus, and I decided to do that too. I was hoping to meet some publishers, show them a chapter from my book, and see if they were interested in publishing it. Alas, they weren't. Thus, I had left Ft. Lauderdale on March 21 and arrived back in Lincoln April 2 via Raleigh and Columbus. My son and daughter-in-law were coming to visit me in Lincoln for Easter, so that was the end of my 2012 winter.

I can't recount all the many kindnesses of my friends in Ft. Lauderdale, so readers will just have to trust me that God was at work making my life lively and lovely that winter. Moreover, I met another special friend from All Saints when I had to move out of Janusz's house the next year. When I told Faye Kartrude that I had to leave before I had time to meet a Lithuanian friend who was coming to Miami in the spring, she generously told me I could stay at her place for a couple of weeks. The next year, I asked her if I could rent a room for a thousand dollars a month, and she said yes, so during the next two years I continued going to Florida in the winter but stayed with Faye instead of at Janusz's, since he had sold his house by then. It was fascinating living at Faye's because she had a sort of Christian community there. She had four helpers to care for her 101-year-old mother. The helpers plus her mother, Faye, and I constituted a Christian community. We all prayed for each other and especially for Faye's mother. It was a joy to share some of my devotional books with Faye and Brenda, the caregiver who worked in the morning, and who has such a big heart. The winter of 2016–17 was the first time I didn't winter in Florida, and I missed my friends and the weather. But the winter in Lincoln was not severe, and I saved my money for a cruise to Europe in the late spring.

Aunt Marcelline's in La Porte

After wintering in Florida, before I bought my apartment in Lincoln in August 2009, I sometimes spent the spring up north with my aunt Marcelline Breese, in La Porte, Indiana. Sometimes I taught at LCC during the fall semester, wintered in Florida from January till March, and then lived April and May with Aunt Marce in La Porte before flying back to Klaipėda for the summer and fall when

I would teach again. June, July, and August were the nicest times in Klaipėda, so I wanted to be there then. In La Porte, I enjoyed seeing the dogwood trees, tulips, and daffodils blooming along the streets. The old Scott-Rumely House on Niles Street and the nearby Rose mansion featured beds of fabulous spring flowers. I thoroughly enjoyed gazing at them on my way to church on Sundays and on my way home from the library on weekday afternoons.

In La Porte, I usually worked on a book at the Carnegie Public Library in the late morning, ate a lunch I packed, worked again in the afternoon, and then came back to have dinner with my aunt in the late afternoon. It was pleasant working at the library because it had three ranks of computers for people to do their email but a few special computers tucked away where patrons could work on longer projects like the one I was doing. What a haven. Moreover, I could check out books in my own name, which I couldn't do in Fort Lauderdale. When I needed a break, I could read the newspapers and magazines and even participate in a book review discussion on Tuesdays once a month plus a weekly writing group on Thursday evenings.

This was the only place I found a writing support group, and it was helpful. The group was unusual. Some wrote science fiction for young people, one fan fiction, another family vignettes, and I nonfiction. It was a fascinating cross-section of people, about half men and half women, some young, some middle-aged. I occasionally get an email from the group, so I know it's still in session.

Research and New Adventures in Retirement

One summer I went to Klaipėda to teach only to discover there had been a misunderstanding and LCC didn't need me. That was disconcerting but turned into a boon because I had time to start a new book. I had found color photographs of Russian women by the Russian photographer Sergei Prokudin-Gorskii in one of the books I had stored at my friend Rosemary's in DC. When looking at them in Florida and after discussing the idea with a friend, the idea of using pictures of women in my next book came to me.

I also wanted to include longer quotes from some of the Russian women writers because one of my friends at LCC had said she enjoyed the quotes in my first book on Russian women, and she would like to have read more by them. That comment lurked at the back of my mind, and eventually it gelled into *Remarkable Russian Women in Pictures, Prose, and Poetry*.

At some point I had discovered Prokudin-Gorskii's color pictures of Russian life around 1914 posted on a Library of Congress website. The pictures were free to use, but publication required seeking permission from his heir, who lived in France. I composed a letter in French and gave it to my French friend Laurent Gontier to check. He was able to improve it—making it smoother and more polite. I had simply written "I request permission ..." but Laurent inserted the more polite form "je voudrais," "I would like to request permission to use your grandfather's slides ...." as the beginning of my letter. Doesn't God provide for us? Giving me a French friend in Klaipėda?

Prokudin-Gorskii's heir replied positively to my request via email, so I began inserting some of his grandfather's pictures into my text. I thought of using some from the Tretiakov Museum in Moscow and some from the Russian State Museum in Saint Petersburg. Eventually, I used pictures from the St. Petersburg film and photo archive instead.

Meanwhile, I couldn't get my publisher AuthorHouse to send my revised memoir about traveling in the Baltics to Klaipėda that summer. Instead, they kept sending it to my Florida address, so I was unable to check corrections of that manuscript that Miriam Gelfand had suggested and I had made the previous April. Once I returned to the States, to Aunt Marce's, Janusz forwarded the disc from Florida, and I received the book cover. Soon, *Falling in Love with the Baltics* was finished and available for readers but with some misspellings. The La Porte Library book club expressed interest in reading my travel memoir, and that was encouraging, but I don't know that they ever did read it.

While I expected to type up a stack of my journals written from 2003 to 2007 during the summer of 2008 in Klaipėda, I didn't get that project finished. Luckily, I was able to store those that were untyped at my friend Tania's dacha. She had an attic, and it seemed like a safe, dry place to keep some boxes of books and papers.

That summer was bittersweet—giving away my furniture, some clothes, and household items. I realized that with the new ninety-day limitation for tourists in most of the EU, I could visit Lithuania but probably never live there again. That was sobering and saddening! When I finally moved out of my flat on August 6, 2008, I realized that perhaps this was a way of freeing me to find a new home in the States. I hadn't thought about this before but decided it might be true. That made moving melancholy but not tragic.

I was able to go to St. Petersburg that summer, and that was a good experience. I took the bus from Klaipėda to Riga one Saturday morning and met my friend Brenda Goodwin there. We had lunch, a beer, and a nice rest in a lovely park that Brenda knew. She had lived in Riga several summers and was well acquainted with the city. I was familiar only with the Old Town, not the larger city. We ate at one of our favorite places on the edge of the Old Town—the Stockmann department store cafeteria—and had time to rest and relax. We'd both fallen that day in the train station and needed to quiet ourselves a bit.

The overnight bus to St. Petersburg left about nine o'clock and it was sad to say goodbye to Brenda, whom I see only about once a year. Still it was exciting to be going to Russia. The white nights meant it never darkened enough to sleep on the bus, but it was enthralling to see the ancient city of Pskov in the pale moonlight as well as the simple farmhouses in the Russian countryside I'd never seen before. As we approached St. Petersburg, I saw signs indicating famous historical sites like Gatchina Palace, the home of Tsar Paul, son of Catherine the Great.

Coming into St. Petersburg was exciting, even though I was tired. We drove through parts of the city I'd never seen. Finally we arrived at Vitebsk Station. It was drizzling slightly, but I soon found a taxi. I had put 500 rubles into my purse since that was the charge the preceding year. I was shocked when the driver told me 1,000 rubles. I said, "No, 500 rubles." There was often a higher price for foreigners than Russians. For Russians the cost to the Christian Seminary was 250 rubles. I knew we paid more for museums, the ballet, and other services, but it had never dawned on me that the taxis charged foreigners more. I wonder if American taxi drivers do this too? I knew from experience that the Central Photo Archive also charged foreigners more for pictures than Russians. Not fair, but life! I shall have to ask some American archivists if we charge foreigners more than Americans to use our services. I wonder!

At least the daily travel on the metro and trolley was the same price and it was cheap—about thirty rubles for the minivan and sixteen rubles for the trolley. Divided by twenty-three, one can see that this was less than one dollar on the trolley, and only slightly more for the minivan. The grocery store near the dormitory charged fairly low prices for hamburger, pasta, and other staples. So living there for a few weeks was inexpensive, except for the taxis.

I found the Central Photo Archive with some effort. I took a minivan from Narvskaya, where the dorm was located, to the downtown, and then the #5 trolley from Gostiny Dvor to Tulskaia stop near Smolny Cathedral. The archives were on Tavricheskaia Street, a few blocks away. When I finally found #69 Tavricheskaia, it turned out the main building was under renovation, and I had to use a side entrance. Eventually I found this entrance and went in. Although the staff had never replied to any of my faxes, they were expecting me. The only problem was that they closed for holidays on July 20, and this meant I had to get all my pictures ordered in a hurry and pay a sur-charge. Eight pictures ended up costing two hundred dollars. Three of the pictures are especially good, so I was satisfied. The archivists were kind and efficient. A French historian also working there noticed that they let us work during their lunch hour but chased all the Russian researchers away. I hadn't noticed this behavior at all.

My Russian was pretty rusty the first few days, so I was grateful for the English speakers at the archive who helped me communicate my needs. Once I decided on eight pictures, we then filled out countless forms that had to be signed by the director of the archive. Then I had to take five thousand rubles to a nearby bank to pay for the archival services before I got the pictures. Then I was supposed to call from the bank to say I had paid. I forgot to do this until several hours later, after I had returned to the dorm, and I was surprised that they were working so late. The hours for researchers were pretty restricted: Monday, Tuesday, and Thursday, 10 to 4.

I thoroughly enjoyed looking at the hundreds of photos of women in the St. Petersburg and Leningrad region from 1890 to 1960. This was a different form of historical research. It was so nice viewing pictures of women who were in medical school in the 1890s and of medical clinics for poor people with women doctors treating them. It was also fascinating to see Soviet organizations in the 1920s and 1930s, and young people in Osoaviakhim/Civil Defense in the 1930s. I was able to buy some of these photos and put them in my books.

The pictures of home life of working class women in the 1890s, 1920s, and 1930s provided glimpses into their lives. Often beds, tables, and chairs occupied the same room, and people seemed to eat, sleep, and study in that space. It was charming to see the huge pillows, or padushka, on the beds, and how neat and tidy they kept their rooms. Some families even had pictures on the wall and plants. Some homey touches are universal.

Other endearing pictures showed young factory workers studying at their place of work. A look at their crowded rooms helped me understand why they studied elsewhere. The women students looked so earnest and hardworking. Only recently have large numbers of working-class Americans been able to go to college with the availability of Pell Grants. That some Soviet workers did so in the 1920s and '30s was significant, and I included their pictures in my book on *Resilient Russian Women in the 1920s and 1930s*.

I also came upon some charming pictures of peasants from the 1930s. One picture showed men and women voting, another resting over lunch, and there in the foreground is a wind-up gramophone. Who would have imagined this? I put this picture in my book *Resilient Russian Women*.

Going to the archives gave structure to my time in St. Petersburg. On Wednesdays, when the archive was closed, I took time to write postcards, do some email at the seminary, explore the neighborhood, and go to an ATM in a nearby mall. When Karen and I had stayed at the seminary dorm, we didn't even notice the mall or any of the nearby restaurants. We mainly went to McDonald's because it was clearly marked and her preference. The malls and shops were in rather dingy buildings, and we had no idea what was inside them. This trip I browsed around, partly from curiosity and partly in remembrance of my friend Dottie West, who always like to shop around to see what's popular. Much to my surprise, all the clothing was made in China. The prices were not cheap, sometimes costing more than in the States. Since I was trying to downsize, I wasn't too tempted to buy anything, although I did admire one gauzy soft orange scarf.

I also found another supermarket besides the one close to the dorm. Shopping there and cooking enabled me to keep my expenses at a minimum. I paid seven thousand rubles for rent, which was about $20 per day; bought food for two to three days at a time for about two hundred to three hundred rubles, paid $100 for my round-trip bus ticket, a few hundred for transportation, $225 for the visa and insurance, and $200 for the pictures from the archive.

I was cooking supper every evening until I met a former LCC colleague who was teaching English to Russian teachers at the St. Petersburg Christian Seminary. I was so delighted to see a friend in St. Petersburg, and was glad that Esther Wiens recognized me too. She was with a group of Canadians who were teaching English to Russian teachers of English. Their students were all high school or university professors, so they were eager learners. Some of them had been engineers during the Soviet period, and when they lost their situations, they retrained as English teachers.

After meeting Esther, my social life improved. I went to dinner with her a few times, had cookies and tea together, and then went to a choral concert at the Anglican Church with her and another Canadian teacher. Providence provides in such surprising ways. I don't know if I would have been lonesome if I hadn't met Esther, but I know I was glad to see her and spend time with her.

I had brought some books with me, but I had already finished reading two of them and could tell the evenings were long. The archives closed at 4 o'clock and it usually took two hours to get home because of the traffic jams on the bridges over the canals. In St. Petersburg only a few intersections cross the waterways, so congestion mounts up near major traffic areas.

I met four fascinating Russian students in the English courses. One was a poet who gave me some of his poetry. That was very touching. I spoke to him one Sunday morning as I waited for the Canadians to go to church. The Russian poet went to a Baptist church, and he was praying for his wife's conversion. That was so poignant. Some of the English students attended the Anglican Church, although most were Orthodox or Baptist. I really enjoyed talking with these thoughtful, well-educated Russians. I toyed with the idea of teaching English there with the Canadians the next summer. However, it was a self-financed project, so it would cost a substantial sum to fly to St. Petersburg and pay for living expenses. I had already done this for several years in Lithuania and didn't know if I wanted to spend several thousand dollars to do this in another venue.

All too soon my time in St. Petersburg came to an end, and I had to go to Vitebsk station to get my overnight bus. I was a little anxious because I wasn't sure at which street corner to wait for the bus. Finally I found the address written in very small letters on my Econolines bus ticket. What a relief! Our bus left on time, but it took us from 8:30 p.m. until 10:30 p.m. just to get out of the city—more gridlock. I think the stopping and starting did something to the bus; at four in the morning it wouldn't go any farther. I finally fell asleep from four to five and missed a call for people with deadlines to take another bus, which had come by. We poked along and finally drew near Riga, where an Econolines bus from Moscow stopped and let us on board. I was wondering if the other bus would make it through the construction around Riga since that also involved a lot of stopping and starting.

The bus was three hours late, so I didn't know if my friend Brenda would still be waiting. She was, and we had time for a small meal and beer before I had to board yet another bus to return to Klaipėda. I was so tired I slept the first two hours. It was a lovely bus, clean and air-conditioned, but screens played non-stop erotic videos. Not my cup of tea. It was nice looking out the window because the bus went to Klaipėda via the city of Sauliai, going through a different countryside than the usual route through Liepāja. I was glad to make the 12:30 bus but was so very tired of sitting more after sitting all night. This was after I had fallen on the trolley tracks in St. Petersburg, and my knees were sore as well as my hip from my previous fall in Riga.

I was so glad to get back to Klaipėda and sleep in my own bed. Unfortunately, I had only a few days before leaving for England to see Irina and Vitaly Petrochenko. I packed, sorted, and packed some more. I was exhausted when

I got the minivan to Kaunas on July 24. Everything went well getting to the airport and flying to England. I hadn't ever been to London Stansted Airport, and it was pretty big. Outside the airport, I waited for a coach to Sheffield. It wasn't marked Sheffield, but Halifax, and I seemed to have missed an earlier one because I was looking for the name Sheffield, not #564 on the front. Fortunately, there were people to talk to as I was waiting, and I bought a newspaper and an ice cream, used the toilet, and didn't mind loitering. But I was tired, having left my apartment at seven in the morning, and knew I had to stay alert until I got on the coach for the last leg of my journey. At nine that evening, I was overjoyed to see Irina at the main bus station in Sheffield.

I hadn't seen Irina and her son, Vitaly, for a few years, so it was good to catch up on their lives. While working full-time, Irina had completed the first year of engineering studies at Sheffield Hallam University, and it seemed Vitaly had grown another five inches. He was eighteen and wanting to get a job and his own apartment—both difficult tasks.

Irina and Vitaly cooked for me every day, and we had several lovely picnics on our outings to the parks. They loved feeding the squirrels at the nearby botanical garden and even took along a bag of nuts. I was touched that nature meant so much to them. Vitaly was so cute when he placed the peanuts on his pant leg for the squirrels, and they climbed up his leg and even jumped onto his lap to be fed. I was surprised to learn that the Irina and Vitaly hadn't been hiking in the Moors on the outskirts of Sheffield. So one day we went to nearby Castleton, had lunch at a pub, and ambled around the hills. Irina is from Ukraine, in the Carpathian Mountain area, and she loves mountain climbing. With my arthritis, I'm not so good anymore, and I rested while they climbed.

Another day when Irina was working at the nursing home, Vitaly and I went to the end of the Totley bus line and found our way to the Moors. We passed the Dore and Totley train station and the apartments where my mother-in-law used to live. I thought of her, John, and Martin when he was only five years old. I enjoyed reminiscing about the old times in my mind. I also thought of James Herriot's novels and the TV series *All Things Bright and Beautiful* while we walked on the Moors. On this trip, we saw two lambs escaping from a field as we too clambered over the fence and barbed wire. It was amusing to see them scamper up the road ahead of us with their little tails wagging. We watched them till they were out of sight and then wondered where they went. Luckily there was no traffic on the road, so they seemed pretty safe running away.

Irina and Vitaly also had not been to the historical town of York, so one day we took the train there—fifteen pounds for a day-return ticket, about thirty dollars in American money. After our time at the cathedral and a picnic on the grounds, Irina and Vitaly were anxious to explore the city. They wanted to walk along the wall and take a river trip. We explored the city a bit together, and I retired to read some papers in the library and visit a small museum. I lacked their stamina for walking long distances. I saw a cute pub map for nineteen pounds and thought of Martin, who does research on the brewing of beer. It amazed me they had a map of all the pubs in York, showing the many local beers and ales available. I enjoyed reading the papers in the local public library. They are one of the things I missed most in Klaipėda. Reading the *International Tribune* online was not the same as actually holding a paper in my hands. In Sheffield one day I had bought the *Guardian* but was a bit disappointed. Much to my surprise, the Sunday edition of the conservative *Daily Telegraph* gave me more to read. In York I enjoyed the art museum, especially some paintings of horses by an artist named Stubbs. They were well executed and very engaging. At five, we met again at York Minster for evensong. A choir from Memphis, Tennessee, was singing, and that was touching.

When we returned to the train station, we found we had just missed a train to Sheffield. As luck would have it though, the next one was held up by an accident farther up the line. Someone said there had been a suicide, but I never saw anything about it in the paper the next day. We had to move from one gate to another but finally got a special train to make up for the one that was delayed. It was delightful looking out the window at the picturesque Yorkshire countryside on our way home.

I had a wonderful time with Irina and Vitaly—a real holiday. I didn't do any work except check over my manuscript *Falling in Love with the Baltics* for general improvements on the corrections I had requested in April. Most of them were done, except where I had said to significantly enlarge a picture; they had only slightly enlarged it. So I didn't know what to do about that. It seemed hard getting what I wanted from AuthorHouse. I was seldom able to speak to the same person there, and that was frustrating. I resolved not to use them to publish my next book.

Irina and I had several days to wander around the city of Sheffield and enjoy the fountains, parks, and winter garden, where we almost always drank our coffee and ate our light lunch. Next to the giant conservatory was a small museum of Ruskin's, a knitting exhibit with an unusual knitted wedding dress and knitted wedding cake and champagne bottle. Across the street was the main library, which was exhibiting Goya prints on the topic of folly. They were macabre and weird but arresting. The permanent collection in the Graves Art Gallery was good, ending with a lovely picture by Sargent. One painting by Edward Burn-Jones took twelve years to finish, so I decided that taking a few years to write a book was not so unusual. I always went to art museums in memory of my friend Tania. I knew she would love to know what was being shown and that she would love to have seen it, so I try to do it for her as well as for myself.

England proved expensive; it was easy to spend five hundred pounds in ten days. About half of the money went for transportation. It cost almost three pounds, about five dollars, to go downtown and back. Since I could buy a monthly bus pass in Ft. Lauderdale for twenty dollars, I found the cost of transport for foreigners in England outrageously expensive. Of course, workers are better paid there than in the United States, so I had to factor that in too. Moreover, students and seniors in England rode free, so someone had to support the bus system.

All too soon August 4 loomed before us, and we had to get up at five in the morning to get to the bus station so I could catch my bus to Golders Green at six. Then I reversed my trip, going from Golders Green to Stansted and flying to Riga instead of Kaunas. In Riga, Brenda again met me, but my plane was early, I passed through customs quickly, and I was able to get an earlier bus than I had expected. We had planned a leisurely dinner of salmon, french fries, and beer, and my catching the 11:00 p.m. bus back to Klaipėda. However, it was good to catch the earlier bus, even though it limited our time together to a few minutes instead of an entire evening. I was so tired of sitting on buses that sitting five more hours to Klaipėda was a bit of an ordeal. Secretly I was also worried whether there would be a taxi at the bus station to get me home that late at night. Fortunately, I found a taxi waiting there, and my final European trip ended well.

The next day and a half I frantically packed and gave away my remaining household goods. LCC friends Eric and Becky Hinderliter graciously took me to supper several nights, so I didn't have to cook. It was hard saying goodbye, but I left Klaipėda on August 6 for Vilnius, where I stayed overnight before taking the plane to Frankfort and Chicago. Despite a delayed takeoff, we were able to make connections in Chicago and my friend Karen Piper picked me up in Michigan City at 8:30—after a fifteen- to twenty-hour trip. Needless to say, I collapsed at Aunt Marce's in La Porte and slept for several days. Then, I was off to Iowa City on August 21 to work on my new book, *Remarkable Russian Women*, at the Obermann Institute.

Iowa City and Retirement

In Iowa City, I stayed with Trinity Church friends Dick and Debra Dorzweiler while doing research at the Obermann Institute, a sort of think tank for scholars at the Oakdale Campus. Iowa City is relatively small, so it was easy to get around using public transportation. I bought a monthly bus pass to use on the city buses going downtown. Once at the university, I could use its free bus service to go from the downtown bus hub to the medical center across the Iowa River, where I boarded another bus at the medical plaza to the institute. I used three buses each morning and evening getting to and from the campuses.

Bus culture is unique to each place, and in Iowa City it became a way of connecting to people and places I had formerly known. Free copies of the *Daily Iowan* student newspaper were available on the university buses, and it was fascinating to read it after being away for several decades. It didn't seem as interesting as when I was a student, but then I hadn't read other good national or international papers and so had not had anything to compare it to in the 1960s. Moreover, I was in the habit of listening to the news on National Public Radio in the morning while doing my exercises, so the *Daily Iowan* news seemed lackluster. The waits between bus stops were not long, and it wasn't too cold until winter set in. In November, my friend Karen Piper came to visit from La Porte, and she brought me a warm coat from her church's thrift shop. I had only a light raincoat since I had been traveling and didn't have a winter coat in my luggage.

The Obermann Institute at this time was located at the Oakdale Campus, in buildings that had been part of a large tuberculosis treatment center in former times. The institute was designed for faculty to work on their research projects without interruption. The faculty came from a broad range of departments: history, German language, and sociology. Once a week, the director of the institute held a coffee to which we were all invited

My son, Martin, and me, Iowa City, 2008

and expected to come. It was a captivating cross-section of the university intellectual community, and the conversation was stimulating. We also had monthly lunches where we had a chance to get to know each other. It was here that I met Professor Lawrence Gelfand and got reacquainted with him. He taught American diplomatic history, so I had known him only slightly when I was a graduate student. At the institute, it felt good to be treated as a scholar again. Through Lawrence, I became reacquainted with his wife, Miriam, who had been my first Russian language teacher at the university in 1962. Since this was Iowa City, where people are so friendly, they invited me to their Oaknoll living facility, and I had dinner with them several times. I even asked Miriam to proofread my manuscript *Falling in Love with the Baltics*. She had many helpful criticisms, and I had corrected it, but I couldn't arrange with the publisher AuthorHouse to make them all, and my book ended up with spelling errors.

I remembered her excellent proofreading skills, however, and was able to enlist her aid with my next two books about Russian women that were published by my helpful publisher Paul Royster at Zea Press in Lincoln. I was fortunate to have Miriam check my work because she was a native Russian speaker and could recognize the misspellings of Russian words and names which an American editor could not. Since she knows English grammar and spelling, and is a meticulous editor, they contained very few spelling errors.

My path had also crossed Miriam's when we both volunteered for Barack Obama's campaign in the fall of 2008. I got involved in the political process through my friends and hosts Dick and Debra Dorzweiler, who took me to a small Democratic house meeting where I put my name on a list to work in the campaign. They called me, and I was happy to spend one or two evenings per week in October making phone calls on behalf of Obama. It was at the Democratic headquarters near the old railroad tracks that I ran into Miriam Gelfand again, and it was so good to see someone I knew.

In time I encountered other old Iowa City friends from the 1960s, and the political work became more fun. Indeed, the whole process was elating, especially seeing so many young people involved in the election. Close to the time of the election, some young people from Illinois even came to Iowa City to help organize people for the election. That amazed me. Another day, Debra and I canvassed her neighborhood, and that drew us together in a special way. I hadn't canvassed since the 1960s when a group of us went to Davenport to work for McGovern. The Iowa City experience encouraged me to do some canvassing later for Obama in Lincoln during the 2012 election.

In 2007 and 2008, I taught one semester a year at LCC and spent part of the year in Florida and additional months in my hometown with Aunt Marce.

I kept wondering: "What will I do with the rest of my life? Where will I live? What will I do in retirement?" I hadn't yet adopted Dostoevsky's motto: "When I'm writing, then I'm being most of all." It took quite a while for me to realize how meaningful writing is, whether it's writing in my journal in the morning or working on a book in the afternoon. Still, for an extrovert like me, it's hard taking the time to be alone to write. Fortunately, I recalled some advice by Leon Uris. He reportedly said: "Apply the seat of your pants to the seat of your chair to write." An Iowa historian had also told me: "You can finish any project if you write one hour per day." And "Don't be afraid to read. Reading often leads to writing." These admonitions stood me in good stead in finishing my dissertation and subsequent books.

While doing some research on a book about Russian women in the Slavic collections of the International and Area Studies Library at the University of Illinois at Urbana-Champaign during the summer of 2009, I discovered that Love Library at the University of Nebraska–Lincoln had a fabulous collection of Russian women's writings. This surprised and pleased me. Already my two friends from Iowa, Elaine and Carole, who lived in Lincoln, had convinced me Lincoln was a possible retirement town. In the summer of 2009, I had found a unit at Pioneer House available for less than twenty thousand dollars, and it was a good investment. The monthly assessment, including all utilities, cable TV, and a handyman to fix things, was about $350. Fortunately, I had sufficient funds in a Metropolitan Life retirement account from the El Paso Community College to buy my unit. Living at Pioneer House has worked out well. The location is great because I can walk the ten blocks to campus or take a bus, which comes every fifteen minutes and costs me ten cents. The bus is helpful when I am having health issues, when the weather is inclement, or when I have heavy books to return to the city or university libraries.

Retirement in Lincoln, Nebraska

The spring after I moved to Lincoln, my friend Karen Piper brought my aunt Marcelline to visit me. While I have only a one-bedroom apartment, Pioneer House has a guest room with two beds, so I have been able to invite friends to stay with me. On the next page is a picture Karen took of my aunt and me at the rose garden near the zoo. It was a cold spring day, and I had my head covered, but my aunt, who is hardier, did not. One day, my aunt and I went to see the film *Amelia*, about Amelia Earhart, at a downtown theater. We enjoyed it, and my aunt was so pleased I could take a bus to go to a movie.

Marcelline and Aunt Marce in Lincoln's Hamann Rose Garden, April 2010

My friend Karen helped me move clothes, dishes, and small household goods to my new apartment from La Porte. Another time, we met in southwest Virginia, and Karen ferried furniture that had been in storage for nine years in her van to Lincoln. Karen and Aunt Marcelline have been great supporters in late years.

Before I began working on my book *Remarkable Russian Women*, I had begun an article on libraries and how they have served as almost sacred spaces, places of consolation and contemplation, "havens from the heartless world of capitalist competition." However, with the advent of computers, the tone of public and university libraries has changed. They seem less sacred, with ranks of computers greeting patrons upon entry. While the law library—the Nebraska State Library—at the capitol in Lincoln is a public library, few

Marcelline at the deserted law library in the Nebraska State Capitol

Sculpture of Abraham Lincoln, west side of the Nebraska State Capitol

use it today. I had thought it might be an ideal place to work on my books, but it lacked the proper atmosphere. It was a little too quiet since it was so empty, its ethos not as amenable to writing, as the picture shows.

In Lincoln, it has been lovely living two blocks from the capitol. I enjoy the proximity to our state legislators and the historic atmosphere, including this Abraham Lincoln statue.

Publishers as Friends and Treasures

In Lincoln, I discovered some of the benefits of old age and was able publish my books *Remarkable Russian Women* and *Resilient Russian Women* with the help of editor/publisher Paul Royster. These books are free to read online as ebooks (easy to find with a Google search of their titles) or to read in paperback for about twenty-five dollars from Lulu (www.lulu.com) or booksellers like Barnes & Noble or Amazon. So far, more than fourteen thousand people have downloaded these digital works online, which has been very gratifying. In the digital format all the pictures are in color, whereas they are black and white in the book format. Both Paul and production specialist Linnea Fredrickson have been encouraging and helpful in publishing my writings. Now, I call them friends and treasures as well as editors. After reading Amor Towles's *A Gentleman in Moscow*, I can say that Paul is a Gentleman in the Ivory Tower of Love Library.

Publishing an ebook in the Digital Commons is a wonderful experience. I receive monthly digital computer reports telling me how many people have downloaded the files and a map showing where in the world the downloads have occurred and sometimes which universities the downloaders may be affiliated with. My reports include readers from all continents and countries, including South Africa, Zimbabwe, Cuba, Iceland, Western and Eastern Europe, Russia, India, Australia, the Middle East, and North America. While I haven't made much money from writing these two books, as one generally doesn't from academic books, it has been extremely gratifying to find so many people all over the world reading my work. What more could a scholar ask for?

Friends in Retirement

Friends Are Treasures

Making friends in retirement has been somewhat like making friends in college. People are my age, and we share similar life experiences. Still, it takes a while, with the exception of getting to know people at Pioneer House. In some ways living there is like living in a college dorm or a small town. There are no secrets. Everyone knows what's going on, and that's OK. Since I don't have a car, Pioneer House friends often provide rides for me, and I'm grateful for this kindness. But this is just one of the many benefits of living there. We also have monthly birthday parties for people, and this has been a good way to get acquainted.

I usually make the birthday cakes, and I enjoy doing this. In addition, we have potluck dinners on holidays like Memorial Day, Fourth of July, Labor Day, Thanksgiving, Christmas, and Easter. These too provide occasions to get to know residents in greater depth. When I recently read a graduating senior's ode to college life in the *Daily Nebraskan* newspaper, I wanted to tell him that similar opportunities would surface throughout life. But, some things we can learn only by living. The availability of friends is probably one of them. In Lincoln, I have made friends at church, Love Library, the university copy center, on the bus, book clubs, in yoga and tai chi classes, and in teaching courses for older adults in Osher Life Long Learning (OLLI). The first course I taught for OLLI was in 2015 and I titled it "Downton Abbey with a Russian Twist." I did a comparative study of English and Russian nineteenth-century aristocratic women. In 2016 I offered a history of Russia in film, providing lectures and using three films by Sergei Eisenstein. A year later, I presented a course on the one hundredth anniversary of the Russian revolutions of 1917 using lectures and various Soviet films. In 2018 I gave a lecture on Amor Towles's book *A Gentleman in Moscow*, which I titled "Life Outside the Metropol." I still enjoy the exhilaration teaching affords, but I find it takes more preparation and effort than it used to. OLLI students mainly want to learn from and be entertained by my lectures. Yet many are interested in Russian history, culture, or music. It's a positive teaching experience but different from my previous experiences.

In Lincoln, one thing leads to another. In the fall of 2017 a city librarian invited me to give a lecture "Life Outside the Metropol." It explored women's experiences, which were different from those of the characters in Towles's novel *A Gentleman in Moscow*. In October 2018 I taught a short class for OLLI on this same topic but discussed Vladimir Tchernavin's experiences as well as those of Alexandra Tolstoy and some other women during the 1920s and '30s.

Chapter IX

Sharing the Journey with Kindred Spirits

After retiring to Lincoln, I began attending St. Mark's on the Campus Episcopal Church. One of the reasons I chose Pioneer House was its proximity to the university and to St. Mark's, which is across the street from Love Library. Our church has been a great community sparked by our intellectually and spiritually challenging priests, Jerry Thompson and Sidnie Crawford; wonderfully creative organist and choir directors, Kurt Knecht and Jessica Marks; and extraordinarily helpful office managers, Gwen Colgrove and Bill Huenemann, as well as a fabulous choir and lots of wonderful parishioners, including some I've gotten to know well. Our priest, Jerry, has provided thoughtful sermons and writings. In one he quoted the English guru Evelyn Underhill, saying "The spiritual life . . . is not a consoling retreat from the difficulties of existence, but an invitation to enter fully into that difficult existence, and there apply the Charity of God." In retirement, I feel more able to do this. Often in my youth I wanted to flee the difficulties of life, but sometimes I now feel able to accept them and enter into them with the Charity of God. Slowly, I have even come to ask God's guidance when writing, planning new trips, and dealing with other life events. I'm getting better at doing this.

I took a course in discernment with a study group at nearby St. Paul's United Methodist Church the second year I was in Lincoln plus two other courses on this topic at St. Mark's in 2017, so I am slowly learning to apply this technique in my life. In some ways, St. Paul's is my second church home. It sponsors instrumental and choral concerts the first Friday of the month, and I love attending these as well as having lunch there afterward.

Soon after coming to St. Mark's on the Campus Episcopal Church, parishioner Roger Wait introduced me to a program of healing called the Order of St. Luke (OSL). Its monthly meetings were nearby at St. Matthew's Episcopal Church. This group has been a source of healing for me, friends, and relations. We had communion and a healing service there the first Saturday of every month, followed by a study of some kind that promotes our spiritual growth. Recently, we also studied discernment. Another friend from St. Mark's, Sarah Fairchild, also belonged to the OSL, so that made a bond between us too. Sarah and Mary Roseberry Brown from St. Mark's re-introduced me to Camp Furthest Out (CFO), which is held each summer in June. I had attended a CFO in Indiana when I was twelve years old and then heard about it again when I was seventy. Each time I was facing a personal crisis and needed prayers to love me back into shape. At twelve, I was deeply disturbed about my alcoholic father and at seventy about the diagnosis of bronchiectasis and lung cancer. This camp proved a great opportunity for healing and spiritual growth. At CFO we have lots of time for personal, small group, and communal prayer. We also have morning and evening meditations. Mary, who is on the board of the camp, asked me to give a meditation after my first year. Her confidence in me helped nudge me back into shape. We all need someone to believe in us and care about us and our soul. During my time in Lincoln, friends in OSL and CFO have gently helped me reconstitute myself in my new home. In the summer of 2017, Mary asked me to be on the board, so that's been an endearing experience. Since writing this segment, my friend Sarah Fairchild has died, and that was traumatic. It was hard to let go of her, but she was so sick that I eventually saw her death as a blessing.

One of the spiritual exercises we do at CFO is writing a letter to God and then a response from God. We put the letters in a self-addressed envelope, and the prayer hostess mails them back to us a year later. It's always touching to read these letters, and I include two:

Letter from me to God, June 24, 2014

>Dear God,
>
>It's so good to have time to talk to you and share my concerns. I've been conflicted since Elaine had the bleeding in her brain. I don't understand or like it. I can't make her healthy again. I know you can, and I ask you to make the blood cells in her body behave. Make her heart behave too. Thank you, Lord.
>
>Lord, I've also been feeling conflicted about a new friend and our blossoming relationship. It's lovely to behold but a little scary too. I feel scared of my own desires.
>
>I think part of it is that my father seemed the sexually active member in our family, and he always seemed out of control. That's how I saw sexuality modeled—either repressed as the model for women in my society, or out of control, the model for men.
>
>I need your help now, dear Lord. I need your guidance in dealing with my feelings and fantasies.
>
>Show me a responsible way to act, dear Lord. Help me discuss this with my therapist.
>
>I remember being crazy in love with John, yet that didn't produce a long-lasting, nourishing relationship.
>
>This time, I don't want to act crazy but responsibly and lovingly. Show me how to do this.

Lord, I ask you to help M. too. She is so frail and needs your help. Maybe she too could find help with my therapist.

Lord, gear me up to share my new book with Miriam in Iowa City and Ann at UNL. Show me the right people to give my manuscript to. Thanks for providing CFO for healing, the balm of Gilead.

Continue to watch over Martin and Donna, and Kathryn and Walt, while I am so distracted by Elaine's illness and my new relationship.

Your ever loving daughter,

Marcelline

Letter from God to me, June 2014

Dear Marcelline,

You're in the right place to hear my word. You are being healed physically, spiritually, and psychologically by the people, songs, prayers, and love that I am pouring out on you. Just receive it all with open arms, heart, mind, and soul. Let me fill you with my grace and then you will be in better balance to love and be loved.

It's OK for a man to love you, and for you to love a man. It's OK.

Just remember to respect and honor yourself as well as your friend. Love yourself as well as him. Keep in mind your codependent behavior. You can let this relationship develop as it does. You don't have to force it, neglect it, or fear it. You can be open to it, and see what it teaches you about him, yourself, and the Great I Am.

Your loving Mother/Father God

A year later, June 30, 2015, I wrote another letter to God, saying:

Dear Lord,

My heart was so heavy when I came to CFO Camp this year. I was worried about the president of Pioneer House, who wanted to cut down "Mac the Magnificent Oak Tree." I was really angry at this fellow and his actions.

I was also angry at my friend for disregarding me, for putting his work ahead of me—of valuing it more than me. I felt abandoned and rejected, hurt and angry.

Slowly, praying with others I have begun to feel less judgmental of these fellows. I have begun to distinguish between the sin and the sinner. I have begun to see them as seriously flawed, as I am too.

Please forgive me, Lord. I liked what P. said last night: "Guess who's God? and guess who's not?"

I feel now like I can leave those who troubled me to you, dear Lord. They're your children too. You love them as well as me. Show me how to love the sinner but not the sin.

Help me cherish myself so I won't need others to cherish me so much. Help me not to idolize a romantic relationship. It can be good but not perfect. Most of all, we need your love.

Sincerely,
Marcelline

Letter from God to Marcelline, June 2015

Dear Marcelline,

You are my beloved daughter. I love you. I created you.

I see that you get bent out of shape sometimes and that you need CFO Camp to love and nudge you back into shape. That's one of its purposes. Other people can love you, care about you, and befriend you.

You may feel abandoned right now since Elaine has gone to Indiana for the summer, and your special friend is working lots of overtime.

You may feel abandoned, but I, your Lord, have not abandoned you. I love you, dear daughter. I know your father never told you he loved you, but probably his father never told him he loved him either. Maybe he didn't have much love to give. But how wise have you been in choosing your lovers? Why did you choose lovers who had no love to give you? You had other choices and chose wrongly.

Moreover, you chose not to believe these men when they said they loved you.

You have ignored some of my messengers who came to you with words of love. Try not to ignore friends at CFO who have words of love for you from me.

There is plenty of love in the world—accept it—at Pioneer House, at church, at CFO, and many other places.

> Tune in to my abundant Love. It's there for you—freely given. Go and sin no more. Accept my forgiveness and love.
>
> Shalom,
>
> Your Heavenly Father

In addition to my CFO friends, I have another church friend named Elly who is a member of St. Paul's Methodist Church. She supplies me with their devotional booklet *The Upper Room*, and I give her the Episcopalian *Day by Day*. We share our faith and a common intellectual and political life. Fortunately for me, she keeps me supplied with good books and magazines like the *New Yorker* and the *New York Review of Books*, which she subscribes to and shares. I then pass them on to my friend Michael at Pioneer House, and we have a round-robin intellectual community. Elly often invites me to luncheons, lectures, concerts, and a film club at St. Paul's, which I enjoy but otherwise wouldn't know about. I feel spiritually refreshed whenever I visit St. Paul's because it has some of the most magnificent stained glass in Lincoln. Sitting there at a service or a concert, I feel holy, bathed in the golden glow of its enormous sanctuary windows. Elly and I also share lunch on Tuesdays after our tai chi class and have time to discuss our personal lives, both problems and triumphs. Elly is a poet, so we also discuss our writings. Indeed, she kindly edited this manuscript for me. What a friend! I especially treasure her friendship because I can share my writing concerns with her.

My oldest and one of my best friends in Lincoln is Elaine. She's a French historian, so we have a common intellectual life to share as well as our spiritual and cultural lives. Elaine and I pray for each other and our friends and relations who are ill. Prayer binds us together in a special way. Elaine extends incredible hospitality at her luxurious townhouse to friends for days, weeks, and even years at a time. She's a generous person, and we share many cultural interests. We are both "culture vultures" and enjoy concerts and plays together. As a professor emeritus of Nebraska Wesleyan University, she receives free tickets to musicals and plays presented there. She often takes me as her guest, which I greatly appreciate, especially since the productions are of such high quality. She's also a Lutheran and invited me to join the Lutheran Women's Book Club when I stayed with her in the 1990s and again when I moved to Lincoln in 2009.

I love this club for lots of reasons: we have fun celebrating each other's birthdays, we enjoy visiting various restaurants in Lincoln for lunch when we meet, and we savor being in the company of other readers. Elaine's church is

Marcelline (left) and Elaine (right) at book club at the Green Gateau restaurant, Lincoln

Marcelline (far right) with the Lutheran Women's Book Club, 2013

as spiritual as St. Paul's and St. Mark's. It has many wonderful programs, especially during Lent. I have attended some of them over the years when I was staying at Elaine's. It also engages in outstanding community service. It is through its auspices that St. Mark's was able to sponsor a refugee family in 2016 and again in 2018. Elaine is one of my special church friends because I can talk to her about my spiritual or personal problems, day or night. She also graciously gives me rides to my doctors, and I value her friendship greatly. Moreover, she enjoys tea and cake as much as I do. I can even invite her to share leftovers, and she doesn't mind.

Another dear friend is Beth Hemmer. She lives in Pioneer House and also belongs to St. Mark's Church, so we have a lot in common. She too helps me with rides to various places, goes with me to concerts, and prays for me and my friends when we need it. When I had cataract surgery, she lovingly and dutifully administered the eye drops four times a day for several weeks. I can count on her when I need help, and that means a lot.

Another close church friend is Michael Johnson, who moved to Pioneer House the year after I did. He's a retired Spanish and French professor, and we share intellectual and spiritual interests. Along with Elly and Elaine, he is one of my closest confidants. He too is a member of St. Mark's, a good prayer partner, and usually gives me a ride to my therapist once a month, a ride to get groceries on Saturdays, and a ride to church on Sunday mornings. He also helps me with the Altar Guild duties one Sunday a month. We often go to Wendy's for lunch after church, and on Thursday evenings he takes me to Whole Foods, where we have dinner and then visit our mutual friend Pat Green, who now lives in assisted living. There we view of one of the Great Courses on Greek, Roman, or Renaissance art. Michael serves on the board of directors at Pioneer House and is a steady influence there. His only flaw is sleeping late. If I want to go to the nine thirty adult forum at church, I have to walk because he doesn't get up early enough to attend it. Michael and I share similar political views, and he and my son get along so well that he accompanies us to Saturday night dinner whenever Martin comes to visit. I am especially grateful to him for his astute reading of this manuscript, his helpful editorial comments, and for explaining the ideas of postmodernism to me. He even lent me a graphic novel about postmodernism.

In St Mark's Adult Forum, I have become better acquainted with our priest, Jerry Thompson, along with several church members, including our assistant priest, Sidnie White Crawford, Professor Robert Stock, Susan Steinbech, Mary Lutz, and Connie Bacchus. Susan, Mary, and I participate in the Lincoln Episcopal Women's Book Club, and Connie shares an interest in Russian Orthodoxy with me. Connie is an artist and quilt maker and has made several memorable quilted frontals and vestments for our church and priest. She has also exposed me to some Orthodox priestly memoirs that have enriched my spiritual and intellectual life. She introduced me to a Russian Orthodox bookstore here in Lincoln, where I discovered additional resources for my writings on Russian women. Once again, God has been providing richly for my spiritual life and growth here.

In retirement, I also renewed an elementary school friendship with Peter Cumerford. He asked me to give a talk at Bethel Bible Church in Chicago in April 2015 to some "Savvy Seniors" about my life as a teacher missionary in Klaipėda, Lithuania. Preparing for this talk drew me back into my time teaching and living in Lithuania from 2000 to 2010. The quote I used for beginning of the talk came from Isaiah 50: "The Lord has given me the tongue of a teacher, that I may know how to sustain the weary with a word."

I thought, at our age, we all grow weary and long for words to sustain us. I realized that one of the words (or phrases) that sustains me is "God provides." We never know how this will happen in the present and future, but we can see how it occurred in the past. I shared some of my teaching and travel experiences with the group and thoroughly enjoyed making the presentation, despite initial trepidation.

Several times, I have gone on retreats to a monastery at Schuyler, Nebraska. Once, our project was drawing a picture of how God had been acting in our lives and had been providing for us in the past. I was amazed to see that by placing markers at ten-year intervals, I could see in retrospect that God had been providing for me quite consistently.

Cultural Life

> My cup runneth over.
> *Psalm 23*

Cultural life in Lincoln is rich and refreshing. There are occasions called First Fridays when all the art galleries in the city are free and open to the public. Some galleries even offer free wine and cheese; others request a small payment for the wine. Needless to say, it's fun going gallery hopping. One of the most unusual galleries is the International Quilt Museum, which Elaine sometimes takes me to because it is not downtown. The Quilt Museum always has fascinating exhibits, from Indian and Pakistani quilts to those made in France at the time of the Revolution. There are even special stories, like those of young Sudanese immigrant girls living in Grand Island, Nebraska, learning to make quilts after school. Some of their quilts showed their dreams of the future—becoming a judge, a doctor, even a football player—while others showed their memories of their homeland. The young girls came from different tribes and spoke different languages, so English was their common language. This Friday evening became a study in cultural understanding. Sometimes I go to the downtown galleries with Elaine, Elly, or an artist friend from Pioneer House, Pat Green.

In addition to the lively art scene and the beautiful Sheldon Museum of Art on the university campus, Lincoln resonates with good music. The university often provides wonderful programs and performances by the music faculty and students. There are countless well-performed symphonies, recitals, and even statewide musical contests. Once I heard the state flute competitions and an international clarinet competition. Another time, a French horn program impressed me. Many of the university concerts are free or cost a mere three dollars for seniors. The only problem is that the concerts are often at seven thirty in the evening, and during the fall and winter months it's dark. When I make the effort to go, however, it's always worth it. Recently, I went to hear the Boston Pops orchestra perform Gershwin's "Rhapsody in Blue." It was a magnificent performance, and I was so glad I had the energy to walk the eleven blocks there and back. The music was so uplifting. Unfortunately, there are not as many classical music concerts in the summer when the evenings are longer and brighter, but there are three venues of outdoor jazz programs then. Some are at noon and some at night. All year long the bars offer music, but I haven't ever been to hear this music. I keep thinking I'll go some evening when the nearby Marriott hotel or Chez SoDo restaurant features a famous jazz band, but I haven't done this yet.

Once, a friend of Pioneer House left free tickets to a jazz concert at a downtown bank, and a fellow resident and I attended. It was an entertaining evening. The bands played on the eighteenth floor of the building, and the view of the city at sunset was superb. The building is also the scene of the Torch Club, a private academic dining club that meets there monthly. Others can buy a yearly membership for dining there. So the concert offered a peek into a hidden part of local society while also showing a rare mix of black and white Lincoln inhabitants.

Neighborhoods

Pioneer House Cooperative, where I live, is about ten blocks from the downtown of the city. It is bordered on one side by historic Lincoln Mall with oak trees and lovely flowers and three quite different statues of President Abraham Lincoln—a typical one at the state capitol, a relaxed informal one sitting on a bench on Lincoln Mall, and one of Abe in his youth holding a plow at the City/County Building. It's reassuring to spend some time with his seated statue discussing our present political problems. He reminds me that when he was president, there were grave problems too.

Two blocks east of Pioneer House stands the state capitol, the governor's mansion, and some lovely nineteenth-century historic homes. Two blocks south of Pioneer House is a Hispanic community. There's a grocery with Spanish-speaking workers and clientele, an ice cream parlor, hairdressers, and a bakery with delicious inexpensive pies and cakes. The prices were such a surprise because when I used to housesit in Florida and patronized a nearby Italian bakery, these same treats cost five dollars each. Of course, the New York style cheesecake and chocolate pie were scrumptious.

One fall Pioneer House resident Michael Johnson and I placed voting posters in the Mexican shops. As a retired Spanish professor, Michael knew how to speak to the owners politely in Spanish. We wanted to register people in the neighborhood to vote, but it turned out that the registration process was too complicated, and it was too close to the election to do it.

I also live only a few blocks from various Democratic party headquarters, and it was fun getting to know the young people working in the Organizing for America office in 2012. I was a bit lonely during the summer when my two friends Elaine Kruse and Carole Levin were gone, so it was a good thing to volunteer at the Democratic office once a week. Sometimes they served pizza, sometimes I baked a cake to take, and sometimes we went canvassing in the neighborhood, and I met fellow Democrats. Also, it was energizing in November to go to some of the fundraisers for various politicians. Lincoln is such a friendly place that even politicking is good natured. In later years, I canvassed for another candidate, State Senator Anna Wishart, in a completely different section of town. Often, the Democrats have an ice cream social, and I have gone to these twice and enjoyed getting to know more people who are like-minded. Of course politics is a bit dismaying at times because Nebraska is such a Republican-dominated state. Democrats win only some city, county, and state legislature elections. Still, winning locally helps boost our spirits.

Not too long ago a new bookstore called Francie & Finch opened near our dynamic neighborhood. The owner, Leslie Huerta, is remarkably friendly and hosts all kinds of events: First Friday concerts by small bands, art and craft shows, journaling with a local artist on Wednesday nights, poetry readings, and so forth. She even featured my books on Russian women during Women's History Month. That meant a lot to me. She also featured books on Queen Elizabeth by my friend Carole Levin. She's a marvel and sells many of the most unusual new books. Needless to say, I've bought quite a few already: a humorous book on England by Bill Bryson; J. D. Vance's *Hillbilly Elegy*, a marvelous memoir about the social crisis in southern Ohio; a book about the Italian author Elena Ferrante (I bought this tome for my sister because she had sent me all four volumes of Ferrante's work about women's lives in Naples after World War II); *A Gentleman in Moscow*; *A Secret Sisterhood*; and even several graphic novels—one about Proust, one about Josephine Baker, and one about a Vietnamese family who immigrated to the States. I love looking at the new books. And Leslie dispenses love along with her books. She really cares for her customers. Often I enter her shop, sit down on a cozy chair, and she brings me some warm cider or cocoa and a cookie. She has made her shop into a cultural and intellectual center, and I appreciate that. She gives the service I don't get at other stores. Her place is an example of small is better.

In addition to this charming bookstore, we are blessed with a variety of restaurants in our neighborhood. Some are Mexican, some are cafés like Cultiva, with great coffee and specialties like crepes and cornmeal pancakes, which I adore. Others—like Billy's, the Green Gateau, and the Cottonwood (now closed)—feature cuisine at higher prices. Some are rather simple affairs catering to the employees at the County/City Building and the capitol. So our neighborhood is well situated, having plenty of places to eat within walking distance. There are also lots of bars, but I'm not part of that scene so can't comment on them. The Cottonwood had live music and drinks on Monday nights before it closed.

Friends

Several years ago a colleague at LCC remarked, "It's all about people," and I've found that to be true. Friends have endeared Lincoln to me. Two friends and historians from my graduate school days at Iowa live in Lincoln. One is Carole Levin, whom I've mentioned several times, and who teaches Tudor-Stuart English history in the UNL Department of History. Another acquaintance in the history department is Ann Kleimola, whom I knew from my times doing research at the University of Illinois in the 1980s. Ann and other university historians amassed an amazing collection of Russian history sources that I have used for my books on Russian women. Once, I again returned to the summer lab for Slavicists at the University of Illinois where I profited from a seminar in Russian history that Ann had organized. So I'm grateful to her for all she's done for Russian history in Lincoln.

Another historian friend—the chief influencer of my decision to move to Lincoln—Elaine Kruse, taught history at Nebraska Wesleyan University. Through Elaine I have also met several other delightful members of the Nebraska Wesleyan faculty, who are also retired: Ron Naugle, an American historian, who recently completed the fourth edition of his text on Nebraska, which I was fortunate to proofread; Joyce Gleason, an economist; Joyce Michaelis, a Spanish professor; and Jean Henderson, a music theory professor. Over the years, Nebraska Wesleyan has contributed to my cultural and intellectual life. Elaine has obtained free tickets to outstanding musical and theatrical performances like *Chicago* and *Electra*, which we attended. Outstanding speakers have also come. I even learned the bus route so I could spare Elaine from having to pick me up all the time. I still needed her to give me a ride home, however, because the buses stop running at 7:00 p.m. I've also met fascinating international students as well as community friends through Elaine, and her friendship has enriched my life.

Elaine, the Joyces, and I sometimes go to films at the Mary Riepma Ross Media Arts Center on the University of Nebraska campus. We have seen first-rate French, Latin American, Korean, Canadian, and Chinese films. A downtown movie theater, the Grand, also has popular films at affordable prices, which I enjoy.

Friends have come into my life in various ways. Living in a cooperative has given me many good friends. One group I met when I first moved to Lincoln was affectionately called the Lounge Lizards. These were the guys who drank coffee together in the morning, read the paper, and talked politics. Sometimes I joined them, but usually I worked on a project and didn't get downstairs early. These men included Herman, who was president of the co-op for several years; Jack, who has been one of the finest raconteurs I've ever known; and Rich, a former construction engineer who has fixed things in my apartment for me. When I have a problem with a kitchen door, hanging a picture on our concrete walls, or restoring a sculpture, I have asked Rich to help, and he has done a superb job. When I was beset with computer troubles, I called Herman the first few years I lived at Pioneer House. He always knew how to solve my dilemma. After he married and moved away, I now ask JoAnne or Theresa to help, since they're computer savvy too. Jack recently married and moved away. Life at Pioneer House changes: some folks die, some move away. Yet good friends remain, and new ones emerge.

In addition to the morning group, there were other friends I made at Pioneer House. These included three artists: Pat Green, Audrey Greve, and Gladys Wiedebein, as well as Jim Cook, a photographer. Pat and I initially shared meals together, organized potlucks, and became best friends. Pat also hosted an art salon on Thursday evenings, and she has continued it in her new abode at Gateway Vista. Jim and I sometimes attend Advent and Lenten services at his nearby Christian Church. At first, Jim and I occasionally took a free bus to a casino in Council Bluffs, Iowa, but we haven't done that for a couple of years. I went mostly for the ride in the countryside, the opportunity to see the mighty Missouri River, and to have a good dinner. Jim went to see the trains closely passing by the casino. He is a better gambler than I am and has won enough to pay for his lunch. I have limited myself to $2.00, and I once won $1.31. That didn't pay for my $10.00 lunch, but it was fun to win—even a little. I was surprised to find that most of the gamblers were pretty middle-class and middle-aged. The casino wasn't filled with the sleazy types I had expected. Everyone was polite. It was Iowa after all. Last winter Jim died. A loss to us all.

Some of the women I've met at Pioneer House included a group who used to assemble in the late afternoon for mail and then watch *Jeopardy* and *Wheel of Fortune* on TV. They also rooted for the UNL volleyball team on TV. Most of them joined the fellows to watch Nebraska football on Saturdays. Sometimes they provided pizza, chili, or cake as they enjoyed the game. I'm not much of a football fan, but I enjoyed seeing everyone all decked out in red attire as they rooted for the Huskers. Some of these women also helped decorate and clean the lounge. When I first came to Pioneer House, Edy gave me a radio, dishes, kitchen utensils, and a vacuum cleaner. I'm also indebted to her for cooking supplies. If I run out of walnuts when making a cake or need sage for the Thanksgiving stuffing, I can count on her to lend them to me.

When I first moved to Pioneer House, there was a grand group of ninety-year-old women. One walked thirty to forty blocks per day. She was an independent spirit, and we both enjoyed reading the Jan Karon series about an Episcopal priest in the Carolinas. The other two are also smart and know a lot about the history of Pioneer House, one having lived here for twenty-nine years! These women inspire me and make me think old age is not so bad. I am sorry to report that two of those women subsequently died in their late nineties. I have lived here ten years now, so some of my good friends have moved to assisted living and some have died. Change—inevitable!

Lincoln Helpers

Two others who have made my life in Lincoln good are my Vietnamese doctor Dr. Chau and dentist Dr. Nguyen, who are very kind, professional, and skilled. It turns out that while I live on the edge of the Hispanic community to the southwest, I also live not so far from the Vietnamese community to the northeast. Luckily for me the doctor and dentist have offices near their community and are also within walking distance for me. This way I don't have to take two or three buses into the suburbs to see a doctor. Sorry to say that since I first wrote this, my medical doctor has moved her office out of the downtown and into the suburbs. Now I have to ask a friend to drive me to her office. Presently, the doctor I see the most is a gynecologist named Marti MacLeod Kozal and her muse practitioner. I experienced a prolapsed uterus in the fall of 2016, and I went to see her for help in treating it. She discovered a few other feminine ailments, so I have gotten to know and appreciate her the past year. I see my pulmonologist, Dr. Fiedler, several times a year for the treatment of my bronchiectasis and Mycobacterium avium complex infection. Antibiotics take care of the MAC, and yoga and tai chi have been helping my lung problem. Initially, Michael Johnson drove me every few months for a CAT scan and appointments. We usually ate lunch at the Bryan Health hospital cafeteria because it offered good, affordable food. He also drove me to see my therapist, Tom Tiegs, who helped me manage my depression and other assorted problems. Then we dined at the Olive Garden Italian restaurant. It's wonderful having Michael as a friend who has time to take me to my medical appointments. Doctor appointments have become more regular as I age. I have been blessed to find excellent doctors here in Lincoln and to have Medicare and Blue Cross insurance cover my expenses. I discovered that I have the "Cadillac Plan" with my insurance, but it covers my costs when I see a doctor in Florida or even when traveling in Europe. Thus, it's worth the expense.

Last but not least among what makes my life in Lincoln good is my church, St. Mark's on the Campus Episcopal Church, across from the university library. Our main priest, Jerry, has been delightful, intellectually thought provoking, yet kind and comforting. He sponsors captivating adult forums on mysticism and discernment. He's very open and generous. I've come to know and love several members at St. Marks, including Beth, Susan, Roger, Michael, Jo, Bob, Peg, Mary, Sarah, Martha, Berwyn, and Connie. Roger is a member of OSL (Order of St. Luke), a healing order, and he invited me to join them, which I appreciated. It's wonderful to be with others devoted to Jesus' healing ministry. He also gives me rides home from church when Michael isn't around. Since Michael and I both live at Pioneer House, I usually ride to and from church with him. Initially I walked, but it's harder to do that now.

Generally, people in Lincoln are thoughtful, kind, and helpful, so God has blessed me in bringing me here. After buying my apartment in 2009, I wended my way south to Florida for the winter. Having my friend Janusz's house to occupy for five winters was a wonderful antidote to the Nebraska winters. Once, I went to Florida by way of Iowa City. There I did some research on my former Russian language professor, Helena Scriabina. It was so enjoyable going through her archive. I found several pictures that I used in my books on Russian women and decided to include the story of her life during wartime in a future book on civilians in World War II. I hadn't realized that in addition to sheltering a Jewish woman in the Caucasus, she also helped French soldiers in Germany at the end of the war. I agree with her philosophy that "one meets good people everywhere."

After a week's hospitality in Iowa City with Margaret and Chuck Felling, old friends from the 1960s, I flew from Moline, Illinois, to Atlanta, Georgia, where I stayed with an old friend, Teresa Sapp, and her family. Terry and I were colleagues at the University of Texas at El Paso, and we stayed in touch after she returned to Georgia. We went to an enchanting Salvador Dali exhibit in Atlanta and to a restful Benedictine monastery. We also enjoyed eating and talking together nonstop. Her son and daughter-in-law cooked for us, so we were spoiled. It was good to meet her family, especially her grandson—the apple of her eye.

From Atlanta I flew to Ft. Lauderdale and had to get used to living there again. At first, it always seems so foreign with its tropical climate and flora. However, with several friends at All Saints Episcopal Church and a few at the nearby Presbyterian church, I felt less lonesome than I did during my first few years. We have a bonny, blonde baby at our church, and he reminds me so much of Martin fifty years ago. I enjoy this toddler in remembrance of my son who is so grown up except in my heart and mind.

Travel in Retirement

My expenses living in a co-op like Pioneer House are minimal, and I am able to save a few thousand dollars each year to travel. Last year I took a cruise from Ft. Lauderdale to Spain and Italy and thoroughly enjoyed myself. I am blessed to do this but also grateful that a lifetime of frugality enables me to live modestly whether I am on holiday or in Lincoln. Indeed, when I was in Florence, Italy, last spring, I enjoyed going to a local grocery store to see what it was like and also to purchase a salad with olives and cheese as well as an Italian beer for my supper. I could have afforded a meal at a nice restaurant but had found the dinners were too big for me. I couldn't eat all the food and couldn't take it back to the convent where I was staying. I found buying a salad at the grocery, buying a meal at a nearby deli, or getting a small meal and a Moretti beer from the friendly gyros café owner made me happy and saved me money. Moreover, these transactions allowed me to interact more with the Florentine natives. I got to know the deli and café owners, and enjoyed talking to them since they both knew English. Indeed, when I needed to make a long distance call to a friend in Germany, I found I could ask the café owner to help me since he grew up in Germany and knew the country code. He was such a nice guy helping me make my call and refusing any payment. How's that for a blessing? When we look around, we find God blessing us in so many unexpected ways and places.

Wholeness

"Breathe on me, Breath of God"

Most of my life I was blessed with excellent health and was not very conscious or grateful for it. However, in the winter of 2009, I was diagnosed in Florida with an untreatable lung condition called bronchiectasis. That was a low blow. I didn't want to believe it and didn't for a couple years. However, I eventually sought a second opinion in Lincoln, and my pulmonologist, Dr. Fiedler, told me I not only had bronchiectasis but possibly lung cancer. That was a real shock. I didn't know what to do. I couldn't believe I had lung cancer because I was still walking a couple miles to the library and eating three meals a day. I thought, "How could I have cancer?" I just didn't believe it. He, as well as the pulmonologist in Florida, wanted to perform a bronchoscopy on my lungs. That frightened me because I had never had many medical tests. I didn't want that procedure and resisted having it for some time. Then, I thought about dying of lung cancer. Finally, I decided I didn't want my son to become an orphan, and I would have the test.

I realized I wanted to live for myself as well as for my son. Absolutely terrified of the procedure, I lived through the bronchoscopy, thanks to the help of my friends who prayed for me at this time. The test was inconclusive, so Dr. Fiedler told me I needed a biopsy to see what the mass in my lungs was. This test showed no cancer but an infection called Mycobacterium avium complex, or MAC. The treatment for it involved three different antibiotics, which I had to take three times a day for twelve months. This cured the MAC but seemed to give me chronic urinary tract infections. Anyway, I was grateful for the healing and for my Pioneer House friend Michael Johnson who drove me back and forth to the hospital where Dr. Fiedler worked. We got to know the cafeteria pretty well because I had to have CAT scans on my lungs every few months for several years. It was a special blessing having Michael for a friend because he is prayerful and also discrete. He didn't talk about my condition to everyone else, and I appreciated that. Today, I don't mind these medical issues as much, but adjusting to the first episode and treatment was hard. In 2017 my pulmonologist informed me that my situation has improved, and that was good news. In January 2018, I got the flu, pneumonia, and MAC again. Those three plus my bronchiectasis just about did me in. Presently, I'm back on three antibiotics again for a year.

For a long time I had been seeking wholeness in other people, places, and things. In the summer of 2011, I attended the Nebraska Camp Furthest Out (CFO) seeking healing for my bronchiectasis. At CFO I felt a curious sense of wholeness, of being in the Kingdom of Heaven here and now. This has been a wonderful reassuring feeling. I sometimes describe the camp as an opportunity to be "loved back into shape" through singing and prayer. I also found a sense of wholeness in the Order of St. Luke and its healing ministry. This group met monthly at St. Matthew's Episcopal Church, and it too has been a godsend, but recently ended. Ever since my divorce, I have attended healing services, seeking wholeness in body, mind, and spirit. It's been an ongoing issue for me but usually more psychological than physical. However, as I've been aging in retirement, I've been seeking healing for my body as well as my mind and spirit.

I've also been working toward wholeness and confidence in my personal life with my therapist, Tom Tiegs. I've been able to share my disappointments, fears, triumphs, and writing problems with him, and he's helped me grow in confidence and assurance, learning how to set better boundaries with others and myself. I've been learning to pay attention to my energy flow and notice whose company energizes me and whose depletes me.

I've come to understand that many friends and relations care about me. This has helped heal the wounded female part of me—the part that always felt too tall, too inadequate, and not good enough. Now I know I am enough—good enough, attractive enough, smart enough. Recently, it felt good to hear a friend describe me as an intellectual. It also felt good to hear another say how nicely I had decorated my apartment. It is cozy enough. It's OK. Indeed, it's fine for me. I have finally learned not to discount myself and my surroundings. Overcoming feelings of gender, class, and family inferiority has been the journey of a lifetime, but it's been a rewarding odyssey.

My relationships with my brother, sister, and son are better than they've ever been. Although I'm sorry to have bronchiectasis and other ailments, I think I've been learning compassion from this chronic disease. I've also come to pray in a new way. I simply ask Jesus to help me walk when my legs hurt, to be with me when I'm frightened in the dentist's or doctor's office, and to watch over me while I'm writing this memoir.

At seventy-nine, I am of the age category in which my friends, relations, and I suffer from such chronic diseases and ailments as diabetes, heart trouble, cancer, blood clots, urinary tract infection, stroke, broken bones, hernia, prolapsed uterus, and even West Nile virus. Several friends have had knee and hip replacements. Most of us have had cataract surgery, and that was another difficult diagnosis for me to accept. It took me five years to decide to get the surgery. In the meantime, my vision had become so poor I couldn't recognize friends from more than ten feet away. While I sometimes get terribly frightened when hard diagnoses are made, I am learning to pray with my friends and to accept illness and ailments as part of the aging process. Thankfully, my cataract surgery was very successful, and I'm grateful to Dr. Mota for his good work and to my Pioneer House friend Beth Hemmer for administering the eye drops for several weeks. She is a godsend. She also helps me get to medical appointments and cares about me.

Reading the book *Being Mortal* has also been helpful. It helps me realize that we all want to live our lives until the end. None of us want to be warehoused into a nursing home. I'm grateful for friends to pray with and for me when I am afflicted, and to have them pray for my friends and relatives when they are suffering. I know God doesn't excuse me from suffering, and I'm thankful for those who share this hard part of my aging journey.

I can now often say, "Thank you, Lord, for life and for another day." I can praise God as the psalmist does in Psalm 103:

> Praise the Lord, Oh My Soul.
> Let all that is within me praise God's gracious name.
> He forgives our sins; heals our infirmities;
> Redeems our lives from the pit;
> Crowns us with Mercy and Loving-Kindness;
> Renews our youth like an Eagle's . . .
> Bless the Lord, Oh my Soul!

Books like *Being Mortal* and *Mr. Owita's Guide to Gardening*, which my Episcopalian women's book club read in the fall of 2016, made me aware of my mortality. Yet when I talk to dear ones about this issue, I realize that our ailments are normal, and the aging process requires adjustment. It's inconvenient. I don't like it, but there it is. Not just for me, but for my friends and relations too. We sometimes discuss death and realize that many of us who have been academics have been blessed with full, rich lives. Our work allowed us to read and study the topics we loved, travel to faraway places, and in retirement experience financial serenity with our Social Security and university TIAA pensions. We all have a great deal to thank God for. In old age, I have returned to simple prayers, and often pray when I feel overcome and can hardly walk home: "Jesus, please walk the next few blocks home with me," or "please heal my afflicted friend in body, mind and spirit." Occasionally, I shake my finger and say authoritatively, "Behave cells!" regarding friends who have serious illnesses. Those last words and actions shock me when they come from my mouth.

Another boon in old age is learning to listen to the spirit when praying and to my muse when writing. If I take the time to listen before doing my devotions, I often hear a song in my heart. Sometimes it's a simple song like "Near to the Heart of God," "Breathe on Me, Breath of God," "Lord of the Dance," "Blessed Assurance," or "There Is a Balm in Gilead." Often the songs that come to mind are Negro spirituals I learned as a youth. Sometimes they are Shaker and church hymns I learned as a child or those that we still sing in church on Sunday. With the aid of the internet, I can find the words that I don't remember and print the entire hymn. When I take the time to stand up and sing and maybe dance around with my tambourine before sitting down to pray, I usually feel enthused and blessed. A couple of years ago, I learned a ditty, "Every little cell in my body is healthy, every little cell in my body is well. Feel so good, feel so swell, every little cell in my body is well." It is sung to the tune of "Shortnin' Bread" ("Mammy's little baby loves shortnin' bread"), and I sing this for myself and for friends who are afflicted in various ways. Since I live alone, I am free to stand up and sing or dance around my apartment and play my tambourine whenever I feel moved.

I've learned that prayers and writing often take on dimensions I hadn't planned at the beginning, just as my life doesn't always proceed the way I plan. My friend Tania in Lithuania used to say "Life corrects our plans." I now think God or the Holy Spirit does.

One of the greatest benefits of living in Lincoln is that I am physically closer to my son and daughter-in-law, closer than I have been for decades. For years we lived hundreds, even thousands, of miles apart, and it's a joy to have my son and daughter-in-law come visit me several times a year. Since they have three cats to which I am allergic, I seldom go to Kansas City to visit them. But

Martin and Donna really like the city of Lincoln, several of the restaurants here, and coming to visit me. They are always very generous in taking me and dear friends to eat at fine restaurants. Martin knows a lot about beer since it's one of the fields of his research. He always helps me order a beer or ale that he thinks I will like. If he's wrong, he drinks it and orders me another one. What a son! At first I drank only the Belgian ale Stella Artois, but I have recently branched out at the Thursday craft beer nights at Whole Foods. There I've learned to try other ales and have found I like the Scottish Old Chub made in Colorado, the Belgian Leffe beer, and almost any beer by the Sierra Nevada Brewery of Chico, California.

One Saturday when Martin and Donna were visiting, they even went on a march with me. Living near the capitol, I can easily get involved in various causes. This Saturday I was demonstrating for Occupy Wall Street and had made a sign to carry. I was glad that my friend Michael wanted to participate and also that Martin and Donna marched. That was a very special time. So although my relationship with my son has always been good, now I get to see him more often, and that's one more special blessing of my old age.

It's good to end my memoirs counting my blessings. While I had initially thought this the end, I have subsequently decided to include a chapter on cooking, baking, and entertaining. So, I'm including a few recipes that my mother passed on to me and that some readers might also enjoy.

Chapter X

Mother's Cooking Legacy

"Simple Can Be Good"

When I graduated from college, I vowed to lead a life different from that of my mother's, and in some ways I succeeded. Much to my surprise, I find I often express my love for my family and friends through sharing food, just as my mom did. Growing up, I wasn't aware that cooking and baking were also creative outlets for mom, but they were, and for me too. Both of us loved baking and trying new recipes. I hadn't realized how many "habits of the heart" I had learned from my mother.

While my mother didn't teach me to cook and bake because she was always in a hurry to get things done since she worked outside the home, she did sometimes let me help. I remember her showing me how to line a cake pan with wax paper by drawing an outline of the pan on the wax paper with a pencil and then cutting the paper lining. This was done after oiling and flouring the pan. Before Teflon, this helped us remove cakes more easily from the pans. While mother didn't teach me how to measure and sift cake flour, I watched her and learned from her example. Since she always cooked from scratch, I learned about peeling potatoes, frying meat, fixing vegetables, and preparing salads. I don't remember her asking me to help her prepare dinner, but my sister and I usually set the table and did the dishes while she did other chores like sweeping the floor in the evening.

When I married, I discovered oven meals were good to make in the winter since everything was ready at the same time. For Sunday dinners, I often baked a small amount of meat (a one pound boneless roast or meatloaf), potatoes, and acorn squash. One of my mother's recipes I used was for meatloaf. It's simple, a good standby, and fail-proof. I never thought much about its being such a simple dish. After living in Lithuania and encountering my friend Laurent Gontier's French cooking, I was embarrassed to invite him and his wife to my place for meatloaf and baked potatoes, but I finally did. Much to my surprise, he said "Simple can be good." I was pleased and had to agree. At his house, however, we always had chicken or pork with plums or other fruit, something more captivating.

Another story about serving meatloaf and baked potatoes in Lithuania involved Adolfina's family. They had never seen baked potatoes and didn't know how to eat them. I had invited my colleague Daryl Culp to this dinner, and they watched him eat to see how they should proceed. I only found out about this from Viktor much later. My German friend Helmut once asked me why it was called meatloaf. I told him it was usually baked in a loaf pan, the sort used for bread, but since I didn't have one of those, I made it in a round casserole dish. Many dishes can be baked in different amounts or kinds of containers.

Mom's Recipe for Meatloaf

1 pound ground beef
1 cup oats
1 cup milk

1 egg
Salt and pepper

Mix all the ingredients together; place in a loaf pan; garnish with garlic, onion, peppers, or ketchup. Bake in a 350 degree F. oven for 1 hour.

Note: This recipe can be altered by substituting one 8-ounce can of tomato sauce for the milk. It can also be doubled or halved and it still turns out. Just bake the meatloaf a longer or shorter time.

The next recipe for apple walnut cake was not something I ate growing up. I had it only as an adult, when Martin and I spent a few weeks with mom in the summer. That was the sort of vacation we could afford, and she was always welcoming. She loved us both and spoiled us. I was happy being spoiled and going to the lake in La Porte. I don't remember making this cake for my family, but Mother and I made it in El Paso when she came to live with me. I made it for my friends Mollie and Birdie there and later for friends in Lithuania.

I can't remember why, but I took some of mother's recipes to Lithuania with me. So I made this cake there, and everyone liked it, as the picture with Victor shows. My Lithuania Christian College friend Alexa Maples took the picture of us. I often made this cake when entertaining Adolfina and her family as well as for Tania and Irina when they came to Friday afternoon English conversation.

Apple Walnut Cake

2 cups sugar
1 cup oil
3 eggs
1 teaspoon vanilla

Mix these four ingredients together.

3 cups flour
1 teaspoon baking soda
1 teaspoon baking powder
1 teaspoon cinnamon
½ teaspoon salt

Sift these dry ingredients together and then mix with the first combined ingredients. Then stir in 3 cups of diced apples and 1 cup of nuts.

The dough will be stiff. Scrape it into a 9-by-12-inch glass baking dish and bake at 350 degrees F. for 45 to 60 minutes.

Garnish with powdered sugar or whipped cream, or serve it plain. Refrigerate anything left over. This cake will last two weeks in the fridge.

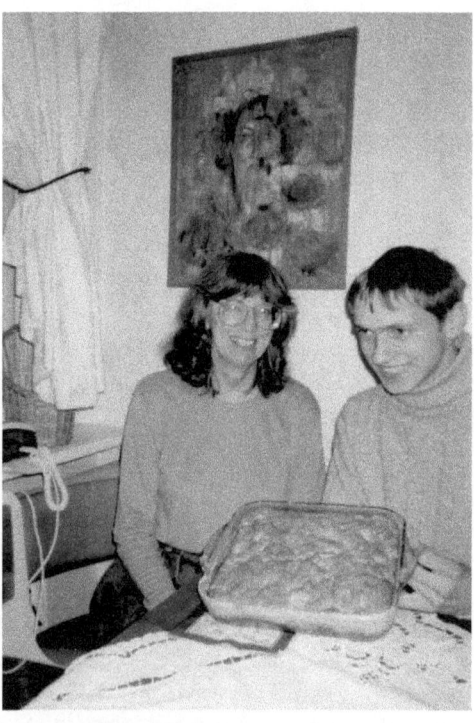

Marcelline, Viktor, and an apple walnut cake in my Klaipėda kitchen, 2005

Note: Not all cake recipes can be adjusted, but this one can. When making half the recipe, use a glass pie pan for the baking dish. I have a gluten-intolerant friend in Lincoln, so I learned I can substitute gluten-free flour for the regular flour. Several friends at Pioneer House like it, so I occasionally make it for our monthly birthday club celebration. (However, I've gotten lazy in old age and now tend to use cake mixes rather than baking from scratch.)

Some of my Lithuanian friends also liked my mother's recipe for pumpkin date nut bread. Another teenage boy about Viktor's age lived in our apartment building, and he too liked to come talk to me. He just loved this bread. I think it was because American desserts are richer and sweeter than those in Lithuania.

Pumpkin Nut Bread

1 cup oil
1½ cups sugar
4 eggs
2 cups pumpkin (1 can)

Mix these four ingredients together.

3 cups flour
1 teaspoon cinnamon
1 teaspoon salt
1 teaspoon baking soda
2 teaspoons baking powder

Sift these dry ingredients together and add them to the batter.

Add nuts, raisins, and dates to the batter.

Put into several prepared loaf pans, or make into muffins.

Bake for 55 minutes at 350 degrees F. for loaves, less time for muffins.

Family Cooking in Iowa City

When I was first married, I really wanted to please and impress my husband, as any bride might. I liked making cakes and found a recipe for Basque cherry cake, which I recollected recently. I also discovered that John couldn't tolerate greasy fried food and wasn't used to it. So, I went to the Iowa City Public Library and found a wonderful international cookbook. From it I learned to make several tasty dishes. Watching my mother use a recipe, I felt confident I could cook or bake anything using a recipe, and I did. I soon learned to substitute chicken, pork, or ground beef for lamb, which is featured in many Balkan recipes, and following are four recipes that I remember from cooking them frequently. I don't make them much anymore because they are designed for a family or large group, not a single person; and peeling and slicing potatoes and onions are time consuming, and I have grown lazy.

Basque Cherry Cake

> Yellow cake mix
> Cherry jam
>
> Mix cake according to the box directions.
>
> Bake in thin layers, eight in all, in round cake pans.
>
> Cool cake. Spread cherry jam between the layers.
>
> *Note:* Today, I don't take the time to make several layers, so I don't make this cake any longer. As I remember, the cake mix called for butter and was like a rich pound cake. I looked up this recipe on the internet (as well as burnt sugar cake, which my mother also made), so if you want authentic Basque cherry cake, use a recipe from there.

Dishes that John, Martin, and I as well as our friends enjoyed when we lived in Iowa City during the 1960s and in England from 1968 to 1970 were moussaka, rice pilaf, and pork and potatoes. While the original moussaka recipe called for sliced eggplant, I used potatoes and also substituted hamburger for lamb.

Moussaka

Sauté peeled and sliced onions, garlic, and potatoes in olive oil.

Sauté hamburger.

Layer the onions, potatoes, and hamburger in a casserole or baking dish.

Add 1 can of tomato paste diluted with 1 quart of water. Add salt and pepper to this liquid. Pour this tomato mixture over the layers.

Spices: Place 3 bay leaves and 2 cinnamon sticks on top of the mixture.

Bake at 350 degrees F. in an uncovered Dutch oven or casserole for 1 to 1½ hours. The dish is done when the potatoes are soft to a fork.

Rice Pilaf

Sauté ½ pound cubed chicken, fish, or other meat.

Sauté one diced onion, 2 cloves diced garlic, 3 sliced celery sticks, and salt and pepper.

Add 1 cup rice, 2 cups water, one diced tomato, walnuts, and raisins.

Bring to a boil and then cook 20 to 30 minutes on top of the stove on low heat until all the water is absorbed.

Note: In the 1960s, I didn't always have walnuts and raisins in my cupboard, and I didn't like tomatoes, so I often omitted those ingredients. Today, I include them. One cup of rice makes a lot, so I don't cook this dish very often these days, or else I make half of it.

Pork and Potato Dish

Sauté 1 pound cubed pork.

Sauté several peeled and sliced potatoes, onions, and garlic, and add salt, pepper, and thyme.

Layer these ingredients in a baking dish or Dutch oven.

Dot with flour, pour ½ cup of white wine and ½ cup of whole milk over the layers, and bake 1 to 1½ hours in a 350 degree F. oven. The dish is done when the potatoes are soft to a fork.

Lithuanian/American Recipes

While living in Lithuania, I heard of three good dishes from colleagues. One was baked oatmeal that my Canadian Mennonite friend Marg Fast told me about, the second was a recipe for scrumptious brownies that Janice Turner from Oklahoma gave me. The third was sauerkraut soup. Needless to say, my Lithuanian friends, especially Tania, loved the brownies. They are very rich because the recipe uses cocoa and chocolate chips as well as oil. While my Lithuanian friends loved the brownies, I only made the baked oatmeal for my own breakfast, and the soup was often for a Sunday soup supper at church or my own consumption. Although the soup was quite tasty, I never thought of it as special enough to serve to guests.

Baked Oatmeal

3 cups oats	1 teaspoon cinnamon
½ cup sugar	1 egg
1 teaspoon salt	½ cup oil
1 teaspoon baking powder	1 cup milk

Mix all the ingredients together. Add raisins and nuts, if desired. Bake at 350 degrees F. for about 45 minutes. Leftover baked oatmeal can be microwaved or fried in the skillet to warm it up..

Brownies

2 cups sugar
1 cup oil
3 eggs

Mix these three ingredients together.

1½ cups flour
4 tablespoons cocoa
1 teaspoon salt
1 teaspoon baking powder
1 teaspoon vanilla
Chocolate chips and nuts, according to taste

Mix in all the remaining ingredients and bake at 350 degrees F. for 30 to 50 minutes, depending on pan size.

Note: These brownies are extremely rich, so don't encourage people to eat more than two at one sitting. Making these brownies in Lincoln recently, I discovered they need to bake only 30 minutes. In Lithuania, I couldn't adjust my oven very well, and they always took 50 minutes.

Sauerkraut Soup

Sauté ½ pound diced pork and chicken, 2 onions, 2 cloves garlic, and 4 sticks celery in butter or oil.

Add several peeled, cubed potatoes and carrots, and one jar or can of sauerkraut. Cover with water, add salt and pepper, and cook for 1 to 2 hours, until the potatoes are tender.

Note: This makes a large pot of soup, so use a big kettle or Dutch oven.

Chapter X

Necessity and Cooking

Sometimes I have developed recipes and cooked food out of necessity. Once I was making bread in Iowa City, and I ran out of flour, so I decided to use some oats. The bread came out well, and I discovered that substitution in recipes is often possible. When I lived in El Paso in the 1990s, I occasionally found myself out of bread, so I turned to my *Joy of Cooking* cookbook and made scones for breakfast. Eventually I discovered that friends like scones for tea as well as breakfast, and so do I, especially with raisins and cranberries in them. Here's recipe for scones. Living alone, it's good to bake and cook small amounts of things, so I often cut this recipe in half.

Since I eat less flour these days, I make the scones less often and haven't tried them with gluten-free flour yet. That may be my next experiment!

Scones

- 2 cups flour
- 2 teaspoons baking powder
- ½ teaspoon salt
- 2 tablespoons sugar
- ¼ cup butter
- 2 eggs
- ½ cup cream or milk

Blend together, working the butter into the flour mixture first and then adding the eggs and cream. Add some raisins or cranberries last. Drop by spoonful onto a baking sheet or bake in a muffin pan. Bake at 375 degrees F. for 15 minutes.

Note: Oil can be substituted for the butter, but butter makes tastier scones.

The following recipe comes from two friends, one in Florida and one in Lincoln. When I can't decide what to take to a potluck or what to cook in the summer, I find this is a handy salad to serve. As for meatloaf, many adjustments can be made with this salad.

Asian Salad

2 packages ramen noodles, crushed
1 head of cabbage, shredded, or one bag of shredded cabbage
1 jar dry-roasted peanuts
2 ounces white sesame seeds
1 bunch green onions, chopped

Toss these ingredients together.

¾ cup olive oil
½ cup rice vinegar
2 tablespoons sugar
1 teaspoon salt

Stir the dressing together and drizzle over the salad. Season to taste with salt and pepper.

Note: This makes a very large bowl of salad. I cut this recipe in half for myself. Even so, it makes a lot, but the salad will keep in the fridge for several days.

CHAPTER XI

Conclusion

Writing conclusions is difficult, and ending this autobiography is no exception. It's hard to know what note to end on without sounding like Pollyanna. In church one Sunday, I was thinking about how our spiritual lives ebb and flow. Then I reflected that my life began in harmony and seems to be ending that way. As a child, I was physically and mentally healthy. I felt safe, secure, and blessed. My early life was in sync.

In elementary school, I became conscious of my family's poverty, and that was disturbing. I wasn't so dismayed that I had a breakdown, but this was the first shadow on my sunshine. In adolescence, I began to feel psychologically and socially alienated. I became aware of the effect of my father's alcoholism on our family life, and I felt awkward about being tall and skinny. I didn't know the term "low self-esteem," but that's what I experienced. However, my physical health remained strong, as did my spiritual life, so I was partly in sync and partly out.

Going to college was a liberating experience, and I felt more together. My athletic skills were valued, I was healthy physically, and I succeeded intellectually—winning tuition scholarships each semester to finance my college study. There, I didn't worry so much about being tall and unattractive since lots of girls didn't date in college. And many of the men were tall. I didn't feel so much like an ugly duckling. The emphasis on study and spiritual life made me feel in harmony with college life.

In graduate school, I encountered the patriarchal bastion of academe and the "old history of male elites." I was unused to tough competition and an all-male atmosphere. I didn't feel like I belonged, and I didn't, but I didn't want to admit it. Since I had won a fellowship to study history, I didn't know what else to do. I was totally bewildered by this experience. When my Russian history advisor urged me to write my M.A. thesis on "The Woman Question in the 1860s," I was upset and confused. How could I be impartial, as the "old" history required? I didn't know then that doing women's history was part of postmodernism. No one told me. I just felt upset. My intellectual and psychological life were in turmoil, Still, I remained healthy physically and anchored spiritually even though many of the male graduate students made fun of religion. My future husband didn't scoff at religion, so that was a consolation. My life was certainly out of sync, and I was glad to meet my future husband, who was not only handsome but seemed to have it all together. While I felt alienated at the university, he relished the anonymity.

Marrying John the second year in graduate school made me feel anchored socially and emotionally. I was happier being in love, making cakes to please him, and caring for our new baby than I was studying. I wasn't used to the high level of competition in my history courses and felt more at ease in the Russian language and culture classes where the students weren't so aggressive, and the female professors were more nurturing. There, I did reasonably well. I wasn't conscious of it at the time, but I was behaving as a dilettante in my European history courses. I wasn't the serious student I had been in college. Becoming a wife and mother may have been my way of rebelling against graduate school—I'm not sure. While I enjoyed my new social status, my intellectual life was not harmonious. I worried if two achieving graduate students could make marriage work. Since my husband was achieving more than I was, I happily put him and his academic career ahead of my own. I avoided my own lack of accomplishment by basking in his. This was easy to do since I admired him so much, and the ethos of the 1960s encouraged my behavior. So, I continued my old traditional behavior and didn't become a liberated, feminist woman until after our divorce.

After sixteen years of marriage, I discovered that love doesn't always work. I grew tired of putting my husband first and wanted to renegotiate our situation. My husband didn't, so we divorced and I had to confront my own insecurities. I returned to graduate school, a more serious person and scholar than I had been earlier. I wanted to try teaching, to see if I could succeed. If not, I knew I would have to find another way to support myself. I loved being a teaching assistant, and I was good at it. My mind was disturbed by the divorce so I couldn't concentrate on writing my dissertation, but I could do simple computations about the census data I was using, and I did those. Becoming my true self took a lot of time and effort. I participated in postmodernism by developing a new feminist theology and a new philosophy of women's and social history. Through it all, I continued to jog one or two miles a day and walk to class and around Iowa City, so I remained physically healthy despite my mental and emotional anguish. Unfortunately, I still loathed my tall, healthy body instead of being grateful for it. I was grateful for my mother and son. Their love at this hard time helped sustain me. Church and university friends also helped. After a couple of years, the pain subsided, and life in Iowa City became pleasant.

Not getting a job and discovering the Adult Children of Alcoholics (ACOA) program in the 1980s helped me achieve greater peace of mind. I accepted my low self-esteem and myself as I was. ACOA helped me deal with the stigma and shame of my father's alcoholism. Today the stigma in American society seems to have shifted to opioid addiction. When I hear people talk about this stigma and shame, I understand. It took me a long time to absorb the idea that alcoholism is a disease, not a moral failing. It seems to take other Americans awhile to understand this addiction too. Sad that our society is so based on shame! While writing this chapter, I remembered reading a book by Anne Schaef called *When Society Becomes an Addict* (1987). She seemed to identify our problems so well.

Digesting the ACOA program took a while. Still, I managed to teach my classes at Iowa, obtain a job at Hamilton College, and later another job at the University of Texas at El Paso (UTEP). I enjoyed teaching and felt satisfied with my performance. However, I still felt low self-esteem and feared publishing my first book, despite the interest of several publishers. This led to the loss of my job at UTEP in 1994. At first I wasn't too dismayed and thought I would get another position, but the market was closed to Russian historians after the fall of the Berlin Wall. My life wasn't ruined, but it felt bleak, especially after the death of my mother, former husband, and several family members and friends in 1997. So my life was socially, emotionally, and financially out of sync in the 1990s. However, I still enjoyed good health and a deep spiritual life at my church.

Getting a one-year job at Radford University in 1999 and then the teaching position at Lithuania Christian College redeemed me financially and intellectually. However, I still felt alone, sad, depressed, and frustrated when I first lived in Lithuania. Slowly, I made Lithuanian, Russian, and American friends and life improved. In retirement, my life is once more in sync. I enjoy financial serenity with Social Security and a small TIAA annuity; I have a rich social life, a deep spiritual life at St. Mark's Episcopal Church, and a positive intellectual life writing books, teaching classes for OLLI, and talking with friends. I enjoy a reasonably healthy body for my age and still walk around. I enjoy my tai chi class at a nearby senior center, and although I have a few chronic illnesses, none are life-threatening. Various chronic diseases have drawn my brother, sister, and me more closely together in old age. In some ways, we have come full circle.

I have experienced fewer banes than blessings in life. My friend Elaine and I often muse about death and dying, arguing that we have been blessed with rich, meaningful lives, and death need not be devastating for us or our families. As academics, we have enjoyed teaching, researching, writing, and traveling. We have experienced the joys of marriage and motherhood as well as the wrenching sadness of divorce. Yet, our lives flourished with friends and the rich intellectual, cultural, and spiritual life in Lincoln. What more could we want? A book titled *Simple Abundance* by Sarah Ban Breathnach discusses financial serenity, and I have found that in addition to social, intellectual, cultural, and spiritual serenity. Writing this book has contributed to my sense of purpose and given me meaningful work for four years. Now I can let it go, hoping readers will enjoy this history of one Midwestern woman muddling through her personal crises and the effects of postmodernism in the late twentieth and early twenty-first centuries.

www.ingramcontent.com/pod-product-compliance
Lightning Source LLC
Chambersburg PA
CBHW031133160426
43193CB00008B/130